The Dominican Republic and the Beginning of a Revolutionary Cycle in the Spanish Caribbean

1861–1898

Luis Álvarez-López

University Press of America,® Inc.
Lanham · Boulder · New York · Toronto · Plymouth, UK

To: Nelson Alvarez, Paulina Morales, César Roque Rosario and Flora Rosario Pérez.

Table of Contents:

List of Graphs

Tables and Charts

Foreword

¡Patria desventurada! ¿Qué anathema
  Cayó sobre tu frente?
Levanta ya de tu indolencia extrema:
  la hora sonó de redención suprema
Y ¡ay, si desmayas en la lid presente!
               - Salomé Ureña, "Ruinas"

(Oh, wretched Motherland! What woe
  Befell your brow
Rise up, already, from your extreme
  Indolence, the time has come
To be redeemed.
And, woe is you, if you are feign in the struggle)

The second half of the nineteenth century presents a very complex and tellingly profound moment in the history of the Dominican Republic. The independence won in 1844 from Haiti, the sister nation inhabiting the island of what was known as *Quisqueya*, *Aity* and later on, *Hispaniola*, was short-lived, as the young nation was soon annexed back to Spain, and independence had to be hard-fought for again in what has come to be known as *la Restauración* of 1865.

Between 1865 and the 1880's the young nation saw as many as twenty-three governments, and *caciquismo* and internecine wars prevailed. This instability is painfully portrayed in Salome Ureña's (1850-1897) civic poetry of the period: a yearning for the establishment of peace, and for a nation to base its highest ideals at the foot of the pedestal of education.

Luis Alvarez' book offers an English-language study of a defining moment in the conceptualization of nation-formation for the Dominican Republic, linking it to the ideals of revolutionary Spanish-Caribbean nations. The chapters range from analysis of the causes behind the annexation of the Dominican Republic to Spain to the steps that brought about a political struggle for the "restoration of independence". The author also offers a snapshot of life in the Dominican Republic during its last years as a colony of Spain.

The book's structure allows for a mid-point introduction of the subject of colonialism to include a comparison of the struggles for independence from colonial Spain in the Dominican Republic and Puerto Rico. An analysis of Ramón Emeterio Betances' ideals and his engagement in the struggle for an independent Spanish Caribbean during the years of 1861-1898 broaden the vision of this monograph in a significant way.

The last chapter focuses on the impact of the Spanish army on the quality of life of the people in Santo Domingo during the last stages of the Spanish colonial dominance 1861-1865, rendering a powerful portrait of the plight of its people. Bibliographical notes and citation of sources complete the contents of this volume.

With this publication, Luis Alvarez makes a contribution to a growing field of study, and responds to the needs of university students who are searching for answers to their questions about the history of the Dominican Republic, its importance to the development of the Spanish Caribbean, and its contribution to the history of humanity.

Daisy Cocco De Filippis, Ph.D.
President
Naugatuck Valley Community College
Connecticut Community Colleges
July 2008

Preface

The purpose of this book is to analyze the history of the Dominican Republic during the second half of 19th century as a Caribbean nation. Focusing on the political independence process of the Dominican Republic, its economic structure and social classes, subsequent annexation to Spain and the Restoration war.

The annexation process of the Dominican Republic to Spain in 1861 opens a new stage in the relationship between Cuba, Puerto Rico and the Dominican Republic. The three islands became part of the Antilles Empire, the last effort of Spain to preserve and renovate its three century old empire in the new world.

Having lost all her colonies in Latin America during the Napoleonic war, Spain become emotionally attached to the last two colonies in the region: Puerto Rico and Cuba. Spain objectives were to preserve the "ever faithful isle of Cuba" and "the pearl of the Antilles: Puerto Rico" from the expansionist policy of the Union and the desire to build a slave based Caribbean empire of the Confederate States. Due to the existence of black slavery in Cuba and Puerto Rico, both territories were extremely attractive for the Southern agrarian expansionism.

Spain developed a foreign policy cemented in a strategic alliance with the Northern European Empires: France, England and Portugal. The main objective of these nations was to preserve the status quo in the Caribbean, allowing Spain to maintain the two remaining colonies. The Northern Empires supported Spain and her colonialist policies in the Antilles. These nations also shared the agreement to curb any North American encroachment in the Caribbean.

The Union developed a foreign policy in support of the status quo, allowing the preservation of Spanish colonialism and black slavery in Cuba and Puerto Rico. Knowing that Spain was the weakest of the Empires in this alliance, the Union chooses to deal with Spain and not to deal with France or England. The United States was waiting for the right moment to take control of the two colonies.

The great alliance of the Northern European empires was used in the case of Mexico to foster the French colonial expansion in the area. Despite the disaster of that effort, Spain used the same alliance to achieve geopolitical supremacy in the Spanish Caribbean. The sense of urgency in the Dominican case was justified by Spain with the thesis of the two enemies; Spain was confronting the Black race and the Anglo-Saxon race, both races were putting in danger the pearls of the Antilles; Cuba and Puerto Rico.

As a result of Spain's expansionist policy, the Dominican Republic becomes a colony of Spain on March 18, 1861. From that moment on, the history of Cuba and Puerto Rico were inextricably intertwined because the colonial models imposed on the Dominican Republic was a reproduction of the Cuban and Puerto Rican colonial societies. The models to transform the Dominican Republic's economy and society were based on Cuba's and Puerto Rico's. The economic resources to undertake this transformation were coming also from Cuba, Puerto Rico and Spain. Despite the differences between the three different islands, the Spanish ruling class believed that the political juncture (United States civil war 1861-1865) was suitable to achieve its political dreams of imperial expansion and was ready to accept the challenges to alter a seventeen years independence country into a colony.

From the economic point of view, the Dominican Republic had the most backward economy structure in the Spanish Caribbean. An agrarian economy based on small farming, cattle, tobacco and cacao production, and without an internal national market. The Dominican economy had also a weak integration into the international market, exporting tobacco, mahogany and other woods, sugars, coconuts, etc.

This subsistence economy rested in the shoulders of an independent peasants group with access to the land. The existence of land ownership known as communal land (*terrenos comuneros)* provided access to the land by the peasants even if they were not the owners of it. The low density of the population and the abundance of land also help to explain why the direct producers were not under pressure to increase the production.

Different from Cuba and Puerto Rico that developed robust plantations systems, after the Haitian Revolution, based on a black labor force, the Dominican Republic was the last Caribbean colony to develop that system, without black slavery and a formal independent country setting.

From a political point of view the Dominican Republic was an independent country, struggling to preserve its political independence against its neighbor, Haiti. The black slavery was abolished twice (Toussaint in 1801 and Boyer in 1844) and the main concern of the ruling class was the annexation to any other European powers or the United States in order to established political stability and preserve their political hegemony.

The preservation of the political independence of the country wasn't the concern of the ruling class. They believe that the country was not prepared to be an independent country. The annexation to another Caucasian empire was a goal of the ruling class to develop themselves as a social class achieving several important objectives:

1-Capital accumulation
2-Political stability
3-Peace with Haiti
4-Whitening of the Dominican Republic with European immigrations.

Different from the Dominican Republic, Cuba and Puerto Rico were colonies of Spain for centuries, with Creole bourgeoisies divided between different political positions to reform the colonial system or to preserve it without the abolition of the black slavery. The struggle for breaking the colonial pact was a commitment of only a fraction of the ruling class. Most of them believed in changing the system without national struggle because they were in fear of "the black perils." They were terrorized by the idea of another Haitian Revolution. This idea also was an obstacle in the struggle for the Cuban independence; always the danger of an anti-white revolution by the black population was an impediment for the ruling class to joint the national struggle for independence.

In the Dominican Republic the same idea of the" black peril" was manipulated by the ruling class to advance the annexationists cause. There is no doubt that President Soulouque was serious about reconquest the Eastern part of the island. But President Soulouque was overthrown and President Fabre Geffrard advanced a proposal for peace and recognition of the Dominican Independence that was refused by Pedro Santana.

The "black peril" in the Dominican case meant the thread of a Haitian invasion to the Dominican Republic and the danger of the "black population" living in the country. Different from Cuba and Puerto Rico "the black peril" was mostly from Haiti as well as from the Dominican black population. The last point became clear with the rebellion of Monte Grande that forced the new government to confirm the abolition of the black slavery with a decree on March 1, 1844.

The annexation to Spain (1861) started a new colonial experiment in the Dominican Republic. The new colonial regime was a total failure. The exclusion of the native ruling class from the state apparatus, over taxation, imposition of the Catholic Church customs, economic exploitation and prejudice and discrimination against blacks and mulattos led to rebellions, insurrections and a liberation war against the Spanish authorities that lasted two years.

The characteristics of the war, class participation, ideology, political alliances, tactics, strategic, class and national consciousness are themes discussed in this book.

The far-reaching impact of the Restoration war in the Spanish Caribbean is not fully understood, some experts in the region don't even mention the war. Other totally ignores a war that contributed to create a political crisis in Spain and opened the possibilities to the independence of Cuba and Puerto Rico.

The example of the Eastern part of Quisqueya defeating the Spanish Empire opened a revolutionary cycle in the Spanish Caribbean that led to military struggles in the three islands and ended with the defeat of the Spanish empire by the United States.

This historical process has been totally ignored. For example Oruno D. Lara in his book *Space and History of the Caribbean*. Princeton: Markus Wiener Publisher, 2006; doesn't even mention the Restoration War (1863-1865) and also ignores the *Grito de Lares* in Puerto Rico (Sept 23, 1868). Franklyn W. Knight in his well known book *The Caribbean: the Genesis of a Fragmented Nationalism*. Oxford: Oxford University Press, 1990, overlooked the Dominican case, not even in a footnote, does he mention the historical process of Dominican Restoration war and the impact in the Caribbean.

In the general history about Latin America, the Dominican Republic and Puerto Rico are not included. This is the case of the Keen, Benjamin and Keith, Haynes, whose book *History of Latin America*. Boston: Houghton Mifflin, 2004. It only includes a chapter about Cuba. David L. Clauson's book *Latin America and the Caribbean. Land and People*. Boston: McGraw Hill, 2006. Clauson used a chapter to analyze the Greater Antilles focusing only in the Ten Year War and José Martí's role as organizer of the 1895 Great War. Both books also miss the crucial role played by the Restoration War in the Dominican Republic and the impact in the Caribbean.

Dominican Republic and the beginning of a revolutionary cycle in the Spanish Caribbean objective is filling this gap in the Caribbean historical knowledge revisiting an ignored but important historical process in the Dominican Republic and the Spanish Caribbean.

Luis Álvarez-López
Manhattan, New York.
May, 2008.

Acknowledgments

In preparing *The Dominican Republic and the Beginning of a Revolutionary Cycle in the Spanish Caribbean 1861-1898,* I have benefited from the collaboration of many colleagues, librarians and friends in New York, Dominican Republic and Puerto Rico.

Beginning with New York I must recognize the enthusiastic assistance of my colleagues in the Puerto Rican/Latin American Department, Apolinar Matos González, Carolina González, Luis Barrios and Christ Aviles for his continued technical support.

Anther group of colleagues in the Department deserves special recognition, Demetri Kapetanakos, Marco Navarros and Edgardo Díaz-Díaz. They reviewed some sections or chapters of the book and made invaluable suggestions that improved its content.

Over the years I have benefited from the expertise, encouragement and assistance from fellow historians and colleagues from the Dominican Republic. Among them Emilio Cordero Michel, current President of the Dominican Academic of Historians 2007-2010, José Chez Checo, Adriana Mu-Kien Sang Ben and Alejandro Paulino.

Doctor Carmen H. Sanjurjo, from Metropolitan State College of Denver, reviewed the text and made important contributions. She was willing to take time from her busy schedule to peruse the manuscript. At the Bronx Community College, Sharon Utakis and Nelson Reynoso encouraged me to finalize the project. Sharon was able to review a few of the chapters and improve their contents of its. At Hunter College, Harry Rodriguez helped me with moral support and words of encouragement. Yesenia Montilla also from Hunter College was a meticulous reader that peruses the manuscript and improves some sections of the book. I am extremely grateful to her.

At the people institute, Ronald Chilsom, David and Margaret Billing and Shadia Alvarez made invaluable suggestions that were incorporated into the book. My Daughter Yadhira Alvarez contributed with some of the graphs and charts in the book and reviewed some of the arguments that I presented. In the same fashion Will Jenkins helped with the analysis of 19th century incomplete data regarding the Spanish army in Santo Domingo.

Sonia Bu, Carlos M. Larancuent and Wilfredo Larancuent made priceless contributions while reviewing the text, graphs and tables as well as making intelligent suggestions that substantially improved sections of the book. They reviewed the book on several occasions and discussed with me some of the hypothesis.

Special thank to Edwin Díaz, who meticulously reviewed all the book chapters and discussed with me some historical facts and argument. He made numerous suggestions that substantially improved the development of the book.

I am grateful for the help of Dr. Mauricio Álvarez, a Microbiology and specialist in immunology for reviewing the chapter on the Spanish Army and the diseases and illnesses they confronted in the new territories.

Finally my wife Miosotis Fabal provided support, assistance and words of encouragement. Needless to said, I am responsible for the points of view, hypothesis and analysis of the present publication.

Seventeen Fundamental Conclusions about the Annexation to Spain and the Restoration War of the Dominican Republic: 1861-1865

First Conclusion: International Context

I characterize Spain's foreign policy in reference to the Dominican Republic during the period of 1844-1855, as a policy of "deliberate disdain" toward Santo Domingo. Spain refused all the efforts of the Dominican government for cooperation in their endeavor to preserve Dominican independence against the attempt of the Haitian government to control the Eastern part of the island.

Spain's rejection of the Dominican Republic's request for mediation, protection and recognition by the young and frail Dominican state was in agreement with her foreign policy. Spain considered the Dominican Republic . . . "Like an evil for the Antilles and our interests, considering the lack of advantages that we can derive from her [the Dominican Republic], the island is an evil we can avoid."[1] [Author's translation]

That is, Spain preferred to safeguard the "colonial status quo" in the Spanish Caribbean by protecting its slave bases in the colonies of Cuba and Puerto Rico, against the example of anti-colonialism and anti-slavery of Haiti and the Dominican Republic. Both countries were politically independent; slavery didn't exist within their borders and they were strategically placed between Puerto Rico and Cuba. Spain considered the existence of both countries as a threat to its colonies in the region because Haiti and the Dominican Republic set the precedents of political independence in the Spanish Caribbean.[2]

This was especially true of Haiti, the first black independent republic, which abolished black slavery twice in the Eastern part of the island (1801 and 1822) during the Haitian domination. Haiti pursued the effort to regain sovereignty of Hispaniola. Spain feared that Haiti, with the United States' support, would succeed in invading the Dominican Republic and establish a Haitian government on the island. The threat was, that "Haiti will be a tool of United States,"[3] and consequently a serious menace to the Spanish possessions of Cuba and Puerto Rico. On the other hand, the Dominican Republic was an independent country without slavery, whose population was comprised mostly of blacks and mulattos, which made it different from other Spanish colonies. Some of its political leaders were also black and mulatto, which was also different from the other Spanish colonies.

Spain's foreign policy established a temporary political alliance with two other northern European empires: France and England, an alliance intended to curb a possible expansion of the United States into the Caribbean. Both the French and British empires showed an interest in maintaining a commercial and political hegemony in the Dominican Republic. Spain was in opposition to American expansion in the region, allying itself with both the French and British empires in order to bring about equilibrium in the Spanish Caribbean and dissuade encroachment by the United States in the region.

Spain's political alliance with England and France was part of a broader coalition, namely the Quadruple Alliance that also included Portugal. This alliance was implemented during the first half of the nineteenth century. The Quadruple Alliance strategically linked Spain to the other northern European empires. Other factors linked Spain to England and France, namely Spain's indebtedness to the former and the fact that a Spanish empress, Eugenia de Montijo, occupied the French Imperial throne.[4]

The idea of a North American expansion toward the Caribbean originated in the Union as well as in the Confederate government. Both developed campaigns of expansionism into the Caribbean. Before the Civil War, the vision that prevailed in the South was to create a proslavery Caribbean empire, with the annexation of Cuba and other Caribbean islands. The possibility of the annexation of Cuba would add a new proslavery territory that would eventually become a state, simultaneously assuring an added southern vote in the American Senate and thereby fortifying the position of the pro-slavery states in Congress.[5]

From the Southern political perspective, the interest in expansionism increased as a result of the Compromise of 1850. According to Martínez Fernández, "the question of territorial expansion ceased to be a national and party issue and became a bitter sectional issue. Many southern statesmen deemed the Compromise of 1850 as a serious political setback that threatened to seal the South's minority status and loss of control over the Senate and the House of Representatives. California statehood disturbed the sectional balance of power in the Senate, giving Free states a clear majority in the upper house. Southern politicians thus began to look for new territories that, once admitted to the Union, would boost slave-state representation. Some white Southerners argued that seven new states could be carved out of Cuba and Puerto Rico and as many as twenty-five out of Mexico."[6]

The strongest supporters of expansionism were southern politicians annoyed with United States internal politics. That is the reason why Mississippi and Louisiana produced the most outstanding filibusters, especially New Orleans, which was the base for the financial and organizational expeditions of Narciso Lòpez in the 1850's. Lòpez was linked to the Havana club, the Creole planters' annexationists' movement whose members believed that the great republic from the North was the best destiny for Cuba because it combined slavery with democracy. Some family members of Narciso Lòpez, such as his nephew José María Sánchez Izñaga and brother-in-law Francisco de Frías (Count of Pozos Dulce) made a financial contribution and gave encouragement for his activities.[7]

The policy of expansionism into the Dominican Republic was mostly a project of the Northern states, located in New York with the support of commercial, financial and shipping interests. The South rejected the idea of expansion into a Caribbean territory such as the Dominican Republic, which had a free dark-skinned population and lacked black slavery. The Dominican Republic was not a concern of the Union during the first years of the Dominican Independence process; instead Cuba was the target of Northern politicians.

The United States' interest in Cuba started with the Founding Fathers. John Quincy Adams metaphor of 1823 is well known, he affirmed . . . "If an apple, severed by a tempest from its native tree, cannot choose but fall to the ground, Cuba, forcibly disjoined from its own natural connection with Spain, and incapable of self support, can gravitate only toward the North American Union, which, by the same law of nature, cannot cast her from its bosom."[8] The thesis of the political gravitation and the no-transfer policy, in which the Union refused to approve the transfer of Cuban sovereignty from Spain to any other third party, became part of the Union's foreign policy toward Spain, in reference to Cuba. Preserving the status quo in the Spanish Caribbean meant keeping Cuba under Spain until the conditions were ripe to make Cuba a United States colonial possession.

Despite the official policy in favor of maintaining the status quo in the Caribbean, the United States, during the 1840s, made multiple attempts to acquire Cuba. The Manifesto of Ostend as well as the plans of Presidents James Polk and Franklin Pierce shows two apparently contradictory faces of United States policy regarding the possessions of the Spanish empire in the Caribbean: maintaining the status quo and the pursuit of expansionism.[9]

At this juncture Spain's foreign policy toward Santo Domingo started to change. It started to consider the existence of Haiti in the western part of the island, as a black independent republic. The eradication of slavery in the Haitian state and its secular pledge to extend its control of the eastern part of the island made the Spaniards interpret this conflict as a clash between two races: black against white. The Spaniards never considered the fact that the majority of the Dominican population was black and mulatto, and they felt great concern about Cuba and Puerto Rico – colonies where slavery existed.[10]

Spain also believed that England and Haiti had a common purpose in the struggle in favor of the abolition of black slavery in the Spanish Caribbean, but Spain's main concern was with the United States and Haiti. She feared that Haiti, with the support of the Union, might possibly overpower the Dominican Republic and, as a result, the other Spanish possessions would be endangered by the hypothetical Haitian plan to build a black empire and to free the black slaves.[11]

The control of the political power in Spain by the Liberal Union party and General Leopoldo O'Donnell, whose government reinstated the foreign policy of military and territorial expansion overseas, contributed to a change in Spain's foreign policy. A similar interventionist policy was applied in the Spanish Caribbean, trying to invigorate the ancient colonial empire with the annexation of

Santo Domingo. The strategic goal of the Spanish foreign policy was to stop American expansionism in the Caribbean and simultaneously to fortify its empire in the Antilles.

Spain's foreign policy toward the Dominican Republic was expressed with clarity in the correspondence of their Minister of State, Calderon de la Barca, to the President of the Counsel of Ministers on March 6, 1854, in which Spain refused to provide either protection or the recognition of its independence, as requested by Ramón Matías Mella on his mission to Europe. In this document, the State Minister expressed the following:

> Spain cannot grant material protection to the Dominican Republic, because of the difficulty of implementing such protection as well as because of the expenses of such commitments.
>
> It would be premature and without any compensation to us, to recognize the independence of said republic.
>
> That it is most important and urgent to avoid conquest by the black people of Haiti, or to be overtaken by American filibusters.
>
> It would be convenient for us to deal with this situation and try to arrange the remedy as soon as possible with the friendly powers that have possessions overseas.
>
> That for now without either destroying or alerting the hopes of the General Mella, in relation to the recognition of independence, we would be able to send to Santo Domingo an agent to report to this Minister and to the General Captains of Cuba and Puerto Rico about the situation of the Republic.[12] [Author's translation]

The fundamental reason that explains the change in Spain's foreign policy toward the Dominican Republic was the North-American Dominican Treaty of 1854 that was perceived by Spain and its allied powers as an instrument to influence the Dominican Republic and from there attack the Spanish colonial possessions.

This commercial treaty also intended to lease part of Samaná to the United States to install a coal fueling station for commercial ships and the American war fleet. The recent experience in America, regarding the expansion in Texas, as well as the swift defeat of Mexico in the 1848 war, along with the appropriation of the territories of California, New Mexico, Utah, Nevada, and Arizona, caused enough apprehension in Spain. The presence of General William Cazneau from Texas and his experience in political expansionism already mentioned, led Spain to appoint a business agent and a Consul, and to the signing of a Treaty of Recognition, Peace, Commerce and Extradition with the Dominican Republic.[13]

Francisco Serrano, Governor of the island of Cuba, understood that Spain's foreign policy should be focused on the Dominican matter. All the efforts of the Overseas Department must focus on the Dominican situation and the national policies of the Americas should focus on the same situation. In his own words, "I am convinced that all the policies of Spain in these regions should be concentrated on this question, in confronting the Americans."[14] [Author's translation] Opposition to United States because they were the only political power that would object to Spanish expansion in the Caribbean and because the Dominican Republic could potentially become the general headquarters of filibusterism in the Antilles.

The Crimean war in Europe, in which England and France fought against Russia, seemed to open the American path toward the Caribbean, in a juncture characterized by the increasing agitation about Cuban annexation by the Union. In this regard, President Franklin Pierce's plans were twofold: To obtain a naval base in the Dominican Republic, and to achieve control of Cuba.

The radical opposition of England and France to the Dominican-American Treaty of October 1854 should be framed within the process of imperial rivalries of the United States with England as a consequence of its fishing rights disputes and their rivalries in Central America as a consequence of the *Clayton Bulwer Treaty* of April 1850. The War of Crimea would deepen these contradictions because England perceived that the Americans were in support of the Russians. The effort of the United States in their aspirations by achieving the signing of the 1854 Treaty with the Dominican Republic was a total failure by the militant opposition of the northern European empires: England, France and Spain. This achievement of the political alliance was an obstacle for the short-term goals of the Union. Such plans also confronted a persistent internal opposition in the United States Congress, especially from the anti-slavery leaders who believed that recognition of Santo Domingo would be the prelude to annexation.[15]

Analyzing the internal affairs of the United States and the impact of the annexation of Santo Domingo by Spain, it is necessary to consider the Civil War in the United States. The Union States and the Confederacy were involved in the War of Secession, which made it impossible for the Union States to protect and apply Monroe Doctrine principles or Manifest Destiny in any part of the world, not even in their own "backyard."

In reference to England, its foreign policy was guided by four basic considerations:

1. To increase commerce with the Dominican Republic and Haiti.
2. To avoid the emergence of a black empire under Haitian leadership.
3. The block the increment of American and French influence in both the Dominican Republic and Haiti.
4. The other element was the issue of slavery. Spain should comply with the English demand of not reestablishing slavery in the new Caribbean territory, on the condition of carrying out the annexation of Santo Domingo by Spain.[16]

France represented no danger for Spain because the annexation of the Dominican Republic was in accord with its international policies to preserve European hegemony in the Caribbean and to curtail the efforts of North American influence in the region. Besides, an express or tacit understanding existed between France and Spain in their political views toward the Antilles and Latin

America. Finally, France was immersed in the effort of maintaining the empire of Maximiliano in Mexico.

Second Conclusion: The Economy and Society during the Years Prior to Annexation

The Dominican economy during the years of 1844-1861, a period known as the First Republic, was based mostly on agricultural products and livestock rearing. Subsistence agricultural production predominated over commercial agriculture, centered on family and community consumption, to be sporadically destined to reach the regional and local markets. At the same time there was a commercial production of tobacco, mahogany and precious woods. The cattle industry produced meat and hides for the neighboring towns. There was also a minor production of coffee, sugar, honey, wax, leather, rum, and the raising of mules and goats. These instances of commercial and subsistence agricultural production were specialized regionally and their process of production and commercialization were linked to intermediary merchants, to foreign merchants, and to the foreign commercial houses situated throughout the country.[17]

These commercial firms were established in the ports of Santo Domingo, Puerto Plata, Azua, Montecristi and Samaná. The economy was, from time to time, connected to the outside world through the exports of a few agricultural products. However, the lack of an internal national market and the deficiency of even a primitive system of transportation, made communications between different regions almost nonexistent. Horses, mules and horse-drawn carts were the only means of transportation.[18]

The agrarian economy was characterized by use of primitive instruments of production, such as hoes and machetes, the lack of a stable labor force and stunted demand. A communal system of land ownership, scarce work capital and small population were also impediments to the development of a commercial agriculture. The ratio of land to population was so huge that only a small number of peasants lacked access to land as tenant farmers, property owners or as sharecroppers.

The land's population density was 10.4 inhabitants per square mile in 1860.[19] Despite these internal impediments, the population was very well adapted to its ecological niche because the production was steadily increasing, as well as international commercialization.

The economic activities in the Southern woodlands were centered on the production of timber and sugar. The production of timber was based on a system of land ownership known as *latifundio* (great state) with a dependent peonage as a main labor force and a primitive system of division of labor. In the coastal section of Azua, the production of sugar was destined for internal consumption and was based on traditional methods.

In the process of production and commercialization of woods, an incipient division of labor began to emerge. The production of timber was carried out by different social groups, such as woodcutters, officials, ox drivers (*bueyeros*), car-haulers and wood speculators. From the early 1800s a substantial class of landowners and wood exporters developed in the south.

Most of the workers in the production process were linked to the monetary economy throughout a system of contracts. The production was destined for the export to the international market through the representatives of foreign commercial houses established in Santo Domingo, Puerto Plata, Montecristi, and Azua. Port cities located in the south, north and in the eastern part of the country.

The few available statistics indicate that the production of mahogany was decreasing for several decades. On the other hand, other less valuable woods showed a curve of ascending growth like *Campeche, Guayacán, Mora* and *Espinillo*. Utilizing the few dispersed statistics we have built a snapshot of the production and export of mahogany (Table 1.1 and Figure 1.1).

Table 1.1: Mahogany Exports 1822-1880

Years	Exports (miles feet)
1822	2,580
1823	2,251
1824	2,102
1825	2,861
1826	1,940
1835	5,413
1836	4,954
1838	4,880
1845	3,223
1855	3,479
1868	1,058
1869	1,256
1872	1,863
1880	1,815

Source: Roberto Cassá, *Historia Social y Económica de la República Dominicana.* (Santo Domingo: Editora Alfa y Omega, 1980), vol.2, 19-20.

Wood production, including mahogany, was linked to the Dominican state through the payment of taxes, which provided the necessary incomes to pay for the import of merchandise related to this economic activity for regional demands of goods not produced in the country.

The cattle ranching production had great economic importance during the colonial period. The decline of the plantation system at the end of the 16th century led to the diminishing of mining and sugar production. As a result of these changes in the economic structure of the colonial society, stockbreeding became

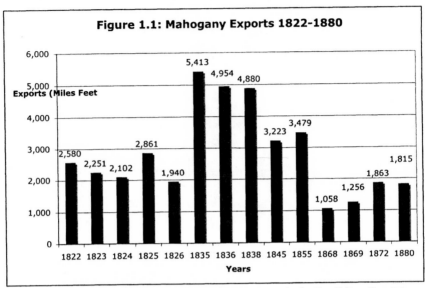

Figure 1.1: Mahogany Exports 1822-1880

Source: Roberto Cassá, *Historia Social y Económica de la República Dominicana.* (Santo Domingo: Editora Alfa y Omega, 1980), vol.2, 19-20.

the most important economic activity. The cattle and ranchers became intrinsically part of the Dominican rural landscape.

During the 17th century as well as the 18th century, the production of cattle increased significantly under the stimulation of foreign commerce. At this stage, the rise of Saint Domingue in the Western part of the island, (the most prosperous French colony in the Caribbean), had a far reaching impact in the Spanish colony of the Eastern part of the island. This neglected and forgotten colony in the Caribbean became a provider of cattle on a grand scale to Saint Domingue, energizing the livestock economy in the different regions, east, west and north.

The multiple impacts of the French Revolution in the colony of Saint Domingue had disastrous consequences for the formally prosperous cattle economy of the oriental part of the island. The Haitian revolution, the abolition of slavery, wars and migrations contributed to the ruining of livestock production. These historical processes diminished the social and economic power of the ranchers, leading to their impoverishment in the colonial society.

By the 19th century, stockbreeding was a declining economic activity of "agonizing persistence." The ranch as a productive unit "lost economic and social power." Nevertheless, the production of cattle was still present in the western zone of the country, in the northwest region, in central Moca, La Vega and Jarabacoa. As in the past economy, livestock production was oriented to the breeding of bovine cattle, pork, horses, donkey, and mules. The cattle were domesticated and also wild. It was utilized for local consumption in meat markets and sporadically exported to be used as a raw material to produce meat and leathers. Moreover, it was used as a means of production in agriculture and in the sugar industry.[20]

The characteristics of the ranches as rural enterprises were still present in the Dominican economy, with a weak connection with the market, the existence of small plots of land *(conucos)* as basic units of production for subsistence, the existence of a limited labor force with easy access to the land, technological primitivism and the extensive use of land.

The cattle rearing economy can be characterized as an economy of subsistence in transition to a market economy. The study of the Protocols of Notaries that had been carried out showed the heterogeneousness of the relations of production that existed. On the one hand, some studies have shown the payment in salaries of laborers and foremen, but also they were given access to small properties inside the ranch, which transformed them into salary workers, but with access to the land. In this way, their position as wage earners was neutralized by the access to the land, which was used for subsistence agriculture production.

On the production of tobacco, the economic and social situations were different from the stockbreeding as well as the production and export of mahogany. Tobacco was produced in the North region, Santiago and the fertile plain, Moca, Villa Gonzalez, etc. Its production for export started during the colonial period. An increment of its production occurred during the Haitian domination and in the subsequent period during the First Republic (1844-1861) when its production showed an ascending curve.

The constant growth of the tobacco exports is explained not only because of external demand alone, but by the development of an economy based on independent peasants who had access to the land. In this commercial production, thousands of direct producers, merchants and intermediaries participated in financing the crop in advance and hiring muleteers who transported the production to the main port of Puerto Plata.

Pedro Francisco Bonó, the first Dominican sociologist, described the dynamism of the tobacco harvest. He stated that:

> Everywhere piles, bags, and packs of tobacco are being hauled, everywhere are warehouses full of this leaf and swarms of workers of sexes, selecting, tying, weighing, and packing. Stores are packed with customers; supplies come and go, in other words, there is an exchange of goods thrice that the rest of the years.[21]

The characteristics of the tobacco industry permitted a relatively easy incorporation of the peasants in its production. The possibility of access to the land, low investment of capital that required the cultivation of the tobacco and the rudimentary and primitive form of its production made its cultivation the broadest and most important economic activity in the northern part of the country.

The cultivation of tobacco was carried out on small and medium properties, which permitted the development of a peasantry, not subject to the exploitation that existed in the cattle zone. The structure of the agrarian property that was created was different from the livestock productions that developed in the east and to the large wooded extensions for the cutting of wood in the South. In the northern region, farmers developed small agricultural properties cultivated by small independent producers. Tobacco was produced for export to Germany, United States, France, Holland, and for local consumption in plug tobacco (*andullos*) and cigarettes generally used among the peasantry. This economic activity was also linked to the development of several domestic-rural industries such as, the making of bags (*serones*) for the transportation of tobacco, the textile industry for the making of cords, threads, hammocks, ropes, and the industry of the muleteers (*recueros*) for the transportation of tobacco from Santiago to Puerto Plata.

I was able to organize Table 1.2 by utilizing the figures of tobacco exports from 1844 through 1868.[22]

Table 1.2: Tobacco Exports 1844-1868

Years	Exports (Hundred Pounds)
1844-1845	30,000.00
1845-1846	34,000.00
1846-1847	28,000.00
1851	65,000.00
1855	50,000.00
1856	55,000.00
1860	80,000.00
1861	70,000.00
1862	30,000.00
1863	30,000.00
1866	30,000.00
1867	67,000.00
1868	123,000.00

Source: Manfred Wilckens, "Hacia una teoría de la Revolución" (2) *Ciencia y Sociedad*, (vol.XXV, no.4-Octubre-Diciembre 2000). Instituto Tecnológico de Santo Domingo. 427-465. Cassá, Roberto. *Historia Económica y Social*. (Santo Domingo: Alfa y Omega, 1980), vol. 2, 19-20.

The exports of other woods to Europe and other markets are shown in Table 1.3 and Figure 1.3.

Third Conclusion: The Internal Political Situation

The third conclusion indicates that the process of annexation to Spain was carried out with the main purpose of maintain political power permanently by a fraction of the dominant class: ranchers, which were headed by Pedro Santana. This fact shows the lack of nationalistic sentiments of this fraction of the class,

Table 1.3: Export of Other Kinds of Woods 1845-1846

Type of Wood	Export (Pounds)
Palo Mora	679,617
Campeche	6,000
Guayacan	170,000
Resina de Guayacan	28,518

Source: Roberto Marte, *Estadísticas y Documentos Históricos de Santo Domingo* 1805-1890. (Santo Domingo: Museo Nacional de Historia y Geografía, 1984), 84.

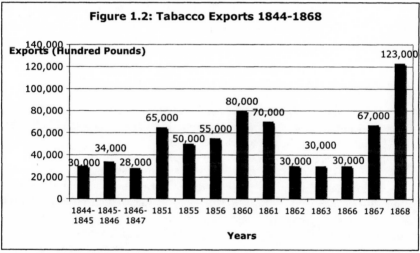

Figure 1.2: Tabacco Exports 1844-1868

Source: Manfred Wilckens, "Hacia una teoría de la Revolución" (2) *Ciencia y Sociedad*, (vol.XXV, no.4-octubre-diciembre 2000),427-465. Instituto Tecnológico de Santo Domingo. 427-465. Cassá, Roberto. *Historia Económica y Social*. (Santo Domingo: Alfa y Omega, 1980). Vol. 2, 19-20.

which was politically dominant, but also shows the political sagacity of this sector that tried to eliminate its progressive tendency toward its political and economic weaknesses, just as evident in the revolution of July of 1857.

This approach explains the process of annexation to Spain as a consequence of a political project elaborated by a fraction of the dominant class, in a suitable international juncture (as has been analyzed in the previous note) and not as a consequence of the Haitian attempts to regain control of the Dominican Republic. [23]

The hostilities between Haiti and the Dominican Republic were solved with a truce of five years and the subsequent proposal of peace by President Fabre Geffrard. The proposal included the recognition of Dominican independence and

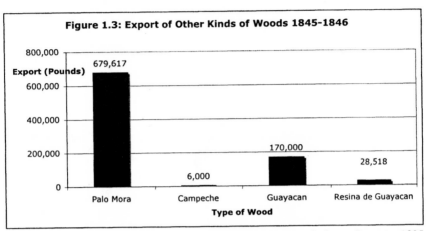

Figure 1.3: Export of Other Kinds of Woods 1845-1846

Source: Roberto Marte, *Estadísticas y Documentos Históricos de Santo Domingo* 1805-1890. (Santo Domingo: Museo Nacional de Historia y Geografía, 1984), 84.

the return of Dominican territories under Haitian possession. Haiti did not constitute any threat to the Dominican Republic but Pedro Santana and the dominant class used it as an excuse to achieve the annexation to Spain.[24]

The idea of annexation of the country to another foreign power was a political project of a sector of the dominant class of the Dominican Republic. This group had the conviction that Dominicans did not have the conditions to have a politically emancipated country, independent of the Haitian politics, to regain the eastern part of the island, which was not in existence anymore. It should be emphasized that in the struggle for the foundation of the Dominican State, since its inception; there had been several annexationist movements. Some were interested in making the country a colony of France, others of England, and a final group of Spain. It is obvious that the Haitian objective of reconquest of the eastern part of the island, previous to the Geffrard government, contributed to strengthening the annexationists' ideas of this fraction of the dominant class during the First Republic (1844-1861), but these ideas were in existence even before the beginning of independence (1844-1861).[25]

Despite these facts, this absurd idea persisted in several forms: some social scientists believe that the annexation to Spain was carried out to avoid the Haitian intent to regain the eastern part of the island. This argument can be considered true but is not the whole truth because this argument does not take into consideration the interests of the dominant class to maintain political power. The objectives of this dominant group were:

1. The use of the state as an instrument for the accumulation of capital and political power.

2. Stopping the political instability in the country by granting the guardianship of the Dominican Republic to a more advanced capitalist nation.
3. Colonizing the country under the wings of a Caucasoid empire to whiten the country and at the same time, to put a stop to the intents of the Haitians of regaining control of the eastern half of the country.

The ranchers and landowners who constituted the dominant class during the First Republic had alienated and racist beliefs, and had a clear political consciousness to end the independence of the Dominican Republic. This group rejected "the idea of a country for all Dominicans," blacks, mulattos, mestizos and whites, that was advanced by the founding father of the country's independence, Juan Pablo Duarte. Promoting white immigration and accusing black and mulatto officers was part of the racist behavior of this dominant group, which desired to whiten the country against the allegedly Haitian threat.[26]

Fourth Conclusion: The Ideology in the Process of Annexation to Spain

The ideological underpinning, from which the process of annexation to Spain was carried out, was based on the idea of the *double danger*. On the one hand, there was the danger of the colonial expansion of the United States, which intended, according to the Spanish colonial authorities, to convert the Dominican Republic into a springboard from which to attack the colonial territories of Cuba and Puerto Rico. The other danger was the Haitian threat because Haiti supposedly intended to regain the Eastern part of the island to build a black empire that would promote the revolt of black slaves in Cuba and Puerto Rico, Spanish colonies where slavery existed. This was the point of view of the native dominant class and also of the Spanish colonial authorities in the Spanish Caribbean, whose strategy was to expand its colonial empire in the Antilles, converting the Dominican Republic into a new colony of Spain.

The idea of the "double danger" was evident in several documents by Pedro Santana and the annexationists' fraction as well as by the Spanish authorities. The reports of the Spanish Consul Mariano Álvarez, sent to the State Department on July 16, 1861, indicated:

Two different races are interested in the acquisition of the beautiful Antilles. One is the black race from Haiti and the other one is the Anglo-Saxon race. Both races are enemies of the Dominican race. If these races achieve their objectives, the Dominican races would disappear from Hispano-America. Both races are still interested in the Dominican Republic. The first one has been defeated but is willing to attack again as soon it recovers from the its defeat, and the second one is the Eagle of the Union, which is impatiently waiting for a good opportunity to control this beautiful land [27] [Author's translation]

Pedro Santana expressed similar ideas in the correspondence that he sent to the Queen of Spain, April 27, 1860. He stated:

> I believe that, this is the best moment to strengthen the relationship between both our countries. If we pass this opportunity, a revolution might take place, which happens frequently in these new Republics and if I become weak, despite that I always defeat the Haitians in the struggle, and a powerful northern nation, take advantages of this situation, what would happen to us? All these circumstances can be a danger not only for the Dominican Republic but also for the other two Spanish possessions in the Antilles.[28] [Author's translation]

The other idea used by one of the brilliant ideologists of the annexation, was the idea that the annexation constituted the possibility of peace. The annexation to Spain constituted a guarantee of peace; therefore,

> We have seen the party's desire to depose its weapons, to abandon voluntarily its trenches and even to lend its sincere and loyal cooperation.[29] [Author's translation]

Of course, the peace was guaranteed by the imperial presence of troops in the new territory. The investments of capital that would come from Spain would maintain territorial integrity in opposition to the supposedly Haitian threat. These conditions would guarantee the political stability that he and his associates anticipated. Seeing the annexation as a consequence of the menace of the Haitian Republic is the same invalid approach that already had exposed Rodríguez Demorizi in their innumerable publications on the annexation, characterized by an anti-Haitian unilateralism.

Fifth Conclusion: State and Society in the Framework of Spanish Colonial Control

The fifth conclusion maintains that the Spanish colonial policy radically affected the relationship that existed between the Dominican state and society during the First Republic. Since the beginning of the colonial society, the omnipresence of the state in the Dominican society was evident in multiple edicts, laws and regulations that attempted to control almost in its totality all the routine behaviors of the inhabitants of the new territory.

The interventionist colonial state promoted the transformation of Dominican society into a colonial territory similar to Cuba and Puerto Rico. Concrete evidence of this seen in the multiple edicts emitted by the Spanish authorities, such as the Edict of Police and Government of October 15, 1862 as well as others, such as the one that required all owners of wagons to pay taxes and obligating them to yield their animals to the Spanish soldiers, when needed.[30]

From the beginning of the Restoration War, the Spanish colonial State became an apparatus eminently repressive against Dominican supporters, collaborators or simply relatives of the rebels who fought for the re-establishment of the republic. These repressive policies were clear in the creation of military commissions to judge the rebels and in the organization of a body of volunteers to struggle against the rebels, and also in the surveillance on the border to avoid the smuggling of weapons to Santo Domingo.

This repressive and anti-insurgent state created a confiscation policy against the rebels. Thus, they seized all kinds of properties: farms, shacks, lands, estates, urban farms, livestock, dogs, and horses. These properties were sold in public auctions. Confiscations occurred in Santo Domingo, Azua and Baní. Figures 1.4, 1.5 and 1.6 show the properties and animals confiscated.

Table 1.4: Confiscated Properties in Santo Domingo

Property Type	# of Properties Confiscated
Huts	100
Houses	39
Small Plots of Land	8
Farms	4
Total	*151*

Source: *Relación de las Propiedades Incautadas por la Comisión Administradora e Investigadora*. Legajo 25, Anexión a España. Archivo General de La Nación, República Dominicana.

The resources generated by these confiscations were utilized to implement a social policy of public assistance in order to gain the population's loyalty to the colonial state, which had been affected by the war. This policy provided services to the Spaniards and to the Dominican population faithful to the Crown; it was especially helpful for those Spaniards returning to Spain, Cuba and Puerto Rico. This social policy provided resources for:

1. The repair of dwellings and properties affected by the war.
2. The exoneration of confiscated rent payments of dwellings.
3. Distribution of rations for families originating from territories controlled by the rebels.
4. The concession of dwellings and farms previously owned by rebels and families loyal to Spain.
5. The payment of passages for the "poor of solemnity" that desired to return to Spain, Puerto Rico, and Cuba.[31] [Author's translation]

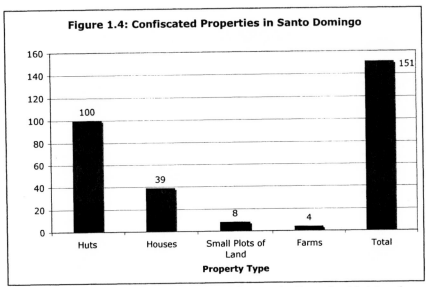

Figure 1.4: Confiscated Properties in Santo Domingo

Source: *Relación de las Propiedades Incautadas por la Comisión Administradora e Investigadora.* Legajo 25, Anexión a España. Archivo General de La Nación, República Dominicana.

Table 1.5: Confiscated Properties in Azua

Types of Properties	# of Properties Confiscated
Urban Farms	114
Small Plot of Land	38
Ranches	2
Total	*154*

Source: *Relaciones de las Fincas Secuestradas los meses de Agosto, Septiembre, Octubre Y Diciembre.* Legajo 25.Archivo General de la Nación. República Dominicana.

Sixth Conclusion: Origins of the War of Restoration and the Incorporation of People in the Struggle for the Reestablishment of the Republic

The sixth conclusion maintains that the main causes for the origins of the Restoration War must be linked to Spain's administrative policies, which hurt the interests of all social groups within the Dominican society: small farmers,

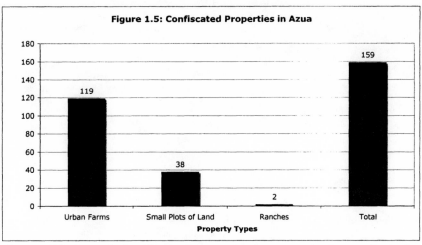

Figure 1.5: Confiscated Properties in Azua

Source: *Relaciones de las Fincas Secuestradas los meses de Agosto, Septiembre, Octubre Y Diciembre*. Legajo 25.Archivo General de la Nación. República Dominicana.

Table 1.6: Confiscated Animals in Bani

Animal Type	# of Animals Confiscated
Donkeys	17
Horses	11
Cows	06
Bulls	05
Calves	03
Total	*42*

Source: *Relación de los Bienes Incautadas a los Rebeldes Perteneciente a los Rebeldes que se han averiguado desde el último Septiembre hasta la fecha*. Legajo 25. Archivo General de la Nación, Repùblica Dominicana.

ranchers, laborers, professionals, merchants, artisans, foremen, military personnel, clergy, freemasons, fruit vendors, landless peasants, etc. The main cause wasn't the political devotion of the Dominicans to their independence, or the development of a national conscience. In fact, a fraction of the Dominican fighters that struggled against Spain were annexationists, especially the followers of the former ex-president Buenaventura Báez.

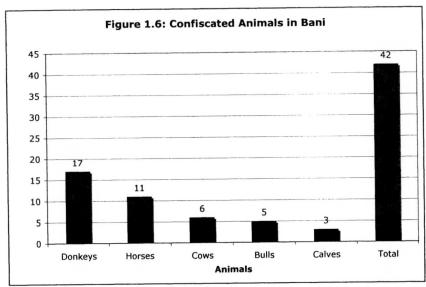

Figure 1.6: Confiscated Animals in Bani

Source: *Relación de los Bienes Incautadas a los Rebeldes Perteneciente a los Rebeldes que se han averiguado desde el último Septiembre hasta la fecha.* Legajo 25. Archivo General de la Nación, Repùblica Dominicana.

Nevertheless, there existed also a political movement that was anti-annexationist and anti-colonial. This movement was comprised of the leaders from diverse minority groups like the *Trinitarian Movement, Liberales Cibaeños,* (liberals from Santiago, followers of the revolution of 1857) and even some of the Baecista's followers. In spite of the accusations of Báez, saying that the rebels were annexationists, the reality is that the documentation analyzed in this study shows with total clarity their position as militant nationàlists in the search for diplomatic support of the United States and other foreign countries.

The global oppression generated by these policies intended to modify subsistence farming and small-scale agricultural production with a model of intensive commercial agriculture in order to export tropical crops to Spain and other nations. That transition to commercial agriculture was difficult to achieve in a country with such a small population and a system of land ownership that made it possible for the farmer to have access to the land.

Some causes were the fiscal exploitation suffered by the Dominican people; indeed, almost all sectors of the society were incorporated into a fiscal policy that pretended to raise the economic resources to finance Spain's colonial project. Part of this fiscal policy was the imposition of a governmental monopoly on tobacco purchases.

Other causes were related to the desire to prohibit everyday customs and activities, such as cock fighting, consensual unions, parties, freemasonry, and the Protestant religion. The imposition of Catholicism, and press censorship, generalized the opposition to Spain.

Additional causes were the prejudice and discrimination against Dominicans, even Dominicans of the ruling class, because they were black and mulattos. To these causes I must add the possibility of the re-establishment of slavery, the imposition of forced labor on the peasants in the construction and maintenance of the roads, plus the enormous difficulties and arbitrariness in the exchange of paper money.

In the final analysis I should mention, the political exclusivity that favored the Spanish's clergy, bureaucracies and soldiers over their Dominican counterparts. For example, Dominican ruling class members who were appointed to high positions in the bureaucracy were replaced by Spanish officers; the Dominican army was separated from the Spanish army and became part of the Colonial Reserve with an inferior salary and the best positions in the Catholic Church hierarchy became a monopoly of the Spanish clergy. All these reasons united Dominicans of the upper classes and the lower classes against the Spanish colonial domain.[32]

Seventh Conclusion: Movements of Opposition to the Colonial Regime, Beginning of the Restoration War and Identities of the Participants

Since the beginning of the annexation to Spain, the movements of political opposition to the colonial regime were varied, such as protest over the loss of the sovereignty, riots against the newly established order, rebellions, the frustrated conspiracy of Meriño, the expedition of Sánchez and Cabral by the Southern border, and the Puerto Plata subversive lampoons. Since the first days of the annexation of Spain on March 18, 1861, the protests were evident. In San Francisco of Macorís, Manuel Rojas, Olegario Tenares and other leaders carried out the first armed protest at the moment that the Spanish flag was raised. In Puerto Plata and in Yamasá the anti-annexionists organized their intents, but they were to no avail. Other protests against the annexation were the revolt of Moca on May 2, 1861, as well as Puerto Plata and Yamasa, as can be seen in the following chart.

Table 1.7 is a chart of the actions of political opposition to the annexation to Spain-1861.

The protests and rebellions of 1861 planted the seeds of the Restoration's War. It was initiated by the rebellion of Neiba on February 9th and the succession of rebellions, which originated in the Northwest region of the country. This was followed by Guayubín, Sabaneta, Montecristi and Santiago, February 21, 1863.

Who were the participants in these rebellions? To which social sectors did they belong? What were their social identities? Examining the different occupations can help to approximate an answer. The seventy-five cases of participants in the rebellions were organized according to occupation. The results are shown in Table 1.7.

Table 1.7: Actions of Political Opposition to the Annexation to Spain – 1861

Date	Place	Facts	Additional Information	Leaders and Participants
March 23, 1861	San Francisco de Marcorís	Armed Protest against the raising of the Spanish Flag	Juan Esteban Ariza fired his weapon killing 30 protestors	Manuel Rojas Olegario Tenares
March 16, 1861	Puerto Plata	Unsuccessful attempt of anti-annexationist conspiracy	Idelfonso Mella said "Up to The Dominican Republic!" when the Spanish flag was hoisted.	Ramón Matías Mella Idelfonso Mella
February and March 1861	Llamaza	Aborted conspiracy of the Republic's Senate	Fernando Arturo Meriño coordinator of the conspiracy.	Fernando Arturo de Meriño
May 2, 1862	Moca	Insurgents attacked fort and army commander	The objective of this rebellion was to hoist the Dominican flag.	José Contreras Juan Pérez Juan Solano
June 1861	The Border near Neyba and the Matas de Farfán	Military expedition from Haiti	The objective was to launch an insurrection against Spain's colonial domain	Francisco del Rosario Sánchez José Maria Cabral Fernando Taveras Víctor George

Sources: Pedro Archambult, *Historia de la Restauración.* (Santo Domingo: Editora Taller), 1981. Rufino Martínez, *Diccionario Biográfico 1921-1930.* (Santo Domingo: Editora de la Universidad Autónoma de Santo Domingo, 1971). Emilio Rodríguez Demorizi, Emilio. *Próceres de la Restauración.* (Santo Domingo: Academia Dominicana de la Historia, República Dominicana, 1963).

Eighth Conclusion: The Problem of the Alliance: Social and Political Forces in the Restoration War

The eighth conclusion maintains that the War of Restoration was a highly popular movement, which had a heterogeneous social character and was the

Table 1.8: Participants in the Rebellion Year 1863

Occupations	# of Participants
Merchants	4
Ranchers/Breeders	8
Militaries	23
Rural Laborers	23
Artisans	12
Public Employees	4
Wood-cutters	1
Total	*75*

Source: *Sumarias de Neyba, Sabaneta, Guayubín, Santiago Y Montecristi*. Colección Herrera, Archivo General De La Nación. República Dominicana.

result of a class alliance. This social alliance brought together farmers, laborers, artisans, landowners, ranchers, merchants, militaries, carpenters, and liberal professionals.

These social forces embodied different political currents: the remnants of the Trinitarian Movement, the Liberal Cibaeños, and the Becistas (followers of President Buenaventura Baez). All these forces had a common political objective: the restoration of the Republic.

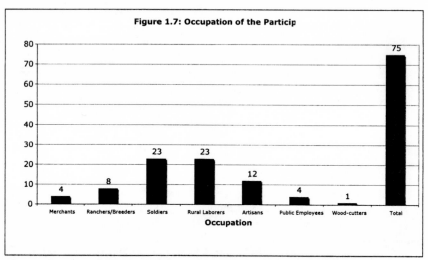

Source: *Sumarias de Neyba, Sabaneta, Guayubín, Santiago Y Montecristi*. Colección Herrera, Archivo General De La Nación. República Dominicana.

Table 1.9: Rebellions that Preceded the Restoration War

Dates	Place	Facts	Other Info.	Leaders of the Rebellion
May 2, 1861	Moca	Attack on military headquarters	Flag captured	José Contreras Cayetano Germosen
February 9,1863	Neiba	Attack on the house of the commander	Weak national movement	Cayetano Velásquez Manuel Chiquito
February 20,1863	Guayubín	Insurrection of the population began with three shots	A rebellion was initiated	Norberto Torres Lucas de Peña
February 21,1863	Sabaneta	Attack on military command	Participation by the members of City Hall	Santiago Rodríguez Antonio Batista Gregorio Luperòn Ignacio Reyes
February 23,1863	Montecristi	Threat to attack the town	Capitulation of the authorities	Juan Antonio Polanco Modesto Belliard
February 24,1863	Guayubín	Insurrection of the population began with three shots	A rebellion was initiated	Norberto Torres Lucas de Peña

Sources: Herrera: *Sumarias de Moca, Neiba, Guayubín, Sabaneta, Montecristi y Santiago.* Santo Domingo, Archivo General de la Nación.

This alliance of classes and political movements was not rare in the historical process of the Dominican Republic. The Dominican independence was achieved as a result of an alliance of classes that joined together nationalists and annexationist sectors.

Theses class alliances were untied when Pedro Santana achieved a military victory over the Trinitarians and *Cibaeños Liberales* after the revolution of 1857. Thus, historically the independence of the Dominican Republic existed during the period that precedes the annexation of Spain in a constant and tense precarious equilibrium, because the conservative ruling class monopolized the political power and continuously conspired to reduce the country to a colonial position.

This social alliance, confronted the Haitian invasions under the hegemony of the ranchers, and especially their maximum leader, Pedro Santana, and the political ideas that they represented. Pedro Santana and the ranchers suffered an overwhelming defeat during the War of Restoration. The other sector of the dominant class also consisted of annexationists with Buenaventura Báez as its leader. His political ideas were based on three main elements as Mu-kien A. Sang shows in Baez's biography: annexionism, anti-Haitianism and conservatism.

Ninth Conclusion: The Spanish Empire Response: An Anti-Insurgent Colonial State

Since the beginning of the uprisings and rebellions, the Captain General began to implement diverse repressive measures to face the pre-revolutionary situation. He decreed a state of emergency in all the Spanish territories of the island of Santo Domingo. Military Commissions were created to judge the "defendants of rebellion against the State."

Some Spanish officers received information that near to the Manzanillo Bay commercial and war ships from the United States were providing weapons and ammunitions to the Dominican revolutionaries. As a result, a state of alert was established. Gabriel Tassara, Spain's representative in Washington, informed the Consul of New York, Boston, Baltimore and New Orleans, to pass any suspicious information to the proper authorities so that they could stop any suspicious cargo directed to Santo Domingo.[33]

Other measures were the organization of the body of volunteers of Santo Domingo, who would share, along with Spanish military, the task of facing the uprising, and the conversion of Puerto Plata into an arrival station for the Spanish troops from Cuba and Puerto Rico.

Thus, the General Captain established an anti-insurgent state–in its colonial version, whose maximum priority was the pacification of the country in a political juncture of colonialist's contradictions that had generated rebellions, uprisings, and war. The anti-insurgent state in Santo Domingo used Cuba and Puerto Rico as strategic bases; from there they received resources, logistics, and a growing quantity of troops. Soldiers were gradually arriving to the country, and the troops were constantly increasing from the onset of the war.

Tenth Conclusion: The Impact of the War on the Economy and Society in Territories under Spanish Control

It was evident that at the beginning of 1864, that the Restoration War had seriously affected the economic structure of the country. The widespread uprising caused a break-up of the national productive apparatus, reducing the labor force and producing a notorious shortage of basic food for the population.

The impact of the war in the Dominican society led to drastic decreases of subsistence production of consumable goods and an excessive increase in the prices of basic staples.

Similarly, the agricultural products for exports, such as tobacco, mahogany and livestock reduced output.

The documents consulted show a clear picture of the effects of the war in the capital's City Hall, where incomes were not able to provide the demand of greater services on behalf of the population threatened by hunger and war.

The fiscal crisis that affected City Hall forced the government to suspend the services of public lighting, to close the Academy of Santo Domingo and to reduce the salaries of the professors of the school of Santa Barbara. Despite all the efforts of the Spanish Overseas Department urging City Hall to provide educational services to its inhabitants, they did not assume financial responsibility for the expenses of education.[34]

Alongside the fiscal crisis, an epidemic of smallpox spread among the Dominican population during the year of 1864. This deepened the difficult economic situation of people from the capital.[35]

The producers and exporters of tobacco and mahogany were seriously affected by the war. Analyzing the statistics on the exports of tobacco, it is evident that there was a dramatic reduction of this export to the German market. For example, in 1861, there were 48,114 quintals exported for the year, to 10,753 quintals for the year of 1864. However part of the production of tobacco in the Cibao region was smuggled through Haiti for the purchase of armaments and materials of war.

The incomes losses of the Commercial Houses, Federico Finke & Ca. that of SS Neuman & Sander, and Juan Kunhardt/Ca. Puerto Plata, demonstrates the negative impact of the war on the merchants. The total loss was approximately $468,530.51 pesos. These merchants exported tobacco to Germany.[36]

Eleventh Conclusion: The Complex Nature of the Restoration War

The Restoration War had a complex nature: it was an anti-colonial and anti-imperialist struggle of the Dominican nation against the Spanish empire by regaining the sovereignty and independence. In this case, I can say it was a war of national liberation.

The war also constituted a sort of civil war. A national minority sector was under the domain of the ranchers, an annexationist fraction under Pedro Santana's control. This fraction aligned with the Spanish troops. They fought against the liberals, nationalists, armed people and unorganized Dominican militias.

It was also a social war, highly popular, where the fundamental social force was constituted by the hundreds of anonymous peasants. Because of the Spanish fiscal exploitation, and by Archbishop Bienvenido Monzón's imposition of Catholic customs, the peasants were gradually incorporated into the fight against an oppressive system. What existed in Bosch's opinion was "a combination of a decidedly national liberation war with an explosive social war."[37]

This popular base of the war and the participation of the liberal intellectuals helped the war to become a revolution, which is explained in the Bulletin of the Provisional Government:

> Different Dominican villages started this war; this was followed by the masses, in a spontaneous way, without suggestions of any species of men of another class. The towns, exasperated by the oppression of the Spanish Government . . . rose simultaneously and took up weapons in defense of their rights.[38] [Author's translation]

The war also was racial in nature; there was the fear amongst large sectors of the black population and mulatto Dominicans that slavery could be reinstated. The examples of Cuba and Puerto Rico where slavery existed and the publicity of the Dominican freedom fighters, emphasizing that the slavery would be reestablished, contributed to the popular sectors perception of the war as an anti-slavery crusade against the white Spaniards who constituted the central nucleus of the Spanish army. The prejudice and the discrimination against the blacks and mulattos in Dominican society were always present in the Spanish colonies.

The Restoration War was an extremely ferocious war, where the Spanish army was defeated by the guerrilla warfare, as the generalized method of fighting, as well as by the terrifying efficiency of the machete. In addition, the Dominicans also caused unmentionable terror among the Spanish troops through the use of fire. Fire served as an offensive weapon against the enemy and topographical conditions and climate, created havoc within the ranks of the foreign army.

The illnesses of the tropics mercilessly attacked the inexperienced troops that came from Spain. The *rámpanos*, yellow fever, dysentery, malaria, smallpox, typhus, and intermittent fevers caused innumerable deaths in the Spanish army. The climate and illnesses became main allies of the Dominican popular army; for example, the number of Spanish soldiers who became sick from dysentery in 1863 in the entire country was 8,698, and the number of Spanish soldiers who suffered from intermittent fevers was 26,584 in 1864.[39]

How and why did the Restoration War become a Revolution? What type of Revolution arose from the Restoration War? A reflection on the Restoration has been advanced by Manfred Wilckens who explains the transition from war to Revolution using the model developed by James C. Davies, in his article "Toward a Theory of the Revolutions." Wilckens explains that the Restoration war occurs in a juncture characterized by a long period of economic growth and social development that is abruptly interrupted, making impossible the aspirations of the economic expectations of the general population. This predisposition created the psychological conditions for the revolution.[40]

Taking into consideration this contribution, it is necessary to carry out a more extensive analysis, which situates the Restoration revolution in the context of the debate on the theory of the revolution that has been developing in the academic world. In that debate is emphasized the contradictory complexity of that social phenomenon called revolution. More than psychological predisposition, there are a multiplicity of variables that must be taken into consideration: economic structure, political junctures, international context, social classes and ideology. However, I shall consider the role played by individuals and popular masses in this contradictory process.[41]

Having presented these considerations, I can indicate the myriad of conflicts and contradictions generated by Spanish administrative policies, plus the objective conditions (pre-revolutionary juncture) for the rise of a social movement of resistance that led to the Restoration War.

The main causes for the rise of the Restoration war were the following:

1. The class contradictions between lower sectors of the society and the Spanish colonial administration, such as, direct producers, landless peasants, and the laborers.
2. The weakening of the dominant class, which was replaced by the Spanish bureaucracy.
3. The development of a widespread animosity against the Spanish colonial government for the exclusion of groups of great influence in the Dominican society: freemasons, Protestants, Dominican soldiers, and Catholic priests.
4. Spain's racist and discriminatory policies alienated a sector of the population, especially the blacks and mulattos.
5. Economic causes were created for the revolution because the colonial government never invested in the infrastructure, which generated a wave of inflation in the entire country; in addition the colonial government taxed the exporting sectors, merchants and professionals.[42]

The fiscal exploitation against Dominicans through a burdensome fiscal policy and racial prejudice against mulattos and black Dominicans constituted the causes that made possible the massive incorporation of the Dominican people in the struggle for the restoration of Dominican independence.

The leadership of the Revolution originated from a strong combination of the old Trinitarian Movement, the Liberales Cibaeños, and a new emerging leadership identify with most of the program of the Revolution of 1857. This leadership was the vanguard that directed the fight by the Restoration of the Republic. Fortunately, the international context favored the Restoration Revolution; due to the fact that the United States was immersed in the War of Secession, it was not able to intervene in the internal situation of the country.

The war enabled the Dominican army to defeat simultaneously the native ranchers' class and the Spanish colonialists, releasing the possibility of reaffirmation of the national conscience in extensive sectors of the country, and serving as an example to the Spanish colonies of Puerto Rico and Cuba.

Lastly, the unification ideology of The Restoration War helped to add to the movement part of the annexationists, who became allied in the struggle against the Spanish Empire.

The regional impacts of the War became evident with the beginning of the Ten Years War in Cuba (1868-1878) and the rebellion of the *Grito de Lares* in *Puerto Rico*, which demonstrated that the Restoration War was the beginning of the end of the Old Spanish empire.

Twelfth Conclusion: Tactics, Strategy and Rearguard

The suitable tactic of the Restoration War was guerrilla warfare, just as described by Ramón Matías Mella in his *Instructions of the War of Guerrilla Warfare* "that gave the excellent results to the Dominican armies in their clash against the disciplined, well coached and better armed Spanish Troops." The instructions said the following:

1. In the present fight and in the military operations undertaken, the use of greater prudence is needed, observing always with greater concern and astuteness so we are not left to surprise, equalizing thus the superiority of the enemy in number, discipline and resources.

2. Our operations should be limited to never risk a general encounter to expose the fortune of luck in battle for the Republic. Make the enemy hostile during the day and at night, to intercept them at rear, their communications, and to their water supply each time that we are able to do that, these are cardinal points that will have to be present as the creed.

3. Attacking them with guerrilla warfare divided by two, three or four, that have a unit of action to their front, by their side, by the rearguard, not leaving them to rest neither during the day nor at night, so that not be owners but that of the land that step on, and surprising them whenever possible. These are rules that we must not stray from.

4. We must never let ourselves be surprised and we must do whatever possible to match them off guard, these are rules that we must not stray from.

5. Our troops must always, when possible, fight camouflaged in the bushes and make use of our knowledge of the forest and the knife and machetes. Every time that we see the possibility to breach security, we must hide inside and to an end to the enemy, we must not present to him a front, however small it may be, with regard to the Spanish troops they are well disciplined and generally superior in number, each time the victory depends on military strategy. They initially would take the advantage and we would be defeated.

6. We must never be caught of guard and be surprised even if it is just one man.

7. Do not allow them to sleep neither during the day nor at night, so that the illnesses wreck havoc on them more so than our firearms. This must be done alone and in small groups. The remainder shall rest and sleep.

8. If the enemy withdraws, find out, if is a false retreat. That is a very common stratagem in war. If is not, continue on to them in the retreat and enforce walk-

ing guerrilla warfare that will attack on all sides, if they advance, cause them to fall in ambushes and assail them with guerrilla warfare. Make every move of the enemy an opportunity to harass them in all the extension of the word...attack them from the swamp, from the forest and make you invisible to them.

9. Complete these war instructions with scrupulousness, while the enemy separates itself from its bases of operation, worse it will be for them if he tried to flee in the country, in a more difficult situation they will be.

10. Organize, wherever you are situated, a service of espionage, to know at all hours of the day and at night the state, their location, the force, the movements and intentions of the enemy[43] [Author's translation]

Using guerrilla warfare, ambush tactics, surprise attacks on the convoys, and using the torch against enemy forts, utilizing fire as an offensive weapon against the Spanish armies, the Dominican army caused havoc to the Spanish military.

The strategic objective of the Dominican armies under the direction of the Provisional Government was the rescue of the sovereignty and the independence by means of expulsion of the Spanish troops.

To make this strategy possible, the Provisional Government had the support of Haiti, which became the rearguard strategic movement in the measure that provided arms, gunpowder and other resources to the Dominican patriots.

The attainment of the goal for the Dominican popular army was based on armed and diplomatic struggles at the same time. There is no doubt that the tactics of the Dominican armies led to the failure of the Spanish armies and to the search for a diplomatic solution.

Thirteenth Conclusion: The Debate over Leadership

Our historiography has maintained a sharp debate about the issue of leadership in the war, trying vainly to find one supreme leader of the war. My conclusions in these notes are in the opposite direction: I will prove that the leadership of the Restoration War was of multiple and heterogeneous character and conforms itself according to its region.[44]

Heterogeneous, because there was a civil leadership comprising one sector of the provisional government: Pedro Francisco Bonó, Ulises Francisco Espaillat, Benigno Filomeno Rojas, etc. There was also a military leadership comprised of Gaspar Polanco, Santiago Rodríguez, Gregorio Luperón, Benito Monción, Pedro Florentino, Eusebio Manzueta and José Cabrera. Each one of these leaders played a role of vital importance in their regions, seeking grass root support in organization, and recruitment of new soldiers. Benito Mención was responsible for the defense of Monte Cristi and the Northwest region. Gregorio Luperón defended Santiago in the north and the east, Gaspar Polanco was chief of operations in Puerto Plata, Pedro Florentino was in charge of the southern region of the country.

Fourteenth Conclusion: The Political Contradiction and the Role of the Revolutionary Dictatorship of Polanco

Given the heterogeneousness and the nature of the social and political forces that confronted the Spanish armies in the Eastern part of the island, it is understandable there were a development of various political contradictions and also the development of several tactics in how to confront the enemy.

In the battle against the Spanish forces, the contradictions originated when the Dominican leaders decided not to follow the Provisional Government's directions. Military leaders such as Gregorio Luperón, Eusebio Manzueta and Pedro Florentino confronted the Spanish army following their own criteria, ignoring priorities, tactics and orders from the Provisional Government.

Inside the Provisional Government, the contradictions had a fundamentally political character and are the result of the different points of view that existed between the Liberal Cibaeños and the Baecistas.

Those contradictions were expressed in the "coup d'etat to Pepillo Salcedo" and in the establishment of the revolutionary dictatorship of Gaspar Polanco, which caused a phase of intransigent radical nationalism.[45] this nationalism translated into a greater belligerence against the Spanish armies. The most notorious examples of this new attitude were the capture of Higuey by the troops of the General Eusebio Manzueta, and the attack on Montecristi, December 28, 1864. Similarly, the different edicts of the provisional government show a line of hardening against the enemy.

An important aspect to consider is the attitude of Polanco and the members of the *intransigent block* in reference to the search for peace. For this group, peace was indissolubly united to obtaining independence and would not be able to be conceived without the recovery of the national sovereignty.

Pepillo Salcedo and the Baecistas favored peace on the basis of the submission of the Dominicans to the Spanish army, signifying the creation of a protectorate or maintaining the Spanish colonial control on Samaná or Montecristi, in exchange for the recognition of independence.

Fifteenth Conclusion: Regional Context, the Restoration War and the Revolutionary Cycle of the Spanish Caribbean

My point of view is that the Restoration War gave an opening to a revolutionary cycle in the Spanish Caribbean, which extended until the end of the 19th century. The cycle had general characteristics and particular accords with the specific realities of each one of the islands in the Spanish Caribbean, with its uneven levels of economic growth and of social and political organization.

Cuba and Puerto Rico constituted colonies of the Spanish empire in which slavery existed, censorship of the press, forced labor and widespread political repression, etc. In the case of the Dominican Republic, its reinstatement of

Spanish control was carried out after 17 years of independent life, without the existence of slavery and with an incipient experience as an independent nation. The first phase of this cycle was the Restoration War 1863-1865, followed by the "*Grito de Lares* in Puerto Rico in 1868, and continued with the *Ten Years war in Cuba*, 1868-1878. It is this first phase of the struggle for independence of Cuba and was it followed, by the second phase of the War of Independence of 1895-1898, which was the last phase of this revolutionary cycle.

The revolutionary cycle ended with the reestablishment of the independence of the Dominican Republic, the independence of Cuba (under the Platt amendment) and with a more than a century old neocolonial system in Puerto Rico, under the United States.

Sixteenth Conclusion: Political Crisis and the Cost of the War for Spain

In my previous publications, I already mentioned the political crisis generated by the Dominican Restoration War in Spain. The downfall of Isabel the Second and the beginning of the democratic republic of 1868-1874 are linked to the economic and political crisis in Spain, but also to the defeat of the Spanish army in Santo Domingo and the abandonment of the Dominican territory.[46]

Information about the cost of war was a major point of debate within the Spanish Parliament in March 1865. In documents available from that time, the cost of the war was estimated to be 392 million of *reales*. Coupled with the number of lives lost, which was 16,000, it became evident that the costs of the war were impossible to sustain for the Spanish Empire

As explained in chapters two and five, the Spanish colonies in the Caribbean contributed to the war in the form of economic resources, soldiers, and officers. Puerto Rico contributed 194,510.94 pesos and Cuba contributed with 1,481, 623.01 pesos. It is also important to note that during the years of 1862 and 1863, both colonies also contributed thousands of soldiers. However, these contributions did not occur without colonial complaints. The Cuban authorities asked the Spanish authorities in Madrid numerous times to be released from monetary contributions to the war in Santo Domingo. Cuba suggested to Spain the creation of direct remittances *(situado)* from Madrid to Santo Domingo.[47]

The contribution from the colonial governments of Cuba and Puerto Rico had a huge impact on the finances of each island. In the case of Cuba (during the year 1863) the colonial government had to borrow 600,000 pesos from the Spanish bank and 170,000 pesos from Messrs I. M. Morales & Co., a private corporation, and smaller sums from many other merchants."[48]

General De La Gándara, the last General Captain in Santo Domingo, estimated that it would be necessary to have a war navy budget of 4,374, 343 *pesos*, a budget of 39, 388, 500 pesos in order to finance the occupation of the Dominican Republic, and an incalculable amount for extraordinary expenses which is believed to be in the realm of 700,000,000 reales. That is to say, General De La

Gándara estimated that the annual expenses for war and occupation would be 787, 777,000 reales.[49]

The cost of the war and the exorbitant number of soldiers killed, injured, sickened and disabled explains the decision of the Narvaez government to abandon the Dominican territory. The Spanish parliament approved a motion recommending the abandonment of Santo Domingo. The Queen of Spain signed the decree that was already approved by the Spanish Cortes annulling the royal decree of May 19, 1861, which accepted the Annexation of Santo Domingo to Spain.

Seventeenth Conclusion: Abandonment of the Territory by the Spanish Troops

General José De La Gándara and his Spanish troops abandoned the territory of the Dominican Republic without signing an exit treaty. The Treaty of Carmelo, which was signed on June 9, 1865, was rejected by the Provisional Government of General Pedro Antonio Pimentel. The reasons for this rejection were the attempts of General De La Gándara to impose harsh conditions on the Dominican Government. He asked for approval of the following demands:

1. The Dominican independence has been a result of the magnanimity of the Spanish nation and Spain has been within its rights waging a war against the Restoration of the Dominican Republic.
2. Compensation to the Spanish State due to the expenses incurred as the result of the incorporation of the Eastern part of the island to the Spanish Empire. Compensation was also due to to the Spanish Empire because of war expenses, and administration of the territory.
3. Respect to people and properties, both Spanish, Dominican interests, as well as other international interests that had been loyal to the Spanish Government.
4. Conveyance of the international trade status of Most Favored Nation.[50] [Author's translation]

The abandonment of the territory was enacted as a result of the Spanish Parliamentary debate and eventual approval of the Real Decree of May 19, 1861. This decree abrogated the existing degree of incorporation of the Dominican Republic to the Spanish Monarchy. The Real Decree of May 19, 1861 was the culmination of a political crisis that was generated by the war due to the enormous expenses incurred; Spain's total failure in achieving the pacification of the country; and, because the Spanish Empire had suffered an extraordinary number of soldiers killed and wounded in the war.[51]

Notes

1. Emilio Rodríguez Demorizi, *Relaciones Dominico-Españolas* (Santo Domingo: Editora Montalvo, 1986), 138.
2. For an in depth discussion of Spanish foreign policy during the period, see Christian Hauch, *Dominican Republic and its Foreign Relations, 1844-1882.* (Ph.D. Diss. Of University of Chicago: Illinois, 1942).Charles Callan Tansill, *The United States and Santo Domingo, 1798-1873. A chapter in Caribbean Diplomacy* (Gloucester: The Johns Hopkins University, 1967).
   Carlos Federico Pérez, *Historia Diplomática de la República Dominicana 1844-1861* (Santo Domingo: Universidad Pedro Henríquez Ureña, 1973). Maria Helena, Muñoz. *Historia de las Relaciones Internacionales de la República Dominicana. El Colonialismo Europeo y las Relaciones Internacionales 1844-1861* (Santo Domingo: Editora de la Universidad Autónoma de Santo Domingo, 1979).
3. David Yuengling, *Highlights in the Debates in the Spanish Chamber of Deputies Relatives to the Abandonment of Santo Domingo* (Washington, Murray and Heister, 1941), 1. (hereafter Yuengling *Highlights).*
4. Eduardo Calleja González and Antonio Fontecha Pedraza, *Una Cuestión de Honor Una Polémica sobre La Anexión de Santo Domingo vista desde España 1861-1865 (Santo* Domingo: Fundaciòn García Arevalo, 2005), 22-23.
5. Luis Martínez Fernández, *Torn between Empires. Economy, Society, and Patterns of Political Thought in the Caribbean, 1840-1878* (Athens and London, 2001), 26-32. (hereafter Martinez Fernandez, *Torn between Empires.)*
6. Martínez Fernández, *Torn between Empires*, 23. The compromise of 1850 was the United States Congress legislation that put limits on the expansion of slavery, but in where it already existed. P. Thompson, *Dictionary of American History.* (New York: MPG Books, Ltd, Bodmin, Cornwall, 2000), 99-100. (hereafter Thompson, *Dictionary).*
7. Louis A. Perez, *Cuba, between Reform and Revolution* (New York: Oxford University Press, 1995), 110. (hereafter Perez, *Cuba).*
8. Pérez, *Cuba,* 108.
9. Ramiro Guerra, *Expansión territorial de los Estados Unidos a Expensa de España y Los Países Hispanoamericanos* (La Habana: Instituto Cubano del Libro, 1975), chaps. 10-11. Manifest of Ostend was the secret memo to President Pierce from U. S. Diplomat in Europe urging the United States Purchase of Cuba for the protection of slavery.
10. Luis Álvarez, *Dominación colonial y Guerra Popular 1861-1865 (La Anexión y la Restauración en la Historia Dominicana) (*Santo Domingo: Universidad Autónoma de Santo Domingo, 1986) ,17-18. (hereafter, Álvarez *Dominación Colonial).*
11. Álvarez-López, *Dieciséis Conclusiones Fundamentales Sobre La Anexión y La Guerra de la Restauración 1861-1865* (Santo Domingo: Editorial Argos, 2005), 23-24. (hereafter Álvarez, *Dieciséis Conclusiones).* Yuengling, *Highlights in the Debates,* 1.
12. Emilio Rodríguez Demorizi, *Relaciones Dominico-Españolas* (Santo Domingo: Editora Montalvo, 1955), 144-145. American filibuster was applied to individual adventures that used military forces to annex Central America and Caribbean countries to United States. Thomson, *Dictionary,* 145.
13. Álvarez, *Dominación Colonial,* 23-25. Pérez, *Historia Diplomática,* chapters 9-10.
14. Álvarez, *Dominación Colonial,* 17-21. Clayton-Bulwer Treaty of 1850 provided that the two countries jointly control and protect what was to become the Panamá Canal.

The treaty was ratified by the Senate and concluded on April 19, 1850. The Columbia Encyclopedia, Sixth edition, 2001.www.bartleyby.com/65cl/Clayton BT.HTML.

15. Tansill, *United States and Santo Domingo*, 178.

16. Hauch, *Dominican Republic*, 137-138. The Monroe Doctrine is the United States foreign policy that effectively claimed hegemony over the whole of the Americas. Arthurs P.Whitaker, *Los Estados Unidos y la independencia de América Latina*. (Argentina: Editorial Universidad de Buenos Aires, 1960), 360-363. *Manifest Destiny* was the phrase used in the 19th century to justify the United States expansionist policies. Thomas E. Skidmore and Peter H. Smith, *Modern Latin America*. (New York: Oxford University Press, 2005), 398-402.

17. Roberto Cassá, *Historia y Económica y Social de la República Dominicana* (Santo Domingo: Alfa y Omega, 1980), vol.2, chapter 16.

18. Hoetink, H. *The Dominican People 1850-1900 Notes for a Historical Sociology* (Baltimore: John Hopkins University Press, 1972), 47-50.

19. Martínez Fernández, *Torn by Empires*, 90.

20. Cassá, *Historia Económica*, chapter 16. Jaime Domínguez, *Economía y Política en la República Dominicana, 1844-1861*. (Santo Domingo: Universidad Autónoma de Santo Domingo, 1977).

21. Ernesto Sagas and Orlando, Inoa. *The Dominican People: A Documentary History* (Princeton: Markus Weiner Publisher, 2003), 107.

22. Sagas and Inoa, *The Dominican People*, 106-109.

23. Jean Price-Mars, *La República de Haiti y la República Dominicana. Diversos aspectos de un problema histórico, geográfico y etnológico*. (Madrid: Industrias Graficas, S.L. 1953), vol 3, 67.

24. Álvarez-López, *Dieciséis conclusiones*, 41.

25. Álvarez, *Dominación Colonial*, 14.

26. Franklyn Franco, "El Racismo en los Inicios de la República." *Isla Abierta*, Revista Cultural, no.674, sábado, (junio 29 de 1966): 8-10.

27. Emilio Rodríguez Demorizi, *Antecedentes de la Anexion a España* (Ciudad Trujillo: Editora Montalvo, 1955), 99-100. Álvarez, *Dominación Colonial*, 36-37.

28. Cesar Herrera, *Documentos para la Historia de la República Dominicana.* (Santo Domingo: República Dominicana, Archivo General de la Nación), vol 1.

29. Manuel de Jesús Galván, *Novelas Cortas* (Santo Domingo: Editora Búho, 2000), 48.

30. *Colección de Leyes, Proyectos y Resoluciones Emanadas del Poder Legislativo y Ejecutivo de la República Dominicana* (Santo Domingo: Imprenta del Listin Diario, 1927), 210-239.

31. Relativo a la suscripción que se abrió para socorrer a la familia de Santiago. Socorro, 1863. Legajo no.25. Santo Domingo: República Dominicana, Archivo General de la Nación.

32. Álvarez-López, *Dieciséis conclusiones*, 55-56. Adriana Mu-Kien Sang, *Buenaventura Báez: El Caudillo del Sur*. (Santo Domingo: Instituto Tecnológico de Santo Domingo, 1987), chap.2.

33. Expediente sobre la Sublevación de Santo Domingo de 1863. *Boletín del Archivo General de La Nación*, no.94, (1952): 291.

34. Anexión a España. Expediente sobre la Academia de Santo Domingo, 1865. Legajo no.35, Archivo General de la Nación.

35. Maria Magdalena Guerrero Cano, *Aspectos sanitarios durante la segunda independencia de Santo Domingo. Su repercusión en Andalucía*. (Sevilla, Imprenta E.E.HA, 1984), 333.

36. Wilckens Manfred. "Dotación de Capital de la Sociedad Rural Dominicana en el Siglo XIX." *Ciencia y Sociedad*, vol. 27. no. 2, (Abril-Junio, 2002): 158-166.

37. Juan Bosch, *La Guerra de la Restauración y la Revolución de Abril* (Santo Domingo: Editora Corripio, 1966), 125.

38. Emilio Rodríguez Demorizi, *Actos y Doctrinas del Gobierno de la Restauración* (Santo Domingo: Editora del Caribe, 1963), 77

39. Guerrero Cano, *Aspectos Sanitarios*, 330-331.

40. Wilckens, Manfred. "Hacia una Teoría de la Revolución: el Caso Dominicano." *Ciencia y Sociedad*, XXV. No. 4. (October -December 2000): 427-464. Davies, James C. "Toward a Theory of the Revolution." *American Sociological Review*, no.1, (Feb. 1962): 5-19. The debate about revolution is in Brian Meek, *Caribbean Revolutions and Revolutionary Theory*. (Barbado, Jamaica: University of the West Indies Press 1993), 7-47.

41. Alcides García Lluberes, Mella y la guerra de guerrillas. *Homenaje a Mella*, Academia DOminicana de la Historia (Santo Domingo: Editora del Caribe, 1964), 253-254.

42. Marino Mejia, foreword to Álvarez-López, *Dieciséis Conclusiones*, 15-18. He sustains a different point of view in reference to the leadership of the Restoration war.

43. Álvarez, *Dieciséis conclusiones*, 73-76.

44. Álvarez, *Dieciséis conclusiones*, 82.

45. Álvarez, *Dominación colonial*, 174-178.

46. Álvarez, *Dominación colonial*, 183-185.

47. Yuengling, *Highlights*, 56-57.

48. Yuengling, *Highlights*, 144.

49. Yuengling, *Highlights*, 57.

50. Álvarez, *Dominación colonial*, 183-184.

51. Álvarez, *Dominación colonial*, 183-185. De La Gándara, *Anexión y Guerra*, vols.2, 319-322.

## 2

Kidnapping the Rebels' Goods: State and Society under the Last Spanish Domination of Quisqueya (1863-1865)

On the analysis of the *Commission for the Kidnapping of the Rebels' Goods* I start with the premise that this commission was an institution of the Spanish colonial government because it administered and implemented the policies delivered by the General Captain, head of the Spanish empire in the new colony.

One of the characteristics of any colonial state is not only the administration of the new territory but also the political dominance of the new colonies by the ruling class. This process of political control generates a class contradiction between different fractions in the ruling class and also in the lower class of the society. In this process the ruling class struggles to impose their dominion in the society.

The colonial government is the center of political power, exercising this power throughout a network of different political institutions whose objectives are to implement the empire's policies in the new colony. In the previous Dominican Republic, these institutions were in charge of the tax system, the Dominican and Spanish Army, the Catholic Church, city councils, productions and regulations, exports and imports with foreign nations, and social customs[1]

Even in a colonial state, the government uses different methods to control the society; one method is political coercion through the use of the army and the repressive apparatus of the State. Another method of control is political persuasion through the use of ideological means of domination, seeking the consent of the citizens by consensus in the civil society.[2]

Based on these premises regarding the colonial government, I can raise the following questions: What were the characteristics of the Spanish Imperial Government in the new Caribbean colony? How was this colonial government structured in relation to the indigenous dominant class and the Dominican lower classes? How did the colonial government function in a context of general war? What state institutions implemented the government's policy in the civil society? Why did the colonial government implement a repressive policy of goods confiscation against the rebels?

Answering these questions will be the objectives of this chapter.

From the Provisional Government to the General Captain

The annexation to Spain occurred on March 18, 1861, and the first measures of the Spanish government were oriented to assure the military's control in the old colony. Another objective was insuring maritime hegemony in the Caribbean Sea and the Atlantic Ocean, which are in close proximity to island.

The annexation by Spain of the eastern part of the island, together with Cuba and Puerto Rico, formed the new Antilles domain, the expansionist dream of the Spanish ruling class to revitalize her colonial possessions in the Caribbean.

The Governor and General Captain of Cuba, Francisco Serrano, instructed Pedro Santana, formal president of the Dominican Republic and main responsible for the annexation to Spain, to appoint a commission to gather the greater amount of information about the colony with the objective of effectively organizing the new colonial territory.

The transition from the commission to the two new governmental offices, known as *Secretarías de Gobernación*, happened in a short period of time. The first office was in charge of the colonial policy and the second was in charge of military affairs until the imperial government established a definitive political system for the colony.

With Pedro Santana having been appointed by the Spanish Colonial Authority General Captain of the new Spanish colony, the most conservative sector of the ruling class achieved the strategic objective of monopolizing the political power.

It was immediately evident that the Spanish colonial authorities realized that Pedro Santana and other members of the ruling class were an obstacle for the development of an effective colonial government. Very soon they realized that this fraction of the ruling class was more interested in itself than in the administration of an effective colonial system. Pedro Santana and his group were interested in the most lucrative situation, and they seemed interested only in a higher salary and good position.[3]

For that reason the Spanish ruling class's interest was in the total control of the state apparatus and institutions. Therefore this fraction of the Dominican ruling class was displaced from the government. In addition, Spanish citizens were appointed as General Captain of the new colony together with the other most important positions in the state bureaucracy.

The transfer of the political power from the Dominican ruling class to the Spanish bureaucracy from Spain, Cuba, and Puerto Rico showed the interest of the Spanish ruling class to reorganize the colony in agreement with the other colonial possessions in the Caribbean.

One of the main obstacles that the new Spanish colonial authority had to confront was Pedro Santana; his attitude was in total opposition to the new Spanish colonial authority, and his lack of cooperation and never ending complaints created an atmosphere of continuous confrontation. Some of his subordinates also abused the discretional power that they controlled; that was the case of Pedro Valverde, Governor of Santo Domingo, who denied the prisoners food and used them to do forced labor. He also sent people to jail for no reason and detained others in a very arbitrary manner.[4]

The reorganization of the colony started during the period in which Pedro Santana was the General Captain of the colony. The creation of new political institutions was oriented to curtail Santana's and some of his followers' power. The new functionaries believed that Spain's strategy in the colony was in opposition to Santana and his associates.

The new authority established two new institutions: *Real Hacienda* and the *Comisaría Regia*. Both institutions curbed Pedro Santana's political power, and veteran administrators from Spain were appointed as heads of these institutions. The appointment of Joaquin M. De Alba as the head of the Real Hacienda is an example of this effort to control Santana's power. De Alba was in charge of the organization of this institution, and he was also responsible for the appointment of the new functionaries, the application of regulations from Cuba and Puerto Rico to the new Spanish colony, and the execution of orders coming from Spain.

Other functionaries from Spain displaced the indigenous ruling class loyal to Pedro Santana. Felipe Dávila Fernández de Castro, Miguel Lavastida, Pedro Delgado, Antonio Madrigal, Miguel Valverde, and Pedro Curiel were replaced by new Spanish officers, which included José Maria Melo, Miguel Tavira, Ramón de la Torres Trassiera, Eugenio López Bustamante, José Porrua y Valdieso, Ramón Pierola, and Manuel Otorena. From then on, these functionaries were in charge of reorganizing the new colony.[5]

The reorganization of the new colony made possible changes in the relationship between the state and society. Beginning with the new colonial control of the country, the colonial state became a more interventionist state institution, making efforts to transform the Dominican policy, economy, society, religion, and culture.

The Spanish bureaucracy tackled the difficult task of colony reorganization: at the beginning it transformed several Dominican institutions such as the Justice System, the Catholic Church, the territorial divisions, the fiscal policy and the Dominican army as well as others. The economic structure was organized following the examples of Cuba and Puerto Rico. On the *Secret Instruction for the Government of Santo Domingo of June 19 1862,* sent to the new General Captain Felipe Rivero, the emphasis was on the immigration of workers from Spain to expand the labor force and on the application of other economic reforms similar to the *Real Cédula de Gracias* of August 10 and 12 1815, 21 and 24 of October from Cuba. This set of legislation applied to Cuba and Puerto Rico, together with the other important economic and social changes, promoted an economic expansion based on the development of commercial agriculture such as tobacco, sugar, and coffee.

The "Secret Instruction" was a program of economic development that included the planting of cotton, expansion of tobacco production and public investments in bridges, roads, and railroads. Analyzing this document it is possible to conclude that the objective of the colonial government was to make feasible the transition from the subsistence agriculture and cattle production to a system of commercial agriculture in the new colony.

The transition to commercial agriculture was possible for a combination of available land, labor forces and capital. In the Dominican society, different from Cuba and Puerto Rico, the only resource available was land; the labor forces were scarce and the capital was almost non-existent. The characteristics of the Dominican rural landscape, especially the system of land ownership known as *terrenos comuneros,* was another impediment to the development of commercial agriculture because peasants were able to use land for subsistence production. The lack of black slaves and the low density of the population were structural obstacles difficult to overcome.[6]

This economic program was short-lived because in the process of reorganizing the colony, the Spanish authorities harmed the interest of almost all social sectors of the Dominican society: peasants, merchants, priests, artisans, army officers, masons, Protestants and professionals. A system of national oppression and exclusion was established throughout the colonial legislation, together with a policy of prejudice and racism against the blacks and mulatos from the country.

It is difficult to establish which of these factors impacted more in the different sectors of Dominican society. The society behaves in a complex and contradictory system of actions and reactions. For example, some of the measures implemented by the colonial government had to be changed as a result of the reaction of different social sectors. In the case of the paper money, conversion to a new currency was not done according to the public's expectations.

The system of conversion of the old currency to the new was slow. While the rejection of bill denominations was seen as a plot by the colonial government that favored its functionaries.

The generalized social tensions created by the cumbersome system of currency conversion led to the changes of the April 1862 law to a set of new regulations that specify the conditions to change the paper money, making the system more favorable for the lower classes of the society.

The new regulations were approved in June 1862 and included two members of the City Council and a committee to review complicated cases. This committee was integrated by functionaries of the general treasury and internal revenues administration.[7]

The fiscal exploitation of the population was another thorny issue that impacted almost all social sectors. The imposition of new taxes, which hit merchants, lawyers, doctors, carpenters, peasants, retail merchants, painters, butcher, and daily laborers and horse-drawn carts created havoc in the Dominican population.

The fiscal pressure over the population can be measured by the fast increment in the amount of taxes imposed during the years of 1862 and 1863. During 1862, the amount of money from taxes was of 302, 741, 61, during the year 1863 the increment was of 705, 325, 00. An increase of more than 100% in income from fiscal contribution in only one year.[8]

Other taxes were imposed on the population, such as, 4% over the value of income from rental houses and a 100% increase in the *Derecho de Patente*. Neither the midwife nor the owner of horse drawn carriages escaped the Spanish fiscal system.

Other events that happened at the moment played an important role, such as, delay in the money coming from La Havana to make the payment for the Spanish garrison and the colonial bureaucracy from Spain. The propaganda and agitation about the idea of reestablishment of the black slavery system in the Eastern part of the island, following the example of Cuba and Puerto Rico, spread throughout the population.[9]

The political ideas and political consciousness played an important role as well, especially among individuals coming from the *Trinitarian* movement and *Cibaeños/as Liberales*. These individuals had clear political consciousness about the need to preserve the national state and maintain a free nation. The incorporation of these groups into the struggle for the reestablishment of the Republic occurred in a critical juncture in the history of the country. They were in total opposition to the annexation of the country to other Europeans empires, which was the ruling class's aspiration.

These groups were a minority in the society, but their opposition to the colonial regime played a pivotal role in the process of struggle that led to the chain of rebellions and Restoration war. But it must be said that the main cause was the multiple contradictions created by the colonial regime in the process of administration of the new territory. Overlooking the fact that the new colony was a formally independent country for 17 years, without the black slavery system and without a tradition of plantations. The labor force coercion as was known in Cuba and Puerto Rico was almost non-existent, a result of the communal land ownership and the low population density.[10]

The colonial model of Cuba and Puerto Rico that the Spanish bureaucracy followed, and its application to the Dominican society, resulted in the creation of a colonial system of global oppression that led to a revolutionary juncture and the development of a social/ racial war with the participation of different social sectors of the Dominican society.

From the General Captain to the Counter-Insurgent Colonial State

Since the beginning of the rebellions and insurrections, the colonial government started to implement a widespread system of political repression in order to contain the pre-revolutionary juncture. They established a military commission to judge those "accused of military plotting against the state, who declare themselves with arms or in favor of government already abolished and incompatible with the political constitution of Spain; those that attended meetings with the objectives of encouraging rebels' plans and those that try to recruit others to separate them from legitimate authority."[11] [Author translation]

The colonial government implemented a system to monitor the United States war ships along the Haitian coast due to the suspicions of collaboration with weapons and military equipment from North Americans. The consuls of New York, Boston, Baltimore, and New Orleans were on alert status to stop any suspicious shipment directed to Santo Domingo.[12]

Other important measures were the edicts organizing in the capital the Spanish volunteer body, which was responsible to confront the rebels together with the Spanish army. The last measure was that Puerto Plata become a station for the arrival of the Spanish army.[13]

Suddenly the Colonial Government was transformed in an insurgent colonial state, whose major priority was the pacification of the country in a political juncture of intensive class struggle and political contradictions that led to rebellions, conspiracies and war.

The contra-insurgent state transformed Cuba and Puerto Rico into centers of support for the Spanish army. From there came the Spanish troops, the Dominican prisoners were also sent to Cuba and Puerto Rico and the sick and dead soldiers went to both colonies. Part of the economic resources to support the war also came from both places, which contributed 88% of the war expenses. The contributions from Cuba and Puerto Rico are in Figure 2.1.[14]

In reference to the Spanish troops, exhibit no.2 and Figure 2.2 show how the number of soldiers was increasing as the war spread throughout the country. In August of 1863 the number of Spanish soldiers was 4,166 troops; that number increased to 10,951 in October, and in December to 14,572. The rapid increment of Spanish soldiers can be explained by the defeat of the Spanish troops in the Battle of September 6, 1863 in Santiago.

During the year 1864, the numbers of troops increased drastically, reaching the amount of 19,494 soldiers. The military strategy of the Governor was to attack the city of Santiago, birthplace of the revolutionary war against the Spanish troops and site of the Provisional government, with a formidable expedition from Montecristi.

The monthly arrival of Spanish troops, based on the monthly average of soldiers coming from Cuba and Puerto Rico, as is shown in Figure 2.2, increased

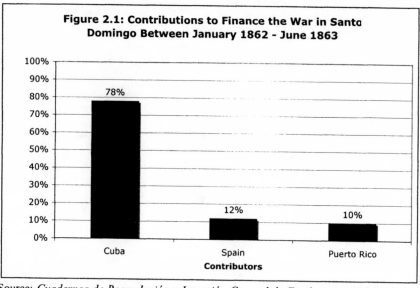

Figure 2.1: Contributions to Finance the War in Santo Domingo Between January 1862 - June 1863

Source: *Cuadernos de Recaudación e Inversión General de Fondos para la Isla de San-toDomingo*, quoted in Jaime de Jesús Domínguez, *La Anexión de la República Domini-cana a España*. (Santo Domingo: Editora de la Universidad Autónoma de Santo Domingo, 1979), 207-210.

the total number of Spanish troops by 44% between August 1863 and June of 1864.[15]

The numbers of Soldiers coming to Española from Spain, Cuba and Puerto Rico increased constantly. However, the steady increment of soldiers, officers, and war equipment (artillery, military health personnel, war engineers, horses and tents) never stopped the spread of the war that extended throughout the entire country. From the rich to the poor and also blacks, mulattos and white, many different Dominican factions engaged in war against Spain. The insurrection became a widespread war against the Spanish troops and the Dominicans who sympathized with Spain.

Beginning in September 1863, the condition of the war changed drastically because what had been a haphazardly organized war against an empire became an organized government sponsored campaign. In the Northern region of the Dominican Republic, specifically in Santiago, a new provisional government institutionalized the nation's opposition to the Spanish Empire.

The development of the Provisional Government contributed to the strengthening of the insurgent movement and the neutralization and weakening of the colonial regime. Four reasons contributed to the inefficacy of the Spanish troops. First, the expansion of the war undermined the colonial state because it could not provide services to the Spanish and Dominican citizens because pacifying the colony was the priority.

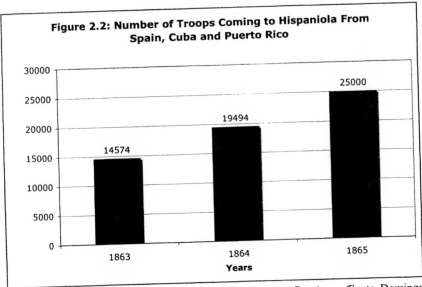

Figure 2.2: Number of Troops Coming to Hispaniola From Spain, Cuba and Puerto Rico

Source: José De La Gándara, *Anexión y Guerra de Santo Domingo.* (Santo Domingo: Editora Santo Domingo: República Dominicana, 1975), 632.

Second, as a result of a drastic decline in governmental income, due to the economic crisis caused by the war, Spain lost a great deal of revenue. The rapid decline in revenues can be explained also because the colonial government had to exempt the payment of taxes in the import of foods from Cuba and Puerto Rico due to the increased inflation. At the same time, the government expenses increased due to the demand of public assistance by the population loyal to Spain and living in the provinces under Spanish domain. Lack of jobs, housing, food and economic resources were the problems faced by these people.

Third, the persistent and daily desertion of officers of the Spanish colonial government weakened it. Documentation shows that the desertion of police officers, priests, military personnel, city council members, and volunteers steadily increased as the war dragged on.

Fourth, the tactic of guerrilla warfare was the best method for waging a war against the highly effective Spanish army. The insurgent army implemented the use of torches and machetes as devastating weapons against Spain and Dominican allies. This usage raised the Spanish army's fear, increasing the overall havoc. The success of guerrilla warfare was also partly due to ample knowledge that the Dominican insurgent army held about the geographical territory of the war. The impossibility of the Spanish army destroying the supply system of the Provisional Government allowed the Dominican guerrillas to constantly attack the Spanish army.

Despite the difficult situation of waging a war in a very hostile environment, the colonial regime created a new repressive institution to confront the propaganda, agitation, and collaboration of the Dominican people with the rebels in Santo Domingo, Baní, Azua and Puerto Plata. This new institution was the Commission to confiscate the goods and properties of the rebels, and their sympathizers.

Origin and Evolution of the Rebels' Goods Confiscations

A large number of property owners have abandoned by their properties (i.e. farms and houses) because the owners are in the insurgent districts as participants in the rebellion or as prisoners or fugitives in the forest. In some cases these properties are under the administration of people without legal authorization of the owners.

The previous situation described is highly negative for the public wealth and demands a fast solution from the government.

Several property owners are outstanding supporters of the rebellion. In that capacity, they lost the faculty over their properties and goods, being fair and in justice, the authority confiscate these and raise some resources to compensate for the damages caused by the rebellion to private and public properties.

The criminal act of the insurrection, the mass assassination, destruction of entire villages by fire, the devastation of extended regions, the unjust pressure and the lawlessness over all kinds of properties results in loss of hundreds of properties, and impoverishment of hundreds of women, children and elderly. These people cannot survive without the assistance of the government.

The authority must protect the properties of such individuals in rebel territories against their will. Some of them are in jails. Others are detained or in other conditions. The duty of the authority is to protect the interest of the people loyal to the Queens and Spain.[16] [Author's translation]

The decree would be applied in City Councils and municipal bodies, which were responsible for the administration of the goods of any person in rebel territory through Commissions appointed with those objectives. These Commissions would receive a 10% of the benefits of each sale and it had the faculty to sell in public auction the perishable merchandise that could be damaged or deteriorated. The money accumulated from the sale or auction had to be used for the City Council to finance a social policy according to some criteria established by it.[17]

Following the decree, City Councils from Baní, Azua and Santo Domingo appointed their Commission to initiate the confiscation and administration of rebel's properties and goods. In Santo Domingo they appointed Leonardo del Monte and Pedro M. de Mena, in Azua, Carlos Eleuterio Deshapte and José Maria Soto, in Baní, José Manuel Báez and Esteban Billini.

Based on the documentation about confiscations, auctions, renting, claims, helps, and property sales, the different commissions initiated a rapid effort to confiscate all the properties of any deserters of the Spanish army from public administration. The number of deserters increased more and more as the war expanded over different regions in the country.[18]

This Commission's tasks and responsibilities were the following:

1. It has to identify rebels' properties, goods and animals.
2. Confiscate and sell such goods in public auction: donkeys, horses, mules, oxen, goats, calves, mare, pigs, farms, houses and portion of land in the cities.
3. Elaborated listing of properties subject to be confiscated: farms in the countryside, houses, pieces of land in the cities, etc. Prepare report about incomes and expenses in the administration of the properties, animals and goods. [Author's translation]

The documentation showed properties confiscated in Santo Domingo, Baní, and Azua.

In Santo Domingo, properties were confiscated from Isidro Contreras, Manuel Rojas, Manuel Araujo, Francisco Páez, Juan Hernández, Pedro Betances, Juan Ruiz, José Maria Cabral, José de la Cruz, Francisco Saviñon, Juan Ramón Fiallo and José Joaquín Machado. The Commission confiscated 100 huts, 39 houses, 8 urban farms and 4 farms (Estancias).[19]

Table 2.1: Confiscated Properties in Santo Domingo

Property Type	# of Properties Confiscated
Huts	100
Houses	39
Small Plots of Land	8
Faros	4
Total	*151*

Source: *Relación de las Propiedades Incautadas por la Comisión Administradora e Investigadora*. Legajo 25, Anexión a España. Archivo General de la Nación, Santo Domingo, República Dominicana.

In Baní animals were confiscated from Jorge Guerra, Pedro J. Rodríguez, Pedro Pablo González, Damián Lugo, Nicolás Vizcaínos, Juan González, Juan Cordero, Joaquín Castillo and Alejandro Soto. The Commission confiscated 17 donkeys, 11 horses, 6 cows, 5 oxen and 3 calves. These numbers are shown in Table 2.2.[20]

Table 2.2: Confiscated Animals in Bani

Animal Type	# of Animals Confiscated
Donkeys	17
Horses	11
Cows	06
Bulls	05
Calves	03
Total	*42*

Source: *Relación de los Bienes pertenecientes a los rebeldes que se han averiguado desde el Ultimo Septiembre hasta la Fecha*. Legajo 25, Anexión a España. Archivo General de la Nación.

Table 2.3: Confiscated Properties in Azua

Types of Properties	# of Properties Confiscated
Urban Farms	114
Small Plot of Land	38
Ranches	2
Total	*154*

Source: *Relación de los Bienes Pertenecientes a los Rebeldes que se han Averiguado desde el último Septiembre hasta la fecha*. Legajo 25, Anexiòn a España. Archivo General de la Nación.

In Azua, properties were confiscated from Gregorio Salazar, Manuel Díaz, Eugenio Santana, Antonio Garrido, Ramón Payano, Teresa Méndez, Ezequiel González, Manuel Medrano, Nicolás Díaz, Raymundo Suero. The Commission confiscated the following properties: 114 urban farms, 38 *conucos*, and 2 farms.[21]

The properties, animals, farms and other goods affected mainly rebel families and relatives. These were living in the rebels' houses and sometimes receiving incomes from the properties and farms.

The confiscations of the properties doubtlessly meant a process of compulsive impoverishment of these families, which lost properties and income. The reaction of these families was to start a wave of claims against the commission's determination. For example, there was the case of Dominga Valencia, who was in charge of three houses for her husband Juan Esteban Aviar. The commission confiscated these houses because Juan was in the *faction*, meaning he was supporting the rebels in the struggle against Spain. The claim of Dominga Valencia resulted in the devolution of the residence that she was living in together with her small son.[22]

Another case was the condition of Dorotea Sanchez, who put to the disposition of the commission two huts and the rent that she was receiving from Manuel Sanchez's properties, allegedly member of the rebel faction. The properties were confiscated, even when she voluntarily advanced the money to the commission. Despite that, she decided to raise complaints against the local colonial officers. Her claim was taken into consideration and the confiscation was suspended. She was basically depending on the rent of one of the houses for livelihood and living in the second one.

Fortunately, she was able to recover the properties because the expropriation decree would have plunged her into misery.[23]

The enormous number of claims faced led to the elaboration of a set of guideline about how to administer the confiscation of rebel's properties and commodities. These guidelines established the prerogatives of the commission members, which were the following:

1. Investigate the properties and commodities of the rebels and register the goods in a book with the necessary specifications.
2. To establish an account with all the incomes from properties rented or commodities sold.
3. Report on a monthly basis to the City Council about the conditions of the urban and rural properties, farms, animals, commodities and incomes deriving from them.
4. The commission is not allowed to make any sale without the City Council's authorization, nor repair houses without a contract and that contract has to be the result of an auction.
5. The furniture or other perishable commodities must be sold in public auction with the authorization of the civil superior government and the report about the sale has to be sent to the City Council.
6. The commission is the money collector and with the monthly reports will prepare a deposit to the existing sums.
7. The commission's income is 80% and 2% to the City Council treasury.
8. Every three months the commission must send a financial report to the City Council President and a report about the overall operation to the Civil Superior Government.[24] [Author's translation]

The guidelines answered some of the concerns raised by City Councils from Bani and Azua, but others were not contemplated in the March 19 1864 decree. The Civil Superior Government addressed other concerns regarding administration of income confiscation and expenses.

The Municipal Council from Bani questioned if it were possible that the children or rebels' relatives had the right to demand payment of the properties that belonged to them and also if they had the right, using the money generated by the properties that had been expropriated, to pay some debt to a third person.

Similar to this claim, the City Council from Azua, received great pressure from the city merchants, who were asking the Commission to use the income from confiscated properties to make payments owed by the rebels. They alleged that this infusion of money would contribute to improve the miserable condition of the local businesses.

Despite the opposition to this claim, the analysis of the documentation showed that its produce payments over certain confiscated properties. The cases of Ramon Fallo, Manuel Machado and Narciso Pastor, whose properties were confiscated, had pending debt with Bernarda Figueroa, Telesforo Objio and Ventura Alfau. Such debts were paid by the Commission.

But one thing was the guidelines and the other was the reality. The lack of income and liquid capital of the City Council made it impossible for them to address some of the ordinary responsibilities faced by the population. Due to that situation, it started to use the economic resources from the expropriation decree as an income to solve some of the pressing issues in the provinces.

This was the case of Azua. The municipal council claimed that they never received a copy of the Instruction of July 12, which provided the use of the economic resources without authorization of the General Administration of Internal Revenues (*Administración General de Reales Rentas*). [25]

According to a communication from Carlos Antonio Deschaste, member of the commission to administer the rebels' properties and commodities from Azua, the City Council from this city made the decision to invest the economic resources from the confiscation decree in some of the pressing needs of the city.

The City Council from Azua invested 401,080 *pesos Fuertes* in the following items:

Tools and road repairs	140.00
Payment to Ignacio Saviñon to pick up garbage in the town	4.00
Payment to capture lost oxen	4.00
Payment to capture cows and oxen from the rebels	20.00
Payment for material to repair the town wagon	20.00
[Author's translation]	

The Azua mayor received a severe reprimand for the convenient interpretation of the March 19 Decree, going beyond it in using the economic resources without the authorization of the colonial government, to solve problems relate to the province.

The colonial government didn't approve of the expenses of the City Council from Azua. They only approved minor expenses related to the capture of cattle. The City Council and the major were obligated to pay 397.80 pesos in a six months period.

The members of the Spanish army and all the staff used by it didn't have to pay the Commission for the use of farms, houses and animals confiscated. The free access to these confiscated properties was considered a just compensation for their efforts in combating the revolutionary action of the rebels.[26]

The Welfare State: The Social Policy of the Commission to Sequester the Rebels' Commodities

Based on the documentation, I can state that the commission implemented a social policy in favor of the Spanish population and in favor of the people loyal to the colonial regime in the country. This policy was implemented in five different manners:

1. Repairs of properties and housing damaged by fire.
2. Payment of the return ticket to Spain of the Spanish colonists and family eager to go back to Spain, Puerto Rico and Cuba.
3. Exemption of payment for rental houses and properties confiscated by the Commission.
4. The distribution of food to the families coming from territories under control of the rebels.
5. Granting of confiscated houses and farms to the families loyal to the Spanish Empire.[27]

The examples of Santiago and Baní shed light on this policy. In the first one, the harsh fire that destroyed Santiago damaged most of the houses, animals and other properties of the neighbors living there. As a response to that, the commission decided to ask for contributions from the more affluent neighbor to raise capital to renovate some of the homes damaged by the terrible fire of 1863.

The colonial government's social policy, financed with the resources of the commission to confiscate the rebels' properties and commodities, joined efforts to help the town of Baní during the year 1865. A decree from the Governor and General Captain assigned 765 pesos with 92 cents to repairs burned buildings in the town, decreasing the miserable situation of the families loyal to the Spanish authorities and investing some capital in the depressed economy of the village.[28]

This social policy also helped a group of Spanish colonists and relatives eager to return to Spain, Cuba and Puerto Rico. The colonial authorities had to provide, free tickets to Manuel Fernandez and family, to Esteban Gato and his brother Felipe from Cataluña and other colonists classified as *pobres de solemnidad*. They lacked economic resources to survive in a city without jobs and affected by skyrocketing inflation.[29]

Another way to assist the families loyal to the colonial regime was to transport them to the cities, which were still under control of the Spanish authorities. These families settled in Santo Domingo, Baní, Azua and Puerto Plata, and received free houses and farms taken away from the rebels. That was the case for Venancio Tejada, Lucia López, Juana Sánchez Ramirez, Juana Sexto and family. The Spanish government exempted them from rent payments because they lacked the money to pay rent.[30']

The application of Venancio Tejada stated…"He is exempt from paying for the dwelling rent that is owed to the government due to the lack of economic resources", he is in such misery that he doesn't have 18 pesos that he has to pay to the government. Venancio, according to the application, is one of the neighbors that suffered more from the excesses of the revolution.[31]

Other families that came from Neyba and Barahona were totally destitute, running from the violence of war. They settled down in the territories still under Spanish control.[32]

The colonial government's social policy, financed with the resources coming from the Commission that sequestered the goods of the rebels, attempted to ameliorate the widespread process of impoverishment of peasants, merchants, ranchers, soldiers, artisans and professionals. Some members of these social sectors decided to immigrate to Santo Domingo, constituting a destitute population living at the expense of the precarious resources of the colonial government in a marginal area of the Old Spanish empire.[33]

Notes

1. Hector Vallecillo y Rudolfs Sonntag, *El Estado en el Capitalismo Contemporáneo* (Mexico: Siglo XX1, 1990), 23.

2. Nicos Poutlanzas, *State, Power, Socialism* (London: NLB Verso, 1980), chapter 1.

3. Nelson Moreno Cevallos, *El Estado Dominicano, Origen, Evolución y Forma Actual, 1844-1892* (Santo Domingo: Punto y Aparte, 1983), 173-185.

4. Emilio Rodríguez Demorizi, *Antecedentes de la Anexión a España* (Ciudad Trujillo: Editora Montalvo, 1955), 275. (hereafter, *Antecedentes*)

5. Jaime de Jesús Domínguez, *La Anexión de la República Dominicana a España SantoDomingo* (Editora Alfa y Omega: Universidad Autonòma de Santo Domingo, 1979), 207-210.

6. Rodríguez Demorizi, *Antecedentes,* 288.

7.Luis Álvarez -López, *Dominación Colonial y Guerra Popular. La Anexion y Restauración en la Historia Dominicana..* (Santo Domingo: Editora de La Universidad Autónoma de Santo Domingo), 88-91.

8. Domínguez, *La Anexión,* 207-210.

9. Anexión a España, 1864. Legajo no. 3, Archivo General de La Nación, Santo Domingo. República Dominicana. Hereafter a shortened reference with the legajo number and Archivo .General de la .Nación. A.G.N.

10. Emilio Rodríguez Demorizi, *Acerca de Francisco Del Rosario Sánchez,* (Santo Domingo: Editora Taller, 1976), 119-127.

11. *Colección de Leyes, Decretos y Resoluciones Emanadas del Poder Legislativo y Ejecutivo de la República Dominicana.* (Santo Domingo: Imprenta Listin Diario, 1927), 250-252.

12. Expedientes sobre la Sublevación de Santo Domingo de 1863. *Boletin del Archivo General de la Nación,* no.94, (1952): 291.

13. Álvarez, *Dominación Colonial,* 168.

14. Anexión a España, Legajo 1864. A.G.N.

15. José De La Gándara, *Anexión y Guerra de Santo Domingo* (Santo Domingo: Editora Santo Domingo, República Dominicana, 1975), vols 2, 630-633.

16. Anexión a España, Legajo 25, 1864. Bandos de Carlos de Vargas, A.G.N.

17. Anexión a España, Legajo 25. A.G. N.

18. Anexión a España, Legajo 25. A.G.N.

19. Anexión a España, Legajo 25.A.G.N.

20. Anexión a España, Legajo 25, Relación de las Propiedades Incautadas por la Comisión Administradora e Investigadora, A.G.N.

21. Anexión a España, Legajo 25, Relación de las Fincas Secuestradas los meses de Agosto, septiembre, octubre, noviembre y diciembre, A.G.N.

22. Anexión a España, Legajo 25, Informe que sobre la petición de Don Eugenio Valencia, emite la Comisión Administradora e Investigadora. A.G.N.

23. Anexión a España, Legajo 25, Documento sobre reclamaciones de Dorotea Gómez.A.G.N.

24. Anexión a España, Legajo 25, Reglamento sobre la Manera de administrar e Investigar los bienes que pertenecen a los individuos comprendidos en el Decreto del Excmo. Sr. Capitán General de esta isla de fecha 19 de Mayo último, aprobado por el ayuntamiento de sesión de 6 de Mayo pasado. A.G.N. Legajos 25, 26, 31, 38, hereafter quote by A.G.N.

25. Anexión a España, Legajo 25, Correspondencia a la Alcaldía Ordinaria de Azua de José Joaquín Pérez, 12 de Agosto de 1864.

26. Anexión a España, Legajo 25, Correspondencia a la Alcaldía Ordinaria de Azua.

27. Álvarez-López, Luis. *Secuestro de Bienes de Rebeldes (Estado y Sociedad En La última Dominación Española),* (Santo Domingo: Editora Argos, 2005), 51.

28. Anexión a España, Legajo 26, Sobre el incendio del día 22 de Febrero del 1865, en el Pueblo de Baní.

29. Anexión a España, Legajo 31.

30. Anexión a España, Legajo 25, Socorro.

31. Anexión a España, Legajo 25, Socorro.

32. Anexión a España, Legajo 25, Ayuntamiento de Azua.

33. Anexión a España, Legajo 38.

## 3

Santo Domingo, Puerto Rico and Cuba: Between National Independence and Spanish Colonialism 1844-1859

Puerto Rico and Cuba, two islands in the Caribbean, had been Spanish colonies since the 16th century, and the Dominican Republic in the eastern part of the island of Quisqueya, was an independent country since 1844. Based on these differences, Spain developed a foreign policy toward the Dominican Republic of "dreadful disdain", rejecting all efforts of Dominican government's diplomacy, which was seeking Spanish mediation, protection and recognition of the frail and young state.

> This foreign policy was stated in the phrase...Santo Domingo is an evil for Our Antilles and Spain's interest, considering not the advantages that we can get out from it, but the wrong doings that we can prevent.[1] [Author's translation]

This view toward the Dominican Republic was more clearly expressed by the General Captain of Puerto Rico, Fernando Norzagaray when he pointed out:

> Of the Dominican Republic nothing should be feared, nor need to be worried. We are empathic to their situation and realize their desire to cause some harm to us. We must be alert because their troubles can reach this island and Cuba. They face a difficult situation. Survival for the Dominicans is almost impossible due to the persistent and continued effort of his enemy the empire of Haiti.[2] [Author's translation]

In spite of this negative view towards the embryonic Dominican state, the General Captains of Puerto Rico and Cuba, paid close attention to the internal and external political climate of the Dominican Republic. A correspondence from the Captain General from Puerto Rico–El Conde de Mirasol–(May 20 1844), stated that:

> A commissioner named Don Pablo Castillo has presented himself to me. He is originally from the Canarias and established for years in the Dominican Republic with the pretension that this General Captainship will assist any movement in favor of Spain, assuring that the sole presentation of a military ship with some available force will be enough to hoist the Castilians flag and return that part of the island to the obedience of the Queen.[3] [Author's translation]

El Conde de Mirasol responded to the daring proposal from Pablo Castillo by stating:

> this General Captain does not have the instruction to perform these acts in those following ways, not even the maritime forces to carry this out.[4] [Author's translation]

But Pablo Del Castillo, aware of France's ambition to occupy the Samaná bay, went further in his proposal, because he believed that Spain should occupy Samaná before the French.

At the onset of the Dominican Independence, the General Captain of Puerto Rico received information and proposals about the possibility of an expansion of the Spanish colonial dominance in the eastern part of the island in contradiction with one of his main allies, France. This information came from Juan Abril, a Spanish merchant who had been living in Santo Domingo for several years.

Nevertheless, this possibility of extending the Spanish domain over the eastern, part of the island, was not easy to accomplish, as a result of the coalition of international forces that influenced the Dominican Republic and the other Caribbean colonies and nations. The northern Europeans empires: Great Britain, France and Spain, defined a foreign policy towards the region oriented to preserve the status quo in the Caribbean. The United States was also interested in preserving the Spanish colonies for Spain, but was also waiting for the right opportunity to gain some territorial expansion in the Caribbean.

The new nation: Dominican Republic, strategically situated between Puerto Rico and Cuba, as well as the existence of Haiti in the western part of the territory, with its anti-slavery position and the desire to reacquire the Eastern part of the island, created an original situation in the Spanish Caribbean, in which the Northern European empires started to play an important role.

The imperial rivalries were manifested from the beginning, not only between European Empires that regularly acted on a common ground in opposition to the United States expansion, but also in reference to the Haitian policy of reconquest of the Eastern part of the island without recognizing the existence of the new Dominican state.

The major interest of Spain during these years was the preservation of the status quo in the Caribbean, keeping safe its colonial control of the "Antillean Pearls", Cuba and Puerto Rico. For the preservation of these colonies, Spain developed a temporary alliance with England and France in order to impede North American expansion in the Caribbean.

The territorial expansion into the Spanish Caribbean had been the historical goal of the United States, as a result of the Union as well as the Confederate States' interests in the region. The interests of the Union went back to the Founding Fathers. It is well known that during Thomas Jefferson's first administration in 1801, he expressed clearly that the interest for the "Pearls of the Antilles" went beyond mere commercial trade. Its geographical proximity to United States, "lying across the opening of the Gulf of Mexico, almost within sight of Florida, could serve in American hands, as a bulwark of defense; while in foreign hands it constituted a danger."[5]

The interest in Cuba was also present in the Southern States. The Confederacy wanted to create a Caribbean empire based on black slavery, in which Cuba would be the epicenter, providing a strong demand for black slaves, a dynamic new market for the south and land in abundance. Other motivations were related to the political juncture in the United States, in which both governments were seeking hegemony in the United States Congress. The Cuban annexation to the South would create another slave state strengthening the Confederate position in the United States Congress.

These reasons led to the growing interest for Cuba. Several initiatives can be mentioned: the development of the annexationists movement in Cuba, Narciso Lopez's expeditions and the multiple attempts by the Union government, from the plots of President's James Polk, Franklyn Pierce and the Ostend Manifest of 1854, and the rejection by United States of England and France's initiatives of Tripartite Convention aimed to preserve Cuba for Spain before the attempt of any individual member to achieve the Cuban annexation.[6]

The increased interest of the Union in the Caribbean and in the Dominican Republic was based on the Monroe Doctrine, which aimed to reduce European control and gradually to expand American influence in the western hemisphere. Guided by the Monroe principles, the Union, since the onset of the Dominican independence, sent commissioners to the island. These Commissioners ended up writing reports about the economic, social, political and racial conditions of the country. This interest in the Dominican Republic, in a period of territorial expansion under the ideological banner of the Manifest Destiny raised concerns to the Spanish colonial authorities in the Caribbean.

In opposition to that, Spain's foreign policy toward the Dominican Republic was characterize by non-participation in the *Joint Mediation* with England and France, whose objectives were to achieve a peace settlement between Haiti and the Dominican Republic. Spain refused to join forces with France and England to achieve peace between Haiti and Dominican Republic. Instead Spain claimed to still have colonial rights over Santo Domingo. This policy was affirmed by Spain's Minister of the State Calderón de la Barca on March 16, 1854, in a Memorandum sent to the Council of Primer Ministers. The document stated:

> That Spain can not concede a protectorate to the Dominican Republic.
> That will be premature and without compensation the recognition of the Republic.
> It is important and urgent to prevent the Dominican Republic from being conquered by the black from Haiti or fall in the hands of American Filibusters.

It would be convenient to deal with this issue and find out a remedy with the international allies.

Without destroying or growing the hopes of Commissioner Ramon Mella, in relation to the recognition of Dominican Independence, you can send to the Dominican Republic an official agent that would inform this Ministry and the General Captain of Cuba and Puerto Rico.[7] [Author's translation]

Spanish foreign policy toward the Dominican Republic started to change as the Union showed interest in the country. At the onset, Spain's main concern was its two colonies: Cuba and Puerto Rico, in need of protection from the filibusters from the North and the black race from Haiti.

At the beginning of 1850s, Spanish concern regarding Puerto Rico and Cuba increased as a result of the Cuban ruling class efforts to replace Spanish colonialism with annexation to the United States. Some members of the Creole bourgeoisie believe that black slavery could be preserved with the United States annexation, reducing tariff payment and maintaining at the same time the North American market. This country was the best of both worlds: combining democratic order with the black slavery system.

In the Dominican Republic, Congress approved legislation promoting foreign migration in April 1852, during President Buenaventura Baez government. The legislation caused a wave of rumors about the possibility of North-American immigration to Samaná with the objective of organizing expeditions against Cuba and Puerto Rico. Similarly to what occurred in Texas, the immigrants will settle down in Samaná overrunning the government and using the territory to attack Cuba and Puerto Rico.[8]

Aware of these news, the General Captains of Puerto Rico and Cuba contributed to changes in Spain's foreign policy, which went from tackling the Santo Domingo's issues based on a temporary alliance with England and France to a more aggressive policy without terminating the alliance with both countries.

The changes in the Spanish foreign policy in reference to Santo Domingo were the following:

1. The Spanish government sent to Santo Domingo an exploratory mission of historian Mariano Torrente.
2. The appointment of a Commercial Agent of Spain in Santo Domingo by the Spanish government.
3. The appointment of Antonio Maria Segovia e Izquierdo as Spanish Consul in Santo Domingo.
4. The signing of a Treaty of Peace, Friendship, Commerce, Navigation and Extradition between the Dominican Republic and Spain, February 18, 1855.[9] [Author's translation]

Eduardo Saint Just, Spanish Commercial Agent, received instructions from the President of the Council of Ministers (11 de September 1854) that stated the following...

> The task that will be carried out in Santo Domingo is extremely important for the conservation of Cuba. The geographic location of this old Spanish possession is in danger because the United States can take control of it. The last information that I received showed me that the danger of Cuba is imminent. According to the news from July 17, an Anglo-American vessel reached Santo Domingo with General Cazneau, which bring authorization from the American government to sign a treaty of commerce with the Dominican Republic, but his main goal is occupy the magnificent Samaná bay with the objective of attacking Cuba in case of a war. The president of the Dominican Republic, Pedro Santana, has been showing sympathy toward Spain and refuses to accept the suggestion from United States, but some of his ministers have been listening to some of the indications of General Cazneau. The interest in United States has been growing as a result of the failure of the Mella mission to Spain, when the previous government refuses to recognize the Dominican independence and provide some protection to this country. The duty that you must carry out in Santo Domingo is to use all possible means to stop the United States ambitious project and dissuade the Dominican government and his president not to accept the concessions asked for by United States...Explain to the Dominican government the disastrous effect for the Dominican independence and for the future of your race if the United States place it's feet upon the island. Used the Consuls from England and France to stop the United States ambition plan for the country.[10] [Author's translation]

Spain's response to the United States plan in Santo Domingo followed the September 11 document from the President of the Council of Ministers, sending to the Dominican Republic and Haiti the exploratory mission of Mariano Torrente. The mission had the support of England and France, showing the existence of a provisional agreement between the three northern European Empires.

Spain also considered taking over the Dominican Republic, claiming that she never resigned the colonial rights that were entitled, and appointed a secret agent to inform to the General Captain of Cuba and Puerto Rico about the political situation in the Dominican Republic.

Torrente's mission led to a report in which he analyzed the Dominican situation in the Spanish Caribbean and the linkages with the Northern European Empires and United States. In his conclusions, he mentions three possible options for the Dominican Republic:

1. Return of the Dominican Republic to the Spanish colonial domain.
2. To establish a protectorate, this would allow Spain control of Samaná Bay, and let it set up some agricultural colonies and a military garrison

3. To defend the territory in order to maintain Dominican independence. [Author's translation].[11]

According to Torrente, the first option was not the best one and its implementation would require joint coordination between France and Spain to impose a colonial regime in both parts of the island. France would resume a colonial regime in the Western part of the island, recovering its former colony and Spain would recover the Eastern part, expanding her Antilles Empire beyond Cuba and Puerto Rico.

Torrente emphasized in his report that the two main enemies that are weakening Spain's colonial enterprise were: United States and Haiti. The United was viewed as an enemy because it hoped to use Santo Domingo to attack Cuba. Haiti and the black race desire were also an enemy as their desire to control Santo Domingo, put in danger Cuba and Puerto Rico.[11]

Despite the proposals of Torrente and the growing enthusiasm in diverse sectors of the Dominican ruling class, Spain's foreign policy didn't change substantially. The Dominican Republic was important to Spain as an instrument to preserve its *Pearls in the Antilles*, especially since the colonies seemed to be in danger.

The Dominican Republic was important to Spain in the context of its imperial domain for two reasons. One, it shared the island with Haiti and it was perceived as a white country, and as a potential ally of Spain in confronting Haiti. Two, the Dominican Republic/Haiti contradiction opened a new dimension for Spain. The two Spanish colonies in the Spanish Caribbean, Cuba and Puerto Rico still had black slavery system, and the Haitian example still represented "the seed of freedom" for blacks in bondages.

Spain's Minister of State analyzed Haiti, using it as an example of a black republic without black slavery, and its impact on Cuba and Puerto. He stated:

If the blacks from Haiti conquer the Dominican Republic, our colony's population from the African race will be in danger, because the black and abolitionist would help the rebellions and insurrection of the slaves.[12] [Author s' translation]

The Dominican–Spanish diplomatic relationships became extremely dynamic as a result of the expansionist design of President Franklin Pierce, who in coordination with the Secretary of State, William Mercy, sent a presidential envoy with the objective of signing a treaty of recognition of the Dominican Republic independence and receive dispensation from the government to:

grant us a site on the coast of the Bay of Samaná, suitable as a stopping place for the United States steamers, and as a place of deposit for coal to be used by its.[13] [Author's translation]

The opposition of England and France frustrated the United States desire to place a base in Samaná and also to sign a Treaty of Commerce, Navigation and Friendship with the Dominican Republic. The treaty was considered as the United States first step toward expansion into the Spanish Caribbean, the colonial authorities from Cuba and Puerto Rico believed that United States would implement the Texan example in the Caribbean, sending a big migration, which would overrun the country and would end with the annexation of the Dominican Republic by the Union.

Based on this assumption, The General Captain of Puerto Rico Fernando Norzagaray, in a letter to the President of Council of Ministers, described the American Commissioner:

> William Cazneau as a man who enriched himself in the real state business in Texas, and with the commodities that supply to the American army in Mexico, he also maintained friendly relations with some people in Havana. Some people believed that the constant travel was more related to pure speculation than diplomacy; nevertheless, other people believed all of this business had a lot of filibusterism.[14] [Author's translation]

In the same document, Fernando Norzagaray, showed some concern about the good disposition of Pedro Santana toward North American, and "if they achieve the goal of annexation of the Dominican Republic, our situation will be critical and is not difficult to predict the negative consequences of our interest in the region."[15]

Puerto Rico, Cuba and Santo Domingo in the Hurricane of United Territorial Expansion

The United State's interest in territorial expansion toward the Spanish Caribbean, especially toward Cuba was very clear, and the General Captains of Cuba and Puerto Rico were both in alert facing the situation. They received detailed information about political, economic and social matters from Santo Tomas, New Orleans, Baltimore, Washington, Boston, and Curacao. The Spanish government, well aware of United States Policy of expansion and also knowledgeable of the Monroe Doctrine basic tenet, became extremely sensitive towards the Spanish colonies in the Caribbean.

The inter-imperialists contradictions in the cases of Cuba and Puerto Rico became even worse because both islands were political colonies of Spain and economic neo-colonies of United States. Since 1765, Havana and San Juan received free trade privileges to negotiate with nations' friend of Spain. These freedoms become more abundant during the Napoleonic war, when the Spanish Caribbean colonies received a permit to negotiate with neutral nations, particularly the United States.

The trading rights of the Spanish colonies in the Caribbean with North America led to a condition of economic dependence with the United States because it became the major external market for both colonies. The trade also developed a common bond of economic interest between the white and Creole planters and the North-American bourgeoisie. A big number of creoles threatened by the narrow local market and the scarcity of capital looked to the big nation of the north for answers. The fact that the black slavery played such an important role in the colonial economies of Cuba and Puerto Rico was also a factor of major attraction to the big nation that combined in a marvelous package a democratic and government with black slavery.

It is not difficult to comprehend that despite the opposition of the Spanish ruling class and the General Captains, a fraction of the colonial ruling class in the Caribbean became annexationists, in favor of being part of United States. For this sector of the dominant class, there was no "colonial contradiction" because they were developing as a social class under the dynamic commerce with the United States. The annexation to the United States also "promised to eliminate the onerous system of Spanish taxation on foreign imports and remove North American tariffs on Cuban products."[16] In a similar fashion the Dominican ruling classes aspiration was the annexation to another Caucasian empire: Spain, showing the colonial mentality of the indigenous dominant classes' throughout the Spanish Caribbean. In the case of the Dominican, the development of a racist overtone created an excuse to achieve the annexation to Spain. The racism of the ruling class used the Haitian policy of re-conquering the eastern part of the Island as the main justification for its actions.

The General Captains of Cuba and Puerto Rico were feverously opposed to the North-American treaty of 1854 or to any other United States initiative in the Spanish Caribbean. The General Captain of Puerto Rico in a letter sent to the Spanish Minister of Overseas, on November 13, 1854 stated:

complicated is the situation of the Dominican Republic, seems to me that the country is breaking up and I have been informing to the Majesty the danger that we are exposed, but my observations have been overlooked and I will reiterate that since the truce between the Dominican Republic and Haiti ended, the Dominican independence is threatened and it is necessary to seek the support of other nations to preserve it. And is it a European question to provide support to them because they are white people and asking for assistance against the black race. If Europe doesn't help, United States will help and all the nations with colonies in the Antilles, will have the enemy at the door. Spain is the one more threatened because of Cuba and Puerto Rico's existence.[17] [Author's translation]

The Attempt to Increase Spanish Hegemony in the Caribbean

Regardless of the political, economic and social differences between Cuba, Puerto Rico and the Dominican Republic and despite the expansionist policy of the United States and Spain, the Spanish colonial authorities concluded that Santo Domingo had two enemies to confront: the Yankees and the Haitians. The solution against these two enemies was to strengthen the Spanish Hegemony in the Hispanic Caribbean with Santo Domingo's annexation to Spain, March 18 1861.

In this way, the Spanish hegemony would expand with a new colony in the Spanish Caribbean. The dream of the Caribbean Empire became a reality, but that dream was the beginning of a nightmare for Spain. The annexation to Spain led to a complex, multidimensional war that opened a revolutionary cycle in the Spanish Caribbean that lasted until the defeat of this Empire in the Spanish- Cuban-Philippines, North-American war of 1898.[18]

Notes

1. Emilio Rodríguez Demorizi, *Relaciones dominico-españolas, 1844-1859* (Ciudad Trujillo: Editora Montalvo. 1986), 138. (hereafter *Relaciones Dominico-españolas).*

2. Rodríguez Demorizi, *Relaciones dominico-españolas*, 161.

3. Rodríguez Demorizi, *Relaciones dominico-españolas*, 14.

4. Rodríguez Demorizi, *Relaciones dominico-españolas*, 8.

5. Philips Foner. *History of Cuba and its relations with the United States*. (New York: Internacional Publisher, 1962), 5.

6-Ramiro Guerra, *La expansión Territorial de los Estados Unidos a Expensa de España y de los Países Hispanoamericanos* (La Habana: Instituto Cubano del Libro, 1975), Capts. 10-11.

Charles Callan Tansill, *the United States and Santo Domingo, 1798-1873. A Chapter In Caribbean Diplomacy* (Massachusetts. Johns Hoskins Press, 1967), 135.

Pedro Mir, *Las Raíces Dominicanas de la Doctrina Monroe* (Santo Domingo: Editora Taller 1984), chapter 2.

7. Rodríguez Demorizi, *Relaciones dominico-españolas*, 144-145.

8. Rodríguez Demorizi, *Relaciones dominico-españolas*, 112.

9. Álvarez, Luis. *Dominación Colonial y Guerra Popular (La Anexión y la Restauración en la Historia Dominicana)* (Santo Domingo: Universidad Autónoma de Santo Domingo.1986), 20-24.

10. Rodríguez Demorizi, *Relaciones dominico-españolas*, 157-158.

11. Álvarez, Luis, *Dominación Colonial*, 18-20. Carlos Federico Pérez, Historia Diplomática de Santo Domingo (1492-1861). (Santo Domingo; Universidad Pedro Henriquez Ureña, 1973) ,260-261.

12. Rodríguez Demorizi, *Relaciones dominico-españolas,* 161. The General Captain from Puerto Rico describes Haiti as the "constant enemy of the Dominican Republic".

13. Tansill, *United States and Santo Domingo*, 133.

14. Rodríguez Demorizi, *Relaciones Dominico-españolas*, 159-160.

15. Louis Pérez, *Cuba Reform and Revolution* (New York: Oxford University Press, 1995), 107.

16. Luis Fernández-Martínez, *Torn between Empires, Economic, Society and Patterns of Political Thought in the Hispanic Caribbean 1840-1878* (Athens & London: University of Georgia Press, 1994.), chapter 3.

17. Luis Álvarez López, *Dieciséis Conclusiones Fundamentales Sobre la Anexión y la Restauración 1861-1865* (Santo Domingo: Editora Argos, 2005), 79.

18. Álvarez-López, *Dieciséis Conclusiones*, 79.

## 4

Ramon Emeterio Betances and the Revolutionary Cycle in the Spanish Caribbean (From the Restoration War to the Cuban Spanish American Philippines War 1864-1898)

Ramón Emeterio Betances was a Puerto Rican, Caribbean and Latin American liberator, who fought tirelessly against the old Spanish Imperialism and the emergent North American Imperialism during the 19th century. Betances also fought for the political independence of the Spanish colonies in the Caribbean and a Federation of Caribbean nations.

He struggled for the absolute political independence of Puerto Rico, Cuba and against the annexation of Dominican Republic to Spain and the United States. He was also a political strategist that used different tactics to achieve his main goal of political independence of Puerto Rico and Cuba.

His political activities extended throughout the Spanish Caribbean's revolutionary cycle, which was initiated with the annexation of the Dominican Republic to Spain in March 1861 and the Restoration war in August 1863; followed by the *Grito de Lares* in September 1868 and the *Grito de Yara* in October, 1868, extending itself to the Cuban-Spanish North American-Philippine war 1895-1898.

Betances's contribution as an abolitionist, revolutionary, political thinker, diplomat, physician and man of science are numerous and need to be analyzed in order to illustrate his role the in revolutionary cycle of the Spanish Caribbean.

Biographical Notes about Betances

Many biographies about Betances are in agreement regarding his origin, he came from a Dominican family settled down in Puerto Rico. He was born in Cabo Rojo, Puerto Rico, on April 8, 1827. He studied medicine in France and graduated as a physician in 1855.

He returned to Puerto Rico from France in 1856 and settled down in Mayagüez.

Betances became known as the doctor of "the poor people and the black people", especially during the cholera morbid epidemic that killed 30,000 habitants, including 5000 slaves. Together with Antonio Blanes, he founded the Hospital San Antonio.[1]

As a concerned citizen he created a secret Anti-Slavery Society, together with the Puerto Rican lawyer, Segundo Ruiz Belvis. He spent a lot of time buying slave children and making them free during baptism in the Catholic Church. As a result of this effort the colonial government of Puerto Rico decided to expel him from the country because he was liberating black slaves in a colonial society that maintain the black slavery system.[2]

He returned to Paris to do scientific investigation and to write literary plays and poems. He wrote the "Vierge de Borinquen", "Les Voyages de Scaldado", published in Le Temps, La Presse and other newspapers. His scientific research about Elephantiasis, Uretrotomia, and Tuberculosis treatment were presented to the Academy of Medicine. [3]

Betances returned to Puerto Rico and immediately started to do some solidarity actions during the Restoration War, which was developing in the Dominican Republic, at the time. His solidarity work with the Dominican Republic began with the annexation to Spain, 1861. In Puerto Rico, following the information, from Félix Ojeda's research, lampoons were circulated on the Puerto Rican streets in reference to the struggle against the Spanish troops. Some of these lampoons abetted the Spanish colonial troops from Santo Domingo to open rebellion against the colonial army sent to the eastern part of the island.[4]

Betances political solidarity with the Dominican Republic led to his second exile from Puerto Rico. From that moment on, his life was filled with the permanent struggle for the independence of Puerto Rico and Cuba. He also struggled against the annexation of Dominican Republic to Spain and United States and fought in favor of the Antilles Federation.

The Historical Context of Betances' Political Actions

Betances lived during a pivotal period in the Spanish Caribbean. It was a period of great economic, social and political transformations, which marked the transition from subsistence agriculture and cattle ranching to the development of an export economy in the region. Examples of these changes were the development of the modern sugar industry, the expansion of the black slavery system and the rise of the peasant class that fluctuated between independent farmers and landless peasants subject to passbook regulations and overexploitation.

The export economy had far reaching affects on the development of new units of production, such as plantations, "haciendas" and cattle ranches. These new units of production led to the origin and expansion of new social classes: owners of plantations and other unit of production, foreign and Creole merchants, independent farmers, landless peasants. Spanish and Foreign merchants were in control of the capital and means of production, and were linked to the international market through the export of raw materials.

The Creole planters and the dominant indigenous class were financially dependent on the Commercial Bourgeoisie from Spain and were also excluded from access to political power. The expansion of the plantation system in Cuba and Puerto Rico led to the expansion of both the Black slavery and the peasant classes tied to the hacienda system.[5]

The increasing productions of sugar, tobacco and coffee as well as rise in exports to the United States led to another contradictory situation in the Spanish Caribbean. The major external market for the Cuban and Puerto Rican production was in the United States, despite the fact that both islands were colonies of Spain. A situation of double colonialism developed: political colonies of Spain and economic dependents of the United States.[6]

The situation of the Dominican Republic was different from those of Cuba and Puerto Rico. The plantation system developed late in 19th century Dominican society, and without a black slavery system. The economic structure was based mostly in subsistence agriculture, cattle ranching and a weak export sector of tobacco production. The primitive agricultural economy and the system of land ownerships known as the communal land system (*terrenos comuneros*), together with low density of the population explained the access to land of large part of the Dominican peasants. The lack of a modern transportation system, weak integration into the international market and the need for a national market made the Dominican economy structure more underdeveloped than those of the Cuba and Puerto Rican economy.

These impediments delayed the development of the plantation system, the social structure that came with it and the country's incorporation into the international market.

From a political point of view, the situation in the Dominican Republic was different than the Cuban and Puerto Rican situations. The country achieved political independence from Haiti in (1844) and the ruling classes were not a foreign governing class that represented the metropolitan country. The ruling class consisted of conservative national elite, without class-consciousness, and a colonial mentality that promoted a pronounced white identity. This ruling class was embodied by the ranchers and property owners. Since the beginning of the independence, they conspired to annex the country to other Caucasian empires using as an excuse the war with Haiti.[7]

The Dominican Republic was not a colony as Puerto Rico and Cuba were; it was an independent Republic with a formal democratic regime, but with a social and economic system similar to a colony. The primitive agricultural economy, the colonial mentality of the ruling class, the white supremacy perspective that it embraced and the existence of Haiti in the Western part of the island, help to explain why the upper class was always eager to return to the colonial regime.

The development of the plantation system in Dominican Republic led to some significant social changes, at the end of 19th century. A ruling class of native and foreigner entrepreneurs developed around the sugar production and an incipient bourgeoisie developed around the tobacco production in Santiago. The Dominican case witnesses a timid process of semi-proletarization in conjunction with a vast conglomerate of peasants and independent farmers. A big number of these peasants were involved in pre-capitalist relation of production, with sporadic access to a regional market and communal system of land ownership.[8]

The economic transformation had far reaching affects on the lower classes. An intensification of the labor force exploitation led to the creation of new mechanisms of control within the labor force: vagrancy laws and the system of peonage. The semi-proletarian peasants became involved in the first stage of the plantation system as cane cutters.

The immigration of new labor forces was also a device use to supply the demand for more workers in an expanding economy throughout the Spanish Caribbean: Coolies, Puerto Ricans, Jamaicans, Haitians, Canaries, etc.

In this economic and social context the political forces in existence were:

1-The Annexationists movement aspired to the annexation of Cuba and Puerto Rico to United States. In the Dominican case, the dominant classes aspired to the annexation to any other Caucasian empire.

2-The autonomist tendency aspired to establish an autonomist regime with Spain, Parliamentarian representation and abolition of Black slavery with reparation as part of the demands of this sector.

3-The separatist, or independents tendency, aspire to break the colonial pact and establish a politically independent nation. The political independence of Cuba and Puerto Rico was a major aspiration for Betances. In the Dominican case, the nationalist tendency sought to maintain a free country with a democratic order and to establish an Antillean Federation. That was the case with Gregorio Luperón and Antenor Fermin from Haiti.[9]

The social structures as well as the economic and political systems were immersed in an international order under the hegemony of the North European empires. It is in the Caribbean where the gathering of interests of imperialist countries occurred because the strategic location of the region in the Caribbean Sea, gave access to the Atlantic Ocean and the Gulf of Mexico.

England, France and Spain maintained a common perspective in avoiding the United States territorial expansion in the Caribbean. Nevertheless, England favored a preservation of the status quo in order to maintain the commercial hegemony in the region; the other two empire's goals were territorial expansion as was evident in the case of France in Mexico and the Annexation of the Dominican Republic to Spain.[10]

Ramon Emeterio Betances, Francisco Basora and the Restoration War

The investigation of Ramón Emeterio Betances in New York, Puerto Rico, Cuba, France and the Dominican Republic shows that he was one of the most tenacious fighters for the independence of Spanish Caribbean people, against the colonial policies of the Spanish and North American Imperialism.

As a man of his time he was one of the most advanced visionaries who fought against the damage caused by colonialism, slavery, racial discrimination, fiscal exploitation and also against the decadence of the Spanish Empire and the emergent expansionism from United States.

The expansionists from the North and from the South were focused on the annexation of the Antilles with their policies of territorial expansion, seeking the hegemony over the northern European empires in the Caribbean and Latin America. Betance was totally opposed to all forms of colonialism, as is shown in the next paragraphs.

The core of Betances's revolutionary work had several basic objectives:

1. The independence of Cuba, Puerto Rico, and the Dominican Republic.
2. Abolition of the Black Slavery system
3. The Antilles Confederation
4. The struggle against colonialism, annexationist, assimilation and autonomy.
5. His diplomatic effort in favor of the Dominican Republic and Cuba.
6. His work as everlasting conspirator for the freedom and independence of the Antilles.
7. His vision as main strategist in favor of the Antillean Confederation with a permanent practice in the anti-colonial and anti-imperialist struggle.
8. His contribution as a physician and man of science dedicated to the study of various tropical diseases.[11]

The investigations about Betances emphasize his multiple roles throughout the course of the Spanish Caribbean Revolutionary Cycle: as an abolitionist, a revolutionary, an organizer of the *Grito de Lares,* (the major attempt of Puerto Ricans to achieve political independence from Spain), and a tenacious opponent of the annexationists President Buenaventura Baez and Silvian Salnave in the Dominican Republic and Haiti respectively. He was also a persistent fighter for the independence of Cuba and the rest of the Antilles, keeping always in mind the liberation, freedom and independences from the oppressive Spanish colonial domination.

I must add his diplomatic skills to his untiring revolutionary efforts, having been appointed First Secretary of the Dominican legation in Paris, personal assistant of Gregorio Luperòn and the person in charge of Dominican businesses in London and Berna. Betances also chose to become a citizen of the Dominican Republic. He promoted several projects for the Dominican Republic, the foundation of national bank and free port and commercial city in Samana.[12]

His revolutionary commitments and diplomatic skills were used to full potential in the *Diplomacia de la Manigua,* in defense of the Cuban insurgent Republic. Two publications emphasize his meritorious efforts. The first one is Felix Ojeda's 1984 book entitled *La Manigua en Paris Correspondencia Dip-*

lomática de Betances, which points out his multiple efforts in achieving the highest goal of independence for Cuba. Of these efforts I will mention the following:

1. The persistent campaign in the French government and in the press to abort the loans that Spain was seeking in the European Banks. The objective of the loan was to finance the Cuban war.
2. To raise economic resources oriented toward the military readiness in the war against Spain.
3. Sending militants from Europe and Latin American into combat in Cuba.
4. The acquisition of weapons and supplies for the Cuban liberating army.
5. Creating solidarity with the political prisoners and Cuban refugees that arrived in Paris.
6. Collect contributions for war from the rich sugar mill owners that lived in Paris.
7. Intervening in the diplomatic negotiations with important figures in the Spanish government, as well as rejecting any agreement not conducive to Cuban independence.
8. Organizing a press corp. to spread the revolutionary view about the war and to respond to false information from the Spanish press.
9. Establish and promote multiple solidarity committees with the Cuban Revolution. An example is the coordination with solidarity committees from France, Italy, an effort to organize with Belgian and Prussia, which supported the Cuban Revolution.
10. He approached the Insurrectional project from the Philippines to cooperate with the Cuban insurgency.[13]

The second publication is a book by Paul Estrade called *Solidaridad con Cuba Libre 1895-1898: La impresionante labor de Betances en Paris*. Estrade in this book discusses in details Betances contribution in the struggle for Cuba and Puerto Rico's independence and also the contribution from the Cuban community in Paris. The solidarity of the socialists and anarchists from France were also analyzed.

In reference to the role of Betances, Estrade stated: "is the organizer and propagandist of The Cuban colony in Paris. He is perfectly conscious of that. His agreement with Marti's strategy is clear, don't expect nothing from Spain, late and miserable reforms, do not expend time seeking for other solutions, independence is the only solution, achieved through a liberation war, popular, fast, unified all the freedom fighters without discrimination of class or race, never believing in the American policy which is always expansionist, prepare together with the independence, the conditions for the Democratic Republic of the future.[14] [Author's translation]

Returning to the Dominican Republic, Betances contribution started with his solidarity work in the Restoration war that he developed in Mayagüez, Puerto Rico, at the beginning of the war. From that period is the following proclamation.

> Rise up Puerto Ricans! Lets show the wretch that robs and insults us, that the Jibaros of Borinquen" (peasants) are no cowards nor executioners, nor murderers of our own brothers...Our cry for independence will be heard and supported by the friends of freedom and there will be no shortage of weapons and money to defeat the tyrants of Cuba, Puerto Rico, and the Dominican Republic. Ramón Emeterio Betances. Down with the Spaniards![15] [Author's translation]

His action of solidarity with the Restoration war resulted in his exile, but he continued this effort in New York City according to the documentation researched. The documents quoted show the role of Betances and Francisco Basora in defense of the reestablishment of the Dominican sovereignty and independence. The first one was appointed agent of the Dominican Provisional Government and the second, Consul of the Dominican Republic.

The first document is a letter from General Melitón Valverde to the Foreign Affairs Secretary (July 16, 1864), in it Betances and lieutenant Dr. Francisco Basora were named agents of the Restoration Revolution, the first one in Paris and the second in New York city. Both were characterized by the document as "honest men, republicans...they work as well with enthusiasm that inspire the desire of men who like them want the independence of their country.[16] [Author's translation]

As agents, both had the ability to raise funds for the Provisional Government, an important task, due to the lack of resources to fight the war against Spanish troops.

A second document dispatched to the Dominican agent in New York, Francisco Basora, to the Secretary of Foreign Affair of the Dominican Republic (February 6, 1865), where it is pointed out that the United States President had sent a message to the Congress recommended the recognition of the Provisional Government of the Dominican Republic. In addition the representative from Massachusetts of the Foreign Affairs Committee recommend the appointment of a diplomatic representative for the Dominican Republic too, which would involve the recognition of the Dominican Republic as a belligerent nation, in opposition to the Spanish Empire.[17]

In reference to Basora, other information confirms the works that he developed, along with others Cuban living in exile. From Doctor Carlos Rama 's book, we know that he was known as a the agent from Santo Domingo, who participated together with Juan Manuel Macias in the Democratic Society of

Friends of America, whose objective was to help the Dominican people in the struggle against Spain.[18]

Betances as a Political Thinker

Betances was not an intellectual or philosopher like Eugenio Maria de Hostos, who spent a big deal of effort thinking, writing and trying to change the political, educational and cultural reality of Latin America. A big effort of Hostos was his struggle against Spanish colonialism in the Antilles and his ideas about the Antillean Federation for the Spanish Caribbean.

His ideas are part of his numerous correspondence, proclaims, articles, speeches, poems, press releases, conferences, press interview and scientific articles, most of it was published in the patriot press of the movement.

A classical document in Betances production is the first proclamation of the revolution, known as the "Ten Commandments of a Free Men" from November 4 of 1867, published in Saint Thomas. This document stated....

The government of Isabel II accused us of being bad Spaniards. The government is lying to us. We are not for separation, we want peace, the Union with Spain, but is on justice to establish certain conditions in this contract. These are the conditions:

1. Abolition of black slavery	2. Right to vote the budget
3. Freedom of religion	4. Freedom of speech
5. Freedom of commerce	6. Freedom of the press
7. Right to bear weapons	8. Freedom of assembly
9. Inviolability of the citizens	10. Right to elect our authorities.[19]

The Ten Commandments of the Free Men constituted a rejection of the Spanish Colonial regime because the demands contain in it, were oppose to the political, economic and social conditions imposed by the colonial regime. These demands are linked to one of Betances pivotal ideas, which were the political independence of Puerto Rico or absolute independence, without string attached.

The idea of absolute independence led him to a permanent confrontation with the Spanish empire and also to a confrontation against the United States emergence as an empire. He was an anti-imperialist always struggling for freedom from the colonial regime, but he knew that this freedom could not be achieved under the current colonial conditions. In a letter, from 1870, from Puerto Principe, He mentioned:

"The Reformist Party or Autonomist persists with a tireless patience, demanding freedom that Spain had no intention to give to her colonies because she doesn't have those freedoms."[20]

In reference to United States, Betances was always opposing the annexation scheme and he was clear when President Grant attempted the annexation of the Dominican Republic. In relation to that, Betances affirmed:

> In this country (Haiti), the government and the people show a great deal of empathy, and are different from the empathy from United States. They protect the Cuban revolution and also sustain the Dominican revolution too. These people had all the essentials to save themselves, but . . . Grant wants Santo Domingo, and that is the danger.[21] [Author's translation]

The most important goal in all his efforts throughout several decades and in different scenarios was the Puerto Rican revolution. He characterized the Puerto Rican Revolution in the proclamation of 1868. When he declared:

> We are around American Republics breeding an immense atmosphere of freedom, but we are the serfs of an absolute king owner of life and properties.
>
> The popular vote is a lie, justice is misleading, the schools are a deception, and commerce is a thief.
>
> To the arms, Puerto Ricans! Let's leave this nefarious condition that portrays us as a people of women and slaves and lets go to Cuba with two flags of the revolution, in conjunction to a free country.
>
> Spaniards that live in the island: our revolution is not based on hate or shame; it is based on love to this country and its inhabitants. If you want to see the cause of justice win unify with us. Let us conquer together, brother, an independent Republic with personal security and respect for our work. For the union of all, peninsular and Creole, conservative and liberal, the revolution must be fast and the impact must be temporary leaving behind only debris. Some in the army struggle, and others in raising funds, all can contribute to the triumph of the justice.
>
> To the armed, inhabitants of Puerto Rico! Free from an arbitrary and corrupt government, let's make the country independent, a more fraternal union searching for progress and civilization.[22] [Author's translation]

The struggle for the independence of Puerto Rico and the other Antilles led to a permanent opposition to the territorial expansion from the United States. From the point of view of the 19th century policy, it means annexation to the United States, which was a political objective of a commercial bourgeoisie and sugar mills owners in the Spanish Caribbean. In a letter to E. Trujillo, Director of "El porvenir" he emphasizes:

> For our Antilles, and for Santo Domingo and Haiti the question of the annexation is already judged and there is no discussion, by instinct the people know in the bottom of the heart how disastrous it is.

It was possible to agitate it in 1868, when some people were quaking in front of disaster of war and the threatening viciousness of the future; they became revolutionary-conservatives and annexationists, for gold ounces, beautiful houses in Havana and by theirs extensive and productive cane fields; no nation can gain its freedom without the crumpling of the building, spilling out blood, setting the hut on fire.

I know them very well and I have seen them in Puerto Rico, Santo Domingo, Haiti, and between the Cubans, these annexationists are outdated.

Rich men, in general, poor old who love their country, but are hopeless and with the only desire to enjoy a day of peace, security and happiness.

They are forgetting the future generations and without thought; they dream that the apples will flourish in Havana and Palms will give coconuts in Washington; both trees will perish because the climate is not suitable for it.[23] [Author's translation]

Ramon Emeterio Betances used all his energy and skillfulness when the Dominican dictator, Buenaventura Baez, attempted to annex the country to United States. It is important to mention that the annexationists' effort during the Second Republic, started with José Maria Cabral when he explored the possibility of renting the Samaná Bay to the United States. But it was with President Baez that the annexationists' plan had a maximum development.

The Baez plan was in agreement with the expansionist fever in the United States, especially the Manifest Destiny policy and the Monroe Doctrine. President Grant was a decisive annexationist; he wanted to be judged in history as the president that added a new territory to the Union.

Baez's annexationist scheme was defeated in the United States senate, but Betances played a crucial role fighting the annexation in "Saint Thomas, Caracas, Curacao, New York and Washington. For all these places, he visited influential individuals, wrote letter and articles, gathered money to buy weapons for Gregorio Luperón and fostered an alliance between the Dominican caudillos in order to establish a United Front against Baez and the annexation.[24]

From Santo Domingo to the Antilles Confederation

Betances's strategy was to assure the Dominican Republic and Haiti's independence, as first steps to achieving political independence for Cuba and Puerto Rico and moving toward the Antilles Federation. The ideas of the Antilles Federation are present in Betances early career, during his year in Paris, he already referred to the idea of the freedom for the Antilles, but it is in Puerto Rico, between the years of 1863-1865 when it started to develop into a more concrete idea of the Antillean Federation.

In the proclamation against Spain, quoted in the book of Felix Ojeda Reyes and Paul Estrade, Betances expressed a clear Antillean perspective when he mentions: "will be not shortage of money and weapons to defeat the despots from Cuba, Puerto Rico and Santo Domingo."[25] A more clear view about the Antillean Federation was articulated by Betances in the last interview with Luis Bonafoux, when stated: "the future of our countries is to form a *Great Antillean Confederation* with 25 millions people". Deported from Puerto Rico in 1864, he came to New York to continue the struggle with Doctor Jose Francisco Basora. Both established the Republican Society from Cuba and Puerto Rico. The foundation document of the Republican society stated: "is our duty to use the means at our disposal to separate Cuba and Puerto Rico from Spain's domain . . . it is only using the weapons that we can earn our rights from the peninsular government to administer our own affairs."[26] [Author's translation]

The research of Cordero Michel has been illuminating in presenting the facts that the Antillean Federation ideas developed in the Dominican Republic during the process of the Restoration war against Spain. The idea grew when the Dominican Provisional Government challenged the Spanish empire with the Restoration war. At the beginning the idea was to establish a geopolitical alliance with Haiti to defend both countries against Spain and the United States, but later to incorporate the other colonies of the Antilles.[27]

The idea of the Dominican Provisional Government was to establish "a respectful and powerful nation and with the islands of Cuba and Puerto Rico to create a Federation capable of challenging the European interests in the Americas."[28] The idea of the Antillean Federation was conceived well in advance during the Dominican Restoration war with the following objectives:

1. Reestablish the freedom, Independence and sovereignty of the Dominican Republic.

2. Consolidate the independence of Haiti, threatened by Spanish colonialism.

3. Defend the oppressed, especially the black slaves, struggle for the abolition of black slavery in Cuba and Puerto Rico and make impossible the reestablishment of black slavery in Santo Domingo.

4. Help by all means necessary to achieve the independence of Cuba and Puerto Rico.

5. Establish the Antillean Confederation to make the Countries stronger and insure their future as free and independent.

6. Maintain the continental equilibrium at this geographical zone, Center of colonial possessions by Spain, France, Holland, England and Denmark and also the center of territorial expansion and the powerful interests of the United States of America.

7. Contribute to the independence of the Antilles and incorporate it to The Confederation after achieving the objective of independence.

8. Achieve the integration of all Latin-American people against his common enemies (following the proclamation of Ramón Matías Mella).[29] [Author's Translation]

The general Gregorio Luperón was "doubtless the historical leader of the future Antillean Confederation" according to Betances. Both developed a lasting relationship throughout several decades, targeting the colonial policies of the decadent Spanish empire and the emergent American Empire as well as they complemented each others struggle in an effort to achieve, social justice and the end of colonialism in the Antilles.

Notes

1. Francisco Moscoso, *Betances para todos los días* (San Juan Puerto Rico: Congreso Nacional Hostosiano. Aurora Comunicación, Inc. 2001), 5. Hereafter *Betances para todos los días.*. Félix Ojeda Reyes, *ElDesterrado de Paris.Biografia del Doctor Ramón Emeterio Betances(1827-1989).(.San Juan: Ediciones Puerto Rico,2001),67.*(hereafter, *Desterrado de Paris).*
2. Luis Bonafaux, *Betances* (San Juan Puerto Rico: Instituto de Cultura Puertorriqueña, 1970), XXV.
3. Bonafaux, *Betances,* XXV. Ojeda Reyes, *Desterrado de Paris*, chapters 1, 2.
4. Félix Ojeda Reyes, Betances, Meriño, Luperòn: Profetas de la Antillanía, Combatientes De Nuestra Libertad. *Ciencia y Sociedad*, vol. 29, no. 4. (Octubre-Diciembre) 2004: 650-651.
5. Luis Martínez –Fernández, *Torn between Empires. Economy, Society, and Patterns of Political Thought in the Hispanic Caribbean 1840-1878* (The University of Georgia Press, Athens and London 1994), 96-113. (hereafter *Torn between Empires).*
6. Martínez-Fernández, *Torn between Empires,* Chapter 3
7. Franco Franklyn, El Racismo en los inicios de la República. *Isla Abierta,* (29 de Junio de 1996): 8-10.
8. Roberto Cassá, *Historia Económica y Social de La República Dominicana* (Santo Domingo: Editora Alfa y Omega, 1980). vol. 2, chapter 16.
9. Jean Ghasmann Bissainthe, La vision antillanista desde la perspectiva haitiana. *Ciencia y Sociedad*, vol. 29, no.4. (Octubre-Diciembre 2004): 616-630.
10. Luis Álvarez-López, *Dieciséis Conclusiones Fundamentales sobre la Anexion y la Guerra de la Restauración 1861-1865 (*Santo Domingo: Editora Argos, 2005*),* 23-26.
11. Bonafoux, *Betances,* Moscoso, *Betances Para Todos los Díaz,* 5-6 y Félix Ojeda Reyes y Paul Estrade, *Pasión por la Libertad (*Río Piedras: Instituto de Estudios del Caribe, 2002), 3-13.
12. Félix Ojeda Reyes, Betances, Merino, Luyeron: Profetas de la Antillana, Combatientes de Nuestra Libertad.. Ciencia y Sociedad(vol.. XXIX, 4, 2004), 651. *El Desterrado de Paris, Biografía del Doctor Ramón Emeterio Betances 1827-1898.* (San Juan: Ediciones Puerto Rico, Inc., 2001), 280-285.
13. Haroldo Dilla y Emilio Godinez, *Ramón Emeterio Betances* (Habana: Casas de Las América, 1983), 345. Félix Ojeda Reyes, *La Manigua en Paris: Correspondencia*

Diplomática de Betances (Centro de Estudios Avanzados de Puerto Rico y del Caribe, en colaboración con el Centro de Estudios Puertorriqueños, Hunter College, City University of New York, 1984), 10-11.

14. Paul Estrade. *Solidaridad con Cuba Libre, 1895-1898. La impresionante labor del Dr.Betances en Paris, 1895-1898* (San Juan: Editora de la Universidad de Puerto Rico, 2001), 35.

15. Ojeda y Estrade, *Pasión por la Libertad, 33.* Note No. 10, stated that the author kept a copy of the document, which is in the Spanish Military Archive. He does not mention the specifics about the Spanish Military Archive (i.e. location). The proclamation had the Betances name at the end. The same document was reproduce in Ojeda, *Desterrado de Paris*, p. 56 without Betances' signature.

16. Ministerio de Relaciones de Exteriores, legajo 15. (Archivo General de la Nación. Santo Domingo, República Dominicana). This document was find out for the author of this book in the Dominican Republic nacional archive and was given by the Dominican historian, Jaime Domínguez to Felix Ojeda Reyes, who reproduces the document in his book, *Desterrado de Paris*, p.57.

17. Ministerio de Relaciones Exteriores, legajo 17. (Archivo General de la Nación. Santo Domingo, República Dominicana.)

18. Carlos Rama, *La independencia de Las Antillas y Ramón Emeterio Betances.* (San Juan: Instituto de Cultura Puertorriqueña), 57.

19. Kart Wagenheim and Olga Jiménez de Wagenheim, *The Puerto Ricans A Documentary History.* (Princeton: Markus Wiener Publisher, 1996.), 61.

20. Moscoso, *Betances para todos los días*, 118.

21. Moscoso, *Betances para todos los días*, 41.

22. Moscoso, *Betances para todos los días*, 21.

23. Moscoso, *Betances para todos los días, 140.*

24. Juan Rodríguez Cruz, Ramón E. Betances y el Proyecto de Anexión de la República Dominicana a los Estados Unidos en 1869. *Revista Caribe.* (Años 1V-V. Num. 5-6. 1983-84): 168.

25. Félix Ojeda Reyes y Paul Estrade, *Pasión por la Libertad (*Editorial de la Universidad de Puerto Rico. Instituto de Estudios del Caribe: Editorial de la Universidad de Puerto Rico), 33. Moscoso, *Betances para todos los días*, 37.

26. Ojeda Reyes y Paul Estrade, *Pasión por la Libertad*, 33.

27. Emilio Cordero Michel, República Dominicana, Cuna del Antillanismo. Revista *Clío* no.165, 71, (Enero-Junio 2003): 230. (hereafter Cuna Del Antillanismo)

28. Cordero Michel, Cuna Del Antillanismo, 232.

29. Cordero Michel, Cuna Del Antillanismo, 233-234.

The Spanish Soldiers in the Last Campaign of Santo Domingo: Diseases, Injuries, Disables and Deaths 1861-1865

A Historical Controversy

There has been a longstanding historical controversy pertaining to the Spanish army during the period of the Annexation and the Restoration War. These different points of view arose in part because the amount of soldiers in the Spanish army that became, sick, wounded, disable or killed during confrontation with the enemy, or due to the tropical diseases that the soldiers suffered.

In general terms, the controversy is characterized by the argument that the Spanish troops never were defeated in new the annexed territory. The tropical climate, the endemic diseases of the country and brusque changes in temperature are the reasons for the abandonment of the Dominican territory after five years of flawed colonialism.

The objective of this chapter is to review this problematic topic, revisiting part of the literature specializing in the subject matter, and some of the sources and chronicles of the war. A mindful and careful study of the sources can bring positive results and also some difficulties in analyzing such a thorny subject.

It is also important to sustain the point of view that the Spanish army was defeated in Santo Domingo, in light of the fact that they were able to win innumerable battles, but in any war it is possible to win many battles and lose the war, which was exactly what occurred.

The most important objective of the Spanish imperial army and its navy station in the Antilles was to preserve the newly annexed territory of the Dominican Republic, which in their view would have fortified their beloved Antillean Empire. This objective was not achieved because the Spanish army was defeated by the Dominican popular army. Using "invisible guerrillas", their blacks, mulattos and ragged whites combatants forced the Spanish army to abandon the Dominican territory.

The Historical Sources

There are a prolific collection of memoirs, medical reports, letters and diaries from the war that enable the historian to make new analysis of the object of studies. The Spanish chronicles of the war that are accessible are results of their publication by the "Asociación Dominicana de Bibliófilos" (Dominican Association of Book Lovers) and are the following: De La Gándara, José. *Anexión y*

Guerra de Santo Domingo.(Santo Domingo: Editora Santo Domingo, 1975), González Tablas, Ramón. *Historia de la Dominación y Última Guerra de España en Santo Domingo.* (Santo Domingo: Editora Santo Domingo, 1975), López Morillo, Adriano. *Memorias sobre la Segunda Reincorporación de Santo Domingo a España.* (Santo Domingo: Editora Corripio, 1983), Rodríguez Demorizi, Emilio also compiled and published various volumes that provide detailed information of the Spanish army and the war. *Diarios de la Guerra Dominico-Española 1863-1865.* (Journal of the Dominican-Spanish War) (Santo Domingo: Editora Del Caribe, 1963). This publication gathered 10 diaries of the war, from the diaries of the headquarters to those written by different Captain Generals and different Columns and Divisions of the Spanish army operating in Santo Domingo. This volume published the report of Andres y Espala, health officer of Santo Domingo from the year 1865, where the Creole disease *rámpano* was described.

Rodríguez Demorizi published two other volumes that contained more information on the Dominican soldiers serving in the Spanish army and Dominican combatants of the Restoration army. *Hojas de Servicio Del Ejército Dominicano 1844-1865.* (Santo Domingo: Editorial Del Caribe, 1968), *Próceres de la Restauración,* (Santo Domingo: Editorial Del Caribe, 1963).

The Dominican Society of Book Lovers published two other Dominican chronicles of the war, which are essential to comprehend this complex historical process. The first is Luperòn, Gregorio. *Notas Autobiografías y Apuntes Históricos.*(Santo Domingo: Editora El Diario, 1974), Rodríguez Objio, Manuel. *Gregorio Luperòn e Historia de la Restauración.*(Santo Domingo: Editora Santo Domingo, 1975).

I should not finish without mentioning recent bibliography concerning the period that offers information regarding the Spanish army in Santo Domingo and the Spanish soldiers that comprise it. The investigation of Maria Magdalena, Guerrero Cano. *Santo Domingo (1795-1865).* (Cádiz: Servicio de Publicaciones de la Universidad de Cádiz, 1986), and her publication about this topic: *Aspectos Sanitarios Durante la Segunda independencia de Santo Domingo. Su repercusión en Andalucia.(* España, Sevilla, 1986). Roblez Muñoz, Cristóbal. *Paz en Santo Domingo* (1861-1865) and *El fracaso de la Anexión a España.(*Madrid: CSIS, 1987). From the Dominican Republic I have the publications of Jaime de Jesus Domínguez. *La Anexión de la República Dominicana a España.* Santo Domingo: Editora Alfa y Omega, 1979. My book *Dominación Colonial y Guerra Popular (La Anexión y la Restauración en la Historia Dominicana.).* (Santo Domingo: Editora de la Universidad Autónoma de Santo Domingo, 1986). Cordero Michel, Emilio. *Características de la Guerra Restauradora, 1863-1865. Clío,* año 70,(junio-diciembre 2002), 91-123. Avelino, Francisco Antonio. Reflexiones sobre la Guerra Restauradora, include in the same journal. González Calleja, Eduardo y Fontecha Pedraza, Antonio. *Una Cuestión de Honor: Una Polémica sobre la Anexión de Santo Domingo vista desde España. (1861-*

1865). (Santo Domingo: Fundación García Arévalo, 2005). And my last two publications: *Dieciséis Conclusiones Fundamentales Sobre La Anexión y La Restauración.* (Santo Domingo. Editora Argos, 2005). *Secuestro de Bienes de Rebeldes (Estado y Sociedad en la última Dominación Española).* (Santo Domingo: Editora Argos, 2005).

War and Disease in History

Historically, there has been a strong relationship between disease and war. There have been multiple wars in which numerous infectious diseases developed, and mysteriously decimated armies. Some historians have stated that wars and diseases are two horsemen of the apocalypse that go hand in hand throughout history. In some wars, a large percentage of "the soldiers were haunted by the specter of infectious disease, maladies as old as man and warfare".[1] For example, "bubonic plague in Jaffa, yellow fever in Haiti, and typhus in Russia are rather prominent examples of how insects and diseases have influenced war. Although not as dramatic or influential, these diseases and others were present in other campaigns in Napoleon's long military career. Epidemic of dysentery, typhoid, smallpox, measles, pneumonia, plague, malaria, typhus and yellow fever decimated the French army during Napoleon long campaign throughout the world.

The British army and the French were victimized by yellow fever in Saint Domingue. The Napoleón Bonaparte dream to build an empire in the Mississippi Valley to stop the English interest in the region failed as result of the French defeat by the Haitian Army. The Toussaint Louverture army defeated the French with the help of yellow fever. General Victor-Emmanuel Leclerc in command of the French army "succumbed of yellow fever himself and 50,000 soldiers, officers, doctors, and sailors may have died from yellow fever".[2]

In the case of the Dominican Republic campaign (1863-1865), the historical situation was similar for the peninsular army, since it set foot in Dominican soil; soldiers were victims of innumerable diseases that diminished the efficacy of the army. The sudden transport of thousands of soldiers, some of them coming from Spain, others from Cuba, Puerto Rico and Mexico, dramatically altered the equilibrium of the urban and rural landscape in Santo Domingo and the other provinces where they settled down: Santiago, Samaná, Azua and Puerto Plata.[3]

The information from the historical sources indicate that there weren't adequate facilities to lodge the number of Spanish soldiers, whom suddenly multiplied the demand for necessary services such as, shelters, foods, diversions, use of military facilities and medical services, even though the Spanish army brought their doctors and nurses with them.

The sudden assembly of so many soldiers in Santo Domingo and the other provinces they inhabited were problematic due to the abrupt changes in temperature. The tropical climate and the rapid changes in the weather along with the pernicious influence of the leafy and exuberant vegetation, created conditions for the development of different diseases.

The troops not acclimated to the tropical temperatures were the first victims. The situation turned more difficult for the Spanish troop in August of 1863, when in subsequent months the war propagated like a dust storm in great part of the nation. The battalions were subject to long and distant forceful marches, improvised attacks from an invisible enemy that used machetes, ruthless torches, and the growing hostile climate whose change in temperature was brisk, and sometimes intolerable for the soldiers. Many soldiers died from asphyxiation under the burning heat and other suffered continuous sickness like: yellow fever, dysentery, malaria, intermittent fever and other diseases.[4]

Doubtlessly, the Spanish lacked antibodies to resist these new diseases, but also the pressure of a war situation, with the rupture of the fragile ecological equilibrium as was already mentioned, made the situation worse. Some of the diseases that the soldiers fell victims of originated from water and infested animals as in the case of malaria, yellow fever, and dysentery.[5]

The Spanish Army in Santo Domingo

The Spanish army in the Dominican Republic was integrated by the Santo Domingo Expeditionary Brigade: Spanish soldiers coming from Spain and from Puerto Rico and Cuba. The Dominican soldiers were the Disciplined Militia, the Provincial Reserve and the Voluntary body loyal to the Spanish army, created at the beginning of the war.

During the heated period of the Restoration war the number of troops that formed part of the army was most likely greater than 60, 000 soldiers. In that sense, the number mentioned by Cordero Michel is close to reality. According to him ". . . Spain came with an army of 63,000 soldiers of all branches: 41, 000 from Spain, and 10,000 from Cuba and Puerto Rico and 12, 000 Dominicans."[6]

Putting together the conservative figures from De La Gándara, which mentions 29,824 soldiers that came from Spain, plus the numbers of Dominican troops organized in artillery, cavalry and infantry which reached 12,000, plus the numbers that came from Cuba and Puerto Rico 10,000, the result is 51,824 soldiers. To this number, I should add a projection of 7,060, from August 1863, (missing data in the Fernández Martínez report) which is the average base in the number of soldiers arriving monthly from Spain during 1861 and 1862. Factoring that number to the amount of Spanish soldiers, the total was 58,884. I must also keep in mind the numbers of volunteers in the Spanish army in Santo Domingo. But that number is unknown. The final numbers are close to the Cordero Michel figure.[7]

This is the Spanish army that faced incessant guerrilla attacks, the offensive torch of the enemy and faced also the tropical climate rigors. This climate was characterized by suffocating heat, rapid changes in temperature and persistent rain throughout some seasons of the year. The diseases came from the unhealthy conditions that existed in the country, exacerbated by the high numbers of soldiers, whom contributed to conditions appropriate for the spread of sickness that victimized the peninsular army.

Hospitals, Infirmaries and Sanitary Personnel

The Spanish army included a group of military health inspectors, which totaled 130. This group included doctors, pharmacists, medical assistant, provisional medics and equipment technician.

These medical personnel worked in hospitals and local infirmaries in different regions of the country. There were hospitals in Santo Domingo, Bani, Samaná, Santiago, Puerto Plata, Concepción de la Vega, Moca, Guayubín, San Juan de La Maguana and Las Matas de Farfán.

The infirmaries were located in San Antonio de Guerra, Dajabón, Santa Cruz, Yabacao, Guaza, Macorís, Juan Dolio, Hato Mayor and Bani.

The duties of doctors, pharmacist, technicians and all other sanitary workers were to attend to the medical necessities of the soldiers and the officials of the Spanish army in Santo Domingo.[8]

The investigation of Guerrero Cano has shown the difficult situations that the peninsular medical personnel faced, beginning with the meager numbers, the unhealthy conditions of the hospitals and infirmaries as well as the insufficient medications to attend the wounded and the sick.

In addition, many hospitals and infirmaries had to be established in the middle of an attack to attend the growing needs of wounded and sick soldiers. As occurred in Santiago and Puerto Plata, the hospitals due to the fires in both places had to be relocated. In the case of Santiago, the hospital was relocated inside a Church close to the fortress of San Luis in Santiago. In the case of Puerto Plata the hospital was moved to the San Felipe fort.

In these hospitals, created in the midst of combat, there didn't exist sufficient numbers of beds to place the sick and wounded. At times the wounded did not have a place to sleep and it was necessary to accommodate two in a bed, some slept on the floor waiting for the death of other soldiers that were badly wounded in order to have access to a bed.[9]

A witness described the difficult situation of these sick and wounded soldiers in the following way:

In the hospital blood was everywhere; it has been three days since the dead have not been evacuated. They were being place under the choir and the stench that the bodies emitted was so unbearable that it was prudent that before sleeping all the doors to the church were opened so that we would not asphyxiate from the pestilence of the cadavers and our wounded. There was a mass of 20 cadavers on our side and somewhere in there were my friends the lieutenants Don Manuel Carrasco, Don Antonio Antolin and Don Antonio Miranda. It has been two days since the sick and wounded have received any insignificant ration of rice and half bread, we lack everything and the medicine has run out.[10] [Author's translation]

The Sick, Wounded, Lost and Death by Enemy Fire: The Battle of September 6, 1863

Following the information from De La Gándara the number of deaths in confrontation with the enemy during the whole Santo Domingo campaign was 448, which was the same number provided by Castel in his historical essay. This figure seems to be wrong; I want to show analyzing some of the historical sources that in the Battle of September 6, the number of dead in confrontation with the enemy was higher than De La Gándara 's number.[11]

Gonzalez Tablas referring to this battle mentioned, the disastrous retreat cost thousand of dead, wounded, and lost men.[12] [Author's Translation]

A letter from José Martínez Moner, reproduced in one of the Journal of the War, (Diarios de la Guerra Dominico-Española) stated that the . . .

The soldiers, countrymen, women, and children of the Division that arrived in Santiago on the way, it is said are 700 people. And in total, between the fire and the attack on the Spanish in Santiago, and other incidents around here, about 1800 men are calculated dead.[13] [Author's translation]

López Morillo offered more conservative number; he indicated that the number of wounded and

killed rose to 390 and of those 205 killed there was one chief, two officers and 161 soldiers' wounded.[14] [Author's Translation]

To this number, I should add, 22 soldiers and one officer whom died in the forceful and long march of the column from Puerto Plata to Santiago.[15]

that in the retreat a big number of Spanish pass away, the road was full of cadavers . . . and in the area around the village of Altamira, with machete attacks by the rebels concluded the rest of the San Quintin.[16] [Author's translation]

Rodríguez Objio affirmed:

The month of September was the bloodiest day that the Restoration registers in their record. The streets parks and around the city were full of cadavers and the quantity made it impossible to bury them.[17] [Author's translation]

Gabriel Garcia described the retreat from Santiago to Puerto Plata of the Spanish troops, already defeated because they abandoned the city, in the following manner:

> The heterogeneous column of soldiers and refugee families of the San Luis Fort began to be attacked merciless by the Dominican army. Going forward, the Spanish column was perpetually attacked with ambushes and surprise attack, the road interrupted by enormous trenches, and the incessant attacks in the front, in the rear, in the flank. In his terrible march, the column has to avoid the main road and walk throughout the forest toward Puerto Plata under a deadly fire from the enemy."[18] [Author's translation]

The sub-tenant Astudillo, which was injured in battle, mentioned that: "the losses, should be considerable in deaths, injures and missing."[19] [Author's translation]

Despite the fact that these sources do not offer clear numbers, but it offers a clear explanation about the magnitude of the Spanish losses in this battle. There is not doubt that the Spanish army losses, the battle and the retreats to Puerto Plata was extremely costly in terms of human life and was higher than the misleading number of De La Gándara.

Diseases, Sick, Wounded and Death since the Onset of the Campaign

Since the beginning of the occupation in the Eastern part of the island, the Spanish troops were victims of multiple diseases, such as, dysentery, yellow fever, intermittent fever, typhoid, "rámpanos", etc.

The amount of soldiers that suddenly arrived to the country created a situation of overcrowding that changed the urban and rural landscape, as I mentioned before. The non-acclimation of the numerous soldiers to the tropical climate, the precarious health services and the geography of the country characterized by exuberant vegetation as well as brusque changes in temperature became a threat for the health of thousands of soldiers coming from Spain, Cuba and Puerto Rico.

Following the information from the medical report of Fernández Martìnez, the expeditionary brigade assigned to Azua, on the borders of Haiti, had to face diseases like dysentery, intermittent fever and typhoid. From 2000 soldiers, 639 became ill and 35 of these passed away.[20]

The health situation was even worse in Samaná, since the beginning of 1861.

The intermittent fever attacks were so aggressive that almost 100% of all sol-diers became sick, and also the yellow fever caused several victims in relation to the number of ill.[21] [Author's translation]

The reports from Luis Golfi and Vargas and Gamir offered some additional information about Samaná. These reports mention the diseases that struck the Spanish soldiers in the province. According to these historical sources, the total numbers of troops was 376, and the sick soldiers were 191.[22] Based on the in-formation from Golfi and Vargas Gamir's reports, I organized Table 5.1 and Figure 5.1. The chart and Figure show the numbers of ill by divisions.

The Spanish soldiers become sick with yellow fever, dysentery, pernicious fever and other diseases. During 1861, the first year of the annexation to Spain other battalions come from Cuba, Puerto Rico and Valladolid. These new arriv-als were victims of several diseases. Based on the figure provided in the memory of Illas and Vidal, I organized Figure 5.2. [23]

Table 5.1 Soldiers Sick by Division in the Spanish Army in Samaná

Division	# of Soldiers	# of Sick
Two Infantry Divisions	211	129
Artillery Division	51	23
Division Engineers	61	23
Prisoners	53	16
Total	376	191

Sources: *Jaime de Jesús Domínguez, La Anexión de la República Domini-cana a España (*Santo Domingo: Universidad Autónoma de Santo Domin-go, Alfa y 0mega, 1979), 257-258. Golfi, Luis. Memoria General Sobre la Bahía y Península de Samaná, quoted in Emilio Rodríguez Demorizi, *Sa-maná, Pasado y Porvenir.*(Santo Domingo: Editora Montalvo, 1945),153-174.

The number of sick soldiers during 1862 increased to 8,027. The troops were victims of the following diseases: yellow fever, intermittent fever, diarrhea, dy-sentery, and scabies. The numbers of soldiers admitted to hospitals were 7,934, from that the number 563 passed away and the disabled were 116. The total numbers of losses were 679, including 178 losses for every 1000 soldiers.[24]

This information is more comprehensible in a chart that includes the num-ber of soldiers sick and the diseases that attacked them during the year. During the three first months, from January to March, (1862) the number of soldiers admitted to the hospital and infirmaries was 1,586 members of the Spanish Ar-my.[25]

During the months of April to June, 1862, the arrival of new troops oc-curred at the beginning of the summer, the changes in temperature proper of the

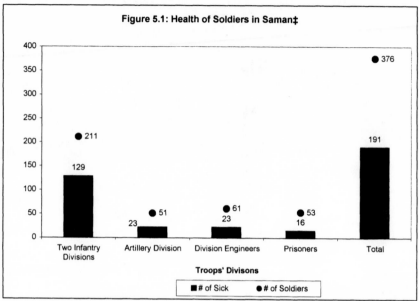

Figure 5.1: Health of Soldiers in Samaná‡

Sources: *Jaime de Jesús Domínguez, La Anexión de la República Dominicana a España* (Santo Domingo: Universidad Autónoma de Santo Domingo, Alfa y Omega, 1979), 257-258. Golfi, Luis. Memoria General Sobre la Bahía y Península de Samaná, quoted in Emilio Rodríguez Demorizi, *Samaná, Pasado y Porvenir.*(Santo Domingo: Editora Montalvo, 1945),153-174.

season created havoc for the soldiers. The health conditions became worse for the troops. The persistent rain of May and the warm weather at the beginning of the summer continued to devastate the troops' health.

The numbers of soldiers admitted to hospitals 3,178. Soldiers who became ill from yellow fever 937, intermittent fever 854, intermittent malign 101, dysentery 210, decease 236 and disable 14.[26]

During the third quarter of the year, from August to October, the health conditions of the soldiers improved. A total of 2,357 soldiers were admitted to the hospitals and infirmaries, plus 450 sick that came from the previous month. The number of sick diminished in great proportion as is shown in the Martínez Fernandez's report.[27]

The fourth quarter of the year 1862, from October to December was less harmful for the troops. The number of ill decreased in the hospitals and infirmaries. The number of soldiers admitted to the hospital was 1, 038, plus 299 that left from the previous months. The number of decease decreased to 98 and disabled were 49. That was not the case of the yellow fever. The other diseases that struck the

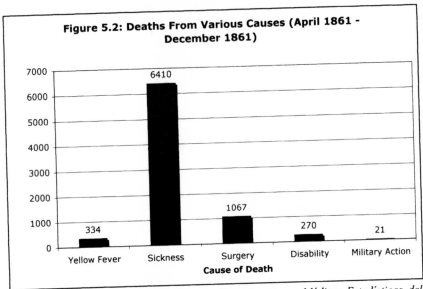

Figure 5.2: Deaths From Various Causes (April 1861 - December 1861)

Source: Juan Fernández Martínez, *Breves Consideraciones Médicos-Estadísticas del Ejército Español en la Isla de Santo Domingo, desde abril de 1861 a julio de 1865.* José De La Gándara, *Anexión y Guerra de Santo Domingo.* (Santo Domingo: Editora Santo Domingo, República Dominicana 1975), 636-648.

Spanish soldiers were not present.[28] The numbers of soldiers sick during 1861-1862 are shown in Figure 5.3.

There is no data available for the months of January to August 1863; Fernández Martinez report doesn't provide any numbers regarding diseases, sick, and dead or disabled soldiers that came to Santo Domingo from Spain or Cuba and Puerto Rico. Beginning in August, the report provided some data for the period August 1863 to June 1864. In terms of ill soldiers, 1,763 became sick of undiagnosed disease, 474 passed away in Cuba and Puerto Rico, and 22 were reported to die in Santo Domingo.[29]

This is a case of "missing information" as a result of faulty data, precisely the most important period, from January to August of 1863, period of social upheavals and generalized aversions toward the oppressive colonial system imposed by the Spanish authority. The beginning of the Restoration War is marked on August 16, 1863. Despite that, there is a method to solve the problem of the missing data, which is using a "regression estimate" using as a base the monthly arrivals of Spanish troops the previous year. Using that methodology, I came with an average number that allowed me to conclude the number of 7000 soldiers is the missing number for that period.[30]

The first six months of the year, from January to August, the army had to confront the Northeast chain of rebellions, which unlock the Restoration war beginning in August 16, 1863. It was a critical juncture for the Spanish army

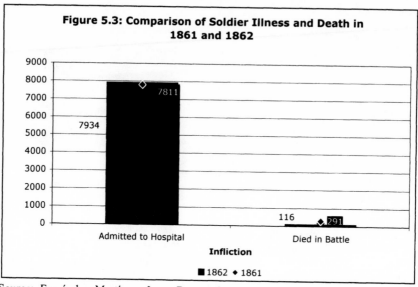

Figure 5.3: Comparison of Soldier Illness and Death in 1861 and 1862

Source: Fernández Martínez, Juan. Breves Consideraciones Médicos-*Estadísticas del Ejército Español en la Isla de Santo Domingo, desde Abril de 1861 a Julio de 1865*. En De La Gándara, José. *Anexión y Guerra de Santo Domingo*. (Santo Domingo: Sociedad Dominicana de Bibliófilos, 1975), 639. Hereafter quote as Fernández Martínez . . .

that had to face an enemy fighting a special war with "invisible guerrillas", waging surprise attacks in front and at the rear of the columns. Due to this these conditions the number of casualties, injures, deaths and disease increased during this part of the year.

The September 6 Battle of 1863, and the retreat of the Spanish army from Santiago to Puerto Plata caused around one thousand deaths and hundreds injured between military and non-military personnel. Other battles, ambushes and attacks to the Spanish army caused a significant amount of deaths and injuries.

Regarding the year of 1864, from January to December, De La Gándara provided some information. The numbers of soldiers injured were 1,249, disabled 375 and returned to the hospital in Spain were 1503. The number of soldiers send to Puerto Rico were 7,005, to Cuba were 2, 314 and in Santo Domingo 3, 413.[31]

The Figure 5.4 shows sick soldiers transported to Cuba, Puerto Rico and Spain.

The investigation of Guerrero Cano is extremely helpful regarding the diseases that ravaged the Spanish army during 1864. She provided an analysis by diseases and geographic location that is crucial to study this topic. Ill and sick soldiers were in hospitals throughout the country: Puerto Plata, Santiago, Santo

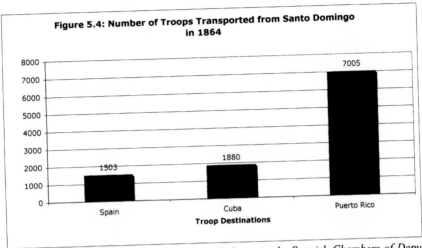

Figure 5.4: Number of Troops Transported from Santo Domingo in 1864

Source: David Yuengling, *Highlights in the Debates in the Spanish Chambers of Deputies Relatives to the abandonment of Santo Domingo.* (Washington: Murray & Heister, 1941), 142.

Domingo, Samaná, Azua, Baní and Montecristi. The soldiers who were ill with Yellow fever, dysentery and intermittent fever are shown in figure 5.5.

For the year 1865 until the last day of the campaign, I used the number from Castel that are reproduced by Guerrero Cano. The chart 5.2 is organized in three different columns with soldier's chiefs and officers, and I consider five variables; sick, injured, deaths in combat, losses and those who returned to Spain. It's crystal clear from the chart that the common soldiers were the main victims of diseases, injures and deaths in combat, followed by the officers. It is evident that the officers received special treatments that made them less likely to become sick, injured or dead in confrontation with the enemy.

The figures for dysentery yellow and intermittent fever are shown in Figure 5.5.[32]

The Table 5.2 shows how some Spanish historians used the numbers to minimize the defeat of the Spanish army in the Restoration War (Figure 5.6 based on the figures found in Table 5.2). The deaths in combats are the same figures used by De La Gándara 448 soldiers, 33 officers and 5 chiefs. These numbers are wrong; I showed that the numbers of deaths in confrontation with the enemy was higher only in the battle of Santiago, September 6, 1863, which led to the establishment of the insurgents Provisional Government in Santiago, heart of the Cibao region.

The number of sick soldiers is also minimized in the numbers provided by De La Gándara. Guerrero Cano's research showed the highest rate of sick soldiers. Only two diseases: Intermittent fever and dysentery count for 35,000 thousands cases. But using this number in order to reach the conclusion that "the

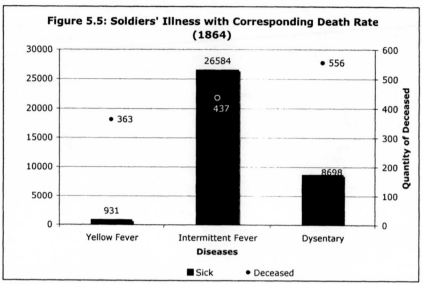

Figure 5.5: Soldiers' Illness with Corresponding Death Rate (1864)

Source: Maria Magdalena Guerrero Cano, *Aspectos Sanitarios Durante la Segunda Independencia de Santo Domingo. Su repercusión en Andalucía.* (Sevilla: Imprenta E.E.H.A.-Alfonso X11, 16.1984), 327-328.

Table 5.2: Soldiers and Officers Sick, Injured, Diseased, Prisoners, and Death in Confrontation with the Enemy

	Chiefs	Officers	Troops
Sick	6	63	6,785
Injured	0	135	1,249
Prisoner and Loss	5	31	603
Deaths In Combat	5	33	448
Returned to Spain Due to Disease	1	21	1,503
Total	*17*	*283*	*10,558*

Source: Maria Magdalena Guerrero Cano, *Aspectos Sanitarios Durante la Segunda Independencia de Santo Domingo. Su repercusión en Andalucía.* (Sevilla: Imprenta E.E.H.A.-Alfonso X11, 16. 1984), 327-328.

Spanish army was not defeated by the Dominican forces, but by elements of nature" is totally a wrong conclusion. This is the same argument used by Yuengling, David, who believed that the Spaniards were not defeated by the Dominican forces, but by elements of nature." The Spanish forces sent to Santo

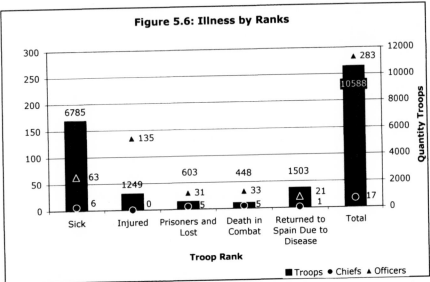

Figure 5.6: Illness by Ranks

Source: Maria Magdalena Guerrero Cano, *Aspectos Sanitarios Durante la Segunda Independencia de Santo Domingo. Su repercusión en Andalucía.* (Sevilla: Imprenta E.E.H.A.-Alfonso X11, 16. 1984). 327-328.

Domingo to put down the rebellions were physically unfit to fight in that climate, and Spain lost a vast amount of men and treasure in its endeavor."[33]

It is difficult to accept that the most backward colony in the Spanish Caribbean, the center of Spanish imperial expansion, defeated the old Spanish Empire, showing that was it possible to overpower it in the Caribbean.

The Spanish imperial government believed that the continuous transfer of troops from Cuba to the insurgent Dominican Republic put in danger this colony, by the absence of a necessary number of troops. Cuba was also present in the decision to abandon the Dominican Republic by the Spanish empire. I conclude emphasizing that the Dominican popular army defeated the Spanish army, using the machetes, torch and guerrilla war. In this effort the endemic diseases of the country and the tropical climate played important roles weakening the foreign army.

Notes

1. Robert K.D. Peterson, *Insects, Diseases, and Military History. The Napoleonic Campaign and Historical Perception.* http://scarab. Msu. Montana.edu/historybug/napoleon/ napoleon.htm. 1. Hereafter Peterson.

2. Peterson. 1. The Haitians Debacle: Yellow Fever and the Fate of the French, 1-4.

3. Diamond, Jared. *Guns Germs and Steel. The Fate of Human Society.* (New York and London: W.W. Norton & Company, 1999). Chapters 11, discuss the origin of animal's diseases in human.

4. Maria Magdalena Guerrero Cano, *Aspectos Sanitarios Durante la Segunda Independencia de Santo Domingo. Su Repercusión en Andalucía.* (Sevilla: Imprenta E. E. H. A.-Alfonso X11, 1986), 318-319. (hereafter, *Aspectos Sanitarios*).

5. Peterson, discuss the multiple etiological factors of human Infectious diseases: concentration of people, the intermixing of population, and diversion of resources. These conditions may lead to a decrease in hygiene and medical care and an increase in malnutrition and famine. 1

6. Emilio Cordero Michel, "Características de la Guerra Restauradora", *Clío,* no. 164, (Junio-Diciembre 2002): 70.

7. Guerrero Cano, *Aspectos Sanitarios,* 320-326.

8. López Morillo, Adriano. *Memoria sobre la Segunda Reincorporación de Santo Domingo a España.* (Santo Domingo: Editora Corripio, 1983), 206. (herafter *Memoria).*

9. López Morillo, *Memoria,* 206.

10. De La Gándara, José. *Anexión y Guerra de Santo Domingo.* (Santo Domingo: Editora Santo Domingo, República Dominicana 1975), 632.(hereafter,De la Gándara, *Anexión y Guerra)*

11. Ramón González Tablas, *Historia de la Dominación y última Guerra de España en Santo Domingo.* (Santo Domingo: Editora Alfa y Omega, 1979) ,159.

12. Emilio Rodríguez Demorizi, *Diario de la Guerra Dominico-Española.* (Santo Domingo: Editora del Caribe, 1963), 102. Hereafter *Diario de la Guerra.*

13. López Morillo, *Memoria,* 120-121.

14. Rodríguez Demorizi, *Diario de la Guerra,* 120-121.

15. Emilio Rodríguez Demorizi, *Antecedentes de la Anexión a España.* (Santo Domingo: Editora Montalvo.1955), 370.

16. Manuel Rodríguez Objio, *Gregorio Luperón e Historia de la Restauración.* (Santo Domingo: Editora de Santo Domingo, 1975), 66.

17. José Gabriel García, *Compendio de la Historia de Santo Domingo.* (Santo Domingo: Ediciones ¡Ahora!, 1975), 435.

18. De la Gándara, *Anexión y Guerra,* 435.

19. De la Gándara, *Anexión y Guerra,* 437.

20. De la Gándara, *Anexión y Guerra,* 638.

21. Emilio Rodríguez Demorizi, *Samaná Pasado y Porvenir.* (Santo Domingo: Editora Montalvo, 1945), 153-174.

22. Jaime Fernández Martínez, Breves Consideraciones Médicos-Estadísticas del Ejercito Español en Santo Domingo.640. Quote in De la Gándara, *Anexión y Guerra,* 641-648. (hereafter Breves Consideraciones).

23. Fernández Martínez, *Breves Consideraciones,* 641.

24. Fernández Martínez, *Breves Consideraciones,* 641-642.

25. Fernández Martínez, *Breves Consideraciones,* 642.

26. Fernández Martínez, *Breves Consideraciones,* 641-642.

27. Fernández Martínez, *Breves Consideraciones,* 643.

28. David Yuengling *Highlights in the Debates in the Spanish Chamber of Deputies Relatives to the Abandonment of Santo Domingo.* (Washington: Murray & Heister, 1941), 142. Hereafter, Yuengling *Highlights.*

29. Guerrero Cano, *Aspectos Sanitarios*, 327-328.

30. Roderick Floud, *An Introduction to Quantitative Methods for Historians*. (Princeton: Princeton University Press, 1975), 176-183.

32 Guerrero Cano, *Aspectos Sanitarios*, 339

33. Yuengling, *Highlights*, 2.

Research, Sources and Bibliography

Primary Sources Unpublished

The research for this book has been conducted in the "Archivo General de la Nación"(National Archive of the Dominican Republic) and in the library of the Dominican Academy of Historian (Santo Domingo) as well as the Dominican Institute Library at City College, Hunter College Library and the New York public Library, New York City.

The main sources for this research are:

Herrera collection on the Annexation to Spain and the Restoration War, 20 vols. Legajos de la Anexión a España, numbers 15, 27, 28, 30, 31, 32, 33, 34, 35 and 36, National Archive, Dominican Republic.
Expediente General de Colonos and Legajos de la Sección de Ultramar, numbers 3525, 3528, 3534, 3536, 3537, 3538. Archivo Histórico Nacional, Madrid.
Records of the Provisional Government of the Dominican Republic, 1863-1864. Libro no.4. Santiago, Dominican Republic.
Relaciones Exteriores, Expediente Consulado Dominicano en New York, no.7. 1868. Archivo General de la Nación
Relaciones Exteriores, Agencia Comercial de los Estados Unidos, 1868. Archivo General de la Nación.
Diario de Las Cortes. Legislatura de 1864 a 1865. Microcard Edition, roll 4319, Centro de Estudios Históricos de la Universidad de Puerto Rico.

Primary Sources Unpublished

Rodríguez Demorizi, E. *Antecedentes de la Anexión a España.* Ciudad Trujillo: Editora Montalvo, 1955.
Rodríguez Demorizi, E. *Relaciones Dominico-Españolas 1844-1859.* Ciudad Trujillo: Editora Montalvo, 1955.
Rodríguez Demorizi, E. *Actos y Doctrinas del Gobierno de la Restauración.* Santo Domingo: Editora Del Caribe, 1963.
Rodríguez Demorizi, E. *Próceres de la Restauración.* Santo Domingo: Editora del Caribe, 1963.
Rodríguez Demorizi, E. *Diario de la Guerra Dominico-Española de 1863-1865.* Santo Domingo: Editora Del Caribe, 1963.

Rodríguez Demorizi, E. *Acerca de Francisco del Rosario Sánchez.* Santo Domingo: Editora Taller, 1976. 119-127.

Rodríguez Demorizi, E. *Hojas de Servicio del Ejercito Dominicano,* 1844-1865. Santo Domingo: Editora del Caribe, 1968.

Rodríguez Demorizi, E. *Samaná, Pasado y Porvenir.* Santo Domingo: Editora Montalvo, 1945.

Secondary Sources

Álvarez-López, Luis. *Historia de la Anexión de Santo Domingo a España,.* M.A. Thesis. Río Piedras: Universidad de Puerto Rico, 1977.

Álvarez, Luis. *Dominación Colonial y Guerra Popular 1861-1865. (La Anexión y la Restauración en la Historia Dominicana).* Santo Domingo: Editora de la Universidad Autónoma de Santo Domingo: 1986.

Álvarez-López, Luis. *Secuestro de Bienes de Rebeldes: Estado y Sociedad en la Última Dominación Española 1863-1865.* Sec. Ed. Santo Domingo: Editora Argos, 2005.

Álvarez-López, Luis. *Dieciséis Conclusiones Fundamentales Sobre la Anexión y la Guerra de la Restauración 1861-1865.* Santo Domingo: Editora Argos, 2005.

Álvarez López, Luis. "Intentos de Producir Algodón en 1862 Durante la Anexión a España," *(*No. 173, 167. Enero-Junio, 2004): 235-244. *Clío.* Órgano de la Academia Dominicana de la Historia.

Álvarez López, Luis. "Santo Domingo y Puerto Rico: Entre la Independencia y el Colonialismo Español." *Revista Dominicana de Antropología (*Enero-Diciembre, 2005): 175-192.

Archambault, Pedro. *Historia de la Restauración.* Santo Domingo: República Dominicana, 1977.

Báez, Evertsz Franc. *Formación Del Sistema Agro exportador en el Caribe. República Dominicana y Cuba: 1515-1898.* Santo Domingo: Editora Universitaria, UASD.1986.

Bergard, Laird W. "Agrarian History of Puerto Rico, 1870-1930." *Latin American Research Review (*3, 1978): 63-94.

Bergard, Laird W. "Dos Alas del Mismo pájaro? Notas sobre la Historia económica comparativa de Cuba y Puerto Rico." *Historia y Sociedad* (1, 1988): 143-54.

Bergard, Laird W. "The Economy Viability of Sugar Production Based on Slaved Labor in Cuba, 1859-1878." *Latin American Research Review* (1, 1989): 95-113.

Bonafoux, Luis. *Betances.* San Juan: Instituto de Cultura Puertorriqueña, 1970.

Bosch, Juan. *La Guerra de la Restauración.* Santo Domingo: Editora Corripio, 1982.

Cassá, Roberto. *Historia Social y Económica de la República Dominicana.* 2 vols. Santo Domingo: Alfa y Omega, 1991.

Cepero, Bonilla, Raúl. *Azúcar y Abolición.* Barcelona: Editorial Critica, 1976.

Corwin, Arthur. F. *Spain and the abolition in Cuba, 1817-1886,.* Austin: University of Texas Press, 1967.

Colección de Leyes, Decretos y Resoluciones Emanadas del Poder Legislativo y Ejecutivo de la República Dominicana.. Santo Domingo. Imprenta Listin Diario, 1927.

Manning, William R. *Diplomatic Correspondence of the United States: Inter-Americans affairs, 1831-1860.* Washington, Carnegie Endowment for International Peace, 1932-39.

Becker, Jerónimo. "La Cuestión de Santo Domingo." *Eme-Eme (.*3, 14: Sept-Oct. 1974):72-92. Santiago. Universidad Revista Católica Madre y Maestra.

Castel, Jorge. *Anexión y Abandono de Santo Domingo 1810-1865.* Madrid, Cuadernos de Historia de las relaciones internacionales y política exterior de España.

Cevallos, Nelson Moreno. *El Estado Dominicano. Origen, Evolución y Forma Actual 1844-1982.* Santo Domingo: Punto Aparte, 1983. 173-185.

Cordero, Michel E. "Características de la Guerra Restauradora, 1863-1865." *Clío,* Órgano de la Academia de la Historia (.164, Junio-Diciembre, 2002):91-123.

Cordero Michel. E. "Gregorio Luperòn y Haití." *Clío.* (152, Enero-Agosto, 1995): 91-123.

Cordero Michel, E. República Dominicana, Cuna del Antillanismo. *Revista Clio.* (165, 71 Enero-Junio 2003): 230-250.

Clawson, David L. *Latin America and the Caribbean Lands and People.* Boston: McGraw Hill higher Education, 2006.

De la Gándara, José. *Anexión y Guerra de Santo Domingo.* 2 vols. Santo Domingo: Editora Santo Domingo, 1975.

Diamond, Jared. *Guns Germs and Steel. The Fate of Human Society.* New York and London: W.W. Norton and Company 1999. The author discusses the origin of animal's diseases in human.

Domínguez, Jaime de Jesús. *La Anexión de la República Dominicana a España.* Santo Domingo: Editora Alfa y Omega, Universidad Autónoma de Santo Domingo, 1979.

Domínguez, Jaime de Jesús. *Economía y Política de la República Dominicana 1844-1861.* Santo Domingo: Alfa y Omega, Universidad Autónoma de Santo Domingo, 1976.

Domínguez, Jorge. *Insurrection or Loyalty: the breakdown of the Spanish American Empire.* Cambridge, Mass.: Harvard University Press, 1980.

Estrade, Paul. *Solidaridad con Cuba Libre, 1895-1898. La Impresionante labor del Dr. Betances en Paris.* San Juan: Editora de la Universidad de Puerto Rico, 2001.

Franco Pichardo, F. *Historia Económica y Financiera de la República Dominicana 1844-1862.* Santo Domingo, Editora de la Universidad Autónoma de Santo Domingo, 1962.

Foner, Philip S. *History of Cuba and its relations with United States.* New York: Internacional Publisher, 1962. 5.

Gil, Guido. *Orígenes y Proyecciones de la Revolución Restauradora.* Santo Domingo: Editora Nacional, 1972.

Godinez Emilio and Dilla Haroldo. *Ramón Emeterio Betances.* La Habana: Casas de las América, 1983.

González Calleja E. and Fontecha Santo Pedraza, A. *Una Cuestión de Honor. Una Polémica sobre la Anexión de Domingo vista desde España 1861-1865.* Santo Domingo: Republica Dominicana.

González Tablas R. *Historia de la Dominación y Última Guerra De España en Santo Domingo.* Santo Domingo: Editora Santo Domingo, 1976.

Guerra, Ramiro. *La expansiòn territorial de los Estados Unidos a Expensa de España y de los Paises Hispanoamericanos.* La Habana: Instituto Cubano del Libro, 1975.

Guerrero Cano, Maria M. *Santo Domingo: 1795-1865.* España: Servicio de publicaciones de la Universidad de Cádiz, 1986.

Guerrero Cano, Maria M. *Disciplina y Laxitud: La iglesia Dominicana en la Época de la Anexión.* España: Servicio de publicaciones de la Universidad de Cádiz, 1989.

Guerrero Cano, Maria M. *El Arzobispo Monzón.* Santo Domingo: Ediciones Arzobispado de la Republica Dominicana, 1991.

Guerrero Cano, Maria M. *Aspectos Sanitarios Durante la Segunda Independencia de Santo Domingo. Su repercusión en Andalucía.* España: Sevilla, 1986.

Guerrero Cano, Maria M. *Santo Domingo En el Periodo de la Anexión a España y Granada Durante el sexenio Revolucionario. Dos conflictos y un arzobispo: Bienvenido Monzón* Resumen de Tesis Doctoral. España: Universidad de Granada, 1984.

Hauch, Charles C. Attitudes of Foreign Governments towards the Spanish Reoccupation of the Dominican Republic. *Hispanic American Historical Review* (no.2, May 1947): 247-268.

Hauch Charles C. *Dominican Republic and its Foreign Relation, 1844-1882* Ph, D. Diss. Chicago: University of Chicago, Illinois, 1942.

Keen Benjamin and Keith Haynes. *A History of Latin America.* Boston: Houghton Mifflin Company. 2004.

Knight W. Franklin. *The Caribbean Genesis of a Fragmented Nationalism.* New York: Oxford University Press.

Lara D., Oruno. *Space and History in the Caribbean.* Princeton: Markus Wiener, 2006. 1990.

Le Riverent, Julio. *Historia Económica de Cuba.* Barcelona: Ariel, 1972.

López Morillo, A. *Segunda Reincorporación de Santo Domingo a España.* Santo Domingo: Editora Corripio, 1983.

Lockward, Alfonso, ED. *Documentos para las relaciones Dominico americanas 1837-1860.* Santo Domingo: Editora Corripio, 1987.

Lúperon, Gregorio. *Notas autobiograficas y apuntes históricos Sobre la Repùblica Dominicana.* 2eds. Santiago: Editorial El Diario. República Dominicana, 1939.

Lluberes,Alcides, Mella y la Guerra de guerrilla. *Homenaje a Mella.* Santo Domingo: Editora del Caribe, 1964.

Martínez-Fernández, Luis. *Torn between Empires. Economy, Society, and Patterns of political thought in the Hispanic Caribbean, 1840-1878.* Athens & London: University of Georgia Press 1994.

Marte, Roberto. *Cuba y la República Dominicana: Transición Económica en el Caribe del siglo XIX.* Santo Domingo: Universidad APEC, 1988.

Marte, Roberto. *Estadísticas y Documentos Históricos sobre Santo Domingo 1805-1890.* Santo Domingo: Banco Central de la República Dominicana, 2001.

Mir, Pedro. *Las Raices Dominicana de la Doctrina Monroe.* Santo Domingo: Editora Taller, 1984.

May, Robert. *The Southern Dream of a Caribbean Empire, 1854-1861.* Baton Rouge: Louisiana State University Press, 1973.

Moscoso, Francisco. *La Revolución Puertorriqueña de 1868: el Grito de Lares.* San Juan: Instituto de Cultura Puertorriqueña, 2003.

Moscoso, Francisco. *Betances para todos los días.* San Juan: Aurora Comunicación, Inc.2001.

Moreno Fraginal, M., Moya Pons, F. and Stanley, Engerman, eds. *Between Slavery and Free labor: the Spanish Speaking Caribbean in Nineteenth Century.* Baltimore: John Hopkins University Press, 1985.

Muñoz, Maria E. *Historia de las Relaciones Internacionales de la República Dominicana. El colonialismo Europeo y las relaciones dominico-haitianas 1844-1861.* Santo Domingo: Editora de la Universidad Autónoma de Santo Domingo.

Nelson, William J. *Almost a Territory: America attempt to annex The Dominican Republic.* Newark: University of Delaware press, 1990.

Ojeda Reyes, F. *La Manigua de Paris: Correspondencia Diplomática de Betances.* San Juan: Centros de Estudios Avanzados de Puerto Rico y el Caribe. En colaboración con el Centro de Estudios Puertorriqueños (Hunter College), City University of New York. 1984.

Ojeda Reyes, F & Estrade, Paul. *Pasión por la Libertad.* San Juan. Editorial de la Universidad de Puerto Rico. Instituto de Estudios del Caribe, 2000.

Peterson K.D., Robert. Insect, Diseases, and Military History. The Napoleonic Campaign   and

Historical.Perception.http://scarab.MsuMontana.edu/historybug/napoleón/n apoleón.htm.1

Pérez, Carlos Federico. *Historia Diplomática de la República Dominicana 1844-1861*. Santo Domingo: Publicación de la Universidad Pedro Henríquez Ureña, 1973.

Perkins, Dexter. *The Monroe Doctrine, 1826-1867*. Baltimore, the John Hopkins Press, 1933.

Poutlanzas, Nicos. *State, Power, Socialism*. London: NLB, Verso Editions, 1980.

Ramas M, Carlos. *La independencia de Las Antillas y Ramón Emeterio Betances*. San Juan, Instituto de Cultura Puertorriqueña, 1980.

Ramos Mattei, Andrés A. Ramón Emeterio Betances en el Ciclo Revolucionario Antillano: Después del Grito de Lares y hasta Abril de 1869. *Revista Caribe*, (5-6, vols. 1V-V, 1983-64), 60-81.

Rodríguez Cruz, Juan. Ramón E. Betances y el Proyecto de Anexión de la República Dominicana a los EE.UU. en 1869. *Revista Caribe*, (5-6,1V-V, 1983). 159-175.

Robles Muñoz, C. *Paz en Santo Domingo 1861-1865*. Madrid, CSIC., 1987.

Robles Muñoz, C. *El fracaso de la Anexión a España. España.* Madrid, 1987.

Rodríguez, Jiménez, J. y Vélez, Canelo, J. *El Pre-capitalismo Dominicano en la Primera Mitad del siglo XIX*. Santo Domingo: Universidad Autónoma de Santo Domingo, 1980.

Rodríguez Objio, M. *Gregorio Luperòn e Historia de la Restauración.* Santo Domingo. Editora Santo Domingo, 1975.

Scarano, Francisco. *Inmigración y Clases Sociales en el Puerto Rico del SIGLO XIX*. Río Piedras: Editora Huracán, 1981.

Sonntag Rudolf and Valecillo, Héctor. *El Estado en el Capitalismo Contemporáneo.* México: Siglo XX1, 1980.23.

Soto Jiménez, J.M. *Los Motivos del Machete. Reflexiones, Apuntes Y Notas para una Interpretación Cuartelaria de la Historia y la Sociedad Dominicana.* Santo Domingo: Editora Corripio, 2000.

Suárez Díaz, Ada. *El Doctor Ramón E. Betances y la abolición de La esclavitud.* San Juan: Instituto de Cultura Puertorriqueña, 1984.

Tansill Callan, Charles. *The United States and Santo Domingo, 1793-1873. A chapter in Caribbean Diplomacy.* Massachussets: John Hopkins University Press, 1967.

Wilckens, Manfred. Hacia una teoría de la Revolución. *Ciencia y Sociedad*, (no.4.Octubre –Diciembre, 2000): 427-465.

Welles, Summer. *La Viña de Naboth*. Santiago: Editorial El Diario, 1939.

Index

Early praise for *Take My Money: Accepting Payments on the Web*

The ability to easily and securely accept payments on the web is critical to any business. *Accepting Payments on the Web* acts as a shining beacon, guiding intermediate and advanced developers through the complexities of setting up a payment system, interacting with third-party processors, and staying within compliance regulations. This book is a must-have for any application developer.

➤ **Nell Shamrell**
   Software development engineer, Chef

Do you need to accept money on the web? No problem! Just follow the steps in Noel Rappin's book and you will be taking money in a blink of an eye.

➤ **Brian Schau**
   Lead developer, Rosving Applications

I've maintained two large payment systems at two different e-commerce companies, and the hard lessons I learned are all captured succinctly in this book. I wish I'd had it years ago.

➤ **David Copeland**
   Author of *Rails, Angular, Postgres, and Bootstrap, Second Edition*

Reading this book has increased my confidence in the daunting task of handling electronic payments. All the topics I'd hoped would be covered are here, along with useful introductions to handy gems and third-party tools.

➤ **Nigel Lowry**
   Company director and principal consultant, Lemmata Ltd.

I would not hesitate to recommend this book to anyone looking to accept payments online. I only wish I'd had this detailed a guide when building some of the systems I've written in the past; it would have saved me a great deal of stress and pain.

➤ **Stephen Orr**
   Senior developer, Siftware

Take My Money
Accepting Payments on the Web

Noel Rappin

The Pragmatic Bookshelf

Raleigh, North Carolina

Many of the designations used by manufacturers and sellers to distinguish their products are claimed as trademarks. Where those designations appear in this book, and The Pragmatic Programmers, LLC was aware of a trademark claim, the designations have been printed in initial capital letters or in all capitals. The Pragmatic Starter Kit, The Pragmatic Programmer, Pragmatic Programming, Pragmatic Bookshelf, PragProg and the linking *g* device are trademarks of The Pragmatic Programmers, LLC.

Every precaution was taken in the preparation of this book. However, the publisher assumes no responsibility for errors or omissions, or for damages that may result from the use of information (including program listings) contained herein.

Our Pragmatic books, screencasts, and audio books can help you and your team create better software and have more fun. Visit us at *https://pragprog.com*.

The team that produced this book includes:

Katharine Dvorak (editor)
Potomac Indexing, LLC (index)
Liz Welch (copyedit)
Gilson Graphics (layout)
Janet Furlow (producer)

For sales, volume licensing, and support, please contact *support@pragprog.com*.

For international rights, please contact *rights@pragprog.com*.

Contents

Acknowledgments

Many people helped me take this book from an idea to a finished project. Among the many who helped are the following:

Katharine Dvorak edited this book and has helped shape the material, make it more consistent, and point out where it needed to be clearer. Susannah Davidson Pfalzer helped get this project started and remains a pleasure to work with.

Several people provided technical reviews and made this a better book with their comments: Zach Briggs, David Copeland, Robin Dunlop, Kenneth Geisshirt, Jeff Holland, Aaron Kalair, Kaan Karaca, Irakli Nadareishvili, Nigel Lowry, Stephen Orr, Martijn Reuvers, Brian Schau, Nell Shamrell, Tibor Simic, Stefan Turalski, and Brian VanLoo.

I've been fortunate to work at Table XI while writing this book, and I thank them for their support. The project that inspired this book was a Table XI client project, and I benefited from the skill and insight of many of my coworkers as we built it.

This book, and most of my career, would not exist without the generosity of the community of developers who write and maintain the open source tools that I use. Thanks to all of you.

Thanks also to my children, Emma and Elliot. You are amazing and wonderful. My wife Erin is my favorite person. I love you.

Preface

A few years ago, I started working on my first web application that required serious payment business logic. The application was a legacy rescue, meaning that the actual core of the payment section already existed—the application already had a payment gateway, which is the third-party service that handles the credit card transaction, and knew how to communicate credit card information.

I was asked to significantly expand the payment logic. You'd think that because the API communication was already in place, the hard part would already be done. I certainly thought that but quickly learned otherwise. Suddenly I had to deal with problems managing inventory, data validation, refunds, administrators who needed to be able to override user rules, security, and fraud. I looked around for information about good practice in this area, and I didn't find much. The different gateway APIs all have documentation and tutorials about how to connect to their servers, some of which are quite helpful; however, I couldn't find answers to my questions as they related to the larger context of the application.

So I fell back on general principles of software development. And I made mistakes. This book comes from somewhere between the things I did right, the things I did wrong, and the things I wish I had done. It is my hope that with this book, you will be able to build your payment application with less stress and without making the same mistakes.

About This Book

When people talk about software design, they often refer to "business logic" as an abstract blob of complexity that they need to manage. The topics in this book cover the literal core of business logic: taking payments, providing a service or good in exchange, managing the flow of money, and reporting finances. Not only are many of these topics arcane in their own right, but they also tend to be the locus of the most tangled and complex logic in any system. And as if that wasn't enough, people tend to react more strongly to bugs or surprises that involve money than they do to bugs that involve, say, the search algorithm.

A payment application can be really rewarding to build—you can actually see the return on investment as genuine money (or at least digital bits that we pretend are money) gets added to your account. But it can also be amazingly stressful to manage, with security concerns, compliance concerns, and the fact that your business may be dependent on the features working smoothly.

Over the course of this book we are going to build a robust web application that takes credit card information in return for goods and services. We will start by building a shopping cart, which is often dependent on a lot of business logic but doesn't have the same dependence on money. We'll use that opportunity to talk about general principles of building complex logic without the added complexity of a third-party payment gateway.

With the shopping cart in place, we'll next look at the basics of taking a credit cart payment, first using Stripe as our gateway, then using Stripe's client-side authentication, and then again using PayPal. Once we have a successful payment in the books, you'll learn about some of the many things that can go wrong in payment processing and how to work around them. And after that, you'll learn how to handle recurring payments in Stripe.

However, taking payments is only part of what you need to do to manage a fully functional payment application. Once we have payments covered, you'll learn about administration and how to bend the rules that sometimes need to be bent. Your business model may also involve making payments, so you'll take a look at that.

Finally, one key difference between financial transactions and many other kinds of business logic is that financial transactions often require interaction with the law. As such, we'll go over three key legal issues that pertain to online payment applications: taxes, reporting, and compliance.

About You

Inevitably, a technical book needs to make decisions about what languages that examples will be presented in and what knowledge we expect the readers will either already have or be willing to learn elsewhere. While I hope that the principles of design and interaction have value outside the specific tools used, the code samples are written in a specific set of tools.

This book uses Ruby and Rails for its server-side code and JavaScript ES6 for its client-side code. I'm assuming that you're already comfortable with

Ruby and Rails and you don't need this book to explain how to build a Rails project, or how JavaScript syntax works. I am not assuming that you have any previous familiarity with payment processing.

About the Project

The web application we are going to build over the course of this book is for a small-town theater company. We'll pretend we've been granted a lucrative contract to create a website for the Snow Globe Theater, a small theater group that brings Shakespeare to the wilds of Alaska. And by "lucrative contract," I mean that we and the person who runs the theater are old buddies, the theater desperately needs to start selling tickets online, and our buddy is calling in some favors.

We'll use a payment gateway and their API to actually process credit card payments and transfer the money to us, but that's only part of the work we need to do:

- Tickets to our shows are a finite resource, so we have inventory management to deal with.

- When purchases are made, we need to notify the user, track the ticket, and update some totals, so we have workflow issues.

- We're going to want to keep an eye on sales, which means reporting.

- We have legal issues to contend with, like taxes and compliance laws.

- Sometimes, bad things will happen in our code, so we need to be able to identify and modify bad data.

- Some of those bad things will be malicious, so we'll look at security.

- Some of those bad things will be deliberate overrides of our normal logic, so we need administration.

Over the course of the book we're going to touch on all of these issues, and by the end, the Snow Globe Theater will have a robust payment-taking machine.

A Note About the Code

Before we add features to the application, I need to say a few words about the application itself. The application uses Ruby on Rails and was built up using Daniel Kehoe's Rails Composer.[1] It uses PostgreSQL as its database.[2]

1.　http://www.railscomposer.com
2.　http://www.postgresql.org

The source code for this application is available as a zip file on the book's web page,[3] which is where you can also find the book's interactive discussion forum. The readme.md file in the code has any other information you will need to start the application, which may include code errata that was discovered after the book was published. Each directory in the zip file is a complete, working version of the Rails application in progress. Code samples throughout the book specify which directory, and therefore, which version of the app, they are from.

Important code note: The code samples presented in the book focus on the business logic and interaction with payment gateways. Often, in the interest of focus, boilerplate code for items like views, controllers, and even sometimes tests are not displayed in the book. The code samples provided have all the fully tested code needed to run the site. Unless otherwise noted, each individual branch is fully tested and has minimal views needed to run the site.

The code samples used throughout this book will show you:

- How to work with the relevant APIs and third-party tools to get something to work.

- How to mitigate complexity, meaning how to manage the business logic for long-term issues of readability, changeability, debugging, and so on.

- How to test. This isn't a book on test-driven development or testing in general, but you'll see examples of testing techniques that are particularly effective in dealing with business logic or third-party libraries. All the code features in the book were written driven with tests, so even where the tests in the book aren't shown, you can still look at the sample application to see further examples of testing in action.

Handling payment logic is complicated, but it is also concrete and quite literally rewarding. Let's go build a website, shall we?

Noel Rappin
noel@noelrappin.com

## CHAPTER 1

Not Taking Payments on the Web (Yet)

Our buddies who run the Snow Globe Theater are eager to be able to sell tickets via their website, but before we can take payments for tickets to *Romeo and Juliet on Ice*, we need to, well, not take payments. In this chapter you'll learn how to enable customers to select the goods they want (tickets, in our case) and put them into a shopping cart for eventual purchase. We first look at the logic behind the data model and then look at how to build the shopping cart feature. The chapter ends with a discussion of the testing techniques we will use throughout the book as we build out our application.

Starting with the shopping cart and not the actual payment gives us a chance to explore the data model and structure of the application before we take money. The financial issues are going to make it all more complicated, so if we can look at the foundations of our application separately, we have less to worry about once we start conversations about dollar signs and credit card numbers.

Understanding the Data Model

I've made decisions about how we're modeling our universe that will have consequences for our code structure throughout our application. Our application starts with a relatively simple data model with the following four ActiveRecord models:

- *Event*—Something you might buy a ticket to see, such as *Julius Caesar* or *Much Ado About Nothing*. Right now, events have only a minimal set of attributes: a title, description and an image_url.

- *Performance*—A specific date and time that an event is performed. The way the data is structured, a performance is what you actually buy tickets for. A performance belongs to an event, and it has a start and end time.

- *Ticket*—What a user actually purchases, which is the right to a seat at a specific performance. A ticket belongs to a performance, and it (eventually) belongs to a user. It also has a price, which we model as an integer number of cents. Behind the scenes, a ticket has a status, which starts as "unsold" and will eventually move to "purchased," with possibly some intermediate steps. It also has an access level—we might have tickets that are available only to certain users.

- *User*—A user is a user, and also our customer. We're using the Devise[1] gem for authentication, which adds a bunch of attributes to the user, including the user's email address and the encrypted password. For the moment, that'll be all the fields we need.

Here's a diagram of how the models relate:

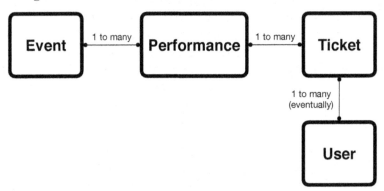

Here are the command-line invocations I used to generate the models. I don't need controllers for all of them, so I used generate model, as opposed to generate resource, which would have created controllers and routes.

```
% rails generate model event name:string description:text image_url:string
```

```
% rails generate model performance \
        event:references start_time:datetime end_time:datetime
```

```
% rails generate model ticket \
  user:references performance:references \
  status:integer access:integer price:monetize
```

The only thing in those commands that isn't standard Rails is monetize as the data type for price. More on that in a moment.

A data model isn't inevitable, and it doesn't need to be a perfect representation of the world. We want the model to be useful, and so we try to structure our data to make our most frequently performed actions easy.

---

1. https://github.com/plataformatec/devise

There are two modeling decisions so far that you should be aware of, a they both relate to the Ticket class. The first is how to avoid floating po numbers; the second is how we choose to model unsold inventory.

Avoiding Floating Point Numbers

We've used a data type of monetize to create our price. The monetize data type comes from the Money Rails[2] gem, and creates two fields in our actual database: price_cents and price_currency. Currency defaults to USD or U.S. dollars, and we won't worry about it for a while. (The data type is monetize and not money because the Rails PostgreSQL adapter already uses money.)

The price of the ticket is saved in the price_cents field, which is an integer and not a floating point decimal. A $10 ticket will be stored with a price_cents value of 1000. Internally, we'll be using the Money[3] and Monetize[4] gems to represent the value as a Ruby BigDecimal. Using integers is a deliberate choice that ensures our math works.

To make this work, we'll need to add the money-rails gem to our Gemfile:

```
gem "money-rails"
```

Floating point numbers are not accurate enough to be used to represent money. Let me explain why that's so, even though floating point numbers certainly seem to have lots of decimal points, which we are taught to think of as very precise.

When Ruby stores a number in memory, integers are stored as exact binary representations of the number. Floating point numbers are more complicated, essentially because they are trying to represent an infinite amount of precision in a finite number of bits.

There are an infinite number of integers, but integers have a finite amount of precision: zero decimal points. Real numbers can have an infinite number of digits of precision after the decimal point, and when representing decimals in computer storage as floating point numbers, that infinite precision needs to be encoded to a finite number of decimals. There are a lot of different ways to encode floating point numbers, but typically they are encoded as a base number and an exponent. For example, the number 10.50 represented as a floating point number would be 105×10^{-1}.

---

2. https://github.com/RubyMoney/money-rails
3. https://github.com/RubyMoney/money
4. https://github.com/RubyMoney/monetize

I'm hand-waving away some of the complexity here; the relevant point for us is that floating point implementations are attempting the impossible: accurately representing the uncountably infinite real numbers in a finite number of bits. And yes, integers are infinite too, but integers are "countable", meaning that given an integer you can always tell what the next integer is. So, a specified small range of integers, like 1 to 100, is finite, but the set of floating points numbers between 1 and 100 is still infinite. And that's as far as I want to take this without digressing into number theory.

Floating point numbers get away with appearing to be infinite by cheating. They don't *really* represent all the numbers; they exactly represent some and approximate the rest. This all sounds super-esoteric, I know, but it will bite you with even simple arithmetic:

```
> 3.01 * 5
=> 15.049999999999999
```

This seems minor; we've only lost a tiny fraction of a cent. When we round for display it will still show as 15.05.

But:

```
> (3.01 * 5) == 15.05
=> false
```

That's a problem. We can't trust floating point numbers to consistently handle equality. In fact, many programming libraries provide "close enough for government work" equality operators for floating point numbers, like RSpec's be_within matcher or MiniTest's assert_in_delta. We also can't trust floating point numbers not to lose cents here and there as our money adds up. People tend not to like it when ordinary monetary calculations lose cents every now and then. The problem is particularly acute when multiplying very large numbers by very small numbers, as you might do in every financial application ever.

Ruby has an internal library called BigDecimal that splits the difference by allowing exact representations of decimals with a specified amount of precision, at the cost of taking a lot more internal memory than a floating point, and being a little harder to instantiate:

```
> require 'bigdecimal'
> BigDecimal.new(3.01, 3) * 5
=> #<BigDecimal:7ffb5c217af0,'0.1505E2',18(36)>
> (BigDecimal.new("3.01") * 5).to_f
=> 15.05
> (BigDecimal.new("3.01") * 5) == BigDecimal.new("15.05")
=> true
```

In this snippet, we're instantiating the BigDecimal objects with a string or with a floating point and a second argument, BigDecimal.new(3.01, 3), in which case the second argument denotes the numerical precision, or the number of significant digits that the BigDecimal will represent exactly.

The BigDecimal math is accurate and does the equality matching without surprise. Via the Money gem, and its related gems Monetize and Money Rails, we'll use BigDecimal internally for all our money arithmetic needs.

Modeling Unsold Objects

The second data modeling decision worth talking about is how we choose to model unsold inventory. This is the kind of decision that can be made casually at the beginning of a project, but one that can have deep effects on later code and whether reporting and processing is easy or hard.

Here are some of the factors that influence the decision:

- We're selling tickets, which are an actual object that exists in the world, and of which we have a finite amount available.

- But, at least before they are sold, there is no particular difference between one ticket and another. (To save all of us a tremendous amount of complexity that is irrelevant to taking payments, we're going to assume tickets are general admission, rather than being for a particular row and seat.)

- After a ticket is sold, we might want to track it as an individual item, if for no other reason than to prevent it from being used twice.

- We're going to have to deal with various sets of tickets at different times: a set of tickets that are for a performance, a set of tickets in a shopping cart, a set of tickets in an order, tickets purchased in a particular time frame for reporting purposes, and so on.

Looking at this very broadly, we have the following options:

Tend toward treating tickets as a counter on the various items they are associated with. In this plan, a performance would start with a ticket_count. When the ticket goes into a shopping cart, we'd increment a hold_count, and create a shopping cart item to associate a number of tickets with a user. When the ticket is purchased, we'd increment a purchased_count and create an order object associating a number of tickets with a user.

Tend toward treating tickets as individual objects in the database. In this plan, when a performance is created, a bunch of ticket objects are created with a status of unsold. When a ticket goes into a shopping cart, we associate it with a user and change its status. Later when the ticket is purchased, we change the status again. In this case, we might not need an explicit shopping cart object—we'd just have tickets in a shopping cart state.

You also can combine these approaches. I've spent a few years working on a site that treats tickets as a counter until they are purchased, at which time ticket objects are created to track the purchased ticket. However, if you are selling something with inventory that is potentially infinite, such as an ebook or a subscription, you can't create individual objects up front.

The counter cache approach is particularly appealing at the beginning of the project, before there are a lot of complex requirements. It can feel minimalist and clever to try to do without explicit inventory models.

These days, my bias is to get inventory explicitly modeled in the database as early as possible. For us, this means creating ticket objects before they are purchased. There are a couple of reasons why I have come to prefer explicit inventory to counter caches. Although just moving counts around seems simpler at the beginning, over time, the number of counts you need to track goes up, and it's really easy to mess up the bookkeeping in ways that are hard to track. It's much easier to create and manipulate arbitrary groups of items if they have their own separate existence in our persistent storage.

Building the Shopping Cart Feature

Now that you understand the data model, let's build our first piece of checkout functionality: adding items to the shopping cart.

Our requirements are simple:

• The user needs to be able to go to the page for an event and select the number of tickets to be purchased for a specific performance.

• The user needs to be taken to a shopping cart page that shows the newly entered items.

That's the happy path, and once we get that in place, I'll talk about some failure scenarios or edge cases.

We'll build our shopping cart feature using test-driven development (TDD), which also gives us an opportunity to see how we'll be writing tests as we move forward. A common TDD process is called *outside-in*, which starts with an end-to-end test that validates the system's behavior externally, and then moves to unit tests that validate the internal pieces of the behavior. Let's first take a look at how to build an end-to-end test.

End-To-End Test

The first step toward building our shopping cart feature is to create an *end-to-end test*. The end-to-end test uses the Capybara[5] gem to automate user actions against our application and validate the output against expectations. The test inputs are simulated typing, selecting, and button-clicking that a user might do, and the output is the markup output of our application. This kind of test is sometimes called a *black-box* test because the internals of the application itself are totally opaque to the test.

Because the test is not dependent on the structure of the code, end-to-end tests are great for smoke tests that validate that everything in your application is working together and working as expected.

Capybara was added in our initial creation of the application by Rails Composer, but I'm adding an additional gem. In the Gemfile, you'll see

```
gem "capybara"
gem "capybara-screenshot"
```

The capybara-screenshot gem automatically captures the HTML and a screenshot for each failed Capybara test, and places them in tmp/capybara. This is very useful when trying to diagnose what's gone wrong in a test.

Capybara doesn't need much explicit setup, but we do have a little bit:

```
cart/01/spec/support/capybara.rb
require "capybara-screenshot/rspec"
Capybara.asset_host = "http://localhost:3000"
```

Our first end-to-end test simulates a user adding an item to the shopping cart, and then checks that the resulting cart page includes the item:

```
cart/01/spec/features/shopping_cart/adds_to_cart_spec.rb
Line 1  require "rails_helper"
   -
   -    describe "adding to cart" do
   -      fixtures :all
   5
   -      it "can add a performance to a cart" do
   -        login_as(users(:buyer), scope: :user)
   -        visit event_path(events(:bums))
   -        performance = events(:bums).performances.first
  10        within("#performance_#{performance.id}") do
   -          select("2", from: "ticket_count")
   -          click_on("add-to-cart")
   -        end
```

---

5.   https://github.com/jnicklas/capybara

```
       expect(current_url).to match("cart")
15     within("#event_#{events(:bums).id}") do
         within("#performance_#{performance.id}") do
           expect(page).to have_selector(".ticket_count", text: "2")
           expect(page).to have_selector(".subtotal", text: "$30")
         end
20       expect(page).not_to have_selector("#22-06-1600")
         expect(page).not_to have_selector("#event_#{events(:romeo).id}")
       end
     end

25 end
```

Let's go through some of the pieces of that code. First off, the spec is in the spec/features/ directory. For tests in that directory, RSpec enables the Capybara API for identifying and manipulating DOM elements. (Capybara has its own syntax for defining tests, which we are not using because it doesn't add much beyond synonyms for existing RSpec functionality.)

On line 4, we do something that's a little unusual in an RSpec test: we load Rails fixtures. You can see how Rails fixtures work by looking at the relevant Rails Guide,[6] or by checking out at *Rails 4 Test Prescriptions [Rap14]*.

I like to use fixtures in end-to-end testing because fixtures can be loaded into the database very quickly, which is a benefit because it allows us to have larger and more realistic amounts of data. (I'm not showing all the fixture definitions here; you can find them in the spec/fixtures directory in the source code.) For our purposes, the fixtures make available an event named :bums, which we reference a few times in the test. I've also modified the db/seed.rb file in the code repo to load the fixtures into the development database when calling rake db:seed.

On line 7, we log in our fake user with the login_as helper, which is defined by the combination of the Devise and Warden[7] gems that we are using for authentication.[8] In order for the Warden helpers to work, some initialization is performed in spec/support/warden.rb:

```
cart/01/spec/support/warden.rb
RSpec.configure do |config|
  config.include Devise::Test::IntegrationHelpers, type: :feature
end
```

---

6. http://guides.rubyonrails.org/testing.html

7. https://github.com/hassox/warden

8. http://blog.plataformatec.com.br/tag/devise

The action of the test happens starting on line 8 and continues through line 13. We use the Capybara method visit to go to the show page for our event. Once we are there, we find the DOM ID that relates to a specific performance using the # shortcut to refer to a DOM ID. We then find a ticket_count pull-down menu, select 2, and click the "Add to cart" button.

The rest of the spec deals with the output of that form submission and checks that it matches expectations. We check that the resulting URL contains the word cart, which is a way of checking that we have wound up at the route for shopping cart display. Within the cart page, we look for DOM IDs that represent the event and performance we selected earlier, and we look to see that two tickets are in the cart. We also check that the other performance and other events are not in the cart.

And that's our end-to-end test. It's a little verbose, but hopefully the fact that it largely depends on DOM IDs and not arbitrary text will keep it from being fragile as we change the web page design.

Workflows

Making this end-to-end test pass involves first creating the initial event show page, creating the resulting workflow that moves things behind the scenes, and then creating the view that displays the shopping cart. Some of these pieces require their own tests.

The initial event controller is pretty straightforward:

cart/01/app/controllers/events_controller.rb
```ruby
class EventsController < ApplicationController

  def index
    @events = Event.all
  end

  def show
    @event = Event.find(params[:id])
  end

end
```

And it has an equally basic pair of view files (plus, I added a link to events_path to the top navigation in views/layouts/navigation.html.slim):

cart/01/app/views/events/index.html.slim
```slim
h2 Upcoming Performances

- @events.each do |event|
  h2= link_to(event.name, event_path(event))
```

cart/01/app/views/events/show.html.slim
```
h1= @event.name

h2 Available Performances
- @event.performances.each do |performance|
  div(id=dom_id(performance))
    .row
      = form_tag(shopping_cart_path, method: :patch) do
        = hidden_field_tag("performance_id", performance.id)
        .col-md-2
          h4= performance.start_time.to_date.to_s(:long)
        .col-md-1
          .form-group
            = select_tag("ticket_count",
                options_for_select((1..10).to_a), class: "form-control")
        .col-md-3
          .form-group
            = submit_tag("Add to Cart",
                class: "btn btn-primary", id: "add-to-cart")
```

What is interesting about the view file is the declaration of where the form is being submitted: form_tag(shopping_cart_path, method: :patch). This means we'll be submitting the form to a route and controller named after our shopping cart. Because I mentioned that having explicit ticket objects meant we didn't need a separate database object for the shopping cart, this may seem surprising.

Even though the shopping cart doesn't need to be stored in the database as its own table (at least not yet), a shopping cart is still a thing that exists in our system, and we'll still be treating it as a resource. In Rails terms, that means we'll have a controller for it and a model, but it won't be an ActiveRecord model. Instead it will be a wrapper around the set of tickets that a particular user might have currently stored in the cart.

Because each individual user will have only one shopping cart, we can treat the shopping cart as a Rails singular resource, adding the shopping cart to the route file as follows:

cart/01/config/routes.rb
```
Rails.application.routes.draw do
  root to: "visitors#index"
  devise_for :users
  resources :events
  resource :shopping_cart
end
```

Because the shopping cart is a singular resource, the controller won't have an index action, and we don't need to pass an ID to the show or update actions.

The form has two fields: a hidden field that represents the performance that the user wants to attend, and a ticket_count field representing the number of tickets being bought. When we submit the form, it sends a :patch method to the shopping_cart_path, which the routing table resolves to the update action of the ShoppingCartsController as shown here:

```
cart/01/app/controllers/shopping_carts_controller.rb
def update
  performance = Performance.find(params[:performance_id])
  workflow = AddsToCart.new(
      user: current_user, performance: performance,
      count: params[:ticket_count])
  workflow.run
  if workflow.success
    redirect_to shopping_cart_path
  else
    redirect_to performance.event
  end
end
```

There's not a lot to this controller action. I like to keep controller actions minimal and put the bulk of the logic in objects that represent the workflow.

The first thing we need to do in the controller is use the incoming performance_id to find the performance object we want to buy tickets to. Then we pass that object, the current user, and the number of tickets to an object called AddsToCart. Once we have the AddsToCart object, we run it. If the result is successful, we redirect to shopping_cart_path to show the cart; if not, we go back to the performance.event page to display the form again.

Why do we put all our business logic in this AddsToCart object, which is, as we'll see, a normal Ruby object that is not connected to Rails? The AddsToCart object uses our ActiveRecord models, such as Performance, Ticket, and User, to manage retrieving objects from the database and saving them back, but the business logic stays in the AddsToCart object. I'll be calling objects like AddsToCart *workflow* objects, because more direct names like "action" or "process" are already heavily used.

The basic idea of using a workflow object is separation of concerns. We have a controller object, which is there to handle interaction with the user request. And we have a model object, which is there to handle interaction with our storage. Traditionally, Rails applications put business logic in the model (you may have heard this referred to as "skinny controller, fat model"). In my experience, this leads to large and unwieldy model classes. The following diagram shows the rough relationships between the objects.

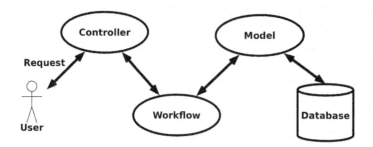

There are many different ways to manage complex business logic, and you can be successful with many of them. I'm not advocating that the setup we'll use in this book of having a bunch of workflow objects to carry the business logic load is the only way to go—just that it's worked for me in the past and that it has a lot of positive qualities. The main negative quality of the workflow structure, again in my experience, is that it can be challenging to combine the common elements of several different workflows that have some shared behavior.

By separating the business logic from the database storage, we are able to place separate features in separate classes that are simpler to understand and test than if we combined everything into the ActiveRecord model. If we do it right, it's easier to find the logic that belongs to a particular activity. The benefit may seem small now, with the logic still pretty simple, but as more complexity is introduced, the separate classes will be better able to handle it.

The code for our workflow object looks like this:

cart/01/app/workflows/adds_to_cart.rb
```ruby
class AddsToCart

  attr_accessor :user, :performance, :count, :success

  def initialize(user:, performance:, count:)
    @user = user
    @performance = performance
    @count = count.to_i
    @success = false
  end

  def run
    Ticket.transaction do
      tickets = performance.unsold_tickets(count)
      return if tickets.size != count
      tickets.each { |ticket| ticket.place_in_cart_for(user) }
      self.success = tickets.all?(&:valid?)
      success
    end
  end

end
```

There's not a lot to it. The initialize method takes the user, the performance, and the ticket count and saves them all in instance variables. I like to have workflow objects use Ruby keyword arguments because it's easier to tell what the arguments are doing when the workflow object is invoked. We also set a success instance variable to false; we'll toggle it if the workflow is successful.

When the workflow is run, call an unsold_tickets method on the performance, which is defined in a moment. If the number of tickets returned by that method isn't the number requested, back out of the method with the result still set to false. If we do get the expected number of tickets, call a method on each ticket called place_in_cart_for, which updates the ticket appropriately (remember, use the ActiveRecord model to interact with the database). If the updates all succeeded, each ticket will be valid, which then becomes the final result of the workflow.

Our Model Logic

We have two dependent methods in the ActiveRecord models to look at. The first grabs some unsold tickets from a performance:

cart/01/app/models/performance.rb
```ruby
class Performance < ApplicationRecord

  belongs_to :event
  has_many :tickets

  def unsold_tickets(count)
    tickets.where(status: "unsold").limit(count)
  end

end
```

If those tickets exist, it returns a Rails association with the appropriate number of tickets. We also have the Ticket method that actually saves the ticket we are adding to the cart:

cart/01/app/models/ticket.rb
```ruby
class Ticket < ApplicationRecord

  belongs_to :user, optional: true
  belongs_to :performance
  has_one :event, through: :performance
  monetize :price_cents

  enum status: {unsold: 0, waiting: 1}
  enum access: {general: 0}

  def place_in_cart_for(user)
    update(status: :waiting, user: user)
  end

end
```

After some ActiveRecord setup, the place_in_cart_for method just does a simple update into the database. Again, the workflow object uses the ActiveRecord object to handle database logic, so the workflow can abstractly say, "Hey, ticket, you are now in Fred's shopping cart," and the ticket translates that into the actual status change, setting the user and the actual database save. There are a couple of other potential failure modes here that we'll look at in Chapter 5, *Failure Is Totally an Option*, on page 81.

The amount of work we've had to do to mark something as saved in a shopping cart may seem minimal. This is probably a good thing; it's a sign that our data model is helping us make common transactions simple.

In the fullness of time, our workflow reports back to the controller that adding tickets to the cart was successful and then redirects to ShoppingCartController#show:

```
cart/01/app/controllers/shopping_carts_controller.rb
def show
  @cart = ShoppingCart.new(current_user)
end
```

All that the show method does is create an instance of our non-ActiveRecord ShoppingCart model and then transfers off to the view. Let's look at the view here, as some of the details are important to the original end-to-end test:

```
cart/01/app/views/shopping_carts/show.html.slim
h1 Shopping Cart

- @cart.events.each do |event|
  h2= event.name
  div(id=dom_id(event))
    table.table
      thead
        th Date
        th Tickets
        th Total Price
      tbody
        - @cart.performances_for(event).each do |performance|
          tr(id=dom_id(performance))
            td= performance.start_time.to_date.to_s(:long)
            td.ticket_count= @cart.performance_count[performance.id]
            td.subtotal
              = humanized_money_with_symbol(@cart.subtotal_for(performance))

h3 Total #{humanized_money_with_symbol(@cart.total_cost)}
```

We're not going to win any style points for design. We are simply asking the cart for a list of events that have tickets, and then for a list of performances, and then to display the performance's start time, the number of tickets, and the subtotal of how much those tickets cost.

Behind the scenes the shopping cart model is basically a wrapper around the list of tickets sharing a user and the :waiting state. Actually, let's show the User's tickets_in_cart method first, which retrieves all the tickets we need:

`cart/01/app/models/user.rb`

```ruby
def tickets_in_cart
  tickets.waiting.all.to_a
end
```

The User model has a has_many association with tickets, and tickets.waiting works because we've defined the ticket status as an ActiveRecord enum. The scope comes along for free. Now we can see the ShoppingCart model (drum roll, please):

`cart/01/app/models/shopping_cart.rb`

```ruby
class ShoppingCart

  attr_accessor :user

  def initialize(user)
    @user = user
  end

  def tickets
    @tickets ||= user.tickets_in_cart
  end

  def events
    tickets.map(&:event).uniq.sort_by(&:name)
  end

  def tickets_by_performance
    tickets.group_by { |t| t.performance.id }
  end

  def performance_count
    tickets_by_performance.each_pair.each_with_object({}) do |pair, result|
      result[pair.first] = pair.last.size
    end
  end

  def performances_for(event)
    tickets.map(&:performance)
        .select { |performance| performance.event == event }
        .uniq.sort_by(&:start_time)
  end

  def subtotal_for(performance)
    tickets_by_performance[performance.id].sum(&:price)
  end

  def total_cost
    tickets.map(&:price).sum
  end

end
```

A shopping cart instance gets its list of tickets by calling the user method, and then contains a number of methods that separate those tickets by performance and perform basic calculations on them. I wouldn't expect this to be the final factoring of this code—it seems to me that a lot of the logic here is generic to a list of tickets rather than a shopping cart, so it's likely that we'll pull that code into some more generic form once we need that logic in multiple contexts. (You could also argue that either ShoppingCart or the AddsToCart workflow could be implemented as a SimpleDelegator of User.)

With all that code in place, our end-to-end test passes and the feature works. Load this into a browser, and you'll be able to add tickets to a shopping cart. You won't be able to do anything else with them yet, but we'll get there.

Unit Testing Our Logic

Before we move on from the shopping cart to payment and checkout (coming up next in Chapter 2, *Take the Money*, on page 21), I want to show some of the tests that I wrote to drive the AddsToCart object because they show a technique that we're going to use as we work with our business logic and third-party services. Specifically, I used RSpec's verifying doubles when testing AddsToCart to isolate the test from the database and allow us to verify the workflow logic without dependency on any other part of the code.

Note that in order to run the tests, you need to have created the PostgreSQL database (rails db:create:all and rails db:migrate), and that PostgreSQL must be running.

Now, the workflow test:

cart/01/spec/workflows/adds_to_cart_spec.rb
```ruby
require "rails_helper"

describe AddsToCart do

  let(:user) { instance_double(User) }
  let(:performance) { instance_double(Performance) }
  let(:ticket_1) { instance_spy(Ticket, status: "unsold") }
  let(:ticket_2) { instance_spy(Ticket, status: "unsold") }

  describe "happy path adding tickets" do
    it "adds a ticket to a cart" do
      expect(performance).to receive(:unsold_tickets)
          .with(1).and_return([ticket_1])
      action = AddsToCart.new(user: user, performance: performance, count: 1)
      action.run
      expect(action.success).to be_truthy
      expect(ticket_1).to have_received(:place_in_cart_for).with(user)
      expect(ticket_2).not_to have_received(:place_in_cart_for)
    end
  end
end
```

```
describe "if there are no tickets, the action fails" do
  it "does not add a ticket to the cart" do
    expect(performance).to receive(:unsold_tickets).with(1).and_return([])
    action = AddsToCart.new(user: user, performance: performance, count: 1)
    action.run
    expect(action.success).to be_falsy
    expect(ticket_1).not_to have_received(:place_in_cart_for)
    expect(ticket_2).not_to have_received(:place_in_cart_for)
  end
end

end
```

There are two tests here that share a common setup. The first one tests the success case of adding a ticket to a cart; the second tries to simulate a specific failure case.

The common setup is done by the series of let statements at the beginning of the test file. Each of them sets up an RSpec *validating double.* Generically, a *test double* is a "fake" object that stands in for a real object that interacts with the code being tested (the name is analogous to "stunt double"). We say the object is fake because instead of processing or logic, the double has canned values that it supplies in response to messages. You'll sometimes see these called "mock objects" or "stubs"; it's the same idea, but "test double" is the more generic term.

For what it's worth, when initially coding I did write these tests before the code, but not using doubles. I went back and refactored the tests to use doubles. There are several reasons why a test double might be preferable:

- To simulate an object that might be expensive to use or might have bad side effects because it's created by a third-party service or because using it has real-world implications

- As a shortcut to simulate failure states that are hard to create otherwise

- To abstract the interface of an object and potentially reduce its dependence on the details of other objects it interacts with

In these two tests, we're doing a little bit of all three. We're using doubles to create objects that otherwise would have to be saved to the database. As much as we Rails developers like to pretend otherwise, the database is a third-party dependency, and it can be slow to create large numbers of objects there.

The second spec is simulating a potential failure case, namely that the performance doesn't have enough tickets to fulfill the order. We do so by explicitly saying that the performance should receive :unsold_tickets and return an empty list. The empty list is what unsold_tickets, itself tested separately, would return if there are no tickets to sell. By directly setting a double on the performance method, we sidestep the need to create an event or ticket objects that would produce the failure mode. Although this case isn't too hard to set up with real objects, other failure cases—which might include networking or database failures—can be hard to automate without using doubles.

And in both cases, we're using the doubles to minimize the amount of interaction the AddsToCart workflow has with other objects. When every interaction potentially requires more test double support, you have an incentive to keep individual objects as isolated as possible.

The first two lines of setup create stand-ins for a User and a Performance using RSpec's instance_double method. By using instance_double, we allow RSpec to validate the methods received from our double against the specified class. If our double is asked to respond to a message that the class does not define, RSpec raises an error.

For example, the first double we create is a fake user: let(:user) { instance_double(User) }. We can specify that the fake user has a particular email address using RSpec and the syntax allow(user).to respond_to(:email).and_return("will@shakespeare.com"). Then user.email, when called, will return will@shakespeare.com. However, we can't specify that the fake user has, say, a favorite food. Even if we try to use the syntax allow(user).to receive(:favorite_food).and_return("cheeseburger"), RSpec will just return the error: the User class does not implement the instance method: favorite_food.

This verification is really useful because it prevents a common problem when using test doubles: the possibility of changes in the object's method names drifting away from the method names used by the double in the test.

For example, say we have a user method called name, and a test that has a double referencing that method: allow(:user).to receive(:name). If we change the name of the underlying method to full_name, then without RSpec's validating double, the test still passes because the test only knows about the double. But with the validating double, we'll get a message saying the User class does not implement the instance method: name and we'll know to change the method under test.

Our last two lines of setup create two tickets using the instance_spy method with a key/value argument status: "unsold", which seeds the double to know about the status method and to have a response ready if called. The instance_spy method creates a validating double just like instance_method; however, it adds the detail that any valid method that is not specified in the double returns nil, rather than throwing an error. Methods that are not defined in the class at all still throw errors. We're doing that here to allow the tickets to save themselves to the database or whatever else they do without this test needing to care about the details.

The test for success adds one additional expectation, which is that the performance double will receive the message unsold_tickets(1) and return a list of one ticket. Using expect instead of allow when setting the exception means that the test will fail if the unsold_tickets message is not received. We then create an AddsToCart workflow, passing it the user double and the performance double.

We run the workflow, and then have three more expectations: we expect the result of the workflow to be true, we expect that the ticket returned as unsold is added into the cart by the method place_in_cart_for, and we expect that the other ticket did not. As far as the AddsToCart workflow goes, this is a complete description of its behavior when run. Additional unit tests (which are in the code base, but that we won't show in the book) verify that the method place_in_cart_for saves the test with the values that we'd expect: changing the status and associating it to a user.

The failure test is nearly identical, but sets up the case where there are no tickets available to be added to the cart by having the performance respond to unsold_tickets by returning an empty list. In this case, we expect the result of the workflow to be false, and we expect that neither ticket will receive the place_in_cart_for message.

Next Up

So far we've established the basic architecture of our payment application, in which our Rails controllers delegate business logic to workflow objects using ActiveRecord models to communicate to the database. We also looked at how to build some shopping cart logic using Capybara and RSpec to write end-to-end and unit tests to drive our architecture decisions. Now that we've got the basic structure of the application covered, it's time to start taking some money.

## CHAPTER 2

Take the Money

Throughout this book we'll look at many different aspects of financial transactions. We'll talk about reporting, administration, legal requirements, and a host of other things. But the key part of taking money from customers is actually taking money from them.

It turns out you can send an API call with a particular set of authentication information to a particular server and this will have the real-world effect of removing money from one person's account and adding it to your account. I don't know about you, but the fact that this is possible still seems magical, even though it happens zillions of times a day all across the world.

In the previous chapter we set up our shopping cart feature. Our users are able to select tickets to a specific performance and are then taken to a shopping cart page that shows the newly entered items. In this chapter we'll use a payment gateway to walk through what you might call traditional credit card processing: users enter their credit card information into a form, then submit it to our server, and our server interacts with a payment gateway to process the payments.

The key to security in payment is to hold on to as little secure information as possible. Persisting your users' credit card data is not actually recommended unless you have either a strong need to hold onto your users' secure information or a strong desire to be hacked and find yourself on the wrong end of a lot of embarrassing headlines. Instead, we'll keep the credit card information briefly in our server's memory as we process the request. It is important to note that even this is not a recommended security practice. Under PCI compliance guidelines (see *Compliance*, on page 307), your server is just as suspect if the credit card information touches it even if the data is not persisted. We'll explore a little bit about why that might be as we go along.

The older server-side credit card processing is the easiest method to think about conceptually, so we'll start there, even though it is *not recommended* from a security standpoint. Once we've got that set up, we'll tweak the process slightly in Chapter 3, *Client-Side Payment Authentication*, on page 45, to allow for a two-step process, where the customer's information is authenticated by the client via an Ajax callback to the payment gateway. This method is even more secure, since the client's private information doesn't even reach our server. Specifically, using the client-side method places you in a much simpler situation when it comes to PCI compliance. Later, in Chapter 4, *PayPal*, on page 59, we'll talk about PayPal, the most commonly used online payment service, which has a different workflow that also keeps users' credit card information off our servers.

To be absolutely clear, the server-side setup in this chapter is just to make it a easier to talk about the Stripe API and the transaction separate from the details of the client-side code. In a real application you absolutely should use a tokenized client-side setup as shown in Chapter 3, *Client-Side Payment Authentication*, on page 45. This chapter's implementation is not the best practice from a security standpoint for a production environment.

Let's get started by looking at payment gateways.

What's a Payment Gateway and Why Do I Need One?

A *payment gateway*, such as Stripe,[1] Braintree,[2] Authorize.net,[3] and others, is a service that mediates financial transactions. On one side of the transaction is the entire global financial system in all its complexity. On the other side is me, some clown with a website. The transaction is just slightly asymmetric.

From our point of view, we want to be able to say, "Here's a customer with a credit card and a transaction," and have the customer's money show up in our account. On the other side, a lot of companies and complexities are involved in that transaction. A typical credit card transaction might involve five or more financial organizations:

- The bank where the purchaser keeps their money
- The bank that issued the purchaser's credit card
- The credit card network (such as Visa or MasterCard)
- The bank that handles credit card transactions on behalf of the merchant
- The bank where the merchant keeps its money

---

1. https://stripe.com
2. https://www.braintreepayments.com
3. http://www.authorize.net

That's a minimum—there may also be interbank networks, insurance companies, governments, and the like. It's brain-melting.

The payment gateway enables us not to have to think about any of this process. We send an API call or two to the gateway, they tell us whether the payment has been successful, and at some slightly future date, the money shows up in our bank account, minus a transaction fee. Gateways also often provide additional services, such as recurring billing, their own fraud protection, some reporting, mediation services for disputes, and on and on.

Setting Up Our First Payment Gateway

We'll be using Stripe as our first payment gateway. In my experience, Stripe is the easiest of the gateways to get started with, but the basic API concepts are the same across most of the gateways that are not PayPal.

Before we do anything with Stripe, we need to set up an account. The account will provide us with API keys that we'll use for authentication, and we'll also get a dashboard with some nice reporting services.

Creating our stripe account is pretty simple. We go to http://dashboard.stripe.com/register and enter an email address and a password. Stripe then sends us an email to authenticate the account, which you must do before you start accepting payments. Once we do so, Stripe takes us to our dashboard, as shown in the following figure.

We'll look at the specifics of this dashboard UI later in Chapter 7, *The Administration Experience*, on page 143, but for the moment there are two particular bits worth noting.

First, in the upper-left corner and below the Stripe logo, is a big-ol' switch that is currently pointed at "Test." Stripe accounts come with a test mode, which has its own API keys that we can use in development and staging so that we can test out the account without racking up actual credit card charges. We're going to stay in Test mode for pretty much all the work we're doing in this book. To start taking real charges in Live mode, we'll need to fill out a form and get approval from Stripe, but we'll talk more about this when we discuss going to production in Chapter 13, *Going to Production*, on page 297.

Second, in the upper-right corner is a menu labeled "Your Account." Within that pull-down menu is a menu item called "Account Settings." If we go there, we see rather a lot of settings. The tab we are interested in is "API Keys." Select this tab, and, as you see in the following figure, we see four API keys.

The circle icon to the right of each key gives you a new random key. (Don't worry, I updated all four keys right after I took this screenshot.) We have separate key sets for Test mode and Live mode. And, as is typical with this kind of API key, the key is split into a publishable key, which we can send out to a client, and a secret key, which should stay on our server. Stripe kindly sets up each key with a prefix telling you what kind of key it is.

As of right now, we're ready to take test credit card purchases with Stripe, and the only thing standing between us and real purchases is creating a short form and getting Stripe's approval.

Now, let's wire our Stripe account into our Rails application.

Telling Rails About Stripe

Now that we have a Stripe account, we need to make sure our Rails application uses that account. As is common for API authentication, we have been given long, random tokens that will be recognized by the API servers. One of those tokens, the public one, will eventually be sent via the browser to the client and used to identify our application to Stripe's servers. The other token, the secret one, will only live on our server and be sent to Stripe. You can't get Stripe to transfer any money without both the public token and the secret token being sent to it.

The trick here is that the secret token is, well, secret. You don't want to pass it around via email or chat, and you don't want it to sit in your GitHub repo. At the same time, the production and staging servers will use different tokens, and you'll most likely want the ability to have individual developers use their own tokens in test mode.

There are several ways to make secret tokens work without exposing them. The one we're picking is simple and flexible, but other ways may make more sense depending on your development environment.

First, we'll add two gems to our Gemfile:

```
gem "dotenv-rails"
gem "stripe"
```

The dotenv-rails gem is what is going to allow us to customize the environment keys securely. This gem is a Rails wrapper for the Dotenv[4] gem, which will be installed as a dependency. The Dotenv gem allows you to set up a file named .env and populate it with a bunch of key/value pairs. When the Rails application starts, the gem places those values in Ruby's global ENV hash, just as though they were defined as systemwide environment variables.

The Stripe[5] gem is the official Ruby interface to the Stripe API. We'll be using it to communicate with Stripe, so we may as well get it in here now.

---

4. https://github.com/bkeepers/dotenv
5. https://github.com/stripe/stripe-ruby

Here is a quick way to add our keys into the system during development:

Create an .env file. But, before you do so, confirm that .env is in your application's .gitignore (or whatever your source control uses to not store particular files)—you do *not* want the .env file to be saved to source control, nor do you typically want it to be on your production server—you'll secure the secrets a different way in production. The format of the .env file is <key>=<value>. Yours should look something like this:

```
STRIPE_SECRET_KEY=sk_test_<YOUR KEY HERE>
STRIPE_PUBLISHABLE_KEY=pk_test_<YOUR KEY HERE>
```

You can also ensure that your environment variables are only used in specific Rails environments by creating files with names like .env.development or .env.test, which allows you to use different keys for live development versus testing.

It doesn't actually matter what you call the environment variables on the left side of each statement as long as you are consistent. As written, we'll now be able to refer to them within our Rails code as ENV["STRIPE_SECRET_KEY"] and ENV["STRIPE_PUBLISHABLE_KEY"].

We're not going to stop there, though. I'd like to add one more layer of indirection using the Rails secrets.yml file. Add the following to the file (you'll need to add it for both the development and test environments):

```
server_charge/01/config/secrets.yml
development: &default
  admin_name: First User
  admin_email: user@example.com
  admin_password: changeme
  domain_name: example.com
  secret_key_base: 837442c904d7b579c6c98618efa4b892abb377865f6e9507070787425f
  stripe_publishable_key: <%= ENV["STRIPE_PUBLISHABLE_KEY"] %>
  stripe_secret_key: <%= ENV["STRIPE_SECRET_KEY"] %>
  paypal_client_id: <%= ENV["PAYPAL_CLIENT_ID"] %>
  paypal_client_secret: <%= ENV["PAYPAL_CLIENT_SECRET"] %>
  host_name: "6e0fd751.ngrok.com"
  authy_key: <%= ENV["AUTHY_KEY"] %>
  rollbar: '7f4b0337a9c14f069cb41c1738298fee'
test:
  <<: *default
  secret_key_base: 8489bb21c9497da574dcb42fea4e15d089606d196e367f6f4e166acb281
```

The &default and <<: *default are bits of YAML syntax that allow us to use our development secrets as the basis for the other environments, so that we don't have to retype identical secrets in multiple environments. The word default is an arbitrary label, and the & is an *anchor*, which signifies that everything subordinate to the label is named by the label. The <<: indicates a merge, and the * indicates a reference to a previous label. Together this means that all the key/value pairs belonging to the label should be merged in at the point of the symbol. Any subsequent keys below the merge override the merged-in key/value.

Now we can refer to the Stripe keys within our application as Rails.application.secrets.stripe_secret_key and Rails.application.secrets.stripe_publishable_key. Note that in production we have the choice of continuing to refer to environment variables or having the secrets.yml file actually contain the keys themselves.

Initializing Stripe

Finally, we need to initialize Stripe by telling the Stripe gem what our secret key is. The Stripe gem passes this to the Stripe server as part of all our Stripe API calls. I do this with a brief file in config/initializers/stripe.rb, which raises an exception on startup if the API value isn't there.

```
server_charge/01/config/initializers/stripe.rb
Stripe.api_key = Rails.application.secrets.stripe_secret_key
raise "Missing Stripe API Key" unless Stripe.api_key
```

That's possibly more indirection than strictly necessary—you could leave out the secrets file and just directly reference the environment variable when setting Stripe.api_key. The main reason to add the indirection is to allow the rest of the application to not care about environment variables, which are, after all, implementation details of the system.

More pragmatically, setting up the API key via the Rails secret file gives us more flexibility when deploying or setting up the application in a different environment. We can either set the environment variables or create a local secrets.yml file with a local API key. Because our application will need to run on different server environments, development environments, and test servers, this flexibility can be valuable.

Charging Cards with Server Authentication

With our Stripe account set up and our application configured to speak to the Stripe API, it's time to actually charge some credit cards.

Stripe offers at least three ways to manage our interaction with the user's credit card data:

- A traditional web form that sends the customer credit card information to the server, to be authenticated by Stripe.

- A custom form that authenticates with Stripe client-side before sending information to the server, which sends the server a one-time token rather than the credit card information.

- Stripe's generic checkout form, which can be added as an overlay to any checkout page. This form behaves like the client-side form but requires less coding and has less flexibility. We're not going to be using this form in the book—we're going to build the form ourselves—but you can look at Stripe's Checkout documentation for more details.[6]

Eventually, all three of these require us to send information to Stripe to actually authorize a payment on the credit card after Stripe authenticates the card.

We're going to start by covering the traditional web form version. It's the least implicit version, and will feel the most familiar to you if you are used to conventional Rails applications. Again, I don't recommend this as a final implementation from a security standpoint, but it is easier to understand. In Chapter 3, *Client-Side Payment Authentication*, on page 45, I'll explain why adding client-side processing is preferable for security.

Our game plan here is to do the following:

- Gather the user's credit card information via a form.

- Authenticate the credit card information and get a token from Stripe confirming that the card is valid.

- Do some bookkeeping within our database, such as change the state of the tickets and create a Payment object.

- Charge the credit card.

- Respond to the result of the card within our data.

First let's look at gathering the user's credit card information.

Gathering Information

The first thing we need to do is obtain credit card information from the user. For the view, we just want a basic form. The easiest place to put that form right now is on the shopping cart page, right below the information about what's in the shopping cart:

---

6. https://stripe.com/docs/checkout/tutorial

```
server_charge/01/app/views/shopping_carts/show.html.slim
h2 Checkout

h3 Credit Card Info

= form_tag(payments_path, class: "form-inline") do
  = hidden_field_tag(:purchase_amount_cents, @cart.total_cost.cents)
  .form_group
    = label_tag(:credit_card_number, "Credit Card Number", class: "sr-only")
    = text_field_tag(:credit_card_number,
        "", class: "form-control", placeholder: "Credit Card #")
  .form_group
    = label_tag(:expiration_month, "Month", class: "sr-only")
    = text_field_tag(:expiration_month,
        "", class: "form-control", placeholder: "Month")
    = label_tag(:expiration_year, "Year", class: "sr-only")
    = text_field_tag(:expiration_year,
        "", class: "form-control", placeholder: "Year")
    = label_tag(:cvc, "Year", class: "sr-only")
    = text_field_tag(:cvc, "", class: "form-control", placeholder: "CVC #")
  .form_group
    = submit_tag("Purchase Cart", class: "btn btn-default", id: "purchase")
```

As written, this form is not going to look great on the screen. We'll deal with the making it both prettier and more user friendly in Chapter 3, *Client-Side Payment Authentication*, on page 45.

In code terms, the form is a bit odd in that it's not an ActiveRecord form—none of the data we're gathering here is ever going to touch our database. (Although you could do this with a bare ActiveRecord::Model, there's no particular advantage to doing so.) On the server side, it's going to be passed to a workflow object.

We're gathering the most basic credit card data here: the credit card number itself, the expiration month and year, and the Card Verification Code (CVC). The CVC is designed to be used to authenticate the card in cases where the merchant cannot inspect the actual card to check for a signature. That describes all web interactions, so we need to gather the CVC number. Because the CVC is designed for authentication, even if for some reason you eventually decide to store the credit card number itself (but *don't do this*), you really are never supposed to store the CVC code. Some web applications also gather the name on the card and the cardholder's zip code, which can be used for further authentication and fraud prevention.

We're also passing the amount being charged as a hidden field. We're not going to use that directly—our purchase workflow will separately calculate the price. Eventually, though, we'll use that as a check to make sure that the amount we are actually charging our customer is the amount the customer thinks he or she is being charged. Customers get unhappy fast if they find out that they have been charged a different amount than they expected.

Before we submit the form, one piece of important security business. We are passing secure information in the parameters of our web request. The Rails application can easily be configured to log that information, and we need to make sure that the credit card information is not logged. This is another way in which even getting credit card information on our server briefly can be dangerous. Happily, Rails has a configuration option to filter specific parameters from showing up in the log. We just need to update it for our secure information:

server_charge/01/config/initializers/filter_parameter_logging.rb
```
# Be sure to restart your server when you modify this file.

# Configure sensitive parameters which will be filtered from the log file.
Rails.application.config.filter_parameters +=
    [:password, :password_confirmation, :credit_card_number,
     :expiration_month, :expiration_year, :cvc]
```

On submission, the form goes to payments_path, which resolves via normal Rails REST actions to PaymentController#create. Our Payment class is an ActiveRecord class, and will need both a database table and a resources :purchase line in the routes.rb file.

We need a data migration to get our Payment model:

```
$ rails generate model payment user:references \
  price:monetize status:integer reference:string \
  payment_method:string response_id:string \
  full_response:json
```

server_charge/01/db/migrate/20160721043026_create_payments.rb
```
class CreatePayments < ActiveRecord::Migration[5.0]

  def change
    create_table :payments do |t|
      t.references :user, foreign_key: true
      t.monetize :price
      t.integer :status
      t.string :reference
      t.string :payment_method
      t.string :response_id
      t.json :full_response

      t.timestamps
    end

    add_index :payments, :reference
  end

end
```

And we'll also need a PaymentLineItem model:

```
rails generate model payment_line_item \
  payment:references buyable:references price:monetize
```

And we need that buyable to be polymorphic (it's a ticket right now, but eventually there will be other buyable things):

server_charge/01/db/migrate/20160721043415_create_payment_line_items.rb
```
class CreatePaymentLineItems < ActiveRecord::Migration[5.0]

  def change
    create_table :payment_line_items do |t|
      t.references :payment, foreign_key: true
      t.references :buyable, polymorphic: true
      t.monetize :price

      t.timestamps
    end
  end

end
```

And then a quick rake db:migrate.

We'll get to the details of the Payment model and what all those attributes are in a moment. Right now, the users are able to look at that form, enter their credit card information, and submit the form.

Processing the Form

Rails routes the submitted form to PaymentController#create. In keeping with the application design we discussed when adding tickets to the shopping cart in *Workflows*, on page 9, the primary goal of the controller is to offload logic to the appropriate workflow items and route the form based on the result. This controller method is no different:

server_charge/01/app/controllers/payments_controller.rb
```
class PaymentsController < ApplicationController

  def show
    @payment = Payment.find_by(reference: params[:id])
  end

  def create
    token = StripeToken.new(**card_params)
    workflow = PurchasesCart.new(
        user: current_user, stripe_token: token,
        purchase_amount_cents: params[:purchase_amount_cents])
    workflow.run
```

```
    if workflow.success
      redirect_to payment_path(id: workflow.payment.reference)
    else
      redirect_to shopping_cart_path
    end
  end

  private def card_params
    params.permit(
        :credit_card_number, :expiration_month,
        :expiration_year, :cvc).to_h.symbolize_keys
  end

end
```

Let's look first at the create method. The main player here is the PurchasesCart
workflow, with a short opening act involving the StripeToken object, which is
needed as an input to purchase a cart. The StripeToken is an object in our
application that contacts the Stripe API. We're being a little bit cute in passing
the parameters to the object, using the private method card_params to slice the
parameters hash down to just the keys that we're interested in and then using
Ruby's double-splat ** operator to unroll the hash into the keyword arguments
that our StripeToken object expects. This is a little shortcut that prevents us
from having to write out the entire hash.

Why do we need a token? Stripe uses tokens to split a transaction into two
actions: authorization and payment.

Authorizing the Credit Card

In the authorization action, the credit card information is sent to Stripe, and
Stripe queries the appropriate banks to determine if it is valid. If it is valid,
Stripe returns a *token*, which we can think of as a special credit card number
that is only good for a single transaction. When we do the payment step, we
send Stripe the token along with the payment amount, and Stripe again talks
to whatever bank systems are needed to make the payment happen. The
token is just a reference to the fact that the card information is valid—Stripe
doesn't do fraud or amount checking until you actually submit the payment.

Once again, some programmer somewhere has taken a simple process like
credit card transactions and added another layer of complexity and indirection
with this token step. In other words, it's Tuesday. Programmers are *always*
adding extra layers of complexity. It's what we do.

Adding separate steps is often the right thing to do, of course. And splitting
authentication off into its own separate step, it turns out, is pretty useful.
Credit card information is radioactive. Powerful, sure, but you also don't want

to handle it directly if you can avoid it. Not only is handling and storing credit card information dangerous, but servers that come into contact with credit card information are subject to legal or regulatory requirements; again see *Compliance*, on page 307.

The authorization step allows us to turn the radioactive card information into a clean token that we can pass around with impunity. The token is only good for one use and it's linked to your particular Stripe API, so you don't need to store it, and the cost if it is found out by some miscreant is much lower.

In order to get a token, we need to contact the Stripe API. Our code for this is the first time we've talked to Stripe directly. It's also our first demonstration of a technique that we're going to see a lot of: using our own code to build relatively thin wrappers around third-party APIs. We do this even if, like Stripe, there's already a Ruby gem that contacts the API.

Here's our StripeToken class:

```
server_charge/01/app/models/stripe_token.rb
class StripeToken

  attr_accessor :credit_card_number, :expiration_month, :expiration_year, :cvc

  def initialize(credit_card_number:, expiration_month:, expiration_year:, cvc:)
    @credit_card_number = credit_card_number
    @expiration_month = expiration_month
    @expiration_year = expiration_year
    @cvc = cvc
  end

  def token
    @token ||= Stripe::Token.create(
        card: {
            number: credit_card_number, exp_month: expiration_month,
            exp_year: expiration_year, cvc: cvc})
  end

  delegate :id, to: :token

  def to_s
    "STRIPE TOKEN: #{id}"
  end

  def inspect
    "STRIPE TOKEN #{id}"
  end

end
```

This is a very thin wrapper around the Stripe::Token object provided by the Stripe gem. It's such a thin wrapper that you might wonder why we're even bothering. Wouldn't it be easier to just call Stripe::Token from the controller directly?

It might be, the first time we use tokens, but it's less likely the more we use them. I tend to wrap all third-party access as a matter of course. Here's why:

- Doing so gives our application a single point of contact with the API, making it easier if the API changes or if we switch to a different provider.

- Because the rest of the application communicates via the wrapper, we can have the wrapper's parameters and methods correspond to our domain and not the API's naming conventions. That's not a huge deal in this case, but we do get to use our full names for the parameters rather than Stripe's abbreviations. (Call me crazy, but I've come to dislike abbreviations in variable names.)

- Having a wrapper keeps the responsibility of dealing with the API in one place, meaning that users of the API in our application don't have to worry about implementation details and can therefore be less complicated.

- It's somewhat easier to test because you can create a test double corresponding to the wrapper rather than having to stub the API itself (although the VCR gem makes stubbing the API not that painful).

We get these benefits for what I think is the relatively small overhead of creating a new class and mapping instance variables to represent that class's state.

As for the class itself, we call the Stripe gem's Stripe::Token#create method with our credit card information. Behind the scenes, the Stripe gem makes an HTTP request to the Stripe API, combining the credit card info with our API key. The Stripe API server returns a JSON representation of a token, and the Stripe gem converts that into an instance of the gem's Stripe::Token class. For the moment, we're assuming failure is not an option, so we'll always get a token when we ask for one.

The Stripe::Token class has lots of attributes, but the only one we really care about is the id, which is the string we'll need to pass back to the Stripe server to actually perform a credit card charge. We've set up the class so we can transparently call StripeToken.new(<args>).id. The delegate command transforms id to token.id, and the token method takes care of the API call.

I want to call your attention to the last couple of lines of the StripeToken class, which override inspect and to_s. These methods are to prevent the credit card data in the StripeToken class from being inadvertently or maliciously logged to some source during the brief time that the class is alive. I might also consider setting the credit card data attributes to nil after the token is obtained. These are the kinds of issues that make keeping the credit card data off the server seem like a really great idea.

Updating the Database

Once we have our token in hand, we use the token as one of the inputs to our PurchasesCart workflow. Before we look at the code, let's see what needs to be done for a successful purchase:

- The ticket objects need to have their status changed in the database.
- We need to create some internal objects to represent the payment.
- The credit card needs to be charged.
- The credit card response needs to be associated with the purchase.

Because we're not concerned about failure steps now, it doesn't matter which step happens first, but all of them need to happen in addition to a few others, such as emailing the customer a receipt or changing some reporting data.

We're going to support our internal reporting with two new ActiveRecord classes, Payment and PaymentLineItem. I'm not crazy about the naming. I wanted to call them Transaction, but that's a name already used often in ActiveRecord. The Payment class will have many PaymentLineItems. The way I have this set up, each PaymentLineItem has a one-to-one mapping with a ticket, which is a little unusual—typically a line item object will have a quantity and a price per unit, but the one-to-one mapping is more in line with our application structure at the moment. You can see the exact list of attributes for each of the classes in the schema.rb file; or we'll talk about them as we come across them. Here's our workflow code to make a purchase:

```
server_charge/01/app/workflows/purchases_cart.rb
class PurchasesCart
  attr_accessor :user, :stripe_token, :purchase_amount, :success, :payment

  def initialize(user:, stripe_token:, purchase_amount_cents:)
    @user = user
    @stripe_token = stripe_token
    @purchase_amount = Money.new(purchase_amount_cents)
    @success = false
  end

  def tickets
    @tickets ||= @user.tickets_in_cart
  end

  def run
    Payment.transaction do
      purchase_tickets
      create_payment
      charge
      @success = payment.succeeded?
    end
  end
end
```

```ruby
def purchase_tickets
  tickets.each(&:purchased!)
end

def create_payment
  self.payment = Payment.create!(payment_attributes)
  payment.create_line_items(tickets)
end

def payment_attributes
  {user_id: user.id, price_cents: purchase_amount.cents,
   status: "created", reference: Payment.generate_reference,
   payment_method: "stripe"}
end

def charge
  charge = StripeCharge.charge(token: stripe_token, payment: payment)
  payment.update!(
      status: charge.status, response_id: charge.id,
      full_response: charge.to_json)
end

end
```

The run method lays out what we need to do at a high level: purchase_tickets, create_payment, charge. It's wrapped in a Rails transaction call, which means that any exception that takes place inside the transaction will cause the database to roll back to its initial state. That's very handy for us, since we don't want partial sets of objects sticking around. It means, though, that we'll use save!, create!, and update! in our workflows, because we want to trigger the exception and force the rollback.

The list of tickets is obtained from @user.tickets_in_cart, which, as discussed in the previous chapter, is a list of tickets that belong to this user and are in the :waiting state. To purchase the tickets, the purchase_tickets method calls the purchased! method on each ticket, which is automatically created for us when we define the status enum in the Ticket class.

We also need to build a Payment object to represent the payment transaction in the database. We put the attributes to that object in the payment_attributes method, which is separated from the create_payment method to allow us to test the attributes without having to touch the database. We give the new purchase the user.id, the purchase amount in cents, an initial status of created, a payment method of stripe, and a reference.

The reference is a unique identifier for each purchase that is not its ActiveRecord ID. We want our own unique reference value for two reasons:

- It's less guessable than an incremental value so it's harder for somebody to guess a URL when using it.

- ActiveRecord only assigns an ID on save. We can assign a reference before the item is saved, which means we can pass the reference to our third-party service before the purchase is saved, should we choose to.

A few classes are going to use references, so we'll implement them as an ActiveRecord concern. We have several ways to guarantee a unique value; here's how we're doing it:

server_charge/01/app/models/concerns/has_reference.rb
```ruby
module HasReference

  extend ActiveSupport::Concern

  module ClassMethods

    def generate_reference
      loop do
        result = SecureRandom.hex(10)
        return result unless exists?(reference: result)
      end
    end

  end

end
```

Then we need to make sure the Payment class has an include HasReference line.

We also create a PaymentLineItem for each ticket, which is just a connection to the ticket, the purchase, and another copy of the ticket price in cents.

server_charge/01/app/models/payment.rb
```ruby
class Payment < ActiveRecord::Base

  include HasReference

  belongs_to :user, optional: true
  has_many :payment_line_items
  has_many :tickets, through: :payment_line_items,
                     source_type: "Ticket", source: "buyable"

  monetize :price_cents

  enum status: [:created, :succeeded]
```

```ruby
def total_cost
  tickets.map(&:price).sum
end

def create_line_items(tickets)
  tickets.each do |ticket|
    payment_line_items.create!(
        buyable: ticket, price_cents: ticket.price.cents)
  end
end

end
```

We duplicate the ticket price in the purchase because we need to have a snapshot of the price that was actually paid. If the ticket price were to change later on, we still have to be able to re-create the actual price the customer paid. This ability to re-create the exact circumstances of the purchase will be a common theme throughout our code.

Making the Purchase

With the Purchase instances created, we now contact Stripe to make the charge. Again, this involves a local wrapper to the Stripe gem object, which we call StripeCharge. We pass it the token object and the purchase object. The StripeCharge then calls Stripe, like so:

server_charge/01/app/models/stripe_charge.rb

```ruby
class StripeCharge

  attr_accessor :token, :payment, :response, :error

  def self.charge(token:, payment:)
    StripeCharge.new(token: token, payment: payment).charge
  end

  def initialize(token:, payment:)
    @token = token
    @payment = payment
  end

  def charge
    return if response.present?
    @response = Stripe::Charge.create(
        {amount: payment.price.cents, currency: "usd",
         source: token.id, description: "",
         metadata: {reference: payment.reference}},
        idempotency_key: payment.reference)
  rescue Stripe::StripeError => e
    @response = nil
    @error = e
  end
```

```ruby
  def success?
    response || !error
  end

  def payment_attributes
    success? ? success_attributes : failure_attributes
  end

  def success_attributes
    {status: :succeeded,
     response_id: response.id, full_response: response.to_json}
  end

  def failure_attributes
    {status: :failed, full_response: error.to_json}
  end

end
```

The important work happens in the instance charge method, which calls the gem's Stripe::Charge#create method with a number of arguments. We need to send the charge the following information:

- The currency (usd for U.S. dollars)
- The charge amount in cents
- The source (in our case the source is the token, so we pass the token ID)

We also send three optional arguments:

- A string description, which customers see on their credit card statements.

- Metadata, which is an arbitrary set of key/value pairs that are associated with the purchase in Stripe. We're sending the purchase reference number.

- An *idempotency_key*, which is a unique identifier we provide for the transaction. "Idempotency" is a computer science term that refers to logic that can be run multiple times without changing the outcome. When we pass an idempotency key to Stripe, Stripe uses that key to make sure that the transaction only runs once on the Stripe server. This is helpful for us because it means we don't have to worry about accidentally sending the same charge to Stripe twice. It is, however, our responsibility to ensure the idempotency key is unique. Happily, we've already got a unique key, so we can send the payment.reference.

When we call Stripe::Charge#create, we again cause an HTTP request to be sent to the Stripe servers with our Stripe IDs. Stripe contacts the necessary banks to actually make the charge happen in the real world. We get back a JSON response that the Stripe gem converts into a Ruby object for us. This response contains a lot of data, which we can split into three categories:

1. Data that is critically important, meaning that bad things will happen if we don't store it, including

   • The id of the resulting charge object. This string, which begins with ch_, is how Stripe refers to the charge internally. We can use this ID to view or update information about the charge. Critically, we'll need this ID to refund the charge. So let's hold onto that.

2. Data that is really nice to have locally, even though we can always retrieve it via the charge ID, including

   • The status of the charge, which in our happy case, is succeeded.

   • The amount of the charge, in cents. We can use this for another level of auditing.

   • The credit card bank and last four digits of the credit card so that we can display "Card ending in 1234" when we show the purchase.

3. Data that is also there and which might be useful someday, including

   • Timestamps, addresses, balance on the account, and so on.

My attitude, which is somewhat due to being burned by this in the past, is to save everything that the gateway is willing to give you. Let's look again at what the PurchasesCart workflow does after making the charge:

```
server_charge/01/app/workflows/purchases_cart.rb
def charge
  charge = StripeCharge.charge(token: stripe_token, payment: payment)
  payment.update!(
    status: charge.status, response_id: charge.id,
    full_response: charge.to_json)
end
```

We take three attributes of the purchase instance: the status, which is an ActiveRecord enum, set to the charge.status return value; the response_id, which is a string, and which gets the charge.id from Stripe; and the full_response attribute, which contains the rest of the response.

To make full_response work using PostgreSQL as our database, the initial migration for the field marks it as type json. (If you aren't using PostgreSQL, make the data type text and use ActiveRecord's serialize method. You'll get most of the same benefit.) Once it's placed in the ActiveRecord, we can access the response data as a hash with string keys, so purchase.full_response["amount"].

If the charge is successful, we save the purchase again, and the PurchasesCart workflow returns success based on whether the charge and the save were successful. On a successful cart purchase, the PurchaseController redirects to a payment#show action, which is basically boilerplate except that we use payment.reference rather than payment.id to form the URL and identify the purchase.

Testing with the VCR Gem

There's one more step to cover while we are still talking about this payment example: testing—specifically, testing our interaction with third-party services. Testing third-party services is hard because they are traditionally located across the network from our little tests, making them slow to access in a unit test situation, and also fragile and hard to run on, say, a train with no Wi-Fi.

The VCR[7] gem makes testing third-party services much easier. The gem monitors the interaction between your test and the rest of the world. If your test makes an HTTP request, VCR intercepts the responses and saves them as a "cassette," which is just a YAML file with a particular structure. The next time you run the test, VCR intercepts the HTTP calls, stops them from going over the Internet, and passes the response from the cassette along to the rest of the test. Effectively, you are stubbing the HTTP call with a real HTTP response from the actual remote server.

This is tremendously useful, allowing us to gain the benefit of fast tests and the benefit of real data from our remote source.

Setting up and using VCR involves only a few steps. First, we need to add it as a gem in the test group of our Gemfile, along with the webmock gem, which actually intercepts the network calls:

```
gem "vcr"
gem "webmock"
```

And there's a little bit of setup that I put in spec/support/vcr.rb:

```
server_charge/01/spec/support/vcr.rb
VCR.configure do |config|
  config.cassette_library_dir = "spec/vcr_cassettes"
  config.hook_into :webmock
  config.configure_rspec_metadata!
end
```

Line by line that configuration does three things: specifies spec/vcr_cassettes as the home of the cassette data that VCR stores; specifies webmock as the underlying source of web mocking; and specifies that we're using RSpec metadata to allow us to say which tests will use VCR.

---

7.   https://github.com/vcr/vcr

The RSpec metadata makes it easy to integrate our tests with VCR, as in this test of our StripeToken wrapper object:

```
server_charge/01/spec/models/stripe_token_spec.rb
require "rails_helper"

describe StripeToken, :vcr do

  it "calls stripe to get a token" do
    token = StripeToken.new(
        credit_card_number: "4242424242424242", expiration_month: "12",
        expiration_year: Time.zone.now.year + 1, cvc: "123")
    expect(token.id).to start_with("tok_")
  end

end
```

That :vcr symbol in the describe block is a piece of RSpec metadata. If VCR is loaded, when RSpec comes across a describe or it method annotated with vcr, the VCR gem is activated. This test just creates a StripeToken and verifies that it sets its ID to some string beginning with tok_. Mostly, it's just testing that all the wires are connected.

When this test runs, it makes a call to the Stripe API. With VCR activated, VCR records the result of the call and places it in the file spec/vcr_cassettes/StripeToken/calls_stripe_to_get_a_token.yml. The spec/vcr_cassettes/ part comes from the configuration file; the other parts are the name of the describe block and the it test.

If you look at that file, you see a bunch of YAML that serializes the exact request made and the entire response. Subsequent runs of the test use that value in place of the real call. In addition, future test runs will fail if the API request call does not match the URL used the first time.

If you delete the YAML file, VCR re-creates it on the next test run. Sometimes, a change in the underlying code will change the set of API calls made and the test fails, in which case deleting the cassette is the way to go. You can force VCR to rerecord its cassettes by adding some settings to the RSpec metadata. Instead of just :vcr, use vcr: {record: :all }. But change it back once the test passes—having VCR record on every test run defeats the purpose. For similar reasons, the VCR cassettes are stored in source control and shared between developers and things like continuous integration servers.

VCR can also be configured to automatically refresh the cassettes on regular intervals, which protects you against the test continuing to work even though the remote API has changed.

We can also use VCR in more complicated tests. The original test I wrote for the PurchasesCart workflow used RSpec test doubles, but if I use VCR, I can use "real" objects with "fake" data:

server_charge/02/spec/workflows/purchases_cart_spec.rb

```ruby
require "rails_helper"

describe PurchasesCart do

  describe "successful credit card purchase", :vcr do
    let(:reference) { Payment.generate_reference }
    let(:ticket_1) { instance_spy(
        Ticket, status: "waiting", price: Money.new(1500), id: 1) }
    let(:ticket_2) { instance_spy(
        Ticket, status: "waiting", price: Money.new(1500), id: 2) }
    let(:ticket_3) { instance_spy(Ticket, status: "unsold", id: 3) }
    let(:user) { instance_double(
        User, id: 5, tickets_in_cart: [ticket_1, ticket_2]) }
    let(:token) { StripeToken.new(
        credit_card_number: "4242424242424242", expiration_month: "12",
        expiration_year: Time.zone.now.year + 1, cvc: "123") }
    let(:workflow) { PurchasesCart.new(
        user: user, purchase_amount_cents: 3000,
        stripe_token: token) }
    let(:attributes) { {user_id: user.id, price_cents: 3000,
                        reference: a_truthy_value, payment_method: "stripe",
                        status: "created"} }
    let(:payment) { instance_double(
        Payment, succeeded?: true, price: Money.new(3000),
                reference: reference) }

    before(:example) do
      allow(Payment).to receive(:create!).with(attributes).and_return(payment)
      allow(payment).to receive(:update!).with(
          status: "succeeded", response_id: a_string_starting_with("ch_"),
          full_response: a_truthy_value)
      expect(payment).to receive(:create_line_items).with([ticket_1, ticket_2])
      workflow.run
    end

    it "updates the ticket status" do
      expect(ticket_1).to have_received(:purchased!)
      expect(ticket_2).to have_received(:purchased!)
      expect(ticket_3).not_to have_received(:purchased!)
      expect(workflow.payment_attributes).to match(attributes)
      expect(workflow.success).to be_truthy
    end

  end

end
```

Here in the let blocks, we create a StripeToken, which triggers an API call. Then we run the workflow in the begin block, which triggers another API call via StripeCharge. VCR records them both, actually creating a separate cassette for each of the four tests. It's worth mentioning that the VCR cassettes do store all the data that is passed to and from the API call, including card numbers and API keys. That shouldn't be a problem in most cases, because you should be using test API keys and fake credit card numbers, but it's worth keeping an eye on.

Next Up

In this chapter, we looked at the basics of traditional credit card processing. We used the Stripe API to send transaction information to the payment gateway, authenticate a credit card, and then trigger a payment. In the next chapter we look at how to authenticate customer information on the client side, which offers valuable security benefits.

## CHAPTER 3

Client-Side Payment Authentication

In the previous chapter we used a traditional form processing workflow to manage a credit card transaction for our Snow Globe Theater payment application. Even though we handled the transaction via our server, we still used the Stripe API in two of the steps: validating the customer's credit card and returning a one-time use token, and using that token to trigger the actual transaction.

One reason why we chose to use a token in this workflow example was to minimize the security risk of passing credit card information around our servers. While limiting the amount of credit card information our servers see is a great goal, an even better goal is to eliminate credit card information from our servers completely.

We can do this. We have the technology.

Specifically, we have the Stripe.js library and encrypted Ajax requests. Rather than submit the credit card information to our server and have our server request a token, in this chapter we're going to have the browser send the credit card information directly to Stripe, return a token, and send the token to our server.

The great thing about this is that it's going to require almost no change to our server-side code beyond the StripeToken class itself. We are, however, going to have to change our view code somewhat, including adding JavaScript to manage the form's interaction with the Stripe API. Let's get started by adding the Stripe.js library to our payment application.

Setting Up Client-Side Stripe

First off, we need to set things up. We need to add the Stripe.js library to our application. Many JavaScript libraries commonly used with Rails have been bundled into Ruby gems so that they can be added to the manifest file of the Rails asset pipeline. Stripe.js is not most JavaScript libraries. In particular, it is important for PCI compliance purposes that you retrieve the Stripe JavaScript file directly from Stripe and not from your own server or a content-delivery system. The most common practice is to directly include the library directly in the HTML header of your layout template, like so:

```
client_charge/01/app/views/layouts/application.html.slim
= stylesheet_link_tag("application",
  media: "all", "data-turbolinks-track" => true)
= javascript_include_tag("#{STRIPE_JS_HOST}/v2/#{STRIPE_JS_FILE}")
= javascript_include_tag("application", "data-turbolinks-track" => true)

javascript:
  Stripe.setPublishableKey(
    "#{Rails.application.secrets.stripe_publishable_key}");
```

We've modified our Stripe setup to choose a Stripe host based on environment:

```
client_charge/01/config/initializers/stripe.rb
Stripe.api_key = Rails.application.secrets.stripe_secret_key
raise "Missing Stripe API Key" unless Stripe.api_key
STRIPE_JS_HOST = "https://js.stripe.com".freeze unless defined? STRIPE_JS_HOST
STRIPE_JS_FILE = Rails.env.development? ? "stripe-debug.js" : ""
```

We're using the Rails environment to determine which version of the Stripe library we load. In production, we load the file stripe.js, which is minified for performance, while every place else we load stripe-debug.js. The debug version is not minified, so if there happens to be a problem, we can examine the code and set breakpoints or loggers or whatnot. The use of global variables in the stripe.rb file is to support a test library that we'll talk about in *Testing the JavaScript via Capybara*, on page 53.

Second, the Stripe library is loaded before our application.js manifest that loads the rest of our JavaScript. This is because we're going to write code that references Stripe, and if Stripe isn't already loaded, that code will fail.

Finally, we use Stripe.setPublishableKey to pass our publicly visible key to the JavaScript library. This line doesn't have to be in our header—we could put it in our JavaScript. However, if the line is inside a Rails template, we can use the already-existing Rails mechanism for keeping the key secret and still get it to the JavaScript. Otherwise we'd have to have a different mechanism, which might include hard-coding the key. Not the end of the world in this case—it is the public key, after all—but duplicating long static strings in your code base often leads to pain.

Now we need to update the form and write some JavaScript.

Re-Form-ing the Form

Let's work on the form first, since it's more straightforward. We need to take the name attribute off the credit card fields so that they are not sent to the server when the form is submitted. However, the Stripe library still needs to be able to identify those form elements. To do so, it requests that we use a data-stripe attribute on those form fields:

```
client_charge/01/app/views/shopping_carts/show.html.slim
h2 Checkout

h3 Credit Card Info

= form_tag(payments_path, class: "form-inline", id: "payment-form") do
  = hidden_field_tag(:purchase_amount_cents, @cart.total_cost.cents)
  .form_group
    = label_tag(:credit_card_number, "Credit Card Number", class: "sr-only")
    input.form-control(placeholder="Credit Card #"
      data-stripe="number" id="credit_card_number")
  .form_group
    = label_tag(:expiration_month, "Month", class: "sr-only")
    input.form-control(placeholder="Month"
      data-stripe="exp-month" id="expiration_month")

    = label_tag(:expiration_year, "Year", class: "sr-only")
    input.form-control(placeholder="Year"
      data-stripe="exp-year" id="expiration_year")

    = label_tag(:cvc, "Year", class: "sr-only")
    input.form-control(placeholder="CVC #" data-stripe="cvc" id="cvc")

  .form_group
    = submit_tag("Purchase Cart", class: "btn btn-default", id: "purchase")
```

This is very much the same form. Because we are no longer using the name attribute, we switched from using the Rails text_field_tag to the more generic HTML input tag (in Slim, that's written as %input). And we've added data-stripe fields. The naming convention for the values of the data-stripe fields comes from Stripe, so Stripe expects the credit card number to be in a field with data-stripe="number".

Adding JavaScript to the Form

With the form in place, we need to intercept form submissions so that we can pass the credit card info to Stripe, retrieve a token, put that token in the form, and then submit the form. This requires a little bit of JavaScript.

I like to use the new ECMAScript 2015 standard for JavaScript (which you may know by its earlier name, ES6), because of its improved support for classes, and some cleaner syntax options. Sadly, ECMAScript 2015 is not implemented fully by any browser yet. But we're not going to let a little thing like lack of browser support stop us.

To use ECMAScript 2015 features, we need to use the Babel library for transpiling, and we're using the beta version of Sprockets 4.0 to power the Rails asset pipeline. Babel takes files written in ECMAScript 2015 and transpiles them to good old-fashioned ES5, which any common browser knows. This process is mostly transparent to us, because Sprockets 4.0 uses "source maps" to display our ECMAScript 2015 code in the browser inspector, while still executing the ES5 code behind the scenes.

In our Gemfile:

```
gem "babel-transpiler"
gem "sprockets", github: "rails/sprockets"
```

By the time you read this, Sprockets 4 may well be out of beta, in which case we don't need to point to the GitHub version. I went back and forth a bit on whether to use Sprockets 3 with a workaround or Sprockets 4 in beta, and decided on Sprockets 4 because of improved source map support as well as trying to be forward looking where I can.

With these gems in place, any file with the .es6 extension is automatically converted to clean ES5 JavaScript. (A full list of features in ECMAScript 2015 is outside our scope here; however, the website for the Babel transpiler[1] has some resources.)

The JavaScript code that I'm about to show may look unusual to you. For one thing, this code uses the new ES6 class syntax. Maybe more to the point, the code treats jQuery and the DOM as third-party dependencies, and in keeping with the ideas we've already talked about for code, it isolates the jQuery and DOM features into their own class.

The code also has three small classes: one represents the form object in the DOM, one handles the user submission, and one handles the response from Stripe after requesting a token.

We start by loading the code. We use $(() => new StripeForm()), where $() is shorthand for jQuery's "on page load event," but all we do there is create an instance of our StripeForm class, which handles the submit event:

```
client_charge/01/app/assets/javascripts/purchases_cart.es6
$(() => new StripeForm())
```

---

1.   https://babeljs.io

The StripeForm class is a small wrapper that sets up the handler for the submit event. It's my normal, perhaps idiosyncratic, practice to set up event handlers inside methods and have the event handler be a single line call to another method. Wrapping the handler makes it easier to manage common state or setup. In this case, we don't have much of either (at least, not yet), so this probably will feel a little verbose:

`client_charge/01/app/assets/javascripts/purchases_cart.es6`
```
class StripeForm {

  constructor() {
    this.checkoutForm = new CheckoutForm()
    this.initSubmitHandler()
  }

  initSubmitHandler() {
    this.checkoutForm.form().submit((event) => { this.handleSubmit(event) })
  }

  handleSubmit(event) {
    event.preventDefault()
    if (this.checkoutForm.isButtonDisabled()) {
      return false
    }
    this.checkoutForm.disableButton()
    Stripe.card.createToken(this.checkoutForm.form(), TokenHandler.handle)
    return false
  }
}
```

The fat arrow => is defined in ECMAScript 2015 as an alias for the keyword function, except that, unlike function, the fat arrow keeps the this scope that it's invoked in. If you've ever done something goofy like var that = this in order to pass a this variable into an anonymous function, well, you don't have to do that any more. The class keyword sets up an object-oriented class that can be instantiated with the new keyword. It's mostly a shortcut for the prototype syntax in older JavaScript. We won't be doing anything fancy with inheritance, but it's worth mentioning that inside the class definition, methods can be defined with just methodName() {}; there's no need for the keyword function, a fat arrow, or any kind of comma or semicolon between method definitions. Also inside a class, constructor() is automatically invoked on new instances.

So, we invoke new StripeForm() and the constructor method of the StripeForm class is called. That method creates a CheckoutForm instance and also calls initSubmitHandler(). The initSubmitHandler() retrieves the actual DOM form from the checkoutForm and ties a method to its submit action.

What's a CheckoutForm? It's a thin wrapper around the DOM and jQuery methods that interact with the actual browser output. Or, to put it another way, it's an attic where I hide the jQuery methods and give them nice names because I find them completely inscrutable, especially when chained together. To be clear, it's not that it's hard to figure out what a particular jQuery method is doing—it's just often nigh impossible to figure out why it's doing that or what purpose that DOM change serves toward the actual goal.

The CheckoutForm class has a few really simple getter methods that find elements of interest, a method that actually submits the form, and a method that appends a hidden field to the form given a name and a value:

```
client_charge/01/app/assets/javascripts/purchases_cart.es6
class CheckoutForm {

  form() { return $("#payment-form") }

  button() { return this.form().find(".btn") }

  disableButton() { this.button().prop("disabled", true) }

  isButtonDisabled() { return this.button().prop("disabled") }

  submit() { this.form().get(0).submit() }

  appendHidden(name, value) {
    const field = $("<input>")
      .attr("type", "hidden")
      .attr("name", name)
      .val(value)
    this.form().append(field)
  }
}
```

Looking back at the original StripeForm, it assigns the handleSubmit method to be called when the form is submitted. The handleSubmit does three things:

- Calls event.preventDefault(), which is a jQuery event method that keeps the form from being automatically submitted at the end of this method. We don't want the form to be submitted until after we hear from Stripe. Returning false also prevents further events from being propagated, again to prevent the form from being submitted until we explicitly say it can.

- Calls the CheckoutForm to see if the button is disabled. If it is, then presumably a checkout is in progress, and we exit rather than resubmit.

- Calls the CheckoutForm to disable the button, which prevents a user from clicking the button and submitting the form twice.

- Calls Stripe.card.createToken, which is defined by the Stripe.js library, and which is the JavaScript version of the Stripe::Token#create method we just used on the server side. It sends credit card information to the Stripe server and returns a token.

The Stripe.card.createToken method takes two arguments. The first is the form element that contains all the fields with the data-stripe attributes. The Stripe library automatically takes the credit card data from the form. The second argument is a callback method that is invoked when the Stripe API returns with token data. In our case, we're using a class method of our TokenHandler class, called, boringly enough, handle. (Honestly, I find the Stripe API here to be a little out of date, and I'd rather Stripe change it to use JavaScript promises rather than a callback handler. My normal policy is not to be too idiosyncratic in code examples, but if you wanted to use a promises version, there's an unofficial wrapper using promises.[2])

The handler method is expected to take two arguments: a status code and the actual response data from the Stripe server. All our class method does is create an instance of TokenHandler, which associates our status and response with a CheckoutForm for DOM data and then handles the event:

client_charge/01/app/assets/javascripts/purchases_cart.es6
```
class TokenHandler {
  static handle(status, response) {
    new TokenHandler(status, response).handle()
  }

  constructor(status, response) {
    this.checkoutForm = new CheckoutForm()
    this.status = status
    this.response = response
  }

  handle() {
    this.checkoutForm.appendHidden("stripe_token", this.response.id)
    this.checkoutForm.submit()
  }
}
```

Once we get the token from Stripe, embed it into the actual form DOM and then submit the form normally, essentially completing the event. We've defined appendHidden and submit on the CheckoutForm class so that we can call them from our TokenHandler. The form then submits. Critically, it only submits the token and the hidden field with the price, since the card data does not have name fields in the markup. and we're back to the data on the server.

---

2. https://github.com/bendrucker/stripe-as-promised

Using the Token on the Server

We have to make surprisingly few changes to our server code for it to work with an incoming token rather than an incoming set of card information. This is where we start to see some benefit from encapsulating parts of our code. If we update our StripeToken object to expect an incoming token rather than credit card data, our PurchaseCart workflow should work without any changes.

Updating the StripeToken class changes the structure of it just a little:

client_charge/01/app/models/stripe_token.rb
```ruby
class StripeToken

  attr_accessor :credit_card_number, :expiration_month,
      :expiration_year, :cvc,
      :stripe_token

  def initialize(credit_card_number: nil, expiration_month: nil,
      expiration_year: nil, cvc: nil,
      stripe_token: nil)
    @credit_card_number = credit_card_number
    @expiration_month = expiration_month
    @expiration_year = expiration_year
    @cvc = cvc
    @stripe_token = stripe_token
  end

  def token
    @token ||= (stripe_token ? retrieve_token : create_token)
  end

  def id
    stripe_token || token.id
  end

  private def retrieve_token
    Stripe::Token.retrieve(stripe_token)
  end

  private def create_token
    Stripe::Token.create(
        card: {number: credit_card_number, exp_month: expiration_month,
              exp_year: expiration_year, cvc: cvc})
  end

  def to_s
    "STRIPE TOKEN: #{id}"
  end

  def inspect
    "STRIPE TOKEN #{id}"
  end

end
```

The keyword arguments in the constructor now include stripe_token. We'd normally expect either stripe_token or all of the other arguments, but we're not doing anything in particular to validate that yet. We could, at this point, remove the credit card data from the StripeToken class, since it should not be used any more.

The actual id method now prefers the stripe_token argument if it exists. If not, it falls back to the token object.

Accessing the token object has also changed. If the stripe_token attribute does not exist, then call Stripe::Token.create as before. If we do have the stripe_token attribute but we still want the entire token object, then call a different method, Stripe::Token.retrieve, which retrieves the token object from the Stripe API.

It's possible that we might want the entire token object, if, for example, we wanted to display something like "Visa ending in …1234" on a checkout page. That information is in the token object.

What we have then is a StripeToken wrapper that hides from the outside world whether it was formed by card information or a token string. Because the method to retrieve the token string from the object hasn't changed, a user of StripeToken, such as our PurchasesCart workflow, doesn't have to change at all.

We do have one minor change to make to the PurchasesController. Because we were passing form arguments to the StripeToken dynamically from a whitelist of form parameters, we need to make sure that stripe_token is among them:

```
client_charge/01/app/controllers/payments_controller.rb
private def card_params
  params.permit(
      :credit_card_number, :expiration_month,
      :expiration_year, :cvc,
      :stripe_token).to_h.symbolize_keys
end
```

Again, we can probably remove the credit card attributes from here, as they are no longer being sent. Our code works, but we do have one issue. Our end-to-end test, which depended on form elements that are no longer being passed to the server, now fails. Let's look next at testing our JavaScript.

Testing the JavaScript via Capybara

If you run the tests without making further changes to them, the end-to-end test in spec/features/purchase_cart_spec.rb will fail. By default, our Capybara-driven feature specs don't use JavaScript, which means the client side of the form can't request a token. And if we don't have a token, the form fails.

In order to make the test pass, we need to run the test inside a container that executes JavaScript. We can do that by setting a JavaScript driver for Capybara, which means Capybara runs the test in a headless web browser engine that includes JavaScript. The Capybara driver we're using is called Poltergeist.[3] Poltergeist connects Capybara to the PhantomJS headless browser, which you also need to install; see the instructions at the website.[4] We need to tell Capybara that we are using Poltergeist.

client_charge/01/spec/support/capybara.rb
```
require "capybara/poltergeist"
require "capybara-screenshot/rspec"
Capybara.asset_host = "http://localhost:3000"
Capybara.javascript_driver = :poltergeist
```

In the test, all we need to do is use RSpec metadata to identify the test as dependent on JavaScript:

client_charge/01/spec/features/payments/purchase_cart_spec.rb
```
describe "purchasing a cart", :js do
```

Adding the :js marker makes the test pass (you may have to delete the existing VCR cassette in spec/vcr_cassettes/purchasing_a_cart, since a different API call is being made), but it opens us up to a few other subtle problems:

- Our test now fires up a headless browser in order to run. That means it's going to be pretty slow. We don't want more of these tests than we need.

- Headless JavaScript tests are notorious for being flaky and prone to intermittent timing failures. That shouldn't be a problem for us yet, but it might be as the code gets more complicated.

Worse, if you look at the VCR cassette for the new test, it contains the call to get the charge made server side, but not the call to get the token made client side. (You can confirm this by disconnecting from the Internet; the test will fail.) The test is only passing because it remakes the call to retrieve the token every time.

This is bad.

We have a couple of options to fix this. There's a JavaScript equivalent of VCR that will do the VCR thing, but inside our headless browser at runtime. The gem is called Puffing Billy,[5] which, according to Wikipedia, is the name of both the world's oldest surviving steam locomotive and a tourist reconstruction of an old railway near Melbourne, Australia.

---

3. https://github.com/teampoltergeist/poltergeist
4. http://phantomjs.org
5. https://github.com/oesmith/puffing-billy

While Puffing Billy works, it's a little finicky in terms of setup, and I've never been 100 percent comfortable with it. Instead, we're going to try an option that seems to have a little bit less configuration, a gem called FakeStripe.[6]

The FakeStripe gem swaps out both our server-side Stripe API and the client-side Stripe API, setting up a local test server to retrieve Stripe calls and spit out canned data, even for token calls coming from JavaScript. This is basically all we want out of our test, so let's give it a try.

First, we need to add it to our Gemfile. Everything goes in the test group, which now looks like this:

```
group :test do
  gem "capybara-screenshot"
  gem "capybara"
  gem "database_cleaner"
  gem "fake_stripe"
  gem "launchy"
  gem "poltergeist"
  gem "selenium-webdriver"
  gem "sinatra", github: "sinatra/sinatra"
  gem "vcr"
  gem "webmock"
end
```

The reason we need to explicitly include Sinatra is a temporary incompatibility between Rails 5, Rack 2, and the current release version of Sinatra. By the time you read this, it might not need to be there.

We've already changed our stripe.rb initializer to use STRIPE_JS_HOST as the source of the stripe.js file, and fake_stripe will use that information. There's one minor change in the VCR setup:

```
client_charge/01/spec/support/vcr.rb
VCR.configure do |config|
  config.cassette_library_dir = "spec/vcr_cassettes"
  config.hook_into :webmock
  config.configure_rspec_metadata!
  config.ignore_localhost = true
end
```

The last line, gnore_localhost, allows communication between the JavaScript browser code and our application not to be blocked by VCR. This is good because Rails has some minor back and forth here that we don't want to deal with.

---

6.   https://github.com/thoughtbot/fake_stripe

Finally, the test itself, with the FakeStripe setup. If you follow the FakeStripe documentation, this setup is a little different because we only want FakeStripe for this test, not for all our tests. We could use it as a VCR replacement, but right now I'm not choosing to go back and redo all those tests.

```ruby
client_charge/01/spec/features/payments/purchase_cart_spec.rb
require "rails_helper"
require "fake_stripe"

describe "purchasing a cart", :js do
  fixtures :all

  before(:each) do
    FakeStripe.stub_stripe
  end

  after(:each) do
    WebMock.reset!
    Stripe.api_key = Rails.application.secrets.stripe_secret_key
  end

  it "can add a purchase to a cart" do
    tickets(:midsummer_bums_1).place_in_cart_for(users(:buyer))
    tickets(:midsummer_bums_2).place_in_cart_for(users(:buyer))
    login_as(users(:buyer), scope: :user)        ,
    visit shopping_cart_path
    fill_in :credit_card_number, with: "4242 4242 4242 4242"
    fill_in :expiration_month, with: "12"
    fill_in :expiration_year, with: Time.current.year + 1
    fill_in :cvc, with: "123"
    click_on "purchase"
    expect(page).to have_selector(".purchased_ticket", count: 2)
    expect(page).to have_selector(
        "#purchased_ticket_#{tickets(:midsummer_bums_1).id}")
    expect(page).to have_selector(
        "#purchased_ticket_#{tickets(:midsummer_bums_2).id}")
  end

end
```

We're requiring the fake_stripe file. Before each spec, we are calling the FakeStripe.stub_stripe method; this resets our Stripe API key, sets the host for our JavaScript file, and uses WebMock to stub calls to the Stripe API so that our API calls are intercepted by FakeStripe to return canned data.

And that's it; the test works. However, if we had been dependent on any of the details of the Stripe response, we would've had some problems, but because this test is mostly concerned with the results in our database, we're fine.

Next Up

In this chapter, we expanded our use of the Stripe API to allow us to validate credit card information without sending that information through our server. We added JavaScript to handle an Ajax call to the Stripe server, and also added gem support for testing JavaScript while still caching HTTP responses.

Now that we've been able to set up a secure way of using Stripe, it's time for us to investigate another way of allowing customers to validate their credit card information without sending it to our server: PayPal.

## CHAPTER 4

PayPal

One day, the theater management gathers our development team to make a simple request. A survey of our website patrons determined that 20 percent of them are refusing to give us their credit card information at all. They'd rather use PayPal to pay us. But we don't offer PayPal.

We sigh. We knew this day was going to arrive.

Although many payment gateways work more or less like Stripe, which we set up in Chapter 2, *Take the Money*, on page 21, PayPal is a popular gateway that uses an entirely different payment process. I'm tempted to call PayPal "a more elegant weapon from a more civilized age," except that it's less elegant, and whether the age was more civilized is debatable.

PayPal tries to solve the exact security issue we just solved with our client-side Stripe solution: allowing users to securely make payments without sending their credit card information directly to our servers. Where Stripe uses an Ajax and token mechanism to keep credit card information off our site, PayPal's workflow asks users to log in and present their personal information to PayPal as part of our site's checkout process. (PayPal does have a service that takes credit card information from business sites; however, because this service isn't commonly used, and its functionality is similar to Stripe, I'm not going to discuss it here.)

In this chapter, we'll set up a PayPal business account and learn how to accept PayPal as a source for authorizing transactions.

Setting Up a PayPal Account

To accept payments via PayPal, you need a PayPal business account. If you already have a PayPal personal account, you really want to keep that separate from your developer account. Here's how to create a PayPal business account, at least as of this writing:

Go to the PayPal website.[1] Click "Sign up" and then "Open a business account." You are directed to the business home page, then click "Get Started."

Now it gets a little confusing. You have three options: "PayPal Payments Standard," "PayPal Payments Pro," and "Already accepting credit cards?" That third option, which is usually called "PayPal Express Checkout" and which for some reason PayPal isn't identifying as such on the site, is the one we want. That's the classic "Check out with PayPal button" experience you are probably familiar with.

To select the Express Checkout option, click "Learn More" following the "Already accepting credit cards?" option and then click "Get Express Checkout." You are now asked to answer a couple of questions about your business and enter your business's URL. Next you are asked for an email address. When you enter your email address you are taken to a "Sign up for a Business account" form with that email address filled in. (It seems we could have gotten to this form in fewer than four pages, but *c'est la vie.*)

The form asks us to enter a legal name and a legal business name (though the help text says, "If there isn't [a business name] then please enter something that best represents what you are doing"). You need to enter a phone number and mailing address as well. Then you go to *another* form for some additional questions about the business. The next page asks for the last four digits of your Social Security number and your date of birth. (Non-U.S. residents, I assume you have something different here.)

Finally, you are able to submit the form and create the account.

The resulting page says, "Welcome to your PayPal Business Account." You'll need to perform additional setup activities to actually take payments, but at this point we are ready to create a test account for our theater application.

To test PayPal in development mode, we need to create what PayPal calls "sandbox accounts," and as far as I can tell, how to do so is completely opaque from the business account page. But once you are logged into your business account, point your web browser to the Sandbox Test Accounts page.[2] You should see two automatically created sandbox accounts, as shown in the figure on page 61.

---

1. https://www.paypal.com
2. https://developer.paypal.com/developer/accounts

For the purposes of this book, we are using two accounts to test our system. One account is our fake business account (moneybook-facilitator@noelrappin.com), and the other account is our fake buyer (moneybook-buyer@noelrappin.com). These accounts are based on the email you used to set up the business account, and you'll start with one business account and one personal account. You can create more from this page if you want.

With our account set up, we can use it as a source of the API keys we need, as well as use it to verify and test our transactions.

Accepting PayPal Transactions

As we build our PayPal transaction manager, we're trying to solve two somewhat separate problems. The immediate problem, of course, is setting up our application to handle PayPal transactions. The larger problem is how to gracefully handle changes to our requirements that break the assumptions the code is already making. In this case, the code we've created so far in this book assumes that all payments use Stripe and take Stripe tokens. As we go forward, we need to be aware that the way we add PayPal into our code base could have important consequences for how easy or difficult it is to make future changes to our business logic.

To accept PayPal for payments, several points in our code need to be adjusted:

- Our shopping cart form needs to allow users to select PayPal as a payment option, and know that if users select PayPal, they don't need to fill in credit card information.

- Once our application receives a user request for PayPal, our application needs to branch off into a PayPal-specific workflow, rather than the Stripe workflow we already have set up.

- As part of the PayPal workflow, our application needs to not complete the entire transaction, but instead tell PayPal about the impending sale. In doing so, the PayPal gem will communicate back to the PayPal REST API and give us a one-time URL associated with the new payment.

- Once PayPal returns a one-time URL, our application needs to redirect users to the URL, where they authenticate in PayPal, choose their payment method, and jump through whatever other hoops PayPal asks them to.

- When PayPal sends a message back to our servers letting us know that authentication is successful, our application needs to be able to finish processing the payment.

From our point of view, the fact that the workflow depends on PayPal sending a message back to our servers makes working with PayPal in test or development mode kind of awkward. In particular, it's difficult to completely run an end-to-end test, and it's also hard to completely test the PayPal workflow when you need PayPal to call back to localhost:3000. We'll go over the code to interact with PayPal first, then talk about how we run this in a developer environment and test.

Setup and Configuration

PayPal has, I think, at least three separate APIs—it's hard to tell because the documentation makes no particular attempt to give a useful overview. In any case, we'll be using the REST version of the API, and the associated official Ruby gem provided by PayPal,[3] which we need to add to our Gemfile. The REST version is the newest version, and the one most likely to be kept up in the future, although it still has some limitations relative to the older APIs.

```
gem "paypal-sdk-rest"
```

The gem comes with a handy install script:

```
$ rails g paypal:sdk:install
                      create  config/paypal.yml
      create  config/initializers/paypal.rb
```

Because we're using the REST API, we'll need to create a REST API app to get credentials. Go to https://developer.paypal.com/developer/applications and then click "Create App" under "REST API apps." Give the app a name—we'll use "Snow Globe Theater" and our development merchant account we created in the previous section. Click "Create App" again, and we now have a page with Sandbox API credentials, including a client ID and secret, which we'll need

---

3.   https://github.com/paypal/PayPal-Ruby-SDK

in a moment. In the upper-right corner is a "Sandbox/Live" toggle similar to Stripe's (shown in the following figure) that we can use when we go live.

We now need to add those credentials to our application using the paypal.yml file. We'll use a trick similar to what we did to add the Stripe credentials. We'll add the actual client_id and client_secret to the .env file and then add them to the secrets.yml file:

paypal/01/config/secrets.yml
```
development: &default
  admin_name: First User
  admin_email: user@example.com
  admin_password: changeme
  domain_name: example.com
  secret_key_base: fc65272c27199652b936c28264bf770f385243f00d91b69f7424ca298466
  stripe_publishable_key: <%= ENV["STRIPE_PUBLISHABLE_KEY"] %>
  stripe_secret_key: <%= ENV["STRIPE_SECRET_KEY"] %>
  paypal_client_id: <%= ENV["PAYPAL_CLIENT_ID"] %>
  paypal_client_secret: <%= ENV["PAYPAL_CLIENT_SECRET"] %>
  host_name: "6e0fd751.ngrok.com"

test:
  <<: *default
  secret_key_base: 8489bb21c9497da574dcb42fea4e15d089606d196e367f6f4e166acb281d
```

As you can see in the previous code, we've also added a host_name field, which will come in handy later on when we need to give PayPal a callback URL.

Next we need to add the environment variables to the file PayPal uses, the paypal.yml file:

paypal/01/config/paypal.yml
```
development:
  mode: sandbox
  client_id: <%= ENV["PAYPAL_CLIENT_ID"] %>
  client_secret: <%= ENV["PAYPAL_CLIENT_SECRET"] %>
```

In the paypal.yml configuration file, the same configuration is duplicated in the test section. We might want to keep this out of source control, similar to the secrets.yml file, so that the staging and production versions can be set directly.

View Update

Our shopping cart view now needs to change to allow users to pick PayPal as a payment option. As usual, the following code won't win any design awards, but it's functional:

```
paypal/01/app/views/shopping_carts/show.html.slim
h2 Checkout

h3 Payment Options

= form_tag(payments_path, class: "form-inline", id: "payment-form") do

  .paypal
    img(src="https://www.paypal.com/en_US/i/logo/PayPal_mark_37x23.gif"
        align="left" style="margin-right:7px;")
    span(style="font-size:11px; font-family: Arial, Verdana")
      | The safer, easier way to pay.
    = radio_button_tag(:payment_type,
        :paypal, false,
        class: "payment-type-radio", id: "paypal_radio")
  .credit_card
    | Credit Card
    = radio_button_tag(:payment_type,
        :credit, true,
        class: "payment-type-radio", id: "credit_radio")

  = hidden_field_tag(:purchase_amount_cents, @cart.total_cost.cents)

  #credit-card-info
    h3 Credit Card Info
```

The rest of the credit card information stays as before, subordinate to the #credit-card-info element, which we've added to allow us to easily show or hide the entire credit card portion of the form.

The use of the specific PayPal logo GIF and tagline is required by PayPal if you are using ExpressCheckout.[4] Otherwise, this code defines a standard set of radio buttons setting a form variable called payment_type.

We need add a tiny sprinkle of JavaScript to make sure the credit card information really does hide. This is the JavaScript class formerly known as StripeForm, with the naming updated to better reflect its new function:

---

4.   https://www.paypal.com/webscr?cmd=xpt/Merchant/merchant/ExpressCheckoutButtonCode-outside

paypal/01/app/assets/javascripts/purchases_cart.es6

```
class PaymentFormHandler {

  constructor() {
    this.checkoutForm = new CheckoutForm()
    this.initSubmitHandler()
    this.initPaymentTypeHandler()
  }

  initSubmitHandler() {
    this.checkoutForm.form().submit((event) => {
      if (!this.checkoutForm.isPayPal()) {
        this.handleSubmit(event)
      }
    })
  }

  initPaymentTypeHandler() {
    this.checkoutForm.paymentTypeRadio().click(() => {
      this.checkoutForm.setCreditCardVisibility()
    })
  }

  handleSubmit(event) {
    event.preventDefault()
    if (this.checkoutForm.isButtonDisabled()) {
      return false
    }
    this.checkoutForm.disableButton()
    Stripe.card.createToken(this.checkoutForm.form(), TokenHandler.handle)
    return false
  }
}

$(() => new PaymentFormHandler())
```

With this code we're adding a new handler to fire on a click to one of the radio buttons and passing the handler to the checkoutForm. We also need to make sure that the client-side call to the Stripe API doesn't happen if the customer selects the PayPal option. You'll also need to add a few methods to the CheckoutForm class, which actually interacts with the DOM:

paypal/01/app/assets/javascripts/purchases_cart.es6

```
paymentTypeRadio() { return $(".payment-type-radio") }

selectedPaymentType() { return $("input[name=payment_type]:checked").val() }

creditCardForm() { return $("#credit-card-info") }

isPayPal() { return this.selectedPaymentType() === "paypal" }

setCreditCardVisibility() {
  this.creditCardForm().toggleClass("hidden", this.isPayPal())
}
```

The customer can now select PayPal as a payment option on our form.

Creating a PayPal Payment

The first point of contact between a PayPal request and our server-side application is the PaymentsController. Given the way we've structured the application, we'd hope that the controller wouldn't change very much at all. Its basic functionality—to take in a request and pass it along to the appropriate workflow—hasn't really changed. The only change is that now there's some logic as to what workflow to choose:

paypal/01/app/controllers/payments_controller.rb
```ruby
class PaymentsController < ApplicationController

  def show
    @payment = Payment.find_by(reference: params[:id])
  end

  def create
    workflow = create_workflow(params[:payment_type])
    workflow.run
    if workflow.success
      redirect_to workflow.redirect_on_success_url ||
          payment_path(id: workflow.payment.reference)
    else
      redirect_to shopping_cart_path
    end
  end

  private def create_workflow(payment_type)
    case payment_type
    when "paypal" then paypal_workflow
    else
      stripe_workflow
    end
  end

  private def paypal_workflow
    PurchasesCartViaPayPal.new(
        user: current_user,
        purchase_amount_cents: params[:purchase_amount_cents])
  end

  private def stripe_workflow
    PurchasesCartViaStripe.new(
        user: current_user,
        stripe_token: StripeToken.new(**card_params),
        purchase_amount_cents: params[:purchase_amount_cents])
  end
```

```
private def card_params
  params.permit(
      :credit_card_number, :expiration_month,
      :expiration_year, :cvc,
      :stripe_token).to_h.symbolize_keys
  end

end
```

The request comes into the create method, which no longer just creates a PurchasesCart workflow; it now has to decide whether to create a PurchasesCartViaPayPal or a PurchasesCartViaStripe.

We now delegate the workflow choice to a create_workflow method, which uses the payment_type parameter to choose which workflow to create, itself delegating to a paypal_workflow or stripe_workflow method. (I broke the individual workflow methods out to make the shape of the creation logic clearer. You could argue that this logic should be pulled out of the controller entirely into some kind of factory object. I might try that if the logic got any more complicated. You could also try to associate the workflows with the payment type using a little more metaprogramming, but I think metaprogramming would be even less clear.) We also changed the redirection slightly to allow the workflow to have an opinion about where to redirect on success, but to provide a default if the workflow doesn't have a better idea.

Managing Similar Workflows

In writing the PurchasesCartViaPayPal class, we are forced to confront the fact that there are significant duplications in functionality between the PayPal and Stripe versions: both workflows have a user and a purchase amount; both need to change the status of a set of tickets; and both need to create a Payment instance to record the financial transaction.

At the same time, the two workflows differ. The Stripe workflow uses a token and actually charges the user's credit card as part of its functionality, whereas the PayPal workflow only provides enough information to redirect the user to PayPal for authentication. The PayPal workflow is actually similar to the first part of the Stripe workflow, the setup, which is a thought that will become more important later on.

It's not much of an exaggeration to suggest that the most important quality for the long-term health of our code is how well it deals with duplication. When dealing with two features that have similar but not identical functionality, we have some choices in how we deal with the duplication.

One possibility is just to ignore the duplication. Ignoring duplication makes sense if you think the duplication is incidental, meaning you think the two pieces of code are just as likely to drift apart or stay similar. (A good example of incidental duplication are RESTful Rails controllers, where the simple case looks common to all of them but is relatively unlikely to stay similar as the cases get more complex.)

You also might temporarily ignore duplication if you aren't sure how to abstract the common parts. To quote software engineer and author Sandi Metz: "Duplication is far cheaper than the wrong abstraction."[5] If you create the abstraction in a way that does not reflect the actual conceptual duplication, then you may be continually making changes that affect both parts of the code in ways that make them more complicated than they need to be.

If you decide that the duplication between two parts of the code is actually inherent in the functionality, then the duplicate code should be separated from the unique code. There are a couple of ways to think about that separation, which are similar but have different implications for how the code might change over time.

We might use *delegation*, and describe the common functionality as a class in its own right, which delegates out to two or more separate classes to handle unique functionality. In our case, this structure would manifest as a single PurchasesCart workflow, which has a Stripe or PayPal payment object as an instance variable that would handle the gateway-specific functionality, perhaps called StripeStrategy and PayPalStrategy.

Alternately, we might use inheritance and describe the common functionality as an abstract parent with two separate child classes that manage the unique part. In our case, we would have an abstract PurchasesCart class, which would then have concrete PurchasesCartViaStripe and PurchasesCartViaPayPal subclasses.

Anything you can do with inheritance, you can do with delegation (inheritance is a form of delegation that is explicitly supported by the language). As a rough rule of thumb, if the part of the functionality that is unique maps really easily to something specific in the data model, I tend to reach for delegation. If the unique part is basically structural tweaks to a common backbone, I reach for inheritance.

There are two code smells to watch out for when factoring code into different pieces. If you are making an if check against the same piece of logic in multiple places in the same class, there's a really good chance you have a candidate

---

5.   http://www.sandimetz.com/blog/2016/1/20/the-wrong-abstraction

for logic to pull out into separate classes and delegate. By doing that, you do the logical if check just once to select which delegate. Then within that delegate object, you never have to check for the condition again. In our case, this means we only need to check once whether the user is making a PayPal or a Stripe payment.

On the flip side, another code smell is putting too much of the behavior of your object in parameters. In our case, this might happen when we first realize that the workflow needs to delegate to either a PayPal or a Stripe payment object, so we pass the class object for that payment as an argument when we create the workflow. So far, so good. Passing classes as arguments can be a great way to make objects flexible. But then we realize that the different payment workflows require us to set the ticket objects to different states (because the PayPal workflow doesn't actually complete a payment). No problem—we can then just pass the expected ticket state as another parameter. But then we realize the payment object needs to be slightly different. No problem—we can add another parameter.

But eventually, that becomes a problem in two ways. First, increasing the number of parameters needed to create a class makes creating the class more complicated and makes the calling code harder to read. Second, the number of parameters dramatically increases the number of weird states the code can get into. For example, what if we create an instance with the PayPal payment object but the Stripe ticket state?

You can use delegation and inheritance together. In fact, the code I'll show you next does both. As I started to plan this code, delegation was immediately attractive because our existing architecture is already partially delegated. There is already a split between the PurchasesCart workflow and the StripeCharge and StripeToken objects. We could just make a PayPalPayment class and adjust the PurchasesCart workflow to take the kind of payment as an option.

Having a single workflow almost works, as far as I'm concerned, but in this case the PayPal and Stripe versions are too different to make the common workflow attractive, so I was faced with either putting more logic in the payment objects than seemed reasonable, or with adding more parameters to the workflow object. Instead, I opted for inheritance.

As shown in the following code, both our PurchasesCartViaStripe and PurchasesCartViaPayPal now inherit from a common PurchasesCart class, which contains common logic (I've kept the word abstract out of the class name on the theory that being abstract is an implementation detail):

```
paypal/01/app/workflows/purchases_cart.rb
class PurchasesCart

  attr_accessor :user, :purchase_amount_cents,
      :purchase_amount, :success,
      :payment

  def initialize(user: nil, purchase_amount_cents: nil)
    @user = user
    @purchase_amount = Money.new(purchase_amount_cents)
    @success = false
  end

  def run
    Payment.transaction do
      update_tickets
      create_payment
      purchase
      calculate_success
    end
  end

  def calculate_success
    @success = payment.succeeded?
  end

  def tickets
    @tickets ||= @user.tickets_in_cart
  end

  def redirect_on_success_url
    nil
  end

  def create_payment
    self.payment = Payment.create!(payment_attributes)
    payment.create_line_items(tickets)
  end

  def payment_attributes
    {user_id: user.id, price_cents: purchase_amount.cents,
     status: "created", reference: Payment.generate_reference}
  end

  def success?
    success
  end

end
```

What counts as common?

- Several attributes needed for a purchase, including a user and an amount of money

- The basic workflow of updating tickets, creating a payment, saving things, and talking to the remote API

- The definition of how to get the list of tickets from the user

- The basic logic of creating a Payment object out of the attributes to the purchase

The main piece that is different is what happens when purchase is called. In the Stripe version, we create a StripeCharge. As you might expect, the PayPal version creates a PayPalPayment:

```
paypal/01/app/workflows/purchases_cart_via_pay_pal.rb
class PurchasesCartViaPayPal < PurchasesCart

  attr_accessor :pay_pal_payment

  def update_tickets
    tickets.each(&:pending!)
  end

  def redirect_on_success_url
    pay_pal_payment.redirect_url
  end

  def payment_attributes
    super.merge(payment_method: "paypal")
  end

  def calculate_success
    @success = payment.pending?
  end

  def purchase
    @pay_pal_payment = PayPalPayment.new(payment: payment)
    payment.update(response_id: pay_pal_payment.response_id)
    payment.pending!
  end
end
```

Our PurchasesCartViaPayPal subclass inherits from PurchasesCart and makes four logical changes:

- When updating the status of the tickets, we move them not to the purchased state, but to a new state called pending because they haven't actually been purchased yet. (There's a minor change to the Ticket class to add pending to the end of the list of possible statuses.)

- We added a redirect_on_success_url that comes from the PayPalPayment.

- The payment method is paypal.

- The actual purchase method creates a PayPalPayment and sets its ID as the response_id in our application's Payment instances.

The PurchasesCartViaStripe class was also changed to reflect that most of its behavior was moved to the superclass:

paypal/01/app/workflows/purchases_cart_via_stripe.rb

```ruby
class PurchasesCartViaStripe < PurchasesCart

  attr_accessor :stripe_token, :stripe_charge

  def initialize(user:, stripe_token:, purchase_amount_cents:)
    super(user: user, purchase_amount_cents: purchase_amount_cents)
    @stripe_token = stripe_token
  end

  def update_tickets
    tickets.each(&:purchased!)
  end

  def purchase
    @stripe_charge = StripeCharge.charge(token: stripe_token, payment: payment)
    payment.update!(
        status: @stripe_charge.status, response_id: @stripe_charge.id,
        full_response: @stripe_charge.to_json)
  end

  def payment_attributes
    super.merge(payment_method: "stripe")
  end

end
```

Now, about that PayPalPayment class. Like the Stripe version, it's a wrapper around an object provided by the vendor's gem. Like the Stripe version, it does some work to create a valid object:

paypal/01/app/models/pay_pal_payment.rb

```ruby
class PayPalPayment

  attr_accessor :payment, :pay_pal_payment

  delegate :create, to: :pay_pal_payment
  delegate :execute, to: :pay_pal_payment

  def self.find(payment_id)
    PayPal::SDK::REST::Payment.find(payment_id)
  end

  def initialize(payment:)
    @payment = payment
    @pay_pal_payment = build_pay_pal_payment
  end
```

```ruby
  def build_pay_pal_payment
    PayPal::SDK::REST::Payment.new(
        intent: "sale", payer: {payment_method: "paypal"},
        redirect_urls: redirect_info, transactions: [payment_info])
  end

  def host_name
    Rails.application.secrets.host_name
  end

  def redirect_info
    {return_url: "http://#{host_name}/paypal/approved",
     cancel_url: "http://#{host_name}/paypal/rejected"}
  end

  def payment_info
    {item_list: {items: build_item_list},
     amount: {total: payment.price.format(symbol: false), currency: "USD"}}
  end

  def build_item_list
    payment.payment_line_items.map do |payment_line_item|
      {name: payment_line_item.name, sku: payment_line_item.event_id,
       price: payment_line_item.price.format(symbol: false), currency: "USD",
       quantity: 1}
    end
  end

  def created?
    pay_pal_payment.state == "created"
  end

  def redirect_url
    create unless created?
    pay_pal_payment.links.find { |link| link.method == "REDIRECT" }.href
  end

  def response_id
    create unless created?
    pay_pal_payment.id
  end
end
```

We create one of these objects with one of our own Payment instances as an argument, and it immediately calls build_pay_pal_payment, which creates the gem object of class PayPal::SDK::REST::Payment.

The PayPal::SDK::REST::Payment class takes in a bunch of key/value pairs that correspond to the somewhat haphazardly documented REST API for payments.

From our perspective, the most important piece of information we send are the redirect_urls. We send two: return_url, which is used if authentication is successful from PayPal, and cancel_url, which is used if the user bails on the PayPal side. These URLs need to be actual live routes that work on our side to do the processing we need to handle the payment or the cancellation.

We also send a list of the items in the transaction and the amount of money being transferred. PayPal, for some reason, wants the amount as a string with two decimal places (15.00), rather than an integer number of cents.

We need two pieces of information about this payment from PayPal. First, we need a URL to send our user to authenticate, and second, we need an ID that we can use to refer to the PayPal payment from our code. We get that information by telling the PayPal API to create the payment, and the PayPal API returns JSON with all the same payment data plus the unique ID and URL coming from PayPal. The PayPal gem abstracts this process a little bit. When we call create on our PayPal::SDK::REST::Payment, it uses the response to update the attributes of that instance.

We don't know which of the URL or ID will be requested first, and we don't want to require users of our PayPalPayment class to have to know that the API call is needed, so we implement the call lazily when the code requests either the URL or the ID with the line create unless created?. The create method delegates to the PayPal::SDK::REST::Payment, and created? returns true if the item has already been sent to PayPal.

Handling the PayPal Callback

Here's our PayPal story so far:

- The user selects PayPal as a payment option.

- Our controller creates a PurchasesCartViaPayPal workflow, which in turn creates a PayPalPayment object and registers that payment with PayPal.

- The PayPalPayment tells us what URL PayPal wants us to redirect to.

- We send the user there and the user authenticates via PayPal.

- PayPal sends the user back to the URL we specified in our PayPalPayment.

How do we catch that request and turn it into the data changes we need to register a payment?

First we need a route. The PayPal responses don't need to be Rails resources, so we can just set up an ordinary route match:

```
paypal/01/config/routes.rb
get "paypal/approved", to: "pay_pal_payments#approved"
```

The controller is fairly simple and mostly delegates to Yet Another Workflow:

paypal/01/app/controllers/pay_pal_payments_controller.rb
```ruby
class PayPalPaymentsController < ApplicationController

  def approved
    workflow = ExecutesPayPalPayment.new(
        payment_id: params[:paymentId],
        token: params[:token],
        payer_id: params[:PayerID])
    workflow.run
    redirect_to payment_path(id: workflow.payment.reference)
  end

end
```

The URL request from PayPal includes three tokens that are passed as query strings in the URL: the paymentId, which we use to recover the PayPal payment data; a PayerID, which PayPal uses to identify the payer on their end; and a token that really isn't used for much.

Most of the work is done by the new workflow, ExecutesPayPalPayment:

paypal/01/app/workflows/executes_pay_pal_payment.rb
```ruby
class ExecutesPayPalPayment

  attr_accessor :payment_id, :token, :payer_id, :payment, :success

  def initialize(payment_id:, token:, payer_id:)
    @payment_id = payment_id
    @token = token
    @payer_id = payer_id
    @success = false
  end

  def find_payment
    Payment.find_by(payment_method: "paypal", response_id: payment_id)
  end

  def pay_pal_payment
    @pay_pal_payment ||= PayPalPayment.find(payment_id)
  end

  def run
    Payment.transaction do
      @payment = find_payment
      execute_ok = pay_pal_payment.execute(payer_id: payer_id)
      return unless execute_ok
      payment.tickets.each(&:purchased!)
      payment.succeeded!
      self.success = true
    end
  end

end
```

We pass the workflow the three data items from PayPal, normalized to Ruby naming conventions. The run method starts off by finding the payment using the PayPalPayment class, which itself delegates to the gem to recover the actual PayPal payment data associated with the payment ID.

The important step from PayPal's perspective is the next one, where we execute the payment. Again, we're calling the method on our PayPalPayment class and it's delegating to the gem. By executing the payment we are telling PayPal that everything is a-okay on our end and PayPal can initiate the transfer of funds. If PayPal tells us the execution was successful, then we transition the tickets to a purchased state, save everything, and call it a success.

Developing PayPal Charges

There's a good chance you've been reading over the last few pages and thinking something along the lines of "That code is all well and good, but how do I make the PayPal callbacks work in my development environment so I can see if it even works?"

Good question.

The problem, as I alluded to earlier, is that we need to send PayPal a URL that PayPal can use to tell our site that the user has authenticated and approved the payment. If you are developing the site locally, then you probably are testing it via something like http://localhost:3000, which is not a URL you can pass to PayPal. You need something that's available on the open network that PayPal can see.

Generically, the solution to this problem is called "tunneling," and requires a known public server that acts as a go-between. We attach our localhost to that public server address, and then PayPal hits that public address, which invisibly tunnels the request to our local server and takes the response and passes it back along to PayPal.

Using Ngrok to Enable Developer Callbacks

There are several ways to manage tunneling. We're going to set it up using a tool called ngrok.[6] Ngrok will give us a publicly visible URL that will automatically tunnel to a port on our local development server.

We're using ngrok because it is free (though it has a paid plan) and simple for somebody who is not a networking expert. As proof I offer myself: I don't know beans about networking, and I got ngrok working relatively painlessly. On the

---

6.   https://ngrok.com

downside, ngrok is a cloud tool, so if passing your development environment through a cloud server is a problem, you might seek alternate solutions.

The first step to using ngrok is to obtain it on your computer. Download links for most common development platforms are available on the ngrok home page. Please note that if you are on a Mac and use homebrew, you must install ngrok using the command brew install homebrew/binary/ngrok2. This is because ngrok 2 is not fully open source, and is therefore not a regular part of homebrew.

Once installed, we invoke ngrok with a single command-line call containing the port we want to tunnel:

```
% ngrok http 3000
```

You'll want to do this before you start our Rails application.

The terminal will switch to a screen display that looks like the following figure (if you try this, yours will look slightly different because the ngrok URL is assigned randomly):

```
ngrok by @inconshreveable                                                    (Ctrl+C to quit)

Tunnel Status         online
Version               2.0.25/2.0.25
Region                United States (us)
Web Interface         http://127.0.0.1:4040
Forwarding            http://303c2da8.ngrok.io -> localhost:3000
Forwarding            https://303c2da8.ngrok.io -> localhost:3000

Connections           ttl     opn     rt1     rt5     p50     p90
                      0       0       0.00    0.00    0.00    0.00
```

What this screen means is that the public URL, http://303c2da8.ngrok.io, will be automatically tunneled to localhost:3000. Pressing ctrl-c from this status page will quit ngrok and sever the connection.

We can now take 303c2da8.ngrok.io and copy it to the host_name entry in the secrets.yml file. We need to do that manually because the ngrok URL will change each time (though automating that step would be nice).

Next we use our Rails program as normal, except that we can enter http://303c2da8.ngrok.io in our browser and it should just work. As we browse using the ngrok URL, you'll see a log of requests show up on the ngrok status screen. You can also use localhost:4040 to see a more detailed log in your browser.

Because we've made the ngrok address our host_name, that address is included in the callback URL we send to PayPal when we make a PayPal purchase. PayPal then uses that address to redirect back to our application, and you can therefore walk through an entire PayPal workflow in a typical developer environment.

Testing PayPal

Automated testing for PayPal payments splits into two parts:

1. Testing the initial call to PayPal, the one that gives us the redirect link. This is quite similar to testing any other third-party interaction, and we can test it with the VCR gem.

2. Testing the result of the callback from PayPal. This is, generally, a pain.

Testing the callback is tricky because, in general, automated testing works best if you can start from a consistent, known state. When testing a callback, though, it's not just our local development environment that has to be in a consistent known state, but also the PayPal server that's sending the callback. This is challenging, and ultimately leads to tests that are too brittle to be valuable.

As kind of the least bad option, we're going to adapt the strategies we've been using for all our third-party library interactions:

- Make the controller code that receives the callback very simple.

- Put most of the complex object in a workflow object that can be tested.

- To make up the difference, use test doubles like they're going out of style.

It's not perfect, but this pattern lets you test the internal logic of your code.

Here's what a PayPal workflow test looks like in practice:

paypal/01/spec/workflows/executes_pay_pal_payment_spec.rb
```ruby
require "rails_helper"

describe ExecutesPayPalPayment, :vcr, :aggregate_failures do

  describe "successful credit card purchase" do
    let!(:ticket_1) { instance_spy(
        Ticket, status: "pending", price: Money.new(1500), id: 1) }
    let!(:ticket_2) { instance_spy(
        Ticket, status: "pending", price: Money.new(1500), id: 2) }
    let!(:ticket_3) { instance_spy(Ticket, status: "unsold", id: 3) }
    let(:payment) { instance_spy(Payment, tickets: [ticket_1, ticket_2]) }
    let(:pay_pal_payment) { instance_spy(PayPalPayment, execute: true) }
    let(:user) { instance_double(
        User, id: 5, tickets_in_cart: [ticket_1, ticket_2]) }
    let(:workflow) { ExecutesPayPalPayment.new(
        payment_id: "PAYMENTID", token: "TOKEN", payer_id: "PAYER_ID") }

    before(:example) do
      allow(workflow).to receive(:find_payment).and_return(payment)
      allow(workflow).to receive(:pay_pal_payment).and_return(pay_pal_payment)
      workflow.run
    end
```

```ruby
  it "updates the ticket status" do
    expect(ticket_1).to have_received(:purchased!)
    expect(ticket_2).to have_received(:purchased!)
    expect(ticket_3).not_to have_received(:purchased!)
    expect(payment).to have_received(:succeeded!)
    expect(pay_pal_payment).to have_received(:execute)
    expect(workflow.success).to be_truthy
  end

  end

end
```

There's only one test with a lot of data needed to support it, which in general I don't love (it might be better not to have separate stubs for each ticket, for example). Anyway, we set up doubles for a payment with two tickets, a user, and the PayPalPayment wrapper object. We also have a real ExecutesPayPalPayment workflow object.

In our setup, we attach the workflow to the local payment object and the remote PayPal payment, so we avoid both the database and the third-party library lookup. In the test itself, we verify that the ticket objects that are part of the purchase have received the purchased! message. We expect the payment to receive a succeeded! call, the remote payment to receive execute, and the overall workflow to be successful.

This test is useful because it sets expectations for what happens when we execute a PayPal payment; it's pretty fast, since it has no third-party dependencies; and it should be reasonably stable. It also assumes, for example, that the PayPalPayment class is already tested.

Next Up

So far, we've seen how to make successful credit card charges via Stripe and successful charges via PayPal. We've been too successful. It's time to see what to do when things go wrong.

## CHAPTER 5

Failure Is Totally an Option

So far in the development of our web application we have been living in a happy world without error. A world where users never mistype long credit card numbers. A world where users never exceed credit limits. A world without fraud, server failures, or bugs.

In short, we have been living in a fantasy world. It's time to enter reality.

When it comes to the vast Murphy's Law universe of things that can go wrong with our application, we have a few goals:

- Validate client data entry before it goes to the API servers to prevent blatant data failures.

- Identify when something has gone wrong inside the code so that the code has a reasonable response.

- Notify administrators so the problem can be addressed.

- Present a graceful error message or response to the user.

- Make sure that data integrity is maintained even if the code fails in the middle of a transaction.

- Identify bad data where possible to indicate that something has gone quietly wrong.

For our Snow Globe Theater application, the cost of mishandling failure can manifest itself in many ways:

- Customers could get tickets without having their credit cards charged.

- Customers could get charged without actually getting tickets. (You really want to avoid this one, especially the version where the customer gets charged, doesn't get tickets, and you don't get notified.)

- Customers could get tickets and get charged, but our records become internally inconsistent.

In this chapter, we look at several ways to handle errors so that the result is graceful from a user's perspective while still making enough noise on the server side to alert us when something has gone wrong.

Client-Side Validation

Let's start with client-side validation, which means validating the credit card data users enter in the shopping cart on the way to making a purchase. Our responsibility on the client side is to prevent customers from sending invalid data to the Stripe API server, and in case of an error in the token API call, inform customers that their purchase has been stopped. In this case, invalid data could mean an invalid credit card number, an expiration date that is in the past, a bad CVC number, and so on.

Stripe maintains the jQuery.payment[1] plugin, which is a jQuery plugin that implements a number of credit card validation functions that we can tie to the form that we created in *Gathering Information*, on page 28. A nice feature of the jQuery.payment plugin is that it has no dependency on Stripe itself; we can use it to validate any credit card form.

There are a couple of things you should know about this code. Although Stripe considers it to have "served tremendously," they consider it feature-complete and will not be adding new functionality to it. Quite possibly it will eventually be replaced by something that is less jQuery based and more modern JavaScript.

Also, because the Ruby gems wrapping this library are also a little old, we're going to just take the raw distributed version of the file and copy it to our code base in vendor/assets/javascripts/jquery.payment.js.[2]

From there, we need to add it to the app/assets/javascripts/application.js manifest, which now looks like this:

```
failure/01/app/assets/javascripts/application.js
//= require jquery
//= require jquery_ujs
//= require bootstrap-sprockets
//= require jquery.payment
//= require turbolinks
//= require purchases_cart
//= require_tree .
```

---

1. https://github.com/stripe/jquery.payment
2. https://raw.githubusercontent.com/stripe/jquery.payment/master/lib/jquery.payment.js

To use the payment plugin, we need to beef up our credit card form's markup. Before, we just threw the form onto the page to quickly get some place to put data. Now, let's actually try to make it look like a partially decent Bootstrap form and put hooks in there that we can use in our ensuing JavaScript.

As shown here, I've pulled the credit card form from *Gathering Information*, on page 28 into its own partial template file, and I've updated the markup:

```
failure/01/app/views/shopping_carts/_credit_card_info.html.slim
h3 Payment Options

= form_tag(payments_path,
  class: "credit-card-form form-horizontal", id: "payment-form") do

  = hidden_field_tag(:purchase_amount_cents, @cart.total_cost.cents)
  = hidden_field_tag(:ticket_ids, @cart.tickets.map(&:id))

  .paypal
    img(src="https://www.paypal.com/en_US/i/logo/PayPal_mark_37x23.gif"
        align="left" style="margin-right:7px;")
    span(style="font-size:11px; font-family: Arial, Verdana")
      | The safer, easier way to pay.
    = radio_button_tag(:payment_type,
        :paypal, false,
        class: "payment-type-radio", id: "paypal_radio")
  .credit_card
    | Credit Card
    = radio_button_tag(:payment_type,
        :credit, true,
        class: "payment-type-radio", id: "credit_radio")

  .bg-danger#error-text

  #credit-card-info
    h3 Credit Card Info
    .row
      .form-group
        .col-sm-2
          = label_tag(:credit_card_number, "Credit Card Number",
            class: "control-label")
        .col-sm-3
          input.form-control.valid-field(data-stripe="number"
            id="credit_card_number")
        .col-sm-1
          = image_tag("creditcards/credit.png", id: "card-image")
    .row
      .form-group
        .col-sm-2
          = label_tag(:expiration_month, "Month", class: "control-label")
        .col-sm-2
          input.form-control.valid-field(placeholder="MM / YY"
            data-stripe="exp" id="expiration_date")
```

```
.row
  .form-group
    .col-sm-2
      = label_tag(:cvc, "CVC", class: "control-label")
    .col-sm-1
      input.form-control.valid-field(data-stripe="cvc" id="cvc")
.row
  .form-group
    .col-sm-3
      = submit_tag("Purchase Cart", class: "btn btn-default", id: "purchase")
```

The new changes have various degrees of importance in terms of processing:

- It is now a Bootstrap form-horizontal, and uses the bootstrap .form-group and grid classes (which all start with col-sm) to handle the arrangement of the fields in the browser. For more details about Bootstrap, see the docs.[3]

- DOM IDs were added to a bunch of the elements that the JavaScript code will use to identify them.

- All fields that will have a validity check now have a DOM class of valid-field.

- A space for a credit card image was added.

- The two text fields for the expiration month and year were changed to a single field, expecting the user to enter something like "12/15."

In my browser, the form now looks like this:

If you are reading this on a screen, notice that the words "Credit Card Number" are green, which is a result of the validation. Basically, what we're doing here is checking the validity of all three pieces of information and only enabling the "Purchase Cart" button if all three items are enabled.

---

3. http://getbootstrap.com/css

To make this happen, we create our PaymentFormHandler class, as before, but we add a new method to the constructor:

failure/01/app/assets/javascripts/purchases_cart.es6

```
constructor() {
  this.checkoutForm = new CheckoutForm()
  this.checkoutForm.format()
  this.initEventHandlers()
  this.initPaymentTypeHandler()
}
```

The new method on the CheckoutForm class, which is called format(), sets up the initial formatting of some of our fields, and also disables the payment button:

failure/01/app/assets/javascripts/purchases_cart.es6

```
format() {
  this.numberField().payment("formatCardNumber")
  this.expiryField().payment("formatCardExpiry")
  this.cvcField().payment("formatCardCVC")
  this.disableButton()
}
```

failure/01/app/assets/javascripts/purchases_cart.es6

```
form() { return $("#payment-form") }

validFields() { return this.form().find(".valid-field") }

numberField() { return this.form().find("#credit_card_number") }

expiryField() { return this.form().find("#expiration_date") }

cvcField() { return this.form().find("#cvc") }
```

We're using the payment method that comes from the jQuery.Payment plugin. The credit card number field, the expiration date field, and the CVC field, which all have trivial finder methods, have the payment method called on them with an argument that tells jQuery.Payment what kind of validation to use on that field. They return true or false based on whether the value of the field matches the validation.

The credit card number formatter limits the credit card field to digits, mandates a length of 16, and inserts a space after each four-digit group. The expiration date field automatically inserts the slash between the month and the date, limits the length, and requires the input to be digits. The CVC field similarly checks the length and limits the input digits.

Now back to the PaymentForm. In our initEventHandlers method, in addition to the submit event for the entire form, we add an event for keyup on any item with the class .valid-field, like this:

failure/01/app/assets/javascripts/purchases_cart.es6
```
initEventHandlers() {
  this.checkoutForm.form().submit(event => {
    if (!this.checkoutForm.isPayPal()) {
      this.handleSubmit(event)
    }
  })
  this.checkoutForm.validFields().keyup(() => {
    this.checkoutForm.displayStatus()
  })
}

initPaymentTypeHandler() {
  this.checkoutForm.paymentTypeRadio().click(() => {
    this.checkoutForm.setCreditCardVisibility()
  })
}
```

This event handler causes the form to check the validity of the credit card fields as a group whenever the customer types a key in any of the fields. This is probably more checks than necessary, but they are pretty fast.

Our event handler calls a displayStatus method on the CheckoutForm. Here's that method, along with all the smaller methods it calls:

failure/01/app/assets/javascripts/purchases_cart.es6
```
displayStatus() {
  this.displayFieldStatus(this.numberField(), this.isNumberValid())
  this.displayFieldStatus(this.expiryField(), this.isExpiryValid())
  this.displayFieldStatus(this.cvcField(), this.isCvcValid())
  this.cardImage().attr("src", this.imageUrl())
  this.buttonStatus()
}

displayFieldStatus(field, valid) {
  const parent = field.parents(".form-group")
  if (field.val() === "") {
    parent.removeClass("has-error")
    parent.removeClass("has-success")
  }
  parent.toggleClass("has-error", !valid)
  parent.toggleClass("has-success", valid)
}

isNumberValid() {
  return $.payment.validateCardNumber(this.numberField().val())
}

isExpiryValid() {
  const date = $.payment.cardExpiryVal(this.expiryField().val())
  return $.payment.validateCardExpiry(date.month, date.year)
}
```

```
isCvcValid() { return $.payment.validateCardCVC(this.cvcField().val()) }

cardImage() { return $("#card-image") }

imageUrl() { return `/assets/creditcards/${this.cardType()}.png` }

cardType() { return $.payment.cardType(this.numberField().val()) || "credit" }

buttonStatus() {
  return this.valid() ? this.enableButton() : this.disableButton()
}

valid() {
  return this.isNumberValid() && this.isExpiryValid() && this.isCvcValid()
}

button() { return this.form().find(".btn") }

disableButton() { this.button().toggleClass("disabled", true) }

enableButton() { this.button().toggleClass("disabled", false) }

isEnabled() { return !this.button().hasClass("disabled") }

isButtonDisabled() { return this.button().prop("disabled") }
```

We've got a helper method named displayFieldStatus, which is called once for each field being validated. It takes two arguments: the field object and a Boolean method for whether the field is valid. Those Boolean methods use jQuery.payment methods such as validateCardNumber, validateCardExpiry, and validateCardCVC. The validateCardNumber method checks the card number against the Luhn algorithm,[4] which is a common algorithm that used to verify that a credit card number is plausibly in use. (To be clear, the Luhn algorithm is not inherent to credit cards; it's just a convenient way to include a checksum as part of an account number that is used by credit card issuers.) The validateCardExpiry method validates that the dates are within ranges and are in the future, and the validateCardCVC validates the length of the CVC number.

In each case, we then adjust the DOM classes using the Bootstrap-provided has-error and has-success classes. If the field is empty, it has neither of the classes; otherwise it has the one that corresponds to whether the field is valid.

Once we've done that, we do something that's not strictly necessary but can be a nice little UI thing: we adjust the displayed image to match the type of card being used. We're using a set of images that is in the public domain via Shopify.[5] Ultimately we use the jQuery.payment method cardType, which determines the credit card type given the credit card number and defaults to the generic "credit" if the card type can't be determined. (In actual practice

---

4. https://en.wikipedia.org/wiki/Luhn_algorithm
5. https://www.shopify.com/blog/6335014-32-free-credit-card-icons

you might want to look to each card manufacturer for their branding rather than use the free icons.)

Finally we set the button status, which is to say that we enable the button if all three fields are valid (this.isNumberValid() && this.isExpiryValid() && this.isCvcValid()). If everything has gone right, this means we can only submit the form if all three credit card fields have useful data.

Because we're doing all this preprocessing, error handling when we do submit the form can be relatively simple:

```
failure/01/app/assets/javascripts/purchases_cart.es6
class TokenHandler {
  static handle(status, response) {
    new TokenHandler(status, response).handle()
  }

  constructor(status, response) {
    this.checkoutForm = new CheckoutForm()
    this.status = status
    this.response = response
  }

  isError() { return this.response.error }

  handle() {
    if (this.isError()) {
      this.checkoutForm.appendError(this.response.error.message)
      this.checkoutForm.enableButton()
    } else {
      this.checkoutForm.appendHidden("stripe_token", this.response.id)
      this.checkoutForm.submit()
    }
  }
}
```

The response we get from the Stripe API tells us if there is an error, so we check for that (this.response.error). If the response is an error, all we need to do is display the error somewhere on the screen, which we do by passing the response.error.message back to the checkoutForm. Then we reenable the button to give the customer a chance to change the data and try again.

Now, because we've done some work to prevent the form from loading unless the fields are all valid, it's actually kind of hard in my experience to simulate an error response. If the card is fraudulent or expired, Stripe will still return a token and will only fail the card when you try to use the token. (If we weren't doing all the validation in our UI, the Stripe.js library does basically the same set of validations before requesting the token.)

Server-Side Failure

We've got our token and we've sent our form to the server for the actual credit card charge. Now we have to deal with a wide array of things that can go wrong in the server request.

We're going to see some code suggestions for handling various kinds of problems that might come up, but it's important to realize that error handling is not a one-size-fits-all kind of proposition. The general principles are going to likely need some adaptation to the specific business logic of your application.

Very broadly, our purchase process has three steps:

- The pre-purchase checklist. We must make sure we have all the data we need, and that the data is valid and in the necessary format.

- The actual API call, which we need to make sure is successful.

- Our response to the API call, which typically involves saving the important parts of the response, some bookkeeping, and notifying the user of a successful outcome.

We have basically the same three steps for both the Stripe and PayPal versions of payment, though the post-purchase step for PayPal within our application is rather minor.

Our response to failure generally depends on what stage the failure happens:

- If the pre-purchase fails, we don't make the API call, possibly don't make any database changes, and return the user back to the credit card form to try again.

- If the API call fails, we usually undo some or all of the pre-flight data change, notify the user, and typically also return the user back to the credit card form.

- If the payment goes through but the code fails after...ugh. This is a bad case. You want to make sure this error is captured and a notification is sent, because there may be some administrative cleanup in your future. In some cases you might need to automatically refund the payment.

When trying to mitigate failure or surprise outcomes, it's often more fruitful to focus on how a problem might manifest itself rather than how it might be caused. In other words, for the purposes of our purchasing workflow, we might check to see whether the amount the user approved is still the amount we calculate as the charge. There might be a lot of reasons why the charge might be miscalculated, and when we try to diagnose a specific problem we'll need to track down the reasons. But when we're just trying to respond, we want to focus on the unexpected state itself, rather than how we got there.

The world is large and complex, and you'll find your application in states you wouldn't have believed possible. Sometimes, it's cheaper to detect and mitigate the problem rather than diagnose and fix it. This can often be the case with intermittent problems that have obvious footprints and unclear causes.

Preventing Pre-Purchase Failure

In the pre-purchase section of our code, we're concerned with making sure that the data coming from the user is valid and can be transmogrified into our initial purchase data.

Our PurchasesCart workflow, as it currently stands, performs the following actions pre-flight, either of which could potentially fail:

- It identifies the tickets in the customer's cart and changes their status to either purchased or pending depending on the type of concrete workflow. It's possible that the list of tickets in the cart has changed from when the user submitted the form, due to administrative action, automated removal of shopping carts, or general chicanery. Similarly, the calculated purchase price might be different from what users think they approved.

- It creates a purchase instance and a set of purchase line items that are saved to the database. This could fail due to a database problem, or we could have a validation on the purchase object that fails for some reason.

The list for your application will differ. No matter what happens, we need to respond appropriately to the customer and make sure our data stays clear.

Which leads me to a brief digression on validations. In a Rails application, you can validate data at several points. The validation can happen in the database layer, either covered by a schema migration (such as null: true), or actually defined in the database itself. You can use ActiveRecord validations to specify features that must be true about the data and that are automatically checked in order to allow it to be saved. Or you can have more ad hoc checks for the coherence of your data that you call manually.

For better or for worse, the design of Rails tends to discourage placing this kind of intelligence at the database level, preferring to have all the data validations defined explicitly in the code base—though Rails 5 does put more foreign key checks at the database level. I'm fine with that (although your DB admin may not be), but if you have other users or non-Rails applications accessing your database, you'll need to be careful.

I also tend to have a somewhat high bar for the use of ActiveRecord validations for both the generic ActiveRecord uses like validating the presence of data, and for more app-specific business logic cases. In my experience it's relatively easy to overconstrain data with validations, leading to problems when your code comes into contact with real-world messiness, or when you need to create weird objects for testing purposes.

My rule of thumb is that, in order to use an ActiveRecord validation, the data violation involved must be so important that it's worth raising an exception and potentially stopping execution rather than having the bad data in the database. For example, when creating a new user, we need an email address and we need that address to be unique. Failure to have a unique address would make it impossible for the user to log in, so that's a validation worth having. On the other hand, requiring a user's last name to be at least two characters long (which is a validation that some sites rather stupidly enforce) is both not that important and likely to infuriate a user whose last name is rejected, so I would be reluctant to use ActiveRecord to enforce that constraint.

In practice, this means that I'm unlikely to actually put ActiveRecord validations on the Purchase and PurchaseLineItem classes, since a failure to save those due to a validation failure would potentially raise an exception and block a purchase, potentially a purchase that has already been charged. Instead, we'll check for data anomalies inside the workflow.

Here's how that looks in our code for the PurchasesCart workflow. We've structured the code a bit to make error handling easier, with the note that we may not have enough logic in all the steps to make this structure completely necessary at the moment. One nice feature for us is that the use of an abstract parent class means that both the PayPal and Stripe workflows can take advantage of these improvements.

We set up the class almost as before, but make the run method more abstract:

failure/01/app/workflows/purchases_cart.rb
```ruby
class PurchasesCart

  attr_accessor :user, :purchase_amount_cents,
      :purchase_amount, :success,
      :payment, :expected_ticket_ids

  def initialize(user: nil, purchase_amount_cents: nil, expected_ticket_ids: "")
    @user = user
    @purchase_amount = Money.new(purchase_amount_cents)
    @success = false
    @continue = true
    @expected_ticket_ids = expected_ticket_ids.split(" ").map(&:to_i).sort
  end
```

```ruby
def run
  Payment.transaction do
    pre_purchase
    purchase
    post_purchase
    @success = @continue
  end
rescue ActiveRecord::ActiveRecordError => e
  Rails.logger.error("ACTIVE RECORD ERROR IN TRANSACTION")
  Rails.logger.error(e)
end
```

Our initialization is mostly the same, except that we're taking in a list of expected ticket IDs and expected price from the form, all in the name of validating that we are charging customers for the goods they expect. We've also added a @continue instance variable set to true. This acts as a brake—if any validation fails, we set @continue to false, and all the life-cycle methods know not to proceed.

We've explicitly changed the run method to be just made up of our three life-cycle methods—pre_purchase, charge, and post_purchase—and at the end of it all we measure @success based on whether we have the @continue value remain true through the entire process. If there's an error inside the transaction, Rails raises the error again after rolling back the transaction. In this case, we catch ActiveRecord errors just so that the failure is passed back to the controller and the user gets a failure screen rather than a 500 error. Your application behavior may be different here.

Our pre_purchase method now does some validation, and then creates our ticket and payment objects:

`failure/01/app/workflows/purchases_cart.rb`
```ruby
def pre_purchase_valid?
  purchase_amount == tickets.map(&:price).sum &&
      expected_ticket_ids == tickets.map(&:id).sort
end

def tickets
  @tickets ||= @user.tickets_in_cart
end

def pre_purchase
  unless pre_purchase_valid?
    @continue = false
    return
  end
  update_tickets
  create_payment
  @continue = true
end
```

```ruby
def redirect_on_success_url
  nil
end

def create_payment
  self.payment = Payment.create!(payment_attributes)
  payment.create_line_items(tickets)
end
```

The actual pre_purchase method checks for input validity first. As mentioned, we check that the purchase amount coming from the user input matches our calculated price (currently tickets.map(&:price), but I'd expect that to get more complex in a real system). We also check the list of ticket IDs, which comes from the form as a string, like "10 2 3", and which we convert into an array of integers, [10, 2, 3]. (If you don't like the idea of having an obviously named field in the user-facing form, you could also encode the price and integers using a hash function or something similar.) You also could validate the existence of the token here, but the charge will do that automatically.

If the validation fails, we bounce right out of the pre-charge check, setting the @continue variable to false for good measure. If the validation succeeds, we do the same tasks we did before: set the ticket status to purchased or pending and create the purchase object. We protect against the event of the database save failing (which is unlikely because neither the Ticket nor the Purchase class has much in the way of validations, so it would have to be a genuine database failure) by using create! and save!, which will trigger exceptions and rollbacks on error. Depending on how we might want to handle other errors, we could also use a rescue clause to set @continue = false. Normally, I like my exceptions to be loud and bubble up, but I can see in some cases wanting to handle exceptions in-house, as it were.

Preventing API Call Failures

After the pre-purchase activities are complete, we move to the actual purchase:

failure/01/app/workflows/purchases_cart_via_stripe.rb
```ruby
def purchase
  return unless @continue
  @stripe_charge = StripeCharge.new(token: stripe_token, payment: payment)
  @stripe_charge.charge
  payment.update!(@stripe_charge.payment_attributes)
  reverse_purchase if payment.failed?
end

def payment_attributes
  super.merge(payment_method: "stripe")
end
```

We now have a guard clause, which prevents us from charging forward if @continue has been toggled.

We also have a few things that change if the purchase actually fails. The StripeCharge#charge method, which we will see in a moment, has adjusted slightly to catch exceptions from the Stripe API, and be able to report on its error status. We've also moved the actual creation of the attributes to be added to the purchase to the payment_attributes method of StripeCharge, on the object-oriented design grounds that it's the StripeCharge instance that knows what its attributes are.

Finally, if the purchase fails, we call a reverse_purchase method. You need to think carefully about what behavior you want if the charge fails. In many cases, it's good enough to have the entire workflow in a database transaction that you just roll back, leaving the database untouched.

For better or worse, we're trying a slightly different tactic here. I've decided that I want to hold on to the failed purchase on the grounds that when the customer complains, I'd like to be able to see evidence that his or her error existed. So we actually don't want to roll back the database in this case—though again, there are many, many cases where that's the preferable choice. We want to keep the new purchase object, but we do need to reverse the ticket objects, which we do in the unpurchase_tickets method. Because the database reversal is not automatic, I'm taking it upon myself to make sure that any further changes to the database that might happen as this logic is made more complicated are also reversed. We also set @continue to false in the reverse_purchase method of the failure case so that the post-charge actions don't happen.

Here are the changes to the error handling behavior of the StripeCharge class:

```
failure/01/app/models/stripe_charge.rb
def charge
  return if response.present?
  @response = Stripe::Charge.create(
      {amount: payment.price.cents, currency: "usd",
       source: token.id, description: "",
       metadata: {reference: payment.reference}},
      idempotency_key: payment.reference)
rescue Stripe::StripeError => e
  @response = nil
  @error = e
end

def success?
  response || !error
end
```

```
def payment_attributes
  success? ? success_attributes : failure_attributes
end

def success_attributes
  {status: response.status,
    response_id: response.id, full_response: response.to_json}
end

def failure_attributes
  {status: :failed, full_response: error.to_json}
end
```

The charge method now rescues a Stripe::StripeError exception, which is the parent class for all errors returned by the Stripe gem, including expired card, mismatch between number and CVC code, insufficient credit, and the like.

In the case of an exception, we hold on to the error object, and then pass it back as part of the attributes to be stored in the purchase in the failure_attributes method. This means that we store the error response in the purchase and give the purchase a status of failed. We can search for the purchase if the customer requests it.

Our post-charge is really simple right now. All we do is check to see if the payment succeeded:

failure/01/app/workflows/purchases_cart.rb
```
def calculate_success
  payment.succeeded?
end

def post_purchase
  return unless @continue
  @continue = calculate_success
end
```

Eventually we'll want to notify the customer, and there may be other data reporting activities that happen after the purchase is in place. Failure at this point is difficult to manage, so one way to deal with it is to do as little as possible after the card is charged.

Preventing PayPal Callback Failures

In addition to the pre-purchase failure conditions that are common to Stripe and PayPal, the PayPal callback has a few possible failures that are unique to that workflow. The failure modes that we need to look out for include

- PayPal may never return to the callback, leaving the payment unfinished. (Alternately, I suppose, it might double-call the callback, though given the structure of the code, that's much less of a problem.)

- We might have a failure retrieving the PayPal record after the callback.

- We might have a failure executing the PayPal payment (which the code as we left it in the last chapter actually already handles).

The PayPal execution is easier in one way that the Stripe call: the ExecutesPayPalPayment workflow is only evoked if the first half of the payment is successful. This makes our code a little bit less complex because we can assume that if we get the callback, then the first part of our transaction has gone right.

It's also worth noting that since the caller of the execute PayPal workflow is PayPal, we have a slightly different burden to display error messages. For example, consider the PayPal::SDK::REST::Payment.find(payment_id) method we call to retrieve the payment data from the PayPal API. As far as our application is concerned, that method will either return a PayPal payment object or throw an exception. It seems fine for us to just raise the exception and send that back to PayPal.

As for the other failures, let's take a look at an updated version of our ExecutesPayPalPayment workflow object:

`failure/01/app/workflows/executes_pay_pal_payment.rb`
```ruby
class ExecutesPayPalPayment

  attr_accessor :payment_id, :token, :payer_id, :payment, :success

  def initialize(payment_id:, token:, payer_id:)
    @payment_id = payment_id
    @token = token
    @payer_id = payer_id
    @success = false
    @continue = true
  end

  def payment
    @payment ||= Payment.find_by(
        payment_method: "paypal", response_id: payment_id)
  end

  def pay_pal_payment
    @pay_pal_payment ||= PayPalPayment.find(payment_id)
  end

  def run
    Payment.transaction do
      pre_purchase
      purchase
      post_purchase
    end
  end
end
```

```ruby
def pre_purchase
  @continue = pay_pal_payment.valid?
end

def purchase
  return unless @continue
  @continue = pay_pal_payment.execute(payer_id: payer_id)
end

def post_purchase
  if @continue
    payment.tickets.each(&:purchased!)
    payment.succeeded!
    self.success = true
  else
    payment.tickets.each(&:waiting!)
    payment.failed!
  end
end

end
```

We've added a @continue instance variable that will work the same way as we used it in the Stripe workflow. We've also restructured the run method into pre_purchase, purchase, and post_purchase; again, this should seem familiar, though we're perhaps stretching the definition of "purchase."

In the pre_purchase method we want to check once again that the purchase being requested by PayPal matches the purchase we think is being requested in our database. Our existing PayPalPurchase object already has both the internal PayPal object and our application's purchase object, so it makes sense to put the matching logic in that class:

`failure/01/app/models/pay_pal_payment.rb`
```ruby
def pay_pal_transaction
  pay_pal_payment.transactions.first
end

def pay_pal_amount
  Money.new(pay_pal_transaction.amount.total.to_f * 100)
end

def price_valid?
  pay_pal_amount == payment.price
end

def pay_pal_ticket_ids
  line_item_ids = pay_pal_transaction.items.map(&:name).map(&:to_i)
  line_items = line_item_ids.map { |id| PurchaseLineItem.find(id) }
  line_items.flat_map(&:tickets).map(&:id).sort
end
```

```
def item_valid?
  payment.sorted_ticket_ids == pay_pal_ticket_ids
end

def valid?
  price_valid? && item_valid?
end
```

When we sent the original purchase to PayPal, we included the price and line_item IDs as part of the API call. We have somewhat convoluted methods called pay_pal_amount, and pay_pal_ticket_ids to extract the information we need from the PayPal object and compare it, in the valid? method, to our Payment object.

Back in the workflow object, the purchase method does the PayPal execute as before, and uses the result to populate @continue.

Finally, the post_purchase method checks to see if all systems are a go using the @continue value. If so, we set all the ticket statuses to purchased and the payment status to succeeded. If not, we return each ticket back to the cart, and mark the payment as failed.

These additions to our PayPal execution protect us from some PayPal-specific failure modes. Later in *Notification*, on page 112, we'll add some notifications to make sure that we find out if these hopefully rare events happen.

Testing for Failure

Automated tests for failure cases are a good way to evaluate the quality of your code structure. In a well-factored program, it should be relatively easy to simulate failure states with a nicely placed test double.

In general, you should test failure states using test doubles and focus tests at the workflow or model level, and not test failure states using end-to-end Capybara tests. End-to-end tests are slow and not great at pinpointing the location of problems. As a result, end-to-end tests may not be much use when dealing with most failure conditions.

Stripe, like most payment gateways, provides dummy credit card numbers that simulate various cases.[6] We've seen 4242 4242 4242 4242, which simulates a successful Visa card, but there are a number of other fake numbers, including 4000 0000 0000 0002, which simulates a declined credit card. Between these credit card numbers and using different inputs and test doubles, we can deal with most failure conditions.

---

6.   https://stripe.com/docs/testing

We can use the automatic failure code in a test that's very similar to our passing tests for PurchasesCart:

failure/01/spec/workflows/purchases_cart_via_stripe_spec.rb

```
describe "an unsuccessful credit card purchase" do
  let(:token) { StripeToken.new(
      credit_card_number: "4000000000000002", expiration_month: "12",
      expiration_year: Time.zone.now.year + 1, cvc: "123") }

  before(:example) do
    allow(Payment).to receive(:create!).with(attributes).and_return(payment)
    allow(payment).to receive(:update!).with(
        status: :failed, full_response: a_truthy_value)
    expect(payment).to receive(:create_line_items).with([ticket_1, ticket_2])
    expect(payment).to receive(:failed?).and_return(true)
    workflow.run
  end

  it "updates the ticket status" do
    expect(ticket_1).to have_received(:purchased!)
    expect(ticket_2).to have_received(:purchased!)
    expect(ticket_3).not_to have_received(:purchased!)
    expect(ticket_1).to have_received(:waiting!)
    expect(ticket_2).to have_received(:waiting!)
    expect(ticket_3).not_to have_received(:waiting!)
  end

end
```

The key part here is the setup, where we build a token using the failed credit card number. Our ticket status spec expects the tickets to have received both the purchase method in the pre-check, and then the return_to_cart method in the reversal after the credit card fails. We're also checking that the purchase status is now failed, that the response contains the Stripe error object, and that the overall job shows that success is false.

We can simulate a database failure by stubbing the create method to raise an ActiveRecord exception.

failure/01/spec/workflows/purchases_cart_via_stripe_spec.rb

```
describe "database failure" do
  it "does not trigger payment if the database fails" do
    expect(StripeCharge).to receive(:new).never
    allow(Payment).to receive(:create!).and_raise(
        ActiveRecord::RecordInvalid)
    workflow.run
    expect(workflow.success).to be_falsy
  end
end
```

This test validates that the StripeCharge object is never created if the database fails. If you want to simulate a failure on the second save, then you change the double definition to allow(purchase).to receive(:update!).and_raise.

Now that we've got a sense of how to manage potential failures via automated tests, let's talk about another way to limit the damage that failures can do: running the transaction as a background job.

Running a Background Job

All of our failure mitigation so far has one limiting factor: the time needed to respond to a web request. As the application currently stands, we're making our Stripe API call inside our user's HTTP request, which is slow. If the Stripe API gave us a temporary error, our best response would be to retry the request in a few moments, but we can't necessarily do that in the space of a typical web request.

Moving our payment processing to a background job, however, allows us to get some response back to the user more quickly, as well as gives us more leeway for robust error handling. Using a background job also makes it easier to integrate other tasks, such as sending a receipt back to the user or integrating with reporting tools.

Using Rails ActiveJob

We're going to use Rails ActiveJob, which was added in Rails 4.2, to handle the logistics of background processing. (A blog post by David Copeland[7] was helpful in putting together this section.) ActiveJob is a Rails front end that can be used via an adapter to feed into several background job tools, including Delayed Job, Resque, Sidekiq, and Sucker Punch. When we write the code to conform to ActiveJob's interface, the background job gem provides an adapter. If we decide to move to a more powerful tool, we can with minimal code change because both tools should work with the ActiveJob front end.

We're going to use Delayed Job[8] for this because it's easy to set up. Let's add it to the Gemfile:

```
gem "delayed_job_active_record"
```

And then run two commands from the command line:

```
% rails generate delayed_job:active_record
% rake db:migrate
```

---

7. http://www.sitepoint.com/dont-get-activejob
8. https://github.com/collectiveidea/delayed_job

The generator creates a database migration and a file bin/delayed_job that we can use to run background jobs. Delayed Job has a very simple execution model. It stores background jobs as basically serialized Ruby bindings inside the same database we use for the rest of our application. When we run the worker, it looks at the database, picks up jobs, and executes them. It may not be the best choice for a very large application because it depends on the same database as the application, which means if the database is being overwhelmed, so are the background jobs.

We tell Rails we're using Delayed Job as our ActiveJob back end by adding a line to the application.rb file:

```
config.active_job.queue_adapter = :delayed_job
```

And we're ready to get started.

Let's create our first job:

```
rails generate job purchases_cart
```

This creates two files: app/jobs/purchases_cart_job.rb, which is our job, and spec/jobs/purchases_cart_job_spec.rb, which is our related test file.

You might be asking why we need a new purchases_cart_job when we already have a perfectly good isolated PurchasesCart workflow object. This is an exceptionally good question, and the answer, for me, has to do with how ActiveJob works.

An ActiveJob class has the following characteristics:

- A class that inherits from ActiveJob::Base
- A method called perform that, well, performs the job

There are two limitations to ActiveJob that make just moving our existing code inside ActiveJob seem less than ideal to me.

First, when you invoke ActiveJob, the perform method is just executed. You don't get a fresh instance of the ActiveJob class, and therefore, creating a complex set of states with instance variables seems out of the question.

Second, while the perform method can take an arbitrary number of parameters, those parameters all need to be serializable by ActiveJob, which means they need to be instances of BigNum, FalseClass, Fixnum, Float, NilClass, String, or TrueClass. Or they can be an instance of a class that includes the Rails GlobalId mixin, which ActiveRecord does, and which can be included by any class that implements def self.find(id). You can also include an array or hash made up of the same set (hash keys need to be a string or a symbol).

The lack of instance variables makes just copying our code over problematic. And because our StripeToken class does not implement the GlobalId mixin (and would be unable to do so without calling back to the Stripe API for its find method), just creating our PurchasesCart workflow in the controller and passing it to the job doesn't work either. Instead, we need to pass the request parameters to the ActiveJob and do all the creation of our business logic objects there.

On the plus side, this simplifies our controller (there are some associated view changes that you can see in the code repo):

failure/02/app/controllers/payments_controller.rb

```ruby
class PaymentsController < ApplicationController
  def show
    @reference = params[:id]
    @payment = Payment.find_by(reference: @reference)
  end

  def create
    workflow = run_workflow(params[:payment_type])
    if workflow.success
      redirect_to workflow.redirect_on_success_url ||
          payment_path(id: @reference || workflow.payment.reference)
    else
      redirect_to shopping_cart_path
    end
  end

  private def run_workflow(payment_type)
    case payment_type
    when "paypal" then paypal_workflow
    else
      stripe_workflow
    end
  end

  private def paypal_workflow
    workflow = PurchasesCartViaPayPal.new(
        user: current_user,
        purchase_amount_cents: params[:purchase_amount_cents],
        expected_ticket_ids: params[:ticket_ids])
    workflow.run
    workflow
  end

  private def stripe_workflow
    @reference = Payment.generate_reference
    PurchasesCartJob.perform_later(
        user: current_user,
        params: card_params,
        purchase_amount_cents: params[:purchase_amount_cents],
        expected_ticket_ids: params[:ticket_ids],
```

```
        payment_reference: @reference)
    end

    private def card_params
      params.permit(
          :credit_card_number, :expiration_month,
          :expiration_year, :cvc,
          :stripe_token).to_h.symbolize_keys
    end

end
```

Basically, we just pass all the incoming parameters, along with the current user, over to the job method, which we invoke using perform_later. This causes ActiveJob to enqueue the job into Delayed Job (or whatever our back end happens to be). Our parameters—a User, a parameter hash, and the payment reference—are all serializable by ActiveJob, so we're good.

We have two other related changes in this version of the controller. We generate the Payment reference before the job and pass it to the job (before, we generated it as part of the workflow when the Payment instance was created), and the PurchasesCartJob, as we will see in a moment, hardwires that it is successful, so it will always redirect based on the new payment reference. We don't change our response based on the success or failure of the job because we can't. The job is headed off into the background queue, so we won't know whether or not it succeeds by the time we need to respond to the request.

We could just send the user to a generic URL that says something like "Thanks for ordering, you'll be getting a receipt shortly," but because we already have the capability to generate a unique ID before the purchase is actually created, we can do something better. We generate the reference before the job starts, passing the reference through to eventually be saved with the purchase. This gives the customer a permanent URL that will eventually have his or her order information. And it also gives us the opportunity to do something fancier on the client side should we choose, such as poll or open up a web socket so that the order information can be displayed as soon as it hits the database.

Using Our Background Job

The PurchasesCartJob itself is just the logic to create the PurchaseJob workflow. Almost all of this is taken directly from the original PurchaseController:

`failure/02/app/jobs/purchases_cart_job.rb`
```
class PurchasesCartJob < ApplicationJob

  queue_as :default

  def perform(user:, purchase_amount_cents:, expected_ticket_ids:,
```

```
      payment_reference:, params:)
    token = StripeToken.new(**card_params(params))
    user.tickets_in_cart.each do |ticket|
      ticket.update(payment_reference: payment_reference)
    end
    purchases_cart_workflow = StripePurchasesCart.new(
        user: user, stripe_token: token,
        purchase_amount_cents: purchase_amount_cents,
        expected_ticket_ids: expected_ticket_ids,
        payment_reference: payment_reference)
    purchases_cart_workflow.run
  end

  def success
    true
  end

  def redirect_on_success_url
    nil
  end

  private def card_params(params)
    params.slice(
        :credit_card_number, :expiration_month,
        :expiration_year, :cvc,
        :stripe_token).symbolize_keys
  end

end
```

The only substantive changes involve the purchase reference. We're taking the purchase reference and passing it along to the workflow, as you might expect. We're also attaching the purchase reference to the tickets still in the shopping cart, which is new (there's an associated database migration to add the payment_reference field to the ticket).

We need to add the payment reference to the ticket so that we can track the ticket through the payment process, and doing so is particularly important now that we are processing the transaction in the background. We no longer really know how much time has passed between the customer submitting the form and the card being processed. In particular, the customer may have legitimately added more items to a new shopping cart in the interim. Under the previous code, doing so would prevent the first purchase from happening because the pre-flight check would see a discrepancy between the total cost presented to the user on the form, and the total cost of the combined purchases that the workflow would find when querying the database. By tagging inventory that is already in the process of being charged, we can prevent this kind of double charging.

Handling Workflow Changes

Our PurchasesCart workflow has to change a little bit, owing to the nature of how background jobs work. If our workflow, now running in the background, throws an exception and does not handle that exception, then the job is sent back to the queue. Typically that means the job will be reexecuted, although the specific behavior is dependent on the back end. By default, Delayed Job will reexecute failures 25 times, with an exponentially increasing wait time in between.

That's great for us because many of the exceptions that we don't handle are going to be due to things like API errors on the Stripe side that might be temporary and would clear if the job is run later. However, our PurchasesCart code has been operating under the implicit assumption that it's never been executed before, and as currently written, rerunning the job with the same incoming data will cause some problems. Specifically, the workflow will create a duplicate Payment record pointing back to the same tickets, and may also try to charge the Stripe API a second time. Stripe's idempotency protection probably prevents it from actually charging, but it seems worth trying to avoid a second call on our end, to be safe.

We need to look at all of our interactions with our database and third-party libraries to make sure they still behave reasonably if they have already been executed before.

In our case, we need to

- Check for validity between the incoming form ticket purchase and the calculated price. If the purchase has already been created, we *probably* don't need to recheck this. But we need to protect against the possibility that the user has added later tickets to the cart since the job started.

- Purchase the tickets before the charge by changing their status. Given our data model, running that again is fine; we'd just be setting the status to a value it already has. Other data models might be less forgiving here.

We don't want to create another purchase or purchase line items if a purchase has already been created, and we don't want to send the charge information to Stripe if we've already done so.

Looking at this from the other direction, we might want to create an exception in certain cases to force a new attempt in the future. Specifically, a database failure on save has a chance of being due to a temporary condition, so triggering an exception here is still useful.

With that, the code doesn't change a whole lot. Our initializer changes slightly to allow the purchase_reference to be passed in:

```
failure/02/app/workflows/purchases_cart.rb
class PurchasesCart

  attr_accessor :user, :purchase_amount_cents,
    :purchase_amount, :success,
    :payment, :expected_ticket_ids,
    :payment_reference

  def initialize(user: nil, purchase_amount_cents: nil,
    expected_ticket_ids: "", payment_reference: nil)
    @user = user
    @purchase_amount = Money.new(purchase_amount_cents)
    @success = false
    @continue = true
    @expected_ticket_ids = expected_ticket_ids.split(" ").map(&:to_i).sort
    @payment_reference = payment_reference || Payment.generate_reference
  end

  def run
    Payment.transaction do
      pre_purchase
      purchase
      post_purchase
      @success = @continue
    end
  end
```

We can then use that reference to see if there's an existing purchase. If there is, we don't need to do any pre-purchase, so we just kick out of the method with a guard clause. Also, we now use the purchase reference to filter the list of tickets in the cart to prevent against a second purchase being in flight from the same user. We also no longer catch errors in the run method, since we now want the error to not be caught so that the job can be rerun (with a slight change to the database failure spec).

```
failure/02/app/workflows/purchases_cart.rb
def tickets
  @tickets ||= @user.tickets_in_cart.select do |ticket|
    ticket.payment_reference == payment_reference
  end
end

def existing_payment
  Payment.find_by(reference: payment_reference)
end

def pre_purchase
  return true if existing_payment
  unless pre_purchase_valid?
```

```
    @continue = false
    return
  end
  update_tickets
  create_payment
  @continue = true
end
```

Completely skipping out the pre-charge is only one choice. In some cases, for example, it might make sense to redo the validation step even if the purchase has already changed if there's reason to believe that an outside factor might have affected validity.

If we decide to pass through the method even if there is an existing purchase, we need to change the create_payment method to be aware of the existing purchase:

failure/02/app/workflows/purchases_cart.rb
```
def create_payment
  self.payment = existing_payment || Payment.new
  payment.update!(payment_attributes)
  payment.create_line_items(tickets)
end
```

All we're doing here is trying to reset the existing purchase to the state it would be in if it had been newly created, most likely changing the status. This might be a little simplistic as our business logic gets more involved. As we currently have this structured, a failed save will raise an exception that will cause the job to be rerun.

Finally, we don't need to charge if we've already got a successful response, as evidenced by the response_id being set in the purchase—this change goes in the Stripe workflow subclass:

failure/02/app/workflows/purchases_cart_via_stripe.rb
```
def purchase
  return unless @continue
  return if payment.response_id.present?
  @stripe_charge = StripeCharge.new(token: stripe_token, payment: payment)
  @stripe_charge.charge
  payment.update!(@stripe_charge.payment_attributes)
  reverse_purchase if payment.failed?
end
```

Now if we run our credit card form in development, we can see that a new row is created in the delayed_jobs table, and when we run the delayed_job task, it gets evaluated, making the API call and charging the user.

Running Multiple Background Jobs

We're doing a lot of checking of existing state in the workflow as it now stands, and it's starting to feel a little fragile to me. If you are following along with the code and the tests in the sample code, you can see that the Stripe tests take a lot of setup, and there's a clear argument that they are too dependent on the internals of Payment. There are a few ways to mitigate that problem.

One way to reduce the amount of internal state is to split the Stripe background job into separate "prepare" and "purchase" jobs, where the purchase job is only created if the prepare job passes. The split already somewhat exists in our code, in that the Stripe job already has pre-purchase and purchase phases. At the end of this, we'll wind up with an abstract payment prepare with concrete versions for Stripe and PayPal, and Stripe and PayPal will each have their own separate purchase job.

Creating multiple jobs clears a lot of the error checking and status checking out of the code (particularly in the later jobs), because we can now assert that previous jobs have been successful; otherwise the current job wouldn't have been created at all. So, many of the @continue markers we've been using in the code will go away.

So, we have the PurchasesController call a PreparesCartForStripeJob, which in turn invokes a PreparesCartForStripe workflow. The job is unchanged except for the name of the workflow being invoked. The new workflow has the logic that we were calling pre_purchase, but with a few small changes:

```
failure/03/app/workflows/prepares_cart.rb
class PreparesCart

  attr_accessor :user, :purchase_amount_cents,
      :purchase_amount, :success,
      :payment, :expected_ticket_ids,
      :payment_reference

  def initialize(user: nil, purchase_amount_cents: nil,
      expected_ticket_ids: "", payment_reference: nil)
    @user = user
    @purchase_amount = Money.new(purchase_amount_cents)
    @success = false
    @continue = true
    @expected_ticket_ids = expected_ticket_ids.split(" ").map(&:to_i).sort
    @payment_reference = payment_reference || Payment.generate_reference
  end

  def pre_purchase_valid?
    purchase_amount == tickets.map(&:price).sum &&
        expected_ticket_ids == tickets.map(&:id).sort
  end
```

```ruby
  def tickets
    @tickets ||= @user.tickets_in_cart.select do |ticket|
      ticket.payment_reference == payment_reference
    end
  end

  def existing_payment
    Payment.find_by(reference: payment_reference)
  end

  def run
    Payment.transaction do
      return if existing_payment
      return unless pre_purchase_valid?
      update_tickets
      create_payment
      success? ? on_success : on_failure
    end
  end

  def redirect_on_success_url
    nil
  end

  def create_payment
    self.payment = existing_payment || Payment.new
    payment.update!(payment_attributes)
    payment.create_line_items(tickets)
    @success = payment.valid?
  end

  def payment_attributes
    {user_id: user.id, price_cents: purchase_amount.cents,
     status: "created", reference: Payment.generate_reference}
  end

  def success?
    success
  end

  def unpurchase_tickets
    tickets.each(&:waiting!)
  end

end
```

And we have some changes to the Stripe-specific part:

failure/03/app/workflows/prepares_cart_for_stripe.rb

```ruby
class PreparesCartForStripe < PreparesCart

  attr_accessor :stripe_token, :stripe_charge

  def initialize(user:, stripe_token:, purchase_amount_cents:,
      expected_ticket_ids:, payment_reference: nil)
```

```ruby
    super(user: user, purchase_amount_cents: purchase_amount_cents,
          expected_ticket_ids: expected_ticket_ids,
          payment_reference: payment_reference)
    @stripe_token = stripe_token
  end

  def update_tickets
    tickets.each(&:purchased!)
  end

  def on_success
    ExecutesStripePurchaseJob.perform_later(payment, stripe_token.id)
  end

  def unpurchase_tickets
    tickets.each(&:waiting!)
  end

  def purchase_attributes
    super.merge(payment_method: "stripe")
  end

end
```

The initializer is the same. We still need all the same inputs to create the purchase. The main difference is that as soon as this workflow creates the purchase, it's done.

Our run method now covers what was done in the original pre_purchase method. We have one genuinely exceptional condition: the purchase object might already exist. My idea here, which may be oversimplified, is that if the purchase already exists, then this job is being called incorrectly and it should just end. You probably want to include a notification to the administrators, or log the failure to a file of failed purchase attempts or send the failure to a notification aggregator like Rollbar. Similarly, we end the workflow if our validity check of the expected charge and items fails. (And similarly, we probably want to tell the user in that case.)

We then create the payment instance and save it, and throw an exception if the save fails. If it succeeds, we wind up in the on_success method, defined concretely in the PreparesCartForStripe class, and we add the actual charge job to the queue. Right now, failure via a database exception causes the setup job to be automatically re-queued; we might also want some other logic to happen at some point.

The change in the run method of the PreparesCart class requires a slight change in the PayPal version as well, changing the name of the purchase method to on_success to make sure it's called.

The new ActiveJob is pretty simple:

`failure/03/app/jobs/executes_stripe_purchase_job.rb`
```ruby
class ExecutesStripePurchaseJob < ActiveJob::Base

  queue_as :default

  def perform(payment, stripe_token)
    charge_action = ExecutesStripePurchase.new(payment, stripe_token)
    charge_action.run
  end

end
```

And the workflow takes the purchase and performs a charge:

`failure/03/app/workflows/executes_stripe_purchase.rb`
```ruby
class ExecutesStripePurchase

  attr_accessor :payment, :stripe_token, :stripe_charge

  def initialize(payment, stripe_token)
    @payment = payment
    @stripe_token = StripeToken.new(stripe_token: stripe_token)
  end

  def run
    Payment.transaction do
      result = charge
      on_failure unless result
    end
  end

  def charge
    return :present if payment.response_id.present?
    @stripe_charge = StripeCharge.new(token: stripe_token, payment: payment)
    @stripe_charge.charge
    payment.update!(@stripe_charge.payment_attributes)
    payment.succeeded?
  end

  def unpurchase_tickets
    payment.tickets.each(&:waiting!)
  end

  def on_failure
    unpurchase_tickets
  end

end
```

Our exceptional condition is if the payment.response_id already exists, meaning the charge has already been made. Again, we choose to just drop out of the charge method in that case, and again, there might be additional notification we want to do. We return a token value to prevent the on_failure clause from being invoked if the payment already exists—we'll see a better way of handling failures in a moment.

Otherwise, we try the charge, save the new data if the charge succeeds, and reverse the purchase if it fails, just as before. We might now want to notify the users on success, which we can do with a basic Rails mailer, and we'd expect to have a system in place to notify administrators if something has gone wrong, which we will cover in the next section.

Notification

Notifying customers of the outcome of their transaction is the important final step of a purchase. Typically, we need to send the customer an invoice. For our Snow Globe Theater application, we also probably need to send the customer an actual ticket, most likely with some kind of identification or bar code so that the use of the ticket can be tracked. And if something has gone wrong, we need to tell customers that they have not purchased the tickets they thought were purchased.

Our application requires two important types of notifications:

- Customers need to be notified of the success or failure of their purchases. This is especially true now that the purchase is in a background job and customers are not immediately taken to a status page.

- Administrators need to be notified of exceptional conditions or anything strange that happens.

We are going to manage these notifications with a combination of Rails ActiveJob exception handing, Rails mailers, and a third-party exception notifier tool.

The customer notification is managed with Rails mailers, which are well described in other places.[9] I did want to quickly mention how to integrate the mailer with our code. First, we create the mailer with a Rails generator:

```
$ rails generate mailer payment_mailer
```

Then we can just put a couple of placeholder mailing methods in place:

failure/04/app/mailers/payment_mailer.rb
```ruby
class PaymentMailer < ApplicationMailer

  def notify_success(payment)
  end

  def notify_failure(payment)
  end

end
```

---

9. http://guides.rubyonrails.org/action_mailer_basics.html

In a full application, we'd have logic to actually send these emails to users.

Then we integrate the notification when we have successes and failures, for example, on a Stripe purchase:

```
failure/04/app/workflows/executes_stripe_purchase.rb
def run
  Payment.transaction do
    result = charge
    result ? on_success : on_failure
  end
end

def on_success
  PaymentMailer.notify_success(payment).deliver_later
end

def on_failure
  unpurchase_tickets
  PaymentMailer.notify_failure(payment).deliver_later
end
```

For administrative notifications, I like Rollbar[10] as a third-party exception notifier and aggregator. It's free for up to 5,000 events handled per month, and then has a series of paid plans. (I admit it feels weird to be recommending a commercial service, but we've spent the last several chapters talking about Stripe, so I think I'll cope.)

Rollbar is pretty easy to set up. Go to the Rollbar home page and create an account. As part of creating a new account you'll be asked to start a first project. Select "Rails" as the framework, and you'll be given a page with a server-side access token. The post_server_token is the one you want.

Now we add Rollbar to our project, first as a gem:

```
gem "rollbar"
```

Then we do a bundle install, and a rails generate using the access token provided by Rollbar:

```
$ bundle install
$ rails generate rollbar ACCESS_TOKEN
```

The generator creates a config/initializers/rollbar.rb file, which includes your access token. Technically the access token is not really secret, but it seems better to me to put it in the secrets.yml file.

I normally turn off Rollbar in development mode by tweaking the rollbar.rb file:

---

10. http://www.rollbar.com

failure/04/config/initializers/rollbar.rb

```
config.access_token =
    Rails.application.secrets.rollbar_server_side_access_token

config.enabled = false if Rails.env.test? || Rails.env.development?
```

At this point, Rollbar is set up and any unhandled error from a Rails controller in staging or production is sent to Rollbar, where it goes on a dashboard, and you can choose to have it emailed, sent via Slack, or any of a jillion other integrations. We also need to integrate Rollbar with our ActiveJobs. In Rails 5, we can do this by including the following line in the project parent ApplicationJob class.

failure/04/app/jobs/application_job.rb

```
class ApplicationJob < ActiveJob::Base

  include Rollbar::ActiveJob

end
```

Then it's a question of walking through all the exit points of our jobs and deciding who we want to notify. The setup job has three unsuccessful ways out: validation failure, preexisting purchase object, and database failure. The customer probably needs to know about a validation failure, since it prevents the purchase from going through. And you will probably want to be notified administratively, because the failure could indicate either a bug or security hole in the application. A database failure should cause the job to be re-queued, so we don't need to tell the customer a final result yet, but we do want to notify the administrators because the failure might indicate a bug or system outage.

One way to trigger these notification responses is to cause an exception to be raised when they occur:

failure/04/app/workflows/prepares_cart.rb

```
def run
  Payment.transaction do
    raise PreExistingPaymentException.new(purchase) if existing_payment
    unless pre_purchase_valid?
      raise ChargeSetupValidityException.new(
          user: user,
          expected_purchase_cents: purchase_amount.to_i,
          expected_ticket_ids: expected_ticket_ids)
    end
    update_tickets
    create_payment
    on_success
  end
rescue
  on_failure
  raise
end
```

We call the exceptions with enough information to investigate later, if needed.

The exception classes themselves are minimal. One for the validity exception:

failure/04/app/exceptions/charge_setup_validity_exception.rb
```ruby
class ChargeSetupValidityException < StandardError

  attr_accessor :message, :user, :expected_purchase_cents, :expected_ticket_ids

  def initialize(message = nil,
      user:, expected_purchase_cents:, expected_ticket_ids:)
    super(message)
    @user = user
    @expected_purchase_cents = expected_purchase_cents
    @expected_ticket_ids = expected_ticket_ids
  end

end
```

And another for the pre-existing payment one:

failure/04/app/exceptions/pre_existing_payment_exception.rb
```ruby
class PreExistingPaymentException < StandardError

  attr_accessor :payment

  def initialize(payment, message = nil)
    super(message)
    @purchase = payment
  end

end
```

And then we use the rescue_from method of ActiveJob to catch the exceptions inside the ActiveJob itself:

failure/04/app/jobs/prepares_cart_for_stripe_job.rb
```ruby
rescue_from(ChargeSetupValidityException) do |exception|
  PaymentMailer.notify_failure(exception).deliver_later
  Rollbar.error(exception)
end

rescue_from(PreExistingPaymentException) do |exception|
  Rollbar.error(exception)
end
```

The rescue_from method takes an exception class and a block as an argument. If an exception of that class is raised, the block is invoked, and the exception is, by default, swallowed, meaning that the job is not re-queued. If we want the job to be re-queued, we can re-raise the exception (or any exception) from within the block.

Inside these blocks, we're explicitly calling Rollbar.error(exception) to send the exception to Rollbar (because we're handling the exception, Rollbar won't see it automatically). And in the case of the validity exception, we're also notifying the customer via a mailer and deliver_later, which puts the mail job in the ActiveJob queue.

In the third exceptional exit point, the database failure, the exception is not caught, so Rollbar gets it automatically, and the job goes back in the queue. Then we only need to worry about making sure we know to look at a bug if one arises, which we can do either by checking Rollbar or by preventing Delayed Job from deleting jobs after their last failed attempt.

Let's see what happens if we add a delayed job initializer file:

failure/04/config/initializers/delayed_job_config.rb
```
Delayed::Worker.destroy_failed_jobs = false
```

The Delayed Job sets a failed_at parameter when a job has failed the maximum number of times. We can then look at those jobs with a different automated task to notify the customer that his purchase has failed.

The PurchasesCartCharge job needs to notify the customer on success or failure, which we can do via a mailer. It also can invoke the PreExistingPaymentException if the order has already been charged. If the Stripe API fails, we can either capture those Stripe exceptions with a respond_with in the job, or just allow the default process to rerun the order and check for jobs that fail out of the delayed job queue.

We can similarly use that PreExistingPaymentException in the executing Stripe job rather than use a sentinel value:

failure/04/app/workflows/executes_stripe_purchase.rb
```ruby
def charge
  raise PreExistingPaymentException if payment.response_id.present?
  @stripe_charge = StripeCharge.new(token: stripe_token, payment: payment)
  @stripe_charge.charge
  payment.update!(@stripe_charge.payment_attributes)
  payment.succeeded?
end
```

Raising the exception prevents the on_failure handler from being executed and reverting the tickets, but we can still configure the ActiveJob to notify Rollbar:

failure/04/app/jobs/executes_stripe_purchase_job.rb
```ruby
class ExecutesStripePurchaseJob < ActiveJob::Base

  queue_as :default

  rescue_from(PreExistingPaymentException) do |exception|
    Rollbar.error(exception)
  end
```

```ruby
  def perform(payment, stripe_token)
    charge_action = ExecutesStripePurchase.new(payment, stripe_token)
    charge_action.run
  end

end
```

Next Up

In this chapter, we looked at how to manage a lot of different failure scenarios, including poorly entered credit card data, errors in contacting the Stripe server, and potential errors in our own data processing. We talked about using automated tests to simulate failure states and using background jobs to allow us to encapsulate failure conditions

Now we're going to add another layer of complexity to our processing by adding recurring subscription billing to our application.

## CHAPTER 6

Subscriptions

So far we've been dealing with discrete transactions. The customer buys something, we charge a credit card, and we all go our separate ways. That's not the only business model on the Internet by a long shot. There's also the option where customers buy a subscription to a service, we continually charge their credit cards, and we (hopefully) never go our separate ways. Even our theater application, which isn't exactly software as a service, could have subscribers who are given perks, such as a certain number of free tickets per month.

Because we don't store the customer's credit card in our application, we need the help of our payment gateway to manage automatic regular payments. Asking customers to re-enter their credit card every month is not a great user experience. Luckily, Stripe has a robust API to manage subscription payments, which we will take advantage of to run our subscription service for the Snow Globe Theater.

We could also set up a subscription service on our end, with some kind of recurring job that charged customers on a regular basis, but the gateway subscription APIs are a better solution for us. Using the gateway allows us to avoid having to store sensitive customer information, and the APIs are already set up to handle complex cases such as a customer changing plans, multiple subscriptions, or canceling.

In this chapter, we'll set up the Stripe API to handle our subscriptions. To make Stripe work for us, we need a new level of integration between our application and Stripe. Not only do we need to tell Stripe the business details of our subscription services, but also we need Stripe to inform us of ongoing payments and the failure of ongoing payments. To do this, we will enable *webhooks*, which are endpoints on our application that Stripe will use to send details of transactions when changes happen via Stripe. (Although we'll be

lking about Stripe here, other payment providers offer similar services, so
e information here should be transferable to various APIs).

et's see how we can add subscribers to our application.

Creating Subscription Plans

From Stripe's perspective, a subscription is a relationship between a *plan*
and a *customer*, both of which are data objects defined by the Stripe API. We
need information about both plans and customers in our own database, so
we'll need analogs of both data objects.

As far as Stripe is concerned, a plan has the following parts:

- An amount, which is what the user is charged per subscription term. In
  U.S. currency, the amount is in cents.

- An id, which we'll store in our database as remote_id to distinguish it from
  our local ActiveRecord database ID. This ID is generated by us; Stripe
  doesn't care what it is, as long as it's unique within our list of plans.

- An interval and interval_count, which specify the length of the term between
  user billings. The interval is one of daily, weekly, monthly, or yearly. The
  interval count, which defaults to 1, specifies the number of intervals in a
  term. If you want to bill the user every 12 days, 3 months, or 7 years, for
  whatever reason, you'd specify that information by using the interval_count.

- A human-friendly name, which can be seen on the Stripe administrative
  dashboard.

- A number of trial_period_days, which defaults to nil (meaning 0). By setting
  this value for a plan, you are stating that all subscribers have this number
  of days as a trial period. Effectively, you are delaying the date of their first
  payment.

Although you can create plans via the Stripe dashboard, we're going to create
them from inside our application and send that information to Stripe because
we need to keep track of the plans locally, especially since we want to add
some additional information to plans. First, we need a database migration to
create an ActiveRecord model for plans:

```
% rails generate model plan remote_id:string name:string \
  price:monetize interval:integer interval_count:integer \
  tickets_allowed:integer ticket_category:string \
  status:integer description:text
```

For our local plan object, we've added the attributes tickets_allowed and ticket_category to deal with the local logic of managing how many tickets a particular subscription entitles a user to obtain. Eventually, we'll have to incorporate this logic into the payment workflow, because a user with a subscription won't need to pay for tickets that are covered.

To use these plan objects to get subscriptions working, we'll need not just a model but also a workflow. Right now, however, the only thing we need in the model is a way to get the remote Stripe object:

subscription/01/app/models/plan.rb
```ruby
class Plan < ApplicationRecord

  enum status: {inactive: 0, active: 1}
  enum interval: {day: 0, week: 1, month: 2, year: 3}

  monetize :price_cents

  def remote_plan
    @remote_plan ||= Stripe::Plan.retrieve(remote_id)
  end

  def end_date_from(date = nil)
    date ||= Date.current.to_date
    interval_count.send(interval).from_now(date)
  end

end
```

We can use a simple workflow to create plans and coordinate them with Stripe. All this workflow does is take a bunch of incoming parameters and pass them along to Stripe, along with some defaults, such as currency:

subscription/01/app/workflows/creates_plan.rb
```ruby
class CreatesPlan

  attr_accessor :remote_id, :name,
      :price_cents, :interval,
      :tickets_allowed, :ticket_category,
      :plan

  def initialize(remote_id:, name:,
      price_cents:, interval:,
      tickets_allowed:, ticket_category:)
    @remote_id = remote_id
    @name = name
    @price_cents = price_cents
    @interval = interval
    @tickets_allowed = tickets_allowed
    @ticket_category = ticket_category
  end
```

```ruby
  def run
    remote_plan = Stripe::Plan.create(
        id: remote_id, amount: price_cents,
        currency: "usd", interval: interval,
        name: name)
    self.plan = Plan.create(
        remote_id: remote_plan.id, name: name,
        price_cents: price_cents, interval: interval,
        tickets_allowed: tickets_allowed, ticket_category: ticket_category,
        status: :active)
  end

end
```

If the Stripe creation is successful, the next step is to create a local plan. If the Stripe creation isn't successful, the Stripe gem will throw an exception and the whole thing will stop.

We're not wiring this to a controller or anything yet; that'll be a part of the administration tool that we will discuss in Chapter 7, *The Administration Experience*, on page 143. Odds are you'll rarely create plans. Let's start with a simple Rake task that will create a few plans:

`subscription/01/lib/tasks/plan_creation.rake`
```ruby
namespace :theater do

  task create_plans: :environment do
    plans = [
        {remote_id: "orchestra_monthly", plan_name: "Orchestra Monthly",
         price_cents: 10_000, interval: "monthly", tickets_allowed: 1,
         ticket_category: "Orchestra"},
        {remote_id: "balcony_monthly", plan_name: "Balcony Monthly",
         price_cents: 60_000, interval: "monthly", tickets_allowed: 1,
         ticket_category: "Balcony"},
        {remote_id: "vip_monthly", plan_name: "VIP Monthly",
         price_cents: 30_000, interval: "monthly", tickets_allowed: 1,
         ticket_category: "VIP"}
    ]
    Plan.transaction do
      plans.each { |plan_data| CreatesPlan.new(**plan_data).run }
    end
  end

end
```

All this does is invoke the CreatesPlan workflow for each of a set of sample plans.

Creating Subscription Customers

To actually create a subscription and have it start charging, we need to create a customer object in Stripe and associate it with a plan. Stripe will create an internal subscription object for that customer-to-plan relationship. So, we need to coordinate user objects between our database and Stripe's API.

To register a customer with Stripe, all we need to do is say, "Hey, Stripe, give me a customer ID" (technically, Stripe::Customer.create). Once the Stripe customer is created, we can actually see it on the Stripe dashboard—we can even do some administration there should we choose. It's our responsibility to coordinate the customer records by adding the Stripe ID to our customer record:

subscription/01/db/migrate/20160730192814_add_stripe_customer_to_user.rb

```
class AddStripeCustomerToUser < ActiveRecord::Migration[5.0]

  def change
    add_column :users, :stripe_id, :string
  end

end
```

There are a few things we can do to make the customer object more useful. First, we can send it a description string and an arbitrary metadata argument. Now when we browse the users in the Stripe dashboard, we'll have a little more context.

Second, we can assign payment sources, such as credit cards, to a customer. This associates the source with the customer within Stripe so that the customer can be charged at a later date. This is useful for subscriptions, since we'll need to keep charging the customer over and over again. It's also useful for regular payments, because it allows customers to check out without reentering their credit card information. Associating a card with a user is so common that the Stripe::Customer.create method can take a credit card as an argument. This credit card can either be a full set of credit card data or a token of the kind we've already been using.

Finally, we can also add subscription plans to a user by passing the Stripe ID of the plan. Once a user has a subscription plan and a payment source associated with that user, Stripe will charge the user and then charge the user again when the plan interval expires. Associating a user with a plan is so common that the Stripe::Customer.create method can take a subscription plan ID as an argument.

For our part, we're still responsible for managing subscription data locally, so we need a place to store it:

```
% rails generate model subscription user:references \
  plan:references start_date:date end_date:date \
  status:integer payment_method:string remote_id:string
```

In our database, a subscription combines a user and a plan. The start date of the subscription, the current end date, and a status are also stored. For payment, we have a payment method and a remote ID, similar to what payments have. We'll continue to update the end date as new payments come in to move it further into the future.

Purchasing a Subscription

The workflow for purchasing a subscription is similar to purchasing an individual item, but there are also differences. On the client page, the user selects a subscription plan and enters his or her credit card information. As before, our application contacts Stripe from the client browser before the form is submitted and we receive a token. Also as before, we take that token and send it back to our server when the credit card form is finished.

From this point on, the server-side logic for a subscription purchase differs. Instead of sending a Stripe Purchase object to Stripe, a Customer object is created and associated with the token, which represents the payment method and our user. Now the subscription transaction is complete, at least from our perspective, and it's up to Stripe to continue to regularly charge the customer's credit card. We also ask Stripe to notify our application about payment events, because our application needs to track whether a user is still a subscriber in good standing. (This tracking is done via webhooks, which we'll look at in *Setting Up Webhooks*, on page 131.)

For our example, we're not going to allow subscriptions and tickets to be purchased together, at least not at first. The logistics of calculating the ticket price of multiple tickets and a subscription at the same time introduce more complexity than is needed right now, and also introduce a whole new failure mode if the initial subscription charge fails after we've already given the user free tickets.

Selecting a Plan

To subscribe to one of the plans we offer, a user needs to select a plan and put it in the cart. Because this book isn't *Selecting Subscription Plans on the Web*, we'll keep this simple. We have a controller with an index method:

```
subscription/01/app/controllers/plans_controller.rb
class PlansController < ApplicationController

  def index
    @plans = Plan.active.all
  end

end
```

And a view:

```
subscription/01/app/views/plans/index.html.slim
h2 Subscription Plans

- @plans.each do |plan|
  .plan(id=dom_id(plan))

    h3.plan-name= plan.name

    .plan-description= plan.description
    .plan-cost= humanized_money_with_symbol(plan.price)

    = form_tag(subscription_cart_path, method: :patch) do
      = hidden_field_tag("plan_id", plan.id)
      .form-group
        = submit_tag("Add to Cart", class: "btn btn-default", id: "add-to-cart")
```

The view simply lists all the plans and gives each plan its very own "Add to Cart" button that submits to SubscriptionCartsController#update.

In an architectural decision that I'll defend mainly because it keeps things clean for explanatory purposes, I'm making completely separate and parallel shopping cart classes for the subscription shopping cart. This approach leads to some slightly duplicated boilerplate in the controller:

```
subscription/01/app/controllers/subscription_carts_controller.rb
class SubscriptionCartsController < ApplicationController

  def show
    @cart = SubscriptionCart.new(current_user)
  end

  def update
    plan = Plan.find(params[:plan_id])
    workflow = AddsPlanToCart.new(user: current_user, plan: plan)
    workflow.run
    if workflow.result
      redirect_to subscription_cart_path
    else
      redirect_to plans_path
    end
  end

end
```

But the controller mostly defers to a simple workflow that creates a new Subscription object:

subscription/01/app/workflows/adds_plan_to_cart.rb

```ruby
class AddsPlanToCart

  attr_accessor :user, :plan, :result

  def initialize(user:, plan:)
    @user = user
    @plan = plan
    @result = nil
  end

  def run
    @result = Subscription.create!(
        user: user, plan: plan,
        start_date: Time.zone.now.to_date,
        end_date: plan.end_date_from,
        status: :waiting)
  end

  def success?
    result.valid?
  end

end
```

All we're doing is creating a new Subscription object with the relevant data. This is, admittedly, basically a one-line workflow (at least at the moment), and could clearly be inlined into the main controller. I'm still holding onto the pattern of putting the business logic in workflow objects, though.

Now, the controller redirects to a show action, which has its own similar view to display the actual subscription cart:

subscription/01/app/views/subscription_carts/show.html.slim

```slim
h1 Subscription Cart

table.table
  thead
    tr
      th Plan
      th Total Price
  tbody
    - @cart.subscriptions.each do |subscription|
      tr(id= dom_id(subscription))
        td= subscription.plan.name
        td.subtotal= humanized_money_with_symbol(subscription.plan.price)

h3 Total #{humanized_money_with_symbol(@cart.total_cost)}

h2 Checkout

= render "shopping_carts/credit_card_info"
```

This view renders the credit card partial, which needs to be augmented slightly to allow it to work for subscriptions and regular purchases:

```
subscription/01/app/views/shopping_carts/_credit_card_info.html.slim
= hidden_field_tag(:purchase_amount_cents, @cart.total_cost.cents)
= hidden_field_tag(@cart.item_attribute, @cart.item_ids)
= hidden_field_tag(:purchase_type, @cart.class.name)
= hidden_field_tag(:stripe_token, "", id: "spec_stripe_token")
```

Here I added a hidden field for purchase_type, which will be the class name of the cart—we'll use this in the resulting controller to select which workflow to run. I made the field that was formerly ticket_ids variable by putting the field name in an item_attribute method. So now it's ticket_ids for a ticket purchase and subscription_ids for a subscription purchase. And finally, I added a blank field for the Stripe token, which is frankly only there so that I can use it via Capybara and write Capybara tests that don't require JavaScript.

The credit card form still submits to the PaymentsController, but it has been augmented slightly to switch to our new subscription workflow:

```
subscription/01/app/controllers/payments_controller.rb
private def run_workflow(payment_type, purchase_type)
  case purchase_type
  when "SubscriptionCart"
    stripe_subscription_workflow
  when "ShoppingCart"
    payment_type == "paypal" ? paypal_workflow : stripe_workflow
  end
end
```

Honestly, this switch logic is getting a little complicated for the controller, or at least it's beginning to look a little ugly to me (and I'm starting to think about refactoring). I'll hold off for now, because further switch logic might be forthcoming.

The new part of this code defers off to a brand-new workflow object, creatively named CreatesSubscriptionViaStripe.

Creating a Stripe Subscription Object

The subscription workflow's main responsibility is to register the subscription with Stripe. Registering involves sending to Stripe a combination of the user information, the subscription plan, and the approved token representing the payment method. We need to do a little accounting on our side to make sure all those objects are correctly associated with each other and with the Stripe information. (We don't handle the actual payment here; Stripe will take care of that after we send the information, so one less thing to worry about.)

Here's the workflow code:

```
subscription/01/app/workflows/creates_subscription_via_stripe.rb
class CreatesSubscriptionViaStripe

  attr_accessor :user, :expected_subscription_id, :token, :success

  def initialize(user:, expected_subscription_id:, token:)
    @user = user
    @expected_subscription_id = expected_subscription_id
    @token = token
    @success = false
  end

  def subscription
    @subscription ||= user.subscriptions_in_cart.first
  end

  def expected_plan_valid?
    expected_subscription_id.first.to_i == subscription.id.to_i
  end

  def run
    Purchase.transaction do
      return unless expected_plan_valid?
      stripe_customer = StripeCustomer.new(user: user)
      return unless stripe_customer.valid?
      stripe_customer.source = token
      subscription.make_stripe_payment(stripe_customer)
      stripe_customer.add_subscription(subscription)
      @success = true
    end
  rescue Stripe::StripeError => exception
    Rollbar.error(exception)
  end

  def redirect_on_success_url
    user
  end
end
```

As with other workflows, the key method here is run. The run method starts
with a validity check similar to the one we ran for ticket charges, comparing
the subscription in the user's cart in the database with the subscription that
the user claims to be submitting via the form. This helps protect against the
possibility of the user messing with the upload data somehow.

If the subscription checks out, a StripeCustomer object is created, which is
another wrapper around the Stripe API. In this case, the StripeCustomer class
is used to hide some details of object creation. Specifically, we're hiding the
fact that we need to make different Stripe API calls if xusers have already

been registered with Stripe than if they have not, but more on that when we look at the StripeCustomer code.

If something goes wrong with the StripeCustomer part, either the customer object will not be valid or we'll get some kind of StripeError. In either case we are bounced out of the method without having saved any new data. If everything checks out, the token and subscription are sent to the customer object, which passes them along to Stripe. We also call make_stripe_payment on the subscription:

subscription/01/app/models/subscription.rb

```ruby
def make_stripe_payment(stripe_customer)
  update!(
      payment_method: :stripe, status: :pending_initial_payment,
      remote_id: stripe_customer.find_subscription_for(plan))
end
```

Here the status is set to :pending_initial_payment, the payment method is set to stripe, and the remote_id is set to the remote ID of the subscription.

With all of that done, we save the subscription and user and pass the successful status back out to the controller. The StripeCustomer class winds up doing some of the heavy lifting here, including all the contact with the Stripe API:

subscription/01/app/models/stripe_customer.rb

```ruby
class StripeCustomer

  attr_accessor :user

  delegate :subscriptions, :id, to: :remote_customer

  def initialize(user: nil)
    @user = user
  end

  def remote_customer
    @remote_customer ||= begin
      if user.stripe_id
        Stripe::Customer.retrieve(user.stripe_id)
      else
        Stripe::Customer.create(email: user.email).tap do |remote_customer|
          user.update!(stripe_id: remote_customer.id)
        end
      end
    end
  end

  def valid?
    remote_customer.present?
  end

  def find_subscription_for(plan)
    subscriptions.find { |s| s.plan.id == plan.remote_id }
  end
```

```ruby
  def add_subscription(subscription)
    remote_subscription = remote_customer.subscriptions.create(
        plan: subscription.remote_plan_id)
    subscription.update!(remote_id: remote_subscription.id)
  end

  def source=(token)
    remote_customer.source = token.id
    remote_customer.save
  end

end
```

Before I walk through this code, a quick behind-the-scenes note on design. The code you see here is after a refactoring pass or two, and initially I didn't have a StripeCustomer class. The first pass of this code used a single Stripe API call to create the customer and associate it with the token and with the plan. One method call didn't seem to justify a full class, but because the API call combined the workflow, users, and subscriptions, it wasn't immediately obvious to me where to put it. After dithering over the decision with the nervousness of somebody expecting a code review from lots of smart readers, I initially placed the call in the User class.

Looking over it, I realized that the code didn't work if the user already had a Stripe customer ID, so I needed to separate the creation or retrieval of the customer and the attachment to the token and subscription. Then it became clear that there was enough logic to justify a separate StripeCustomer class. Technically, this could have all stayed in User, but I've seen that movie, and it ends with a 1,000-line User-zilla class that nobody wants to touch. It wouldn't be completely crazy, though, to have this StripeCustomer be a SimpleDelegator to a user object.

As for the code itself, the most important part is the remote_customer method, which looks to see if the user already has a stripe_id. If so, it makes the retrieve API call; if not, it both uses the create API call to create a new user and sets the user's stripe_id to the new remote ID.

Other helper methods allow us to translate our structure to the Stripe API. The source= method allows us to pass one of our StripeToken objects and extract the ID from it and guarantee that our customer saves with the new ID. The add_subscription method allows us to extract the remote plan ID associated with a subscription and create a Stripe subscription object associated with it. Finally, the find_subscription_for method takes in a local plan object and returns the Stripe subscription object associated with that plan.

If the workflow succeeds, Stripe knows about our subscription. If we set the subscription plan with a trial period, it would make sense for us to fully activate the subscription. That's a great choice for many services. However, in the specific case of our little theater ticketing application, we don't want to fully activate the subscription before a charge goes through. That opens up an easy way for users to commit fraud: create a subscription on a bad card and use the subscription quickly before Stripe bounces the payment. So, to fully activate our subscriptions, we need Stripe to notify us that a payment has gone through. We need Stripe webhooks.

Setting Up Webhooks

With our application as it is written, Stripe immediately charges the user's credit card for a new subscription (because no trial period is specified in the plan), and won't tell us about it unless we go looking for the information in the Stripe dashboard.

That's a problem. We need Stripe to tell us about user subscription events. We'd like the opportunity to review invoices before the customer is charged (for example, the user may qualify for a discount that lowers the charge). And we'd definitely like to know if the user cancels or if the card is declined so that we can end the subscription.

To receive this useful information from Stripe, we need to give Stripe a *webhook*, which is a URL in our app for Stripe to send event information. In response to events that happen on the Stripe server, Stripe will send a POST request to a URL that we provide. We provide a single URL and optionally filter the list of events that will trigger a Stripe call. Switching between the events is our responsibility.

Although there are a few gems that provide some shortcuts for handling stripe events—such as with the StripeEvent[1] gem and the Stripe Rails[2] gem—we're going to build this ourselves.

First we specify a route in our routes file:

```
subscription/01/config/routes.rb
post "stripe/webhook", to: "stripe_webhook#action"
```

Then we need a generic controller action to handle the stripe events. I've set this one up so that it's very simple for us to add new events as we wish to handle them:

---

1. https://github.com/integrallis/stripe_event
2. https://github.com/thefrontside/stripe-rails

```
subscription/01/app/controllers/stripe_webhook_controller.rb
class StripeWebhookController < ApplicationController

  protect_from_forgery except: :action

  def action
    @event_data = JSON.parse(request.body.read)
    workflow = workflow_class.new(verify_event)
    workflow.run
    if workflow.success
      render nothing: true
    else
      render nothing: true, status: 500
    end
  end

  private def verify_event
    Stripe::Event.retrieve(@event_data["id"])
  rescue Stripe::InvalidRequestError
    nil
  end

  private def workflow_class
    event_type = @event_data["type"]
    "StripeHandler::#{event_type.tr('.', '_').camelize}".constantize
  rescue NameError
    StripeHandler::NullHandler
  end

end
```

In keeping with our other controllers, this controller mostly just defers out to a workflow object to do the actual work. Unlike our other controllers, this one has a dynamic, metaprogram-ish way of picking a workflow.

All the events go into the action method, where the first thing we do is parse the raw JSON into a hash. Then we need to do two things: verify the event and pick a workflow class.

The verify_event method is slightly paranoid, though what it does is recommended in Stripe's official documentation. Even though Stripe sends an entire event via JSON, we're just pulling the ID from that event and re-requesting it via Stripe::Event.retrieve. This prevents us from being spoofed by somebody sending us fake events. As to why Stripe even bothers sending the rest of the event data in the request (you may remember that PayPal just sends the ID in their callbacks), I don't know. If the event retrieval triggers an error, we return nil. It'll be the responsibility of the eventual workflow to handle that nil.

The workflow_class method dynamically picks the class of the workflow by inflecting on the name of the StripeEvent. So, a Stripe event named something like invoice.payment_succeeded turns into the class StripeHandler::InvoicePaymentSucceeded. If the class doesn't exist, the Rails constantize method throws an exception, which we catch and return a NullHandler class. By scoping all our dynamic classes inside the StripeHandler module, whose name does not come from the incoming event, we limit the amount of damage that a weird or fraudulent request can cause.

The NullHandler does nothing and just lets us use the object system to handle the basic logic:

```
subscription/01/app/workflows/stripe_handler/null_handler.rb
module StripeHandler

  class NullHandler

    def initialize(event)
    end

    def run
    end

    def success
      true
    end

  end

end
```

Once we verify the event and get the workflow class, we run the workflow and return either a success or an error status back to Stripe.

All this means is that the only thing we need to do to start handling a new event is create a properly named workflow class and new events will automatically be passed to it. On a large scale there are faster ways of handling all these checks, but we're nowhere near that scale yet.

Supporting the Stripe Subscription Life Cycle

Now that we have a mechanism in place to capture Stripe events, we need to decide what events we should actually handle. And in order to decide that, we need to look at what events Stripe will send.

There is a set of events that Stripe sends to initialize a new subscription and a set of events that are sent around each new subscription payment. Most of these events we don't really care about, but Stripe sends them anyway (if we want, the Stripe administrative dashboard has a setting to limit the events being sent).

When we initially create our subscription via our workflow, Stripe should trigger two events:

- customer.created
- customer.subscription.created

At the end of the trial period, or immediately if a trial period is not specified, Stripe creates three more events, assuming that the charge succeeds:

- invoice.created
- charge.succeeded
- invoice.payment_succeeded

We explicitly create a customer and a subscription as part of our workflow, so it's perhaps not surprising that Stripe acknowledges those events with callbacks. We don't actually need to use these, but an alternate implementation of our application might, for example, wait for the customer.created callback to associate the customer with the remote Stripe object.

We don't explicitly create an invoice, though. To Stripe, an invoice is an internal object that represents an individual payment for a subscription. It's the successful payment of an invoice that activates the subscription.

The first time through for a new subscription, Stripe generates an invoice when the trial period ends, sends the invoice.created event, and immediately tries to charge the payment source, most likely resulting in nearly immediate charge.succeeded and invoice.payment_succeeded events also being sent.

When the payment comes due for the next subscription time unit, Stripe generates the same three events:

- invoice.created
- charge.succeeded
- invoice.payment_succeeded

This is one exception. On all subsequent payments, Stripe waits, according to the documentation, "approximately one hour" after creating the invoice to make the charge. This is explicitly to allow our application a chance to adjust the invoice. We might want to do that, for example, if the user had earned a credit, or gone over a limit and owed more than Stripe would have assumed.

Capturing an Event

In our subscription process as it exists so far, we want to capture the invoice.payment_succeeded event. We don't at the moment have a reason to adjust the subscription amount, so the invoice.created event isn't really interesting to us, and charge.succeeded seems like too broad of an event to catch. (Stripe will send a callback after every successful charge, not just the subscription-related ones.)

All we need to do to start capturing this event is create the appropriately named class. It then needs to take an event as an argument to the constructor, respond to the run message, and respond to success at the end, like so:

```
subscription/01/app/workflows/stripe_handler/invoice_payment_succeeded.rb
module StripeHandler

  class InvoicePaymentSucceeded

    attr_accessor :event, :success, :payment

    def initialize(event)
      @event = event
      @success = false
    end

    def run
      Subscription.transaction do
        return unless event
        subscription.active!
        subscription.update_end_date
        @payment = Payment.create!(
            user_id: user.id, price_cents: invoice.amount,
            status: "succeeded", reference: Payment.generate_reference,
            payment_method: "stripe", response_id: invoice.charge,
            full_response: charge.to_json)
        payment.payment_line_items.create!(
            buyable: subscription, price_cents: invoice.amount)
        @success = true
      end
    end

    def invoice
      @event.data.object
    end

    def subscription
      @subscription ||= Subscription.find_by(remote_id: invoice.subscription)
    end

    def user
      @user ||= User.find_by(stripe_id: invoice.customer)
    end

    def charge
      @charge ||= Stripe::Charge.retrieve(invoice.charge)
    end

  end

end
```

With Stripe event naming, the first part of the name of the event indicates what type of object is described in event.data.object, which in this case is an Invoice. So this class has some helper methods to extract the invoice, subscription, user, and charge objects. (A full listing of all the fields for all Stripe objects can be found in the Stripe API documentation.[3])

The run method does six things:

- Returns without action if the event is nil.

- Changes the status of the associated local subscription object to active—it might already be active, if the subscription is ongoing, in which case this has no effect.

- Updates the end date of the associated local subscription to match the new plan period.

- Creates a new Payment object so that we have a local record of the payment for our own record-keeping. The maybe slightly odd thing I'm doing here is going back to Stripe to get the entire charge record to put in the full_response attribute. I'm doing this to be consistent with ticket purchases (where we already had the charge object), but it is an extra API call that may not, strictly speaking, be necessary.

- Creates a line item to go with that payment, using the polymorphic relationship between line items and anything that is buyable.

- Returns success if it has gotten this far without failing.

Our error handling here can be relatively coarse, at least to start. If any of the lookups for subscription or user or the like fail, this will return an error code to Stripe. We need to know about the error, but Stripe doesn't really care what our response is at this point.

Once we've received the payment notification callback from Stripe, we can then check for the active status of the subscription—in our case, that means that the status is active and the end_date is in the future:

```
subscription/01/app/models/subscription.rb
def currently_active?
  active? && (end_date > Date.current)
end
```

---

3. https://stripe.com/docs/api

Modifying Subscriptions

At some point customers might want to change or remove their subscriptions, and being a big believer in customer service, we should allow this.

Canceling a subscription is significantly easier to handle, if much less helpful for our bottom line, than modifying a subscription. Canceling a subscription looks something like this:

subscription/01/app/workflows/cancels_stripe_subscription.rb

```ruby
class CancelsStripeSubscription

  attr_accessor :subscription, :user

  def initialize(subscription_id:, user:)
    @subscription_id = subscription_id
    @user = user
    @success = false
  end

  def subscription
    @subscription ||= Subscription.find_by(id: subscription_id)
  end

  def customer
    @customer ||= StripeCustomer.new(user)
  end

  def remote_subscription
    @remote_subscription ||=
        customer.subcriptions.retrieve(subscription.remote_id)
  end

  def user_is_subscribed?
    subscription_id && user.subscriptions.map(&:id).include?(subscription_id)
  end

  def run
    return unless user_is_subscribed?
    return if customer.nil? || remote_subscription.nil?
    remote_subscription.delete
    subscription.canceled!
  end

end
```

We pass the workflow a subscription_id and a user, we verify that the subscription and user both exist locally and remotely, and verify that the user actually owns the subscription. If all that is in place, we simply call delete on the remote subscription object and change the status of the local subscription to canceled. We keep the local subscription around because we'll want it for reporting purposes.

Stripe cancels the subscription immediately by default and does not credit the user for any unused portion of the subscription fee. If you want to wait until the subscription period ends to actually cancel the subscription for some reason, you can pass the argument at_period_end: true to the delete method. Stripe will send a webhook with the customer.subscription.deleted event at the end of the period.

Changing the plan is conceptually similar, but has some wrinkles in how Stripe handles the change. Here's the simplest version:

```
subscription/01/app/workflows/changes_stripe_subscription_plan.rb
class ChangesStripeSubscriptionPlan

  attr_accessor :subscription, :user

  def initialize(subscription_id:, user:, new_plan_id:)
    @subscription_id = subscription_id
    @new_plan_id = new_plan_id
    @user = user
    @success = false
  end

  def new_plan
    @plan ||= Plan.find_by(id: new_plan_idw)
  end

  def subscription
    @subscription ||= Subscription.find_by(id: subscription_id)
  end

  def customer
    @customer ||= StripeCustomer.new(user)
  end

  def remote_subscription
    @remote_subscription ||=
        customer.subscriptions.retrieve(subscription.remote_id)
  end

  def user_is_subscribed?
    subscription_id && user.subscriptions.map(&:id).include?(subscription_id)
  end

  def run
    return unless user_is_subscribed?
    return if customer.nil? || remote_subscription.nil?
    remote_subscription.plan = new_plan.remote_id
    subscription.update(plan: new_plan)
    remote_subscription.save
  end

end
```

Most of the same data retrieval methods are here (we could create a common abstract class for both of these workflows), except at the end, a new plan value is set both locally and remotely and saved. The status of the subscription isn't changed, though that may be an oversimplification.

What happens on the Stripe side depends on the difference between the two plans: whether there is a change in cost and/or a change in frequency.

A change in cost is actually easier to explain. Sort of. By default Stripe does not immediately charge users when they change a subscription plan, even if they increase the cost of their subscription. Instead, Stripe prorates the change in cost, up or down, over the remaining portion of the subscription and applies that amount to the next subscription payment.

For example, let's say we offer plans that cost $10 and $16 per month. If the user upgrades from the $10 plan to the $16 plan one-third of the way through the month, the user pays nothing at the time, but the next bill is $20 ($16 for the next month plus $4 because we spent two-thirds of the previous month at the higher rate). If the user downgrades from the $16 plan to the $10 plan at the one-third mark of the following month, the next payment is just $6 ($10 for the new month and a $4 credit for two-thirds of a month at the lower rate).

There are a couple of ways around this proration. You can disable it entirely by setting remote_subscription.prorate = false before saving the remote subscription. This causes the customer to be billed the normal amount for the new plan starting with the next cycle. You can also specify the amount of time Stripe should use to calculate the next month's bill by setting a proration_date attribute. Stripe recalculates proration to the second, so if your subscription price is quite large, it's possible that there might be a difference between the price you show a user and the price you actually bill two minutes later. Finally, if it bothers you that customers are getting their subscription upgrades for a delayed payment, you can force a payment of their current balance by explicitly creating a new invoice, Stripe::Invoice.create(customer: user.stripe_id). This will trigger a payment of the current balance.

Two other circumstances cause Stripe to attempt to bill the user immediately if the subscription plan changes. First, if the user switches from a free plan to a paid plan, Stripe will trigger the invoice immediately, and will do so as part of the save action, not as part of a future webhook. If the payment fails, Stripe will throw an error and will not update the remote subscription. And second, just to throw one more wrinkle at you, if the new plan is on a different billing interval, then Stripe will change the billing date to the current date and trigger an immediate invoice and charge, just as it would have if the subscription had just started.

Exactly how deep in the weeds your code needs to get to handle these issues depends on what kinds of plans you offer. If you don't have any free plans, and all of your plans have the same interval, then you get off pretty easy. If not, then you'll need to make sure that you properly listen for invoice and subscription events that might indicate a change in the subscription status.

Handling Payment Failures

Another way subscription status can change is if the customer's credit card rejects a subscription payment. Given the details of the application as we've written it, we actually don't need to respond to these events. Because our subscriptions have an end date that is only updated when a payment is received, we could just silently let a payment failure go by. Once the end date had passed, our ticket application would no longer recognize the subscription as active.

Still, Stripe will send us these events, and it's probably a good idea for our local application to be in sync with Stripe.

Stripe's behavior in response to failed payments can be modified in the Stripe administrative dashboard. Stripe allows up to four failed attempts and lets you specify whether the interval between attempts is one, three, five, or seven days. The default is to retry three days after the first failure, five days after the second, and seven days after the third. At the end you can choose to cancel the subscription, just mark it unpaid, or leave it alone.

After each failed payment, Stripe sends a charge.failed and invoice.payment_failed callback, and if you cancel, it sends a customer.subscription.deleted event. We can catch the latter event and update our subscription model's status like this:

```
subscription/01/app/workflows/stripe_handler/customer_subscription_deleted.rb
module StripeHandler

  class CustomerSubscriptionDeleted

    attr_accessor :event, :success, :payment

    def initialize(event)
      @event = event
      @success = false
    end

    def remote_subscription
      @event.data.object
    end
```

```ruby
    def subscription
      @subscription ||= Subscription.find_by(remote_id: remote_subscription.id)
    end

    def run
      subscription&.canceled!
    end

  end

end
```

In this case, the data passed with the event is a Subscription. We find the local counterpart in our database. If the local counterparts exists, we just change its status to canceled, and the ActiveRecord enum method will automatically save the record.

Next Up

We've now covered the basics of taking in both individual and repeating payments. However, transacting with the payment gateway is only part of managing a robust commercial website. Over the next few chapters we'll look at other aspects that are critical to the long-term health of your business. We'll start with administration. Yes, it's that important.

## CHAPTER 7

The Administration Experience

Raise your hand if you've ever shipped a substandard administrative interface under time pressure because it was "just" for the admins. Raise your other hand if you ever regretted that decision.

If you noticed a slight pause, that was because it's hard for me to type with both my hands in the air.

Over the long term, the quality of your administrative tools is going to make a huge difference in the effectiveness of your application. There will be bugs, and special cases, and user requests, and refunds, not to mention the regular administrative tasks of creating data to be consumed by the front end. For every special case, or every unforeseen need, if you don't explicitly give your administrators the tools to manage it, they will improvise. And that will not always be the best thing. Legacy data can be as big a drag on future development as legacy code.

What I call "administration" covers a lot of ground, including the following:

- Content management. For our application's purposes, administration especially includes adding new events, performances, and subscription plans for sale.

- Being able to see dashboards and reports of the current status of the site. We'll talk more about this in Chapter 10, *Reporting*, on page 211.

- Being able to trigger purchases outside of the user-facing site, especially purchases that might break business rules in some way.

- Troubleshooting and fixing customer problems and weird states that the data might get into.

There's a rough ladder to administrative tools. At the top of the hierarchy are tools that are prepared by the developers and specifically designed to allow them to solve specific problems. As we go down the ladder, the tools become more general, more technical, more flexible, and harder to control:

1. The most polished set of tools are ones that are explicitly developed for the application for administrators to use to update the site and site data.

2. Next are one-off scripts or cron jobs that are explicitly written, tested, and run, but are somewhat outside the administrators purview.

3. If you don't have a one-off script, the next step is random access to the Rails console to directly manipulate data.

4. And, when all else fails, there's random access directly to the database to directly manipulate data.

Ideally, you want to have as much activity as you can manage at the top level, where it can be monitored and controlled by the full weight of your application code. However, the tighter you make the rules for dealing with data, the more likely it is that some changes will need to bypass those rules and be handled at the level of the Rails console or the database. That's not usually a good sign, though I know of one pretty big Rails shop that did a lot of customer service requests via a developer and the Rails console for rather a long time.

Please note: If you are doing business in the United States and working with the financial records of a publicly traded company, the law known as the Sarbanes-Oxley Act of 2002 (SOX)[1] may place some limitations on who can access financial data. In particular, you may need to strictly separate people who work on code in the system from people who can administratively access the running system data. Please consult a lawyer if you think this may describe you.

Over the next few chapters, we'll talk about how to control who has access to your administrative functions, how to allow administrators the ability to bend or break business logic, and how to make sure that granting administrators those abilities doesn't lead to a huge tangle of bad data.

Let's start by looking at the simplest administration tool available to us: Stripe's own dashboard.

---

1.   https://en.wikipedia.org/wiki/Sarbanes%E2%80%93Oxley_Act

Using Stripe's Administration Dashboard

Possibly the easiest place to start our administrative journey is with the tools that Stripe makes available. Stripe's dashboard provides access to customer and payment histories with search and edit capability. You can refund items via Stripe and add additional charges to known credit cards. It's a quick way to get some administrative capability, and by using Stripe's webhooks, it's even possible to integrate activity on the Stripe dashboard with our application.

If you log into Stripe after making a test payment, you'll see the Stripe dashboard, as shown in the following figure. (Yours will look a little different depending on what kind of payment you made.)

Stripe gives us a nice line graph of our incoming money volume for the past week, as well as the raw number of successful charges and the number of customers created. If you click "Payments" in the left column, a screen more focused on payments appears, as shown in the figure on page 146.

This screen shows a list of recent payments and includes the payments' Stripe IDs and the time of the transactions. You can also find payments by searching on the Stripe ID. You can export payment data to a CSV file. You can also create your own payment here. Stripe provides a dialog box to take credit card information.

Additionally, if you click one of the payment IDs, you see a detail page for that payment, as shown in the figure on page 147.

This page has all the information that was sent to us in response to the payment, plus some extras, such as the amount Stripe takes for its fee. You can also see the exact logs of both the charge API call and the token API call used for the charge. You can also do some administrative work, such as updating the description, reporting fraud, or requesting a refund. As a first step, it might be easier to process refunds through Stripe and catch the event in a webhook than it is to build a full refund structure in our own app. In addition, you can create a new transaction if you just want to charge some money to somebody for some reason.

The Customers tab has a similar amount of information about subscriptions. You can see the credit cards customers are paying with, the plans they are subscribed to, the payments they've made, and all their invoices. You can also see the next invoice and when it's scheduled, and a log of all events and API calls relating to each customer. Again, using Stripe's own dashboard is not a bad first step toward getting your administration off the ground.

Setting Up Your Own Administrative Dashboard

Although the Stripe dashboard is lovely, it's not going to help us manage inventory or enter details of our little theater's events or performances. For that, we need our own administration tools.

Administration tools get a bum rap in part because it often seems like they are just the basic, most boring kind of web programming: create a form, submit the form, put the results in the database. Repeat. And though that's often true,

it's also true that administration tools are often boring right up to the point where they become critical—and needed to have been completed last week.

We're going to use a tool to quickly set up basic administrative features because having a basic administrative UI is the foundation of more complex administrative logic. There are a number of Rails tools that more or less automatically generate Create/Read/Update/Delete (CRUD) interfaces for your models. The idea is that we can burn through the basic, most straight-forward parts of our administrative tool without much effort, and reserve as much time as possible for the complicated stuff.

The administrative generators are nice and can be useful. The problem is that you think you have a lot of models that can be administrated via a basic CRUD interface, and maybe a few exceptions. What you actually have is maybe one or two models that actually have a basic CRUD interface. And a lot of exceptions. So many exceptions.

Let's set up one of the administrative tools and take a look at what I mean by exceptions.

The tool we're using here is ActiveAdmin.[2] We're using it largely because it's fairly stable (despite being pre-1.0 for a long time) and because it seems to be the first tool in this area to catch up to Rails 5. I'm also keeping my eye on Administrate,[3] which is in early development stages from Thoughtbot.

To set up ActiveAdmin, we need to add some gems to our Gemfile:

```
admin/01/Gemfile
gem "activeadmin", github: "activeadmin/activeadmin"
gem "active_admin_theme"
gem "inherited_resources", github: "activeadmin/inherited_resources"
gem "ransack", github: "activerecord-hackery/ransack"
gem "draper", "> 3.x"
gem "sass-rails", github: "rails/sass-rails"
```

The important one is activeadmin, the active_admin_theme is there because I like it better than the default ActiveAdmin styles, and the rest are to cover versions that are compatible with Rails 5. Eventually, they should all catch up.

And then from the command line, get started with this:

```
% bundle update
% rails g active_admin:install --skip-users
```

This generates several files, including an app/admin directory, adding the admin route to the routes.rb file, some JavaScript and CSS attributes, and a migration to allow administrators to add arbitrary notes to any item. We're running with --skip-users because we've already got a User object defined and we're already using Devise, so we don't need it.

If we now hit localhost:3000/admin, we see this functional administrative interface:

---

2. https://github.com/activeadmin/activeadmin
3. http://administrate-prototype.herokuapp.com

We've got a title bar with a dashboard, a place for comments, and our users table. We are looking at the User index page, with our one created user. ActiveAdmin also puts a group of filters on the side by default.

Next, we want to add administrative functionality for our remaining models. We can do so from the command line:

```
$ rails generate active_admin:resource Event
$ rails generate active_admin:resource Payment
$ rails generate active_admin:resource Plan
$ rails generate active_admin:resource Subscription
$ rails generate active_admin:resource Event
```

That's basically all our ActiveRecord models, except Performance, which we will tack on to the Event screen, and PaymentLineItem, which we will add to the Payment screen.

And so, we have basic administrative CRUD. Well, sort of.

We haven't actually limited access to administrators yet, which we'll do in Chapter 8, *Administration Roles*, on page 155. And there's a lot of business logic that the generic active admin doesn't know about:

- We can arbitrarily associate users and subscriptions on the user page.

- We can edit Stripe IDs, which we don't want to let admins do.

- Our associations, like Payment and PaymentLineItem or Event and Performance, can't be handled yet.

- We can't actually charge a credit card.

You get the idea. Some of these can be handled by judicious tweaking of the ActiveAdmin setup pages. Some, like events and performances, probably should have custom pages entirely. Some, like payments, probably need a lot of extra validation rules and payment rules and the like.

First, let's build a little bit more of the administrative UI by cleaning up one of the pages.

The event page has a couple of issues worth tweaking:

- We probably don't need the image_url, created_at, or updated_at in the index page. Actually, we probably want the image to be uploadable.

- It'd be nice to be able to add and see performances and maybe available tickets.

Here's some of what might work:

```
admin/01/app/admin/event.rb
ActiveAdmin.register Event do
  config.sort_order = "name_asc"

  filter :name
  filter :description

  index do
    selectable_column
    column :id
    column :name
    column :description
    actions
  end

  form do |f|
    f.semantic_errors(*f.object.errors.keys)
    f.inputs do
      f.input :name
      f.input :description
      f.input :image_url
    end
    f.inputs do
      f.has_many :performances, heading: "Performances",
                                allow_destroy: true do |fp|
        fp.input :start_time
        fp.input :end_time
      end
    end
    f.actions
  end
end
```

ActiveAdmin has a big domain-specific language (DSL) to define the various parts of its interaction. This file shows a few pieces.

The sidebar filters are defined by filter <attribute>. Further arguments to that method call allow you to define what kind of filter to use; otherwise it infers the best type based on its kind.

The index method takes a list calls to column, which determines the columns to be placed in the index page. The form method is mostly a wrapper around the Formtastic DSL for defining forms.[4] ActiveAdmin also lets you override controller actions, add custom markup, and do a number of other things. Full details can be found in the documentation.[5]

---

4. https://github.com/justinfrench/formtastic
5. https://github.com/activeadmin/activeadmin/tree/master/docs

Setting Up a Point of Purchase

I'm going to admit right up front that this particular section may not be totally applicable to every reader. But bear with me. It's fun, and makes for a surprisingly effective, and slightly disturbing, demo.

Snow Globe Theater is, of course, a theater. As such, it has a box office. However, in the case of the Snow Globe, it's quite a bit more "box" than "office." It's small. At the box office, people come in and want to buy tickets right there, not even over the Internet or anything.

Asking those people to stand in the lobby and access the website on their phones was dismissed as poor customer service, so the theater would like to build a point-of-purchase system that would allow an employee in the box office to swipe a credit card just like a real store and incorporate that into the application's workflow.

The ingredients of our point-of-purchase system are simple. We need a USB credit card reader, which is available online for something like $20, and we also want the jQuery.cardswipe plugin.[6]

The cardswipe plugin doesn't have a standard Rails packaging, so we're going to have to take the source and put it into a file in our vendor/assets/javascripts directory.[7] We also need to add it as //= require jquery.cardswipe to the manifest file in app/assets/javascripts/.

I would be remiss if I did not point out that the author of this plugin intends it for use in low-security applications, like, say, a private card for a health club, and does not consider it secure enough for payment processing. Which is why we only use it as a shortcut to data entry that we still pass through to Stripe for full data validation and fraud protection. We still don't hold on to the credit card data, and we still don't let it touch our server.

Now we need a place to enter credit card information. Luckily, we already have one, namely the user-facing shopping cart. Rather than build up a duplicate administrative-facing purchase system, we're going to cheat a bit and augment the user-facing one with a couple of administrative features. This is often a handy shortcut to getting customer-service types of administrative work in place, by giving administrators somewhat augmented access to the tools that already exist.

---

6.   https://github.com/CarlRaymond/jquery.cardswipe
7.   https://raw.githubusercontent.com/CarlRaymond/jquery.cardswipe/master/dist/jquery.cardswipe.js

In this case, administrators need to give an additional piece of information to the checkout. Because almost by definition the administrator is buying the ticket for somebody else, that person needs to be able to enter the eventual user somehow on the form. And we're going to give administrators the ability to swipe a credit card.

Add the fields to the credit card form above the existing credit card information:

admin/01/app/views/shopping_carts/_credit_card_info.html.slim
```
- if current_user.admin?
  #admin_credit_card_info
    h3 Administrator info
    .form-group
      .col-sm-2
        = label_tag(:user_email, "User Email", class: "control-label")
      .col-sm-2
        input.form-control(name="user_email" id="user_email")
```

This lets the admin enter an email address for the user. The DOM ID is there just to give the JavaScript something to look for to determine whether or not to display the email field.

On the server side, we'll need to translate that address to a user we can associate the purchase with. What do we do if there isn't an existing user in the system with that email address? That is an interesting question. Strict data integrity would imply that we should have the administrator explicitly create a full user first. But, if this is meant to be a point-of-purchase box office, speed is also important, and it may be better for our customer service to create a minimal user from just the email and ask the user to complete their profile later.

As a first pass, let's try this:

admin/01/app/controllers/payments_controller.rb
```
private def pick_user
  if current_user.admin? && params[:user_email].present?
    User.find_or_create_by(email: params[:user_email])
  else
    current_user
  end
end

private def stripe_subscription_workflow
  workflow = CreatesSubscriptionViaStripe.new(
      user: pick_user,
      expected_subscription_id: params[:subscription_ids].first,
      token: StripeToken.new(**card_params))
  workflow.run
  workflow
end
```

If there's an existing user, we use that user, if there isn't we create one with the email, and if the user isn't an admin, we just take the current_user.

We need some JavaScript code to integrate with the form code we've already written to take the swiped card data and fill it into the form correctly:

admin/01/app/assets/javascripts/purchases_cart.es6
```
$(() => {
  if ($("#admin_credit_card_info").size() > 0) {
    $.cardswipe({
      firstLineOnly: false,
      success: CheckoutForm.cardswipe,
      parsers: ["visa", "amex", "mastercard", "discover", "generic"],
      debug: false,
    })
  }
  if ($(".credit-card-form").size() > 0) {
    return new PaymentFormHandler()
  }

  return null
})
```

The actual USB card swiper sends what the operating system interprets as keypress events; the cardswipe library looks for a particular character combination at the beginning of the card data as a cue to start parsing.

The $.cardswipe command sets up the details of how we're parsing the data coming from the card. Specifically, we're allowing the library to use stock parsers for American Express, Visa, Discover, and MasterCard. If we're doing some kind of weird custom card processing, we can define our own parser. The firstLineOnly command makes parsing faster if you know you are only parsing standard U.S. bank cards, and success defines a callback to handle the data on a successful swipe. In our case, we're calling back to some methods on our CheckoutForm object:

admin/01/app/assets/javascripts/purchases_cart.es6
```
class CheckoutForm {

  static cardswipe(data) {
    new CheckoutForm().cardswipe(data)
  }

  cardswipe(data) {
    this.numberField().val(data.account)
    this.expiryField().val(`${data.expMonth}/${data.expYear}`)
    this.cvcField().focus()
  }
```

After parsing, all we do is take the parsed data and drop it into our form and then let our existing Stripe validators take over. We put the focus onto the cvc field input because the point of the CVC number is that it is not stored on the magnetic stripe and so must be typed in by hand. We want to type it in by looking at the card. From that point, the sales process can continue as before.

We can also bind some additional events to the card swipe, which allows us to let the user know that the scan is processing and notify the user of failure.

And that's all you need to set up your own card swiping point of sale, or just a way to freak out coworkers when you ask them for their credit cards so that you can test your scanner. Either way, it's fun, and might still be valuable for another few months until swiping credit cards is replaced by embedded chips, NearField Communication (NFC) payment, retina scans, or whatever else happens in the battle between credit cards and credit card fraud.

Next Up

You may have noticed a slight oversight in our administrative tools, which is that we haven't defined what an administrator is, how you become one, or how we limit certain actions to certain users. Authentication and authorization are the focus of the next chapter.

## CHAPTER 8

Administration Roles

Building an administration interface only solves part of your problem. Once the interface is in place, administrators are gonna administrate. By its very nature, administration involves circumventing the normal business logic of your application.

In this chapter, we'll look at how to manage the authentication of administrative users to allow them to make changes that normal users cannot. We'll also discuss two common administrative capabilities of a business site: the ability to grant refunds and the ability to manage discounts. In the next chapter, we'll talk more generically about an administrator's ability to break rules and how to maintain data integrity in the face of those changes.

Authentication and Roles

The most critical fact about your administrative tools is that they are only available to a small subset of users. Typically, those users are employees of your company, volunteers, or in some other way specifically chosen. Often you have some greater control over the administrative users' environments, and so can mandate the use of a specific browser. It's also usually easier to offer training to administrative users, and so we have the persistent idea that we can offer administrators less polished interfaces because they have the system knowledge and incentive to deal with poor interfaces.

Defining User Types

Let's talk about the subset of users issue. There are two related issues: we need to identify that certain users have special privileges, and we need to check for those privileges when a user tries to do certain actions.

Authentication is not an area that has been kind to one-size-fits-all toolkits; it seems to be an area where there is a lot of idiosyncratic logic custom to each application. The authentication tools that have been successful have mostly provided a framework to easily define and call your local authentication logic, rather than provide shortcuts for common authentication patterns.

At a high level, there are two models for user privileges:

- In the first model, user abilities are concentric, meaning that each new level is a superset of the previous level. So, you might have regular users and customer service users who can do everything a regular user can, in addition to editing other users' information. Then there are admins, who can do everything a customer service user can, plus they can create new events and give away free tickets. Finally, you might also have super-admins who can do everything.

- In the second model, user abilities are not concentric. One way this might happen is if you have multiple kinds of transactions and admins who can only deal with one of them. So, our theater might have a box office and a merchandise stand, and somebody might have box office access to manage ticket transactions, but not merchandise access to add new merchandise, and neither one might have the ability to refund purchases or add new events.

By and large, if you can possibly conceive your authentication logic as being concentric, your life will be easier: it's easier to determine what a user has access to, and it's easier to write the logic that limits access. The concentric pattern of, say User to Admin to Super Admin, is common for a reason. It's conceptually simple and applicable to a wide range of concerns.

That said, if your company has more complicated logic, then it does. Only you know how paranoid you have to be about over-granting access.

My generic recommendation is that if your access is concentric, the easiest way to model access in your database is to have a single field in your User table with an access level, which can be a string (user, admin, superadmin) or an integer (0 = user, 1 = admin) depending on your taste. We use a Rails enum in this application.

There are a couple of patterns here that I think you should avoid. A common starting place is to just have a Boolean admin field. That's fine as far as it goes, but it does not adapt well when authentication logic gets more complicated, which often leads to the next step of adding additional Boolean fields until you have several such fields in the users table. For concentric access patterns, this is overkill and can lead to problems if the set of Boolean fields are not kept consistent (a user who has admin = true, but customer_service = false, for example). This pattern maybe works a little better if the access is not concentric, but it still requires a database change for each new access type, which is not ideal.

When you have a series of Boolean fields in a single table, the common mitigation is to normalize the database by creating a separate table. This might be a roles table with a list of all possible roles, and then a roles_users join table to create a many-to-many relationship between roles and users.

For our theater application, we've preset the User class to have a role attribute, and we've set up an ActiveRecord enum with the roles, enum role: {user: 0, vip: 1, admin: 2}. One thing to be careful of when using ActiveRecord enums for authentication is that you can't depend on the order of the values matching the relative rank of the roles. As currently written, our roles do line up like that: user has less power than vip, which has less power than admin, but if we add another role after admin, we don't want to be forced to reorder the enum listing (which is dangerous).

In practice, this means avoiding code like the following:

```
def admin_powers?
  role >= admin
end
```

and instead explicitly enumerating role combinations like this:

```
def admin_powers?
  role.in?(:vip, :admin)
end
```

You want to be careful with default values. I set up the role attribute like so:

```
add_column :users, :role, :integer, default: 0
```

I can get away with setting the default to 0, because I've explicitly set the lowest attribute level in the enum to zero. In other cases, you might need to handle default values differently, but you want to make sure that a user with an unspecified role has no special privileges.

Using Pundit to Set Up Authentication

We have to limit our ActiveAdmin dashboard to only administrative users, and we also want to start giving administrators access to parts of the site that other users don't have. For example, a useful first step before setting up an entire administrative interface is to give administrators access to already existing display and edit resources that belong to other users. Typically users can only see and edit their own profiles. But, rather than create a separate administrative user page, we could start by giving administrators the ability to view and potentially edit another user's profile. We just need to manage permissions.

The Pundit[1] gem is used to define authentication rules, making it easy to check whether a user has the authority to perform a specific action on a specific piece of data. We'll add it to our application to support limiting access to data based on the user making the request. And along the way, we'll also lock down our ActiveAdmin site.

As the site currently stands, we have a very minimal user dashboard that shows the user their subscriptions. Let's augment that very slightly, and give it an edit page. Here's the controller:

admin/01/app/controllers/users_controller.rb
```
class UsersController < ApplicationController

  before_action :load_user

  def show
  end

  def edit
  end

  def update
    @user.update(user_params)
    authorize(@user)
    render :show
  end

  private def load_user
    @user = User.find(params[:id])
    authorize(@user)
  end

  private def user_params
    params.require(:user).permit(:name)
  end

end
```

If you look at that controller quickly, it looks like I've made an egregious security error by selecting the user to display based merely on the params[:id] value that is incoming from the request URL. In general, trusting incoming data from the user is a bad idea, and the basic root of many security issues. Often, for a user page like this, you'd use current_user as the user to display.

---

1. https://github.com/elabs/pundit

In this particular case, though, we're covered. Before we display the view, we call authorize(@user), which invokes Pundit. Pundit is then responsible for determining whether the user is authorized to see the page, and it throws an exception if the user is not authorized.

Let's make sure Pundit is set up, and see how Pundit's authorization works.

First, we need the Pundit gem in our Gemfile—if you've been following along with the code base in the example, it's already there:

```
gem "pundit"
```

We can then generate the boilerplate setup:

```
rails generate pundit:install
```

This generates one file—a policy file—that we don't really care about right now. It's boilerplate, and we will use a more specific version.

We also need to make some changes to the ApplicationController file so that our Pundit setup will be available to all our controllers:

admin/01/app/controllers/application_controller.rb
```
class ApplicationController < ActionController::Base

  protect_from_forgery with: :exception

  include Pundit

  rescue_from Pundit::NotAuthorizedError, with: :user_not_authorized

  def authenticate_admin_user!
    raise Pundit::NotAuthorizedError unless current_user&.admin?
  end

  private def user_not_authorized
    sign_out(User)
    render plain: "Access Not Allowed", status: :forbidden
  end

end
```

There are some things in this file that are new and authorization-related.

First, we include pundit, which makes the authorize method available to all our controllers. This part is necessary to use Pundit, although you don't need to have this call in the ApplicationController; you could choose to include Pundit individually in any controller that needs it.

In the next line, we use the Rails rescue_from feature, which allows us to designate a handler for an exception whenever a controller throws that particular exception. The rescue_from functionality is useful any time you have significant commonality over how an exception is handled across the application. Because it's common to want to handle all authorization errors similarly, rescue_from is a great way to make that happen.

Let's hold off on exactly what that rescue_from does for a second, and instead focus on what happens when we make that authorize(@user) call back in the UsersController.

When you call authorize, Pundit uses four pieces of information to determine what to do:

- The name of the controller, which in this case is UsersController
- The name of the action, which in this case is show
- The actual object for which access is desired, which in this case is @user
- The currently logged-in user, which is taken from the current_user method

This may be a little confusing because we are looking at a user record, and the current user is also, well, a user object. Usually, the object we are trying to deal with—which Pundit calls a *record*—is not the same class as the current user.

Given those pieces of information, Pundit looks to create an instance of a policy class. By default, it derives the name of the policy class from the type of the object passed to authorize. We've passed in a user, so Pundit looks for a UserPolicy class. Once that policy object is initialized, Pundit calls a method derived from the controller action. The show action means that Pundit will look for a show? method. You can change the default behavior in a number of useful ways; for details, see the Pundit documentation.[2]

Here's the entire policy class:

admin/01/app/policies/user_policy.rb
```ruby
class UserPolicy

  attr_reader :user, :record

  def initialize(user, record)
    @user = user
    @record = record
  end

  def same_user?
    user == record
  end

  def show?
    same_user? || user.admin?
  end
```

---

2. https://github.com/elabs/pundit

```
def update?
  same_user? || user.admin?
end

def edit?
  same_user? || user.admin?
end
```

```
end
```

The authorization methods in Pundit are expected to return a Boolean value. If the method returns true, the action is authorized and it proceeds. If the method returns false, the action is not authorized, and Pundit throws a Pundit::NotAuthorizedError exception.

Our rule for show?, edit?, and create? is to return true if the logged-in user doing the lookup is the same as the user being looked up, or if the logged-in user is an admin.

If Pundit throws an exception, we can catch it anywhere. As mentioned earlier, I've chosen to use the Rails rescue_from mechanism to create a global handler:

admin/01/app/controllers/application_controller.rb
```ruby
class ApplicationController < ActionController::Base

  protect_from_forgery with: :exception

  include Pundit

  rescue_from Pundit::NotAuthorizedError, with: :user_not_authorized

  def authenticate_admin_user!
    raise Pundit::NotAuthorizedError unless current_user&.admin?
  end

  private def user_not_authorized
    sign_out(User)
    render plain: "Access Not Allowed", status: :forbidden
  end

end
```

That handler uses Devise's sign_out method to log the user out and displays a plain "Access Not Allowed" method, which is a little on the cold side, but you are free to do anything you want here. Redirecting to root and displaying a flash message is another common option, as is logging the access for later perusal.

I have also added an authenticate_admin_user! method that checks to see if the current user is an administrator, and if not, throws the same Pundit exception. This method has nothing to do with Pundit, except that the exception is a useful way to trigger consistent behavior. Instead, this method is called by

ActiveAdmin. If you go to the config/active_admin.rb method, you'll see a line that is commented out:

```
config.authentication_method = :authenticate_admin_user!
```

Uncomment that line, and ActiveAdmin will check with the authenticate_admin_user! method before hitting any ActiveAdmin page. It's also possible to integrate ActiveAdmin with Pundit to give finer-grained control; see the docs for more information.

Testing Authentication

You can test your authentication logic by setting up user situations in RSpec controller tests.

admin/01/spec/controllers/users_controller_spec.rb
```ruby
require "rails_helper"

RSpec.describe UsersController, :aggregate_failures do

  let(:logged_in_user) { create(:user) }
  let(:other_user) { create(:user) }

  describe "access to show and edit" do

    before(:example) do
      sign_in(logged_in_user)
    end

    it "allows a user to view their own page" do
      get :show, params: {id: logged_in_user}
      expect(response).to be_a_success
    end

    it "blocks a user from viewing another user's page" do
      get :show, params: {id: other_user}
      expect(response).to be_forbidden
      expect(controller.user_signed_in?).to be_falsy
    end

    context "logging in as an admin" do

      before(:example) { logged_in_user.admin! }

      it "allows an admin to view another user's page" do
        get :show, params: {id: other_user}
        expect(response).to be_a_success
      end

    end

  end

end
```

Here we test all three setups for the show action: a user viewing his own page, a user viewing another person's page, and an admin viewing another person's page. You can also write similar tests for update? and create?.

If you do not like running the authentication logic in controller tests, you can also make them feature tests almost as is. Instead of accessing the actions via get, you would simulate a page with the Capybara visit method. Alternately, you can unit test the policy classes by explicitly creating something like UserPolicy.new(logged_in_user, other_user) and directly testing whether show? returns true or false.

Now that we've got some authentication, let's apply it to the most common administrative financial task: issuing refunds.

Issuing Refunds

One of the first things we need to allow administrators to do is refund purchases. In a way, refunds are a miniature of everything that caused me to want to write this book, which is to say that their apparent API simplicity covers a tremendous amount of business logic complexity.

Refunds are actually even easier in the Stripe API than purchases, since we don't need to validate a credit card or other purchase method. In fact, we could choose to do refunds from the Stripe dashboard and just catch a webhook on our side to process the data.

But there are all kinds of issues we need to deal with:

- Who can authorize a refund?
- How does somebody authorize a refund?
- Can we issue a partial refund? If so, does that mean we can allow multiple refunds of the same purchase?

Beyond those issues, we have a pervasive system issue. We potentially have all kinds of places in our code base—in reporting, in redemption, and so on—that assume that a purchase can not be undone and always lasts forever. Allowing refunds means we can no longer make that simplifying assumption.

Modeling Refunds

Let's say we have a disgruntled customer, or a customer who realizes she has a conflict for a performance, and we decide to refund her purchase because we are nice people who believe in the value of customer service.

First, we need to decide how to represent refunds in our database. I think there are basically two options:

- Add a refunded_amount_cents field to our Payment table, and when a payment is refunded, update the payment appropriately.

- Add a new "payment" record for a refund, with a negative price, and associate it with the original purchase.

I'm going to choose the second option, even though it's slightly more complicated. Here's why:

- By and large, the more we can treat payment records that are already in the database as immutable, the easier our record keeping is going to be.

- The question of how to store our responses from the payment gateway is easier if each interaction with the database has its own record.

Also, in the category of "things you don't think are ever going to happen until they do," there's the multiple partial refund. As in: "we've bought four tickets to the show, but now George and Martha can't make it. Can you refund two of the tickets?" Then later, "Fred can't make it either, so can you refund one other ticket?" This leaves us with one active ticket and three refunded ones over two transactions. Ugh. (Just to get this on paper, if somebody ever wants to undo a refund, just create a new transaction and pretend the earlier stuff never happened. Everybody will be happier that way.)

So we need a little bit of extra data to handle the creation of these new refund payments:

```
admin/01/db/migrate/20160802212114_refund_columns.rb
class RefundColumns < ActiveRecord::Migration[5.0]

  def change
    change_table :payments do |t|
      t.references :original_payment, index: true
      t.references :administrator, index: true
    end

    change_table :payment_line_items do |t|
      t.references :original_line_item, index: true
      t.references :administrator, index: true
      t.integer :refund_status, default: 0
    end
  end

end
```

That's a column in the Payments class that references the original payment if the payment is refund, and another to reference the administrator who triggered the refund, for audit purposes. The PaymentsLineItem class gets the same columns, plus a new column to store refund status.

Before we get this in code, there's one other data modeling issue we need to tackle, which is a little more specific to our particular application. Let's say we've got 100 tickets for a performance. Somebody buys two, which leaves us with 98, but then he refunds the tickets. This should get us back to 100 tickets, which we can do either by changing the state of the ticket objects back to unpurchased or by creating two new ticket objects.

Refund Code

To make our lives easier, we are going to limit refunds to either an entire purchase or an entire purchase line item. (Honestly, though, if we really wanted to make our lives easier, we'd forget that the entire concept of "refunds" even existed and take up something less stressful, like juggling fire.)

It makes the most sense to put a refund button inside the individual show view for the Purchase and PurchaseLineItem views in our administration dashboard. To do this, we're going to customize the ActiveAdmin view, for which, I think it's going to be easier if we have a dedicated PurchaseLineItem page:

```
% rails generate active_admin:resource PaymentLineItem
```

We need to update the Payment admin panel both to be more usable and to have a button for a refund:

```
admin/01/app/admin/payment.rb
ActiveAdmin.register Payment do
  filter :reference
  filter :price
  filter :status
  filter :payment_method
  filter :created_at

  index do
    selectable_column
    id_column
    column :reference
    column :user
    column :price
    column :status
    column :payment_method
    column :created_at
    actions
  end
```

```
show do
  attributes_table do
    row :reference
    row :price
    row :status
    row :payment_method
    row :user
    row :created_at
    row :response_id
    row :full_response
  end
  active_admin_comments
end
action_item :refund, only: :show do
  link_to("Refund Payment",
      refund_path(id: payment.id, type: Payment),
      method: "POST",
      class: "button",
      data: {confirm: "Are you sure you want to refund this payment?"})
  end
end
end
```

We're setting a filter, index columns, and what to display on the show page. The action_item block gives us a button in the header of the show page to refund the payment. That data: {confirm:} is important, causing Rails to pop up a JavaScript alert to confirm the refund before passing it along, which is an important safety feature.

Along the same lines, you might be tempted to put the "refund" button in the index page to save the click into the show page. Most of the time, this is a bad idea. Having multiple, very dangerous buttons next to each other increases the chance that somebody will accidentally fat-finger one of them and cause problems, especially if they are on a mobile device. Call it a "rule of thumb."

Another good idea, which I'm not implementing here, is to have the refund button trigger a pop-up that allows the administrator to make a note that can be stored in the database for future reference. ActiveAdmin's comment system can be used instead.

The link_to takes us to a controller. I've decided to make this a separate RefundsController. Eventually, we might use a Refunds resource to list all refunds for reporting purposes.

Our plan is to have the controller call a workflow to do local setup, and then spawn a background job for communication with Stripe.

Here's the controller:

```ruby
admin/01/app/controllers/refunds_controller.rb
class RefundsController < ApplicationController

  def create
    load_refundable
    authorize(@refundable, :refund?)
    workflow = PreparesStripeRefund.new(
        refundable: @refundable,
        administrator: current_user,
        refund_amount_cents: @refundable.price_cents)
    workflow.run
    flash[:alert] = workflow.error || "Refund submitted"
    redirect_to redirect_path
  end

  VALID_REFUNDABLES = %w(Payment PaymentLineItem).freeze

  private def load_refundable
    raise "bad refundable class" unless params[:type].in?(VALID_REFUNDABLES)
    @refundable = params[:type].constantize.find(params[:id])
  end

  private def redirect_path
    params[:type] == if params[:type] == "Payment"
                     then admin_payments_path
                     else admin_payments_line_item_path
                     end
  end

end
```

We've seen most of the basic structure here. The tricky part is that the thing we are refunding could either be a Payment or a PaymentLineItem.

The code loads the payable based on its class, and then we use Pundit to authorize the action. Even though the controller action is create, we actually want to authorize refunds separately from other controller actions; therefore, the code explicitly states that Pundit should check for a refund? action.

The policy is really simple right now. The action is okay if the user is an administrator:

```ruby
admin/01/app/policies/payment_policy.rb
class PaymentPolicy

  attr_reader :user, :record

  def initialize(user, record)
    @user = user
    @record = record
  end
```

```
def refund?
  user.admin?
end

end
```

The code needs a nearly identical PaymentLineItemPolicy class as well.

We pass the refundable, the currently logged-in administrator, and the amount of the refund to the workflow object. No matter what the workflow does, our response is the same: we redirect to the index path for the class being refunded and display a message.

The workflow's main jobs are to validate that the refund is legal, and then update the status of all our database objects to prepare them for the Stripe background job. Remember, we decided that for each refund, we'll generate a new payment object.

Here's the code for the setup workflow:

admin/01/app/workflows/prepares_stripe_refund.rb
```
class PreparesStripeRefund

  attr_accessor :administrator, :refund_amount_cents, :payment_id,
      :success, :refund_payment, :refundable, :error

  delegate :save, to: :refund_payment

  def initialize(administrator:, refund_amount_cents:, refundable:)
    @administrator = administrator
    @refund_amount_cents = refund_amount_cents
    @refundable = refundable
    @success = false
    @error = nil
  end

  def pre_purchase_valid?
    refundable.present?
  end

  def run
    Payment.transaction do
      raise "not valid" unless pre_purchase_valid?
      self.refund_payment = generate_refund_payment.payment
      raise "can't refund that amount" unless
        refund_payment.can_refund?(refund_amount_cents)
      update_tickets
      RefundChargeJob.perform_later(refundable_id: refund_payment.id)
      self.success = true
    end
  rescue StandardError => exception
    self.error = exception.message
    on_failure
```

```ruby
  end

  def on_failure
    self.success = false
  end

  def generate_refund_payment
    refundable.generate_refund_payment(
        amount_cents: refund_amount_cents, admin: administrator)
  end

  def update_tickets
    refundable.tickets.each(&:refund_pending!)
  end

  def success?
    success
  end

end
```

The interesting part, as with other workflows, is in the run method.

We have a simple pre-flight validation, which for now, is just that the refundable object is actually there. Then, the code tries to generate_refund_payment, which means asking our refundable object to create its own refund version of itself.

If we're refunding a payment, we create a new payment with the appropriate fields and then loop over our line items and ask them to do the same:

```ruby
admin/01/app/models/payment.rb
class Payment < ActiveRecord::Base

  include HasReference

  belongs_to :user, optional: true
  has_many :payment_line_items
  has_many :tickets, through: :payment_line_items,
                     source_type: "Ticket", source: "buyable"
  belongs_to :administrator, class_name: "User"
  has_many :refunds, class_name: "Payment",
                     foreign_key: "original_payment_id"
  belongs_to :original_payment, class_name: "Payment"

  monetize :price_cents

  enum status: {created: 0, succeeded: 1, pending: 2, failed: 3,
                refund_pending: 4, refunded: 5}

  def total_cost
    tickets.map(&:price).sum
  end
```

```ruby
def create_line_items(tickets)
  tickets.each do |ticket|
    payment_line_items.create!(
        buyable: ticket, price_cents: ticket.price.cents)
  end
end

def sorted_ticket_ids
  tickets.map(&:id).sort
end

def generate_refund_payment(amount_cents:, admin:)
  refund_payment = Payment.create!(
      user_id: user_id, price_cents: -amount_cents, status: "refund_pending",
      payment_method: payment_method, original_payment_id: id,
      administrator: admin, reference: Payment.generate_reference)
  payment_line_items.each do |line_item|
    line_item.generate_refund_payment(
        admin: admin,
        amount_cents: amount_cents,
        refund_payment: refund_payment)
  end
  refund_payment
end

def payment
  self
end

def maximum_available_refund
  price + refunds.map(&:price).sum
end

def can_refund?(price)
  price <= maximum_available_refund
end

def refund?
  price.negative?
end
end
```

Note that we've added a self-join at the top of the Payment class, so a payment can have_many refunds. A payment that is a refund also belongs_to its original payment. Because of how we are handling the data, the clearest way to tell whether a payment is a refund or not is to check if the price is greater than or less than zero.

Creating refund versions of the line items, however, is more challenging because we need to consider two possibilities. If we're creating a refund item as part of refunding an entire purchase, we need to attach the line item to that purchase. But if we're creating a refund version of a line item, that can happen in two different scenarios: the line item is being refunded either on its own or as part of a larger payment.

We can handle that situation a little awkwardly by optionally passing the refund payment to the line item when it exists, and if it doesn't exist, creating a payment, like this:

```
admin/01/app/models/payment_line_item.rb
class PaymentLineItem < ApplicationRecord

  belongs_to :payment
  belongs_to :buyable, polymorphic: true

  has_many :refunds, class_name: "PaymentLineItem",
                     foreign_key: "original_line_item_id"
  belongs_to :original_line_item, class_name: "PaymentLineItem"

  enum refund_status: {no_refund: 1, refund_pending: 2, refunded: 3}

  delegate :performance, to: :buyable, allow_nil: true
  delegate :name, :event, to: :performance, allow_nil: true
  delegate :id, to: :event, prefix: true, allow_nil: true

  monetize :price_cents

  def generate_refund_payment(admin:, amount_cents:, refund_payment: nil)
    refund_payment ||= Payment.create!(
        user_id: payment.user_id, price_cents: -amount_cents,
        status: "refund_pending", payment_method: payment.payment_method,
        original_payment_id: payment.id, administrator: admin,
        reference: Payment.generate_reference)
    PaymentLineItem.create!(
        buyable: buyable, price_cents: -price_cents,
        refund_status: "refund_pending", original_line_item_id: id,
        administrator_id: admin.id, payment: refund_payment)
  end

  def original_payment
    original_line_item&.payment
  end

  def tickets
    [buyable]
  end

end
```

There's one other subtlety, which is that we make Payment and PaymentLineItem slightly API-comparable by defining Payment#payment and PaymentLineItem#tickets, which enables us to not have to worry about whether the generate_refund_payment returns a Payment or a PaymentLineItem.

I'm sure at this point you are getting impatient and wondering why we can't just call the blankety-blank refund method and be done with it. And sure, you could. But six months later when some accountant asks why there's a $250 discrepancy between your records and your bank account, there's some pain in your future.

Back to the workflow. After we call generate_refund_payment.payment, we've guaranteed that we're holding onto the new payment object that is being refunded. There is one safeguard we can use to check to see that the payment hasn't already been refunded: calling can_refund?. can_refund? compares the refund amount requested with the price of the object, minus any money that has already been refunded.

If that check passes, we update the ticket objects by putting them in a new refund_pending status. We don't return them back to the available pool until after the refund has been fully processed. If everything is still good, we create a background job. If anything has raised an exception, we roll back the transaction and return a failure state.

Like our other background jobs, the RefundChargeJob is a thin wrapper around a workflow instance:

admin/01/app/jobs/refund_charge_job.rb
```ruby
class RefundChargeJob < ActiveJob::Base

  include Rollbar::ActiveJob

  queue_as :default

  def perform(refundable_id:)
    refundable = Payment.find(refundable_id)
    workflow = CreatesStripeRefund(refundable)
    workflow.run
  end

end
```

By now, we can guarantee that the refundable object is a Payment, because even if it was originally a PaymentLineItem, we created a new Payment object to handle the refund.

The workflow object is similar to the charge objects, but a little simpler, because we don't have to worry about tokens:

admin/01/app/workflows/creates_stripe_refund.rb
```ruby
class CreatesStripeRefund

  attr_accessor :payment_to_refund, :success, :stripe_refund

  def initialize(payment_to_refund:)
    @payment_to_refund = payment_to_refund
```

```ruby
    @success = false
  end

  def run
    Payment.transaction do
      process_refund
      update_payment
      update_tickets
      on_success
    end
  rescue StandardError
    on_failure
  end

  def process_refund
    raise "No Such Payment" if payment_to_refund.nil?
    @stripe_refund = StripeRefund.new(payment_to_refund: payment_to_refund)
    @stripe_refund.refund
    raise "Refund failure" unless stripe_refund.success?
  end

  def update_payment
    payment_to_refund.update!(stripe_refund.refund_attributes)
    payment_to_refund.payment_line_items.each(&:refunded!)
    payment_to_refund.original_payment.refunded! if stripe_refund.success?
  end

  def update_tickets
    payment_to_refund.tickets.each(&:refund_successful)
  end

  def on_success
    RefundMailer.notify_success(payment_to_refund).deliver_later
  end

  def on_failure
    unrefund_tickets
    RefundMailer.notify_failure(payment_to_refund).deliver_later
  end

  def unrefund_tickets
    payment_to_refund.tickets.each(&:purchased!)
  end

end
```

The workflow is split into process_refund, update_payment, and update_tickets. Processing the refund is delegated to a StripeRefund class that is analogous to the other wrappers we've used to talk to third-party libraries. We'll get to that in a second.

If the refund is successful, we need to handle the bookkeeping in our database, which means updating the status and response ID from the Stripe call, and also updating the stars of all the affected PaymentLineItem instances. We also need to go back to the original payment and mark it as refunded.

That's not all, friends. We also need to handle the ticket management, meaning that we need to mark the existing ticket objects as refunded, but return new tickets to the general pool so that they can be repurchased. This step is particularly specific to applications that have inventory. If you are just selling a service, you most likely don't have to manipulate inventory.

The Ticket class needs a method to handle a successful refund:

`admin/01/app/models/ticket.rb`
```ruby
def refund_successful
  refunded!
  new_ticket = dup
  new_ticket.unsold!
end
```

First, change the status of the ticket to refunded; then duplicate the ticket using the ActiveRecord dup method, and set the status of the new ticket back to unsold.

If the Stripe status and all the database stuff saves successfully, the workflow returns success and notifies the user via email; otherwise it returns failure.

Our actual StripeRefund class is similar to our StripeCharge class:

`admin/01/app/models/stripe_refund.rb`
```ruby
class StripeRefund

  attr_accessor :payment_to_refund, :response, :error, :amount_to_refund

  def initialize(payment_to_refund:, amount_to_refund: nil)
    @payment_to_refund = payment_to_refund
    @amount_to_refund = amount_to_refund || -payment_to_refund.price_cents
  end

  delegate :original_payment, to: :payment_to_refund

  def refund
    return if original_payment.nil?
    @response = Stripe::Refund.create(
        {charge: original_payment.response_id, amount: amount_to_refund,
         metadata: {
             refund_reference: payment_to_refund.reference,
             original_reference: original_payment.reference}},
        idempotency_key: payment_to_refund.reference)
  rescue Stripe::CardError => e
    @response = nil
    @error = e
  end
```

```ruby
  def success?
    response || !error
  end

  def refund_attributes
    success? ? success_attributes : failure_attributes
  end

  def success_attributes
    {status: :refunded,
      response_id: response.id, full_response: response.to_json}
  end

  def failure_attributes
    {status: :failed, full_response: error.to_json}
  end

end
```

There's a single API call to Stripe::Refund.create at the heart of this class. As far as the Stripe API is concerned, we only need one piece of information to trigger a refund: the Stripe ID of the payment being refunded, which we store as the response_id of the original purchase—not the purchase object that we created for the purposes of managing the refund. We can optionally pass an amount to refund (in cents) to the Stripe call. If no amount is passed, Stripe assumes that the entire purchase should be refunded. As with our purchases, we also pass across some metadata to store on Stripe to make it easier to look up items on the Stripe dashboard, and we pass an idempotency_key to prevent the refund from being triggered twice.

If the call fails, we hold on to the error. If it succeeds, we hold on to the response.

Applying Discounts

It's another fine day in the Snow Globe Theater offices when the phone rings. It's ConHugeCo, a local business. ConHugeCo would love to take its staff to a production of *Much Ado About Nothing*, and they are willing to buy hundreds of tickets.

But they want a 25 percent discount.

As the site currently exists, we have no good way to offer this price, short of creating or editing a whole bunch of ticket objects, which creates other problems. Instead, we'd like to allow the purchase to go through as normal, but apply a discount to it.

I wasn't sure I wanted to talk about discounts and discount codes here—they tend to be extremely specific to the domain you are working in. But nearly every business that exchanges money on the web has some kind of discount code process, and if you are anything like me, your first implementation has some flaws.

I want to talk about discounts here, but mostly from the administrative side. There are multiple ways to allow users to enter codes, from having an extra field in the form to offering different URLs, and I'm not really covering the UI issues here.

A quick overview of important points:

- You very much want discount codes to be their own items in the database. They should have many-to-many relationships with the purchases, purchase line items, and inventory items they are applied to.

- You need to always be able to re-create the exact price calculation that happened when the item was originally purchased. Toward that end, it's a good idea to make the discount amounts immutable once a discount code is used. Also, in much the same way we copy the actual price paid to a purchase object, it's a good idea to copy the exact discount amount used to calculate the purchase.

- Adding discounts adds two new complexities to the payment process: calculating whether a given discount applies to a purchase, and the complexity of calculating the price given a discount. Keeping it simple is a really good idea.

Discount Objects

Let's write some code. We will start with a database migration for our new DiscountCode class:

```
$ rails generate model discount_code code:string \
  percentage:integer description:text \
  minimum_amount:monetize maximum_discount:monetize \
  max_uses:integer
```

This generates a migration for the DiscountCode model. We also need to add some fields to the Payment model:

admin/02/db/migrate/20160803000629_create_discount_codes.rb
```
class CreateDiscountCodes < ActiveRecord::Migration[5.0]

  def change
    create_table :discount_codes do |t|
```

```
      t.string :code
      t.integer :percentage
      t.text :description
      t.monetize :minimum_amount
      t.monetize :maximum_discount
      t.integer :max_uses

      t.timestamps
    end

    change_table :payments do |t|
      t.references :discount_code
      t.monetize :discount
    end
  end

end
```

A DiscountCode has the following fields: a code, which is the short text the user types in to use the code; a percentage, which is an integer value (presumably 0 - 100) for the percentage discount; and a description field, which is, well, a description. Then I added three fields that sit in for whatever business logic you might want to use to determine whether the code applies. I've got minimum_amount_cents as in: you need to purchase at least $50 to get the discount; maximum_discount_cents, as in: no more than $10 off no matter how many you buy; and maximum_uses, as in: an individual user can only use the code twice. I guess that it'd also be common to have a start and an end date.

As far as associations go, I've made a simplifying assumption to keep us from going any further into the weeds than strictly necessary. Discount codes only apply to entire purchases, and the user has one shot to enter a discount code as part of the checkout process. That means we don't need to store the discount code in the session or with the shopping cart tickets or anything. It also means that Payment is the only other class that needs to have a relationship with discount codes. We'll store the actual calculated discount as part of the payment. Using monetize sets up the field with a default value of zero, so the existing happy path won't be disrupted.

Before we can continue, we need to make one more quick stop to add discount codes to our ActiveAdmin dashboard:

```
% rails generate active_admin:resource DiscountCode
```

Discount Workflow

To get the code working, the first step is to add a form field to our checkout form:

```
admin/02/app/views/shopping_carts/_credit_card_info.html.slim
.form-group
  .col-sm-2
    = label_tag(:discount_code, "Discount Code", class: "control-label")
  .col-sm-2
    input.form-control.valid-field(name="discount_code" id="discount_code")
  .col-sm-3
    = submit_tag("Apply Code", class: "btn btn-primary", id: "apply_code")
= hidden_field_tag(:active_discount_code, "")
```

This gives us a place to enter the discount code, a button to submit it even if the purchase button is still invalid, and a hidden field to store the active code if one exists.

If we submit the checkout form, control goes to the PaymentsController. If there's a new discount code, we throw it into the session and put control right back to the shopping cart:

```
admin/02/app/controllers/payments_controller.rb
def create
  if params[:discount_code].present?
    session[:new_discount_code] = params[:discount_code]
    redirect_to shopping_cart_path
    return
  end
  workflow = run_workflow(params[:payment_type], params[:purchase_type])
  if workflow.success
    redirect_to workflow.redirect_on_success_url ||
        payment_path(id: @reference || workflow.payment.reference)
  else
    redirect_to shopping_cart_path
  end
end
```

The reason we kick control back to the shopping cart is because we need to display the shopping cart with the new, discounted price to give the user a chance to either change the discount code or purchase the items. Another option would be to have the discount code input field be its own form and pass it to a dedicated controller action for discount codes.

On the ShoppingCartController side, all we do is take that code that we placed in the session and pass it along to the shopping cart:

admin/02/app/controllers/shopping_carts_controller.rb

```
def show
  @cart = ShoppingCart.new(current_user, session[:new_discount_code])
end
```

(As an aside, I might consider hiding the session set and retrieve behind a method so as not to have the two methods be mutually dependent on the specific key being used in the session hash.)

We now have a data modeling issue—because we *always* have a data modeling issue. Until now, we have been calculating the price of an order by simply taking the sum of the tickets involved—code that we have possibly unnecessarily duplicated in both the ShoppingCart and Payment classes.

Over time, both ShoppingCart and Payment need to be able to recalculate the price from a set of tickets. Even if ShoppingCart can do the initial work, the Payment class will need to be able to reproduce it for reporting and auditing purposes. We really don't want this logic to be duplicated. And we're only at the beginning of the business complexity here; we're going to need a place to add transaction fees, shipping fees, taxes, or any other possible quirks as our application gets more complicated.

The answer is PriceCalculator, a new class that takes a list of tickets and a promotional code, and outputs the final price of the tickets. Not only does having a class here prevent our duplication problem, it's also a good place to handle increasing price complexity.

To work right now, the PriceCalculator needs a list of tickets and an optional discount code. Hey, the shopping cart has both of those things:

admin/02/app/models/shopping_cart.rb

```
attr_accessor :user, :discount_code_string

def initialize(user, discount_code_string = nil)
  @user = user
  @discount_code_string = discount_code_string
end

def discount_code
  @discount_code ||= DiscountCode.find_by(code: discount_code_string)
end
```

```
def total_cost
  PriceCalculator.new(tickets, discount_code).total_price
end

def tickets
  @tickets ||= user.tickets_in_cart
end
```

We're using the PriceCalcuator as a service that the shopping cart can invoke when it wants to calculate total price.

The PriceCalculator, at the moment, coordinates pretty closely with the DiscountCode class:

admin/02/app/services/price_calculator.rb
```
class PriceCalculator

  attr_accessor :tickets, :discount_code

  def initialize(tickets = [], discount_code = nil)
    @tickets = tickets
    @discount_code = discount_code || NullDiscountCode.new
  end

  def subtotal
    tickets.map(&:price).sum
  end

  def total_price
    discount_code.apply_to(subtotal)
  end

  def discount
    discount_code.discount_for(subtotal)
  end

end
```

While the code is now more complicated than the price calculation was at the beginning of this chapter, it's not actually all that bad. What we used to call the total is now calculated by the subtotal method, and the total_price method defers to the discount code to calculate the discount, as does the discount method.

There is a boundary, though. The price calculator knows about the list of tickets and only tells the discount code object the subtotal. This is a clean separation right now, though I can imagine future business logic that might disrupt it (for example, discount codes that only apply to specific performances). Eventually we might grow to have one or more DiscountCodeApplicationRule class to handle the complex logic.

The discount code has the math you might expect to support the discount, the minimum amount constraint, and the max discount constraint:

```ruby
admin/02/app/models/discount_code.rb
class DiscountCode < ApplicationRecord

  monetize :minimum_amount_cents
  monetize :maximum_discount_cents

  def percentage_float
    percentage * 1.0 / 100
  end

  def multiplier
    1 - percentage_float
  end

  def apply_to(subtotal)
    subtotal - discount_for(subtotal)
  end

  def discount_for(subtotal)
    return Money.zero unless applies_to_total?(subtotal)
    result = subtotal * percentage_float
    result = [result, maximum_discount].min if maximum_discount?
    result
  end

  def maximum_discount?
    maximum_discount_cents.present? && maximum_discount > Money.zero
  end

  def applies_to_total?(subtotal)
    return true if minimum_amount_cents.nil?
    subtotal >= minimum_amount
  end

end
```

One quirk of the collaboration is that the PriceCalculator uses the Null Object pattern, meaning that if it cannot find a discount code instance matching the code it's been given, it creates an instance of a class called NullDiscountCode, rather than holding on to the nil value.

I've defined NullDiscountCode as a subclass of DiscountCode where the percentage has been hard-coded to zero:

```ruby
admin/02/app/models/null_discount_code.rb
class NullDiscountCode < DiscountCode

  def percentage
    0
  end

end
```

What's great about the NullDiscountCode is that, with the percentage set to zero, all the other calculations (so far) just work. This means that our PriceCalculator doesn't have to continually check to see if the code object is nil, making the calculator code that much simpler.

Purchase Workflow Code

With our price calculator and discount code incorporated into the shopping cart, we just need to make sure that they are incorporated into the purchase itself. Mostly, this means making sure that the promo code and discount amount get saved along with the purchase. This requires some slight changes to our existing purchase workflows.

First, we need to pass the discount code into the workflow. I'll do this for both of our product payment codes. We'll leave off subscriptions, except to note that recurring discounts on Stripe subscriptions need to be created as Stripe objects, in much the same way that subscription plans do:

```
admin/02/app/controllers/payments_controller.rb
private def paypal_workflow
  workflow = PreparesCartForPayPal.new(
      user: current_user,
      purchase_amount_cents: params[:purchase_amount_cents],
      expected_ticket_ids: params[:ticket_ids],
      discount_code_string: session[:new_discount_code])
  workflow.run
  workflow
end

private def stripe_workflow
  @reference = Payment.generate_reference
  PreparesCartForStripeJob.perform_later(
      user: current_user,
      params: card_params,
      purchase_amount_cents: params[:purchase_amount_cents],
      expected_ticket_ids: params[:ticket_ids],
      payment_reference: @reference,
      discount_code_string: session[:new_discount_code])
end
```

Because the active discount code is stored in the session, we just need to pass it along to the workflows—we don't want the workflows to have a dependency on the details of the session.

And because we combined the Stripe and PayPal purchase options into a common parent class, all our common discount handling code can get placed in the parent PreparesCart class. (If you look in the full application source, you'll see separate specs for each child class.) In the Stripe case, we also need to pull the parameter through the PreparesCartForStripeJob.

```
admin/02/app/workflows/prepares_cart.rb
attr_accessor :user, :purchase_amount_cents,
    :purchase_amount, :success,
    :payment, :expected_ticket_ids,
    :payment_reference, :discount_code_string

def initialize(user: nil, purchase_amount_cents: nil,
    expected_ticket_ids: "", payment_reference: nil,
    discount_code_string: nil)
  @user = user
  @discount_code_string = discount_code_string
  @purchase_amount = Money.new(purchase_amount_cents)
  @success = false
  @continue = true
  @expected_ticket_ids = expected_ticket_ids.split(" ").map(&:to_i).sort
  @payment_reference = payment_reference || Payment.generate_reference
end

def discount_code
  @discount_code ||= DiscountCode.find_by(code: discount_code_string)
end

def price_calculator
  @price_calculator ||= PriceCalculator.new(tickets, discount_code)
end

delegate :total_price, to: :price_calculator
```

Some of this is just boilerplate; we add the discount code as a parameter, and also as an attribute, and we set up a method to extract the discount code object give the code string. A little more subtly, we place our new PriceCalculator into the calculation of the price for the purpose of detecting validity.

Later on, after the purchase is successful, we add the discount code and the amount discounted to the attributes that we save to the database:

```
admin/02/app/workflows/prepares_cart.rb
def payment_attributes
  {user_id: user.id, price_cents: purchase_amount.cents,
   status: "created", reference: Payment.generate_reference,
   discount_code_id: discount_code&.id,
   discount: price_calculator.discount}
end
```

And with that, we've now entered the wonderful world of discount codes.

Next Up

Discount codes and our other rule changes in this chapter begin to beg the question: as administrators get more power to change the business rules, how can we continue to ensure that our data is valid?

The next chapter addresses that issue from different directions, including enhanced login security, smarter validations, and more complete auditing.

## CHAPTER 9

Administration and Data Security

Administrators and customer support staff, by their very nature, are both necessary and disruptive to your site and its data: necessary, because no application will ever be able to anticipate the needs of users or the weird states they will somehow manage to get their data into, and disruptive, because administrators have the leeway to break the business rules your application depends on. They also potentially have access to secure data.

In this chapter, we'll look at the issue of maintaining data integrity and security in the face of administrative needs. We'll cover how to handle data validity, auditing, and increased security, and I'll go over a few other tricks that might be valuable.

Breaking the Rules

Sometimes you've gotta break the rules.

Some of the rules. There are other rules that you should never, ever break. For example, tax law. Don't break that rule. PCI (Payment Card Industry) compliance is a good rule, too.

But some of your business rules...that's another story.

Here's a scenario: We've set up our nice point-of-sale box office with our neat little USB credit card swiper and we're swiping away. Along comes a customer who pulls out her wallet, revealing green pieces of paper. Apparently, even in our technological future, cash is still legal tender. We don't want to turn her away, but our business rules mandate a trip to a credit card payment gateway.

And another one: We get a call from the CFO of a good-sized local business. She says they'd love to buy a couple hundred tickets, but at that price, she can only pay with an invoice and purchase order. We can't support that right now, either.

Or: We'd like our box office personnel to have the discretion to arbitrarily offer tickets at a reduced price. We could do that with discount codes, but frankly, that's a pain, and eventually a scenario is going to come up where you are just going to want to change the price of an item for one purchase.

Let's get these rule-breaking possibilities in the code. It doesn't take much code to handle these cases, in part because I simplified the cases a little, and in part because the long-term problem isn't the checkout code.

Continuing our UI decision to allow the administrator to use an augmented version of the user checkout page, here we give an administrator the option for cash or invoice purchases, and make the actual amount a text entry field and not just a hidden field:

```
admin/03/app/views/shopping_carts/_credit_card_info.html.slim
- if current_user.admin?
  .form-group
    .col-sm-2
      = label_tag(:purchase_amount,
        "Purchase Amount Override ($X.XX)", class: "control-label")
    .col-sm-2
      input.form-control(name=:purchase_amount_cents
        id="purchase_amount"
        value=humanized_money(@cart.total_cost))
- else
  = hidden_field_tag(:purchase_amount_cents, @cart.total_cost.cents)
```

We now have what is either an interface issue or a data issue: the hidden field for non-admins (which is what we use to check the payment calculation on the server) is stored as an integer number of cents. Asking the administrator to enter the amount as an integer number of cents seems to be begging for trouble, so we need to allow the more traditional currency formatting. This means that on the server side, we need to convert the entered amount to integral cents somewhere. And we need to error out if the format is bad. (If you listen carefully, you can hear the sound of a can of worms being opened.)

On the server side, we need to make the controller logic more complex to allow for the possibility of a cash purchase. (Tests for all these cases, by the way, exist in the spec directory of the admin_03 branch.)

```
admin/03/app/controllers/payments_controller.rb
def create
  if params[:discount_code].present?
    session[:new_discount_code] = params[:discount_code]
    redirect_to shopping_cart_path
    return
  end
```

```
  normalize_purchase_amount
  workflow = run_workflow(params[:payment_type], params[:purchase_type])
  if workflow.success
    redirect_to workflow.redirect_on_success_url ||
        payment_path(id: @reference || workflow.payment.reference)
  else
    redirect_to shopping_cart_path
  end
end

private def run_workflow(payment_type, purchase_type)
  case purchase_type
  when "SubscriptionCart" then stripe_subscription_workflow
  when "ShoppingCart" then payment_workflow(payment_type)
  end
end

private def payment_workflow(payment_type)
  case payment_type
  when "paypal" then paypal_workflow
  when "credit" then stripe_workflow
  when "cash" then cash_workflow
  when "invoice" then cash_workflow
  end
end

private def pick_user
  if current_user.admin? && params[:user_email].present?
    User.find_or_create_by(email: params[:user_email])
  else
    current_user
  end
end

private def cash_workflow
  workflow = CashPurchasesCart.new(
      user: pick_user,
      purchase_amount_cents: params[:purchase_amount_cents],
      expected_ticket_ids: params[:ticket_ids],
      discount_code: session[:new_discount_code])
  workflow.run
  workflow
end

private def normalize_purchase_amount
  return if params[:purchase_amount].blank?
  params[:purchase_amount_cents] =
      (params[:purchase_amount].to_f * 100).to_i
end
```

Here we've added a call to normalize the purchase amount if the administrator has entered an amount. We're basically punting on the malformed amount, though.

The biggest logic change is in the run_workflow and payment_workflow methods, which now have a two-way switch on both the purchase and payment types. This amounts to nested case statements, and I think it's ugly and may be time to refactor to something a little more data-driven and meta-programmy. The new CashPurchasesCart is the destination of both the cash and invoice payments, and it creates its own workflow class. The CashWorkflowClass is less complex than our other workflows, as it doesn't need to talk to a gateway at all:

admin/03/app/workflows/cash_purchases_cart.rb
```ruby
class CashPurchasesCart < PreparesCart

  def update_tickets
    tickets.each(&:purchased!)
  end

  def on_success
    @success = true
  end

  def payment_attributes
    super.merge(
        payment_method: "cash", status: "succeeded",
        administrator_id: user.id)
  end

  def pre_purchase_valid?
    raise UnauthorizedPurchaseException.new(user: user) unless user.admin?
    true
  end

  def on_failure
    unpurchase_tickets
  end

end
```

The only logic here as written is that a cash transaction needs to be overseen by an administrator. But if there is an administrator, anything goes.

In practice, we might need to have some logic here to distinguish between a cash purchase, where the money is presumably in our hands at the end of the transaction, and an invoice, where we most likely have to track the eventual payment.

Finally, we tweak the PreparesCart to allow for the case where the administrator has entered a custom amount:

admin/03/app/workflows/prepares_cart.rb
```ruby
def amount_valid?
  return true if user.admin?
  purchase_amount == total_price
end
```

```ruby
def tickets_valid?
  expected_ticket_ids == tickets.map(&:id).sort
end

def pre_purchase_valid?
  amount_valid? && tickets_valid?
end
```

Once again, we are just bypassing the checks if an administrator says it's okay. There's a trade-off here: we may be making it harder to see an actual bug if an administrator happens to trigger it.

There are a couple of other features you might want to add in this case. You might want to capture the actual value of the purchase before the administrator's meddling (it might be useful for accounting purposes). You also might want to specially log or notify a superior when an administrative discount happens. We can do the first by tying the cash workflow to the price calculator; the second can be done with a logger or audit tool.

Keeping Data Secure

I hope at this point you are starting to get a feel for how our business logic and administrative tools have implications for the integrity of our data. Our little theater does not have tremendously complex business logic yet, and yet if we were asked to verify the status of our records manually, we'd have some trouble.

Not only do our administrators have the ability to set a price on any purchase, as the application is currently written, they also have the ability to go into the ActiveAdmin UI and change the details of any purchase that has already happened. And even if we were to limit that kind of access to the administrative tools, there's still always a way to get in. Somebody might be able to access the Rails console on production. Or just access the database.

(In case it ever comes up, making random one-off fixes via the Rails console is much preferable to doing so directly in the database, mostly because any Rails validations or callbacks will still be performed.)

Over the next few sections, we'll take a look at security, not just through the lens of restricting access to parts of the application, but also in terms of the integrity of the data—the kind of security that helps you sleep at night.

Auditing

The most basic step in data integrity is an audit trail. Who changed this data, when did they do it, and what change did they make? Having such a record is useful not just to try to catch miscreants, but also to be able to revert well-meaning mistakes, bugs, and the occasional case where users manage to get themselves into a weird state and we can't figure out how.

The PaperTrail[1] gem adds the ability to track changes and revert objects to your ActiveRecord models. It's easy to install, basically works in the background, and continues to be under active development.

Install PaperTrail by adding it to the Gemfile:

```
gem "paper_trail"
```

And then:

```
% bundle install
<lots of output>

% rails generate paper_trail:install --with-changes
    create  db/migrate/20160803022616_create_versions.rb
    create  db/migrate/20160803022617_add_object_changes_to_versions.rb
```

All we get is a couple of database migrations. I'm not going to copy the exact code over because there are a lot of comments. If you are using MySQL, though, you should read the migration text because you need to manually modify the file. The rest of you only need to read the file if you want a sense of what a headache it must be to run an open source project that has to install seamlessly on multiple databases.

The gist, however, is that with the PaperTrail gem we get a database table called versions with item_type and item_id fields, which store the identity of the object being archived; a big, big, big text field, which serializes the data of that object; a created_at field; and then a string field called whodunnit, one called event, and one called object_changes (which effectively stores a diff).

Next, run the migration to add the table to our database:

```
% rake db:migrate
<lots of output>
```

We only need to do two things to activate PaperTrail. For every model that we want to be tracked, we need to add the following line:

```
has_paper_trail
```

---

1.   https://github.com/airblade/paper_trail

I am adding it to DiscountCode, Event, PaymentLineItem, Payment, Performance, Plan, Subscription, Ticket, and User. In the case of User, we have one additional piece of configuration to add to the has_paper_trail command:

```
admin/04/app/models/user.rb
has_paper_trail ignore: %i(sign_in_count current_sign_in_at last_sign_in_at)
```

The problem is that Devise sets a number of attributes on the user automatically when the user logs in. We don't really want PaperTrail to create a new version of a user on every login—that seems kind of pointless—and so we tell PaperTrail to ignore those fields. If the change to the user is limited to those attributes, then PaperTrail won't trigger a new version.

We also need to add one line to the ApplicationController in order to allow PaperTrail to add user information to each version:

```
before_filter :set_paper_trail_whodunnit
```

By default, PaperTrail uses the current_user method to determine whodunnit, but that can be overridden if needed.

Now let's go into the ActiveAdmin tool and do something stupid. I'm going to go into the console and edit a payment so that price_cents is now 2000 instead of 3000. In an attempt to "fix" things, I go back in and change it to 1000.

Oops.

If we now look at the versions table in the database, we can see that it has grown two rows, one for each of my saves. Each row has an item_type of Payment, and an item_id of the payment I tweaked. The whodunnit field is my user ID, and the object field is a YAML representation of the state of the object before the given change. So the first row has the initial state of the object, and the second row has the state of the object after my first edit. (If you'd rather have the whodunnit field allow you to actually get the User instance, you can try the PaperTrail GlobalId[2] gem, which adds an ActiveRecord global ID like the ones ActiveJob uses to each version.)

I can access those versions from the Rails console (the output here has been edited for clarity):

```
> p = Payment.find(2)
> p.versions
[#<PaperTrail::Version>, #<PaperTrail::Version]

> p.version
nil
```

```
> p.live?
true

> p.previous_version
<#Payment>

> p.next_version
nil

> p.version_at(1.day.ago)
<#Payment>
```

The versions method returns a list of PaperTrail version instances, and the version method returns the current instance being looked at, or nil, if the current version is the live version. In this case, next_version returns nil because the instance we are looking at is live, and previous_version returns a new instance of Payment created from the YAML data in the versions table.

This API makes reverting the widget to an older state pretty straightforward:

```
> p = p.version_at(1.day.ago)
<#Payment>

> p.save
```

Saving in this case both restores the Payment instance to the older state, *and* creates a new Version to reflect the bad state that we are moving from. However, because we're doing this from the console, whodunnit isn't set. You can manually set it for a console session with PaperTrail.whodunnit = <whatever>, which might not be a bad thing to put in your Pry or IRB initialization script.

If the original object has been destroyed, PaperTrail gets a version that you can use to restore:

```
> t = Ticket.last
<#ticket>

> t.destroy

> v = PaperTrail::Version.find(5)
<#PaperTrail::Version>

> t = v.reify
<#Ticket>

> t.save
```

You need to look up the correct version in the PaperTrail table for this to work. But the deleted ticket is placed back into the database table and a new version is created. This likely means that if you have PaperTrail turned on, you don't also need a soft-delete tool like acts_as_paranoid.

PaperTrail does not, by default, store the difference between two versions. You can kind of get this by creating the initial migration with rails generate paper_trail:install --with-changes, which gives you an object_changes column in the table that stores the changes on an update. This is not super-sophisticated, so any complicated diff management you'll need to build yourself.

You can add metadata to each version by adding a meta option to the has_paper_trail call:

```
has_paper_trail meta: {status_string: :status_string}
```

The keys here are arbitrary symbols, and the values are symbols that are method names in the class. The method will be called and stored at that symbol in each new version. This might make it easier to search the version table for calculated properties.

PaperTrail doesn't store association data by default, and the ability to do so is described as "experimental," but, generating the table with rails generate paper_trail:install --with-associations will also generate a version_associations table that attempts to store the status of has_one and has_many associations. There are limitations here, mostly that association changes that don't go through Rails callbacks won't be triggered, which means that directly setting the association to an array won't be noticed. There are some other limitations listed in the documentation.[3] The docs also describe other options for changing what triggers a PaperTrail version, how many old versions to keep, and the like. The documentation is quite thorough as to how to customize PaperTrail.

PaperTrail isn't perfect, and it's not a substitute for regular database backups, which we'll talk about more in Chapter 13, *Going to Production*, on page 297. It's going to basically double your write throughput to your database (because each save triggers the creation of an associated PaperTrail version), and it's going to more than double the size of your database over time. If those scaling issues make you or your devops team nervous, you might want to explore a more custom tool.

PaperTrail only gives us the infrastructure for auditing, and exactly what we do with that infrastructure is up to us. Allowing administrators to see past information and undo it can be very useful.

Consistency Checks

In a few different places in this book so far, I've recommended being conservative in the amount of ActiveRecord and database validations you add to

---

3.   https://github.com/airblade/paper_trail

your code that might block a payment from occurring, on the grounds that there are a lot of potential data validations that are potentially less important than letting the payment go through. Still, allowing payments to happen doesn't let us off the hook for checking the consistency of our data. Not only might invalid data sneak through, but also we might have genuine bugs in our application code, especially surrounding the coordination of payment with inventory or services.

One way of checking for consistency is to actually write a script that checks for consistency. Here's a sample, implemented as a Rake task:

admin/05/lib/tasks/consistency_test.rake
```ruby
namespace :snow_globe do

  task check_consistency: :environment do
    inconsistent = Payment.all.reject do |payment|
      TicketPaymentConsistency.new(payment).consistent?
    end
    if inconsistent.empty?
      ConsistencyMailer.all_is_well.deliver
    else
      ConsistencyMailer.inconsistencies_detected(inconsistent).deliver
    end
  end

end

class TicketPaymentConsistency < SimpleDelegator

  attr_accessor :errors

  def initialize(payment)
    super
    @errors = []
  end

  def consistent?
    success_consistent
    refund_consistent
    amount_consistent
    errors.empty?
  end

  def success_consistent
    return unless success?
    inconsistent_tickets = tickets.select { |ticket| !ticket.purchased? }
    inconsistent_tickets.each do |ticket|
      @errors << "Successful purchase #{id}, ticket #{ticket.id} not purchased"
    end
  end
```

```
def refund_consistent
  return unless refund?
  inconsistent_tickets = tickets.select { |ticket| !ticket.refunded? }
  inconsistent_tickets.each do |ticket|
    @errors << "Refunded purchase #{id}, ticket #{ticket.id} not refunded"
  end
end

def amount_consistent
  expected = payment_line_items.map(&:price) - discount
  return if expected == price
  @errors >>
      "Purchase #{id}, expected price #{expected} actual price #{price}"
end

end
```

There are many, many different ways to implement a task like this, so take this with a grain of salt, and be prepared to adapt the idea to the specifics of your application.

What I've built here is a Rake task that runs a consistency check on every Payment. The consistency check itself is written as a TicketPaymentConsistency class that is a SimpleDelegator wrapper around Payment. Right now, it runs three checks:

- If the payment succeeds, all of the tickets attached to it should also have a successful status.

- If the payment is a refund, all of the tickets attached to it should have a refunded status.

- We should be able to infer the cost of the payment from the cost of the line items, minus any discount. This one is likely a little too simplistic.

The code for these checks is a little more complicated than it might otherwise be because we are holding on to error messages for reporting purposes. We run each check for each payment; then if any check has added something to the errors attribute, we declare the payment "inconsistent," and eventually pass it along to a mailer that will send an email to somebody to tell them they need to look at something. This implementation sends an "okay" email so that we can differentiate between "everything is okay" and "the script crashed."

One interesting side effect of writing out a script to test consistency is that it acts as a check of our architecture and data modeling solutions as well. For example, I note here that the status for a successful purchase is succeeded and the status for a successful ticket is purchased. There might be a good reason for that, but it also might be worth looking at. It also occurred to me as I put this together that I have no way to check the amount of tickets on each purchase. It might be useful to put that amount separately in the Payment data to have that cross-checked, too. Similarly, I find myself wanting a capacity data attribute on each Performance so that I could check that the number of outstanding tickets matches. Another check that I didn't do here would be to match the payment amount with the returned payment amount from Stripe, which we have held onto.

This script's execution time will increase as the number of payments increases, and if a payment has already checked as consistent, it doesn't need to be rechecked unless something has changed. So you might add a consistent_at time stamp attribute and then not recheck any payment whose consistent_at time is later than the updated_at time of the payment or its line items or associated tickets. You also might want to run it against a database read replica or backup; see Chapter 13, *Going to Production*, on page 297 for details.

I recommend having a task like this tied to a cron job and run it regularly—how often it runs depends on your traffic flow, but I think at least daily is probably smart. We'll talk about how to set this task up when we talk about production environments in Chapter 13, *Going to Production*, on page 297.

One-Off Changes

Many of these audit and consistency features are dependent on changes happening through Rails. Inevitably, you'll be asked to make one-off changes in the data. Possibly a bug or bad data entry has left the database in a weird state that can't be fixed from the administrative UI, or there's been some external change in data that needs to be reflected in our database, or who knows.

One-off Rake tasks are very useful here, because they are easy to invoke from the command line of your production application. I recommend placing tasks that you expect to be one-off cleanup tasks in a subdirectory of lib/tasks so you don't confuse them with code you might want to keep using. Please remember, there is really no such thing as a "one-off" task—you'll probably need to run it multiple times in development to get it right, and then in staging, and then in production. And once it exists, it will often find a way to be used again. So, keeping even "one-off" tasks clean and well written will pay off.

Other times, you are going to want to directly interact with the production console or database. This is not exactly, you know, recommended behavior, but I've done it and you've done it or will do it, because sometimes getting something cleaned up fast is necessary.

A quick checklist of things to think about for one-off changes:

- If it's possible to make the change inside the admin UI, do it that way.

- If it's not possible, why not? Consider making the change possible in the admin UI, especially if it is something you are being asked to do regularly.

- Prefer making the change via the Rails console, then directly in the database, if possible. That way, the change will be picked up by PaperTrail, updated_at, validators, and the like.

- If you do need to go in via the database for some reason, I will argue that using a GUI like Sequel Pro[4] is less error prone than a command line.

- If you do go in via a command line, start by declaring a transaction so you can roll back if you make a mistake. If possible, do this with somebody sitting next to you to confirm production data changes as you make them.

- When you are done, exit and close the window. I close the terminal app to be sure, but don't leave an open line to the production data hanging open. It's too easy to lose track and type commands to the wrong terminal.

- If possible, don't do this at 2:30 a.m. when you are exhausted.

That should do it. Good luck!

If you do find yourself in a situation where you think people are messing with your data via the database rather than Rails, there are some tools at your disposal. In Chapter 13, *Going to Production*, on page 297, we'll talk about database backups and replicas. Another thing you can do is save a special column in your models as an MD5 hash of the other columns (updated in a Rails ActiveRecord callback) so at least you'd be able to detect database changes that didn't go through Rails. I've never quite been paranoid enough to try that, but I've clearly been paranoid enough to think about trying it. You might be in a situation where you are sharing data with other applications that are also modifying it, in which case you need to be very careful about validating data.

Two-Factor Authorization

Because administrators have access to a lot of user data, administrator accounts are particularly valuable. Passwords are not exactly as secure as we'd like them to be or as effective in preventing breaches. Let's take the next security step and add two-factor authentication to our administrative

---

4. http://www.sequelpro.com

accounts. (There's no real reason not to offer two-factor to everybody, but we're talking about administrators here.)

The idea behind two-factor authentication is that we combine something users know—their passwords—with something users have—their phones. Implementations of two-factor authentication predate smartphones, but what used to require the distribution of a dedicated authentication fob can now be handled with SMS or a smartphone app.

We're going to use Authy[5] as our two-factor authentication source on the general rule of allowing tools built by security experts to handle our security. Authy is a commercial service with a free tier that we're going to take advantage of.

When we add users to our system, we send Authy the user's email address and cellphone number. Authy sends us back an authy_id. It's our responsibility to associate that authy_id with the user. We don't actually need to permanently store the cellphone number.

Later, when the user logs in, assuming the password matches, we tell Authy that this particular user is trying to log in. Authy sends a message to the user that includes a token. The user needs to enter that token into our site in order to fully log in.

So, in order to integrate Authy into our site, we need to

- Sign up for Authy.
- Make it possible to give users an Authy ID.
- Intercept the Devise login process to require the second factor for full login.

You can sign up for an Authy account on the Authy Developer web page.[6] As I write this, there's a big button on the web page that says "Get Your Free API Key." You don't have to tell me twice. I push it.

Authy will ask you for a username and password and a cellphone number. Authy will immediately send a token to the cellphone to confirm that everything is above board and valid.

From here on in, I'm using what is (as I write this) Authy's beta dashboard. I hope it will have some kind of similarity to what you see on your screen as you walk through these instructions some time in the future.

---

5.   https://www.authy.com
6.   https://www.authy.com/developers

I click "Create Authy Application," and then "Create Your First App." I name the app and I decline any integrations at the moment. You should see a screen that looks more or less like the following screenshot:

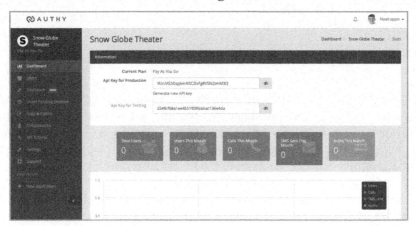

Hey, API keys! That's something we already know how to deal with!

We're now done with Authy's website for the moment. There are some other handy things we can do there, like see all our registered users and also how many authentications we've done in the billing period. Right now, though, let's turn our attention back to our code.

Authy's Ruby integration is handled with a Ruby gem conveniently named authy. We need to add it to our Gemfile:

```
gem "authy"
```

There's no other explicit setup, but we do want to get that API key in there, so let's add a config file:

```
admin/05/config/initializers/authy.rb
require "yaml"
Authy.api_key = Rails.application.secrets.authy_key
Authy.api_uri = "https://api.authy.com/"
```

And then add this line to the secrets.yml file, along with the other secrets:

```
authy_key: <%= ENV["AUTHY_KEY"] %>
```

Now, we need to be able to store the Authy ID with each user, which means we need a database migration:

```
admin/05/db/migrate/20160803032825_add_authy_to_user.rb
class AddAuthyToUser < ActiveRecord::Migration[5.0]

  def change
    change_table :users do |t|
      t.string :authy_id
    end
  end

end
```

All we need is to add authy_id as a string field on User. We're not saving the cellphone number to our database. We could, but because Authy will hold onto it for us, we don't actually need to. So on the general principle of not storing any private data unless strictly necessary, we decide not to hold onto the phone data.

Now we need to coax ActiveAdmin into letting us enter a phone number for our users even though we don't actually have a phone number attribute. (Of course, one way to work around this would be to actually have a phone attribute, but we've already decided not to do that.)

So to do this, simply add attr_accessor to the User class. (We're not going to use it for anything, really, but ActiveAdmin will get upset if we try to make a form field without there being an accessor.)

```
admin/05/app/models/user.rb
attr_accessor :cellphone_number
```

Small changes to our Adminstrate form and controller help us send the cellphone information along to Authy.

See if you can spot the small change we made to the list of form fields in the user dashboard so as to put the cellphone form on the form:

```
admin/05/app/admin/user.rb
ActiveAdmin.register User do
  permit_params :email, :password, :password_confirmation

  index do
    selectable_column
    id_column
    column :email
    column :current_sign_in_at
    column :sign_in_count
    column :created_at
    actions
  end

  filter :email
  filter :current_sign_in_at
```

```
filter :sign_in_count
filter :created_at

form do |f|
  f.inputs "Admin Details" do
    f.input :email
    f.input :password
    f.input :password_confirmation
    f.input :cellphone_number
  end
  f.actions
end

permit_params :email, :password, :password_confirmation, :cellphone_number

controller do
  def update
    @user = User.find(params[:id])
    if params[:user][:password].blank?
      @user.update_without_password(permitted_params[:user])
    else
      @user.update_attributes(permitted_params[:user])
    end
    return if @user.admin? && params[:user][:cellphone_number].blank?
    authy = Authy::API.register_user(
        email: @user.email,
        cellphone: params[:user][:cellphone_number],
        country_code: "1")
    @user.update(authy_id: authy.id) if authy
  end
end
end
```

Notice that we are overriding the ActiveAdmin controller from within our ActiveAdmin page.

We handle the actual update ourselves, using ActiveAdmin's version of Rails strong parameters, and Devise functionality to make sure that we can safely update the user even without entering a password. After that's done, grab the @user again. If the user is an administrator, and if a cellphone number was added in the form, we make a call to Authy::API.register_user with the user's email, the cellphone, and the country code. (We're making the assumption that all our administrators are U.S.-based, which is probably not a permanent assumption.)

Authy returns an object, and we take the id from that response and save it to the authy_id of the user.

This takes care of the entering cellphone data and registering it with Authy side of the equation—though, looking at the code, I'm thinking it might be worth refactoring the Authy code into either the User class or a really simple wrapper class. Maybe?

Now that the we have associated a user, an email address, a cellphone number, and Authy, we need to use that information as part of the login process. Because our login process is controlled by Devise, we need to override some of what Devise gives us to take the two factor authentication into account. (There is a devise-authy gem that will do some of this work for us, but it looks as if it hasn't been updated in a while, and it was a little too automatic for this use case, so I decided not to use it.)

In order to do this, we need to get Devise to give us a place to put the code that we want to add. Luckily, Devise is somewhat expecting this kind of request and provides some generators to give us some boilerplate locations for our code. The act of logging in is handled by Devise in the SessionsController (as in, creating, updating, or deleting a new session). To get an overridable version of the SessionsController, invoke the following generator:

```
rails generate devise:controllers users -c=sessions
```

The resulting SessionsController class is a subclass of Devise::SessionsController, meaning that we don't need to re-create functionality—the Devise parent class already has it—we can just override the parts we don't like.

Before we look at our SessionsController, there's one quick piece of bookkeeping. We need to use the routes.rb file to tell Devise that the new controller exists:

admin/05/config/routes.rb
```
devise_for :users, controllers: {
    sessions: "users/sessions"}

devise_scope :user do
  post "users/sessions/verify" => "Users::SessionsController"
end
```

We're adding two different routes to the route file: in the first line, we're telling Devise that our new sessions controller takes control of sessions. In the second, devise_scope, we're adding a brand-new route called verify, which is also in our new SessionsController.

And here is the beginning of our lovely SessionsController in all its glory:

admin/05/app/controllers/users/sessions_controller.rb
```
def create
  @user = User.find_by(email: params[:user][:email])
  if @user&.authy_id.present?
    if @user&.valid_password?(params[:user][:password])
      session[:awaiting_authy_user_id] = @user.id
```

```
      Authy::API.request_sms(id: @user.authy_id)
      render :two_factor
    else
      render :new
    end
  else
    session[:awaiting_authy_user_id] = nil
    super
  end
end
```

There's a lot to unpack here. The create method is where Devise rouses control after the user submits the email address and password in the sign-in form. The parameters come in as params[:user][:email] and params[:user][:password].

First, we need to find the User record in question, which we do by searching the database on the incoming email. If we find a matching user, we check to see if the user has an authy_id. (Remember, the &. operator acts like :try, and avoids nil errors.) If there is no user, or the user doesn't have an authy_id, we drop to the else clause, which calls super, meaning we get the normal Devise login behavior.

If we do have a user and an authy_id, we follow up by checking that the user's password is valid using the Devise valid_password? method. If not, we fall back to the login form. If so, we continue trying to get the second factor. Usually, if the user matches the password, we'd sign in the user, but we're in a brave, two-factor world, so we have more to do.

Now comes the Authy part. We put the user ID into a session variable, which is a marker that a two-factor session is in progress. Then we make the all-important Authy::API.request_sms call. We pass it the user's authy_id. And then we render a very simple form waiting for the user to enter a new token:

admin/05/app/views/users/sessions/two_factor.html.slim
```
h2 Verify Your Code

= form_tag(users_sessions_verify_path) do
  .form-inputs
    = text_field_tag(:token)

  .form-actions
    = submit_tag("Enter Token")
```

Behind the scenes, Authy receives the request_sms call. What it does next depends on what it knows about the user's phone. If it knows that the user has Authy's native app, it sends a push notification telling the user to open the native app and read the token there, as shown in the figure on page 204.

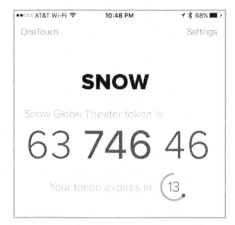

Otherwise, it sends the user an SMS text to the number it has on file, like this:

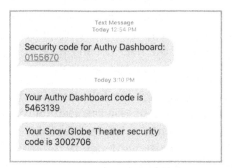

The user enters that number and submits the form, taking us back to the verify method of the SessionsController:

admin/05/app/controllers/users/sessions_controller.rb
```ruby
def verify
  @user = User.find(session[:awaiting_authy_user_id])
  token = Authy::API.verify(id: @user.authy_id, token: params[:token])
  if token.ok?
    set_flash_message!(:notice, :signed_in)
    sign_in(User, @user)
    session[:awaiting_authy_user_id] = nil
    respond_with @user, location: after_sign_in_path_for(resource)
  else
    session[:awaiting_authy_user_id] = nil
    flash.now[:danger] = "Incorrect code, please try again"
    redirect_to users_sessions_two_factor_path
  end
end
```

In the verify method, we start by re-creating the user from the session ID we stored in the create method. We then send another Authy API call, Authy::API.verify, sending it the user's authy_id and the token the user just entered.

Authy responds with a token object. If that object is ok?, the user verifies and we can now sign the user in. We set a flash message, and then we use the Devise sign_in method to actually sign the user in and set the session and all that. We unset the session variable and then we redirect the user to wherever the after sign-in path is.

If the token is not okay, we set a different flash message and redirect the user back to the two-factor form to re-enter the token.

And we're done—except for one thing. There's a tiny quirk in Devise and how it searches for current_user. Essentially, if you ask Devise for current_user and there is no current user, Devise actually checks to see if there is a form sub-mission in process with a username and password. If so, Devise authenticates and logs the user in. Normally, this is great, because it means that we don't have to worry about any controller before_actions that might depend on the user being logged in.

In two-factor authentication, though, this is a real pain in the neck, because the underlying Devise mechanism doesn't know that we're not finished with the authentication process, and it will heedlessly both log the user in *and* show us the form awaiting the token. This is not helpful.

To mitigate this problem, I did two things. Well, three, if you count screaming at the computer while I tried to figure out why the heck the user was being logged in.

The first thing I did was block the paper trail whodunnit filter from running, because that filter calls current_user:

```
admin/05/app/controllers/users/sessions_controller.rb
skip_before_action :set_paper_trail_whodunnit
skip_after_action :warn_about_not_setting_whodunnit
```

Second, I overwrote current user to just return nil if we are in the middle of a two-factor transaction:

```
admin/05/app/controllers/application_controller.rb
def current_user
  return nil if session[:awaiting_authy_user_id].present?
  super
end
```

And then it works! Two-factor security is ours.

Two-factor authentication isn't perfect, though. Recently, an activist was hacked despite having two-factor authentication because hackers talked his phone company into re-targeting his phone's SIM card. The native apps are therefore preferred to the SMS-based authentication.

Simulating Users

It's not unusual for customers to have issues with the website that are specific to their circumstances—something in their data or history with the site that is causing a strange condition.

It'd be great if you could log in as the user, but we don't save user passwords in any way that's recoverable. However, we can do the next best thing: we can use Devise to allow our administrators to temporarily assume the identity of a user.

This is actually rather easy to do technically, but it comes with a host of secondary issues. Simulating a user login is potentially dangerous and opens you up to privacy concerns that we've spent most of this book trying to avoid. You need to be very careful with this feature.

All that said, it's still useful, so I'm going to show you how to do it. We need to add the ability to simulate a user to our ActiveAdmin UI, which means we need to have ActiveAdmin give us the view file so we can add the link. We can get ActiveAdmin to give us a button on the show page to simulate a user:

admin/06/app/admin/user.rb
```ruby
action_item :refund, only: :show do
  link_to(
      "Simulate User", user_simulation_path(id_to_simulate: resource.id),
      method: :post, class: "action-edit",
      data: {confirm: "Do you want to simulate this user?"})
end
```

That's still pretty boilerplate, but it does talk to a route we haven't defined yet, so let's fix that by adding to the route file. Rather than add non-RESTful routes to an existing controller, I've decided to create a new resource and controller that doesn't directly correspond to an ActiveRecord model:

admin/06/config/routes.rb
```ruby
resource :user_simulation, only: %i(create destroy)
```

We are only ever going to have one simulation in a session, so the resource can be singular. The create action starts a simulation and destroy ends one. We'll need to pass the create action the ID of the user to be simulated, but the destroy action doesn't need any arguments—all it needs to do is revert the active simulation.

The controller methods are short but sweet:

```
admin/06/app/controllers/user_simulations_controller.rb
class UserSimulationsController < ApplicationController

  def create
    @user_to_simulate = User.find(params[:id_to_simulate])
    authorize(@user_to_simulate, :simulate?)
    session[:admin_id] = current_user.id
    sign_in(:user, @user_to_simulate, bypass: true)
    redirect_to root_path
  end

  def destroy
    redirect_to(admin_users_path) && return if simulating_admin_user.nil?
    sign_in(:user, simulating_admin_user, bypass: true)
    session[:admin_id] = nil
    redirect_to admin_users_path
  end

end
```

When we create a simulation, we grab the user being simulated, given the ID. We then authorize, using Pundit, and a pretty simple policy:

```
admin/06/app/policies/user_policy.rb
def simulate?
  user.admin? && !same_user?
end
```

You can simulate if you are the admin and if you are not trying to simulate yourself.

If the authorization succeeds, we store the administrator's id in a session. Doing so allows us to put the administrator back as the current user, and also allows us a place to check to see if a simulation is currently in progress. Then we actually use Devise and Warden to make the user being simulated the logged-in user, using the bypass option to prevent the user's tracking data, such as the last login time or login count, from updating.

Now as far as the system is concerned, the logged-in user is no longer the administrator but the user being simulated. It's really, really important that the administrator always is aware of being logged in as a different user. Bad things can happen if the administrator forgets.

So let's lend a hand by putting a permanent message on the page if a user is being simulated. The way this app is structured, all the flash messages are in a particular partial called _messages. Let's add one:

admin/06/app/views/layouts/_messages.html.slim

```
- flash.each do |name, msg|
  - if msg.is_a?(String)
    .alert(class="alert-#{name.to_s == "notice" ? "success" : "danger"}")
      button.close(
        type="button" data-dismiss="alert" aria-hidden="true") &times;
      div(id="flash_#{name}")= msg

- if simulating_admin_user
  .alert.alert-danger
    button.close(aria-hidden="true"
      data-dismiss=alert type="button")
      | &times;
    div
      | You are simulating #{current_user.email}
      = link_to("End Simulation", user_simulation_path, method: :delete)
```

We define the simulating_admin_user in ApplicationController, along with one other small helper method:

admin/06/app/controllers/application_controller.rb

```
def user_for_paper_trail
  simulating_admin_user || current_user
end

def simulating_admin_user
  User.find_by(id: session[:admin_id])
end
helper_method :simulating_admin_user
```

The simulating_admin_user method just returns the User instance corresponding to the session variable where we stored the identity of the administrator running the simulation. If it returns nil, there's no current simulation. If there is a current simulation, we put a link up to undo the simulation, which goes to the destroy action of our UserSimulations controller.

That destroy method undoes the simulation by retrieving the administrative user and re-signing him or her in, again bypassing Devise's tracking. Finally it redirects back to the administrative user's screen, where the whole thing started.

There is one other helper method defined in the ApplicationController to discuss: user_for_paper_trail. If the administrative user makes changes while simulating an ordinary user for later audit purposes, it's important that we retain the identity of the administrative user who was actually responsible for the change. The user_for_paper_trail method is automatically called by PaperTrail's whodunnit and allows us to detect a simulation and use the administrator.

There are a lot of other possibilities for simulation if you need more security or auditing. You could have a special log of simulation starting and ending, for example. You could also prevent certain actions, like purchases, from being invoked by a simulating admin. You could automatically revert a simulation after a given amount of time. Or make administrators re-two-factor authenticate before simulating. It all depends on what makes sense for your application.

Blocking Email

One last tip, which is more development than administrative, I suppose.

When we are developing an app or when it is in staging, we want to prevent emails from going out to potentially unsuspecting users. I always associate this with simulating users because I once actually was simulating a user in a development environment, triggered an email message, and sent that user a very surprising receipt. What we want is for emails not to go out to users when we are developing.

Fortunately, tools exist to help us. Let's add a couple to our Gemfile:

```
admin/06/Gemfile
group :development, :staging do
  gem "mail_interceptor"
  gem "email_prefixer"
end
```

We added two gems: MailInterceptor,[7] which actually blocks and redirects email, and EmailPrefixer,[8] which attaches the app name and environment to the subject line of the email.

The group listing is a little weird. We want these gems to be in play for development and staging environments, but not for production and also not for testing—test emails don't get sent anyway, and we might want to actually see the test emails in order to debug them.

After we bundle install, we need to add one brief configuration file:

```
admin/06/config/initializers/mail_interceptor.rb
unless Rails.env.test? || Rails.env.production?

  options = {forward_emails_to: "noel@noelrappin.com",
             deliver_emails_to: ["@snowglobetheater.com"]}

  interceptor = MailInterceptor::Interceptor.new(options)
```

---

7. https://github.com/bigbinary/mail_interceptor
8. https://github.com/wireframe/email_prefixer

```
    ActionMailer::Base.register_interceptor(interceptor)
    EmailPrefixer.configure do |config|
      config.application_name = "Snow Globe"
    end
  end
end
```

Again, we only initialize these tools if we are not in the test or production environment.

MailInterceptor has two settings. The forward_emails_to setting is a single email or list of emails. Any email sent by the app and not covered by the other setting is sent to these email addresses and not to the recipient designated by the app. The deliver_emails_to setting is a list of strings. If any string is a partial match with the recipient of the email, the email proceeds normally. You could use this, for example, to allow QA testing to proceed with known account names.

After we define the settings, we create the interceptor and register it with ActiveMailer.

Finally, the EmailPrefixer gem just takes the application name as a configuration option and adds it to the subject lines of email messages, as in [Snow Globe] or [Snow Globe Staging].

Next Up

We've covered a lot of different administrative functions in the last few chapters. It's now time to go back to some more advanced functionality that our application is going to need as we move toward launch. In the next chapter we're going to look at some reporting features; then we'll look at making payments and paying taxes, and finally, we'll talk about issues involving in moving to production.

## CHAPTER 10

Reporting

The Snow Globe Theater is thriving. Customers are buying tickets, nobody seems to have found any lurking edge-case bugs, the subscribers are subscribing, and the theater's proprietors are happy with us. Yay for happy clients!

There's just one more thing. There's always one more thing.

They'd like some analytical data.

Nothing fancy, just some current inventory, daily revenue, weekly revenue, website analytics. Not to mention the kind of sales reports you might have to show to an accountant.

In this chapter, we'll explore some basic code to get these kinds of reports to your customers. Specifically, we'll talk about converting largish amounts of your data into two-dimensional arrays suitable for external use. In doing so, I'm going to make some simplifying assumptions. I'm going to assume that you are not, at least initially, going to interface with any high-powered enterprise reporting engine or contact management software. The focus is going to be on things we can do relatively simply with the tools at hand.

Using ActiveAdmin Reporting

Let's not overlook the simplest tool available. Every one of us has access to an analytic tool of tremendous power, which for many just sits idle or underused. I refer, of course, to spreadsheets. Even if you don't have Microsoft Excel, free alternatives are available and quite powerful.

One of the best features of a standard spreadsheet program is that it accepts a common input format that is fairly easy to generate: comma-separated values (CSV) files. One of the quickest wins you can get in reporting is to make your application emit data in the CSV format so that you can add that data into a spreadsheet and do any statistical fireworks you want.

JSON is also commonly used as a format for communication between applications. For our purposes, we'd like ours to be able to emit JSON files so that a client-side graphing tool can use them. And here's a great thing about our application as it stands right now: it already does this. To a point. ActiveAdmin, which we installed in Chapter 7, *The Administration Experience*, on page 143, offers CSV, XML, and JSON output as an option on all of its index pages. Head to any of our application's ActiveAdmin index pages and you'll see:

> Download: CSV XML JSON

Subtly but usefully, ActiveAdmin streams the CSV file so that it starts sending data before the file is complete. Streaming makes the app feel more responsive to the user and can prevent timeouts (especially if you are on Heroku,[1] which has a very tight timeout limit). You'll appropriate this technique in a bit when we create our own CSV data. This is not true for JSON or XML, both of which are a little harder to stream.

By default, the ActiveAdmin links return all the database attributes of the class in schema order. That's unlikely to be exactly what you want, so ActiveAdmin has a small DSL to allow you to customize the CSV output. (As far as I can tell, you can't customize the JSON or XML output.)

Let me demonstrate by turning the Payments CSV into something you might be more likely to use:

```
reporting/01/app/admin/payment.rb
csv do
  column(:reference)
  column(:date) { |payment| payment.created_at.to_s(:sql) }
  column(:user_email) { |payment| payment.user.email }
  column(:price)
  column(:status)
  column(:payment_method)
  column(:response_id)
  column(:discount)
end
```

This DSL, which starts when the csv method is called with a block, takes a series of calls to the column method. If column is called without a block, ActiveAdmin assumes the value is a method of the same name. If column is called with a block, the argument to the block is the instance being converted, and the value of the block is the value of the CSV cell. In either case, the symbol or string argument to column is humanized and used as the column

---

1.   https://www.heroku.com

name in the header row (you can pass a humanize-name: false option if you want to skip the humanizing part). Any option that Ruby's FastCSV library takes for CSV generation can be passed as a key/value pair to the initial csv call. If you have global CSV configurations, you can set them in the config/initializers/active_admin.rb file with a config.csv_options = { WHATEVER }.

Finally, the CSV file is returned as a file, suitable for import into the spreadsheet of your choice.

Rolling Your Own Data

A limitation of the ActiveAdmin data setup is that it allows only one CSV definition per class, and that class needs to already be something ActiveAdmin is handling. You're likely going to want multiple windows on the data, and CSV representations of data that isn't quite a database table.

The ActiveAdmin DSL for CSVs is nice, though, and it'd be valuable to be able to appropriate it. Turns out that, while the ActiveAdmin::CSVBuilder is not a lot of code, it's somewhat tightly coupled to ActiveAdmin and Rails controllers and views, and is a little more abstract than we need it to be.

So, I took the liberty of pulling out the CSV builder code and adapting it to be a lot more generic. First, I removed a few references to controllers and view contexts, which we don't need and which limited how data could get into the builder. Second, I refactored the code a bit to match the naming conventions and style of this app, and also because I'm fussy about code. Third, the code is now designed to start converting to just a two-dimensional array.

Take a look at this code. The first part is the ReportBuilder class—the other classes are described internally to that class. The class takes a set of options and a block. We expect the block to have a set of column calls to define the report format:

```
reporting/01/app/reports/report_builder.rb
# Inspired by the the ActiveAdmin::CSV builder class defined at
# https://github.com/activeadmin/activeadmin
# The ActiveAdmin code is Copyright (c) Greg Bell, VersaPay Corporation

class ReportBuilder

  attr_reader :columns, :options
  attr_accessor :humanize_name

  def initialize(options = {}, &block)
    @columns = []
    @options = options
    @block = block
    @humanize_names = options.delete(:humanize_name)
  end
```

```ruby
def csv_options
  @csv_options ||= options.except(
      :encoding_options, :byte_order_mark, :column_names)
end

def column(name, _options = {}, &block)
  @columns << Column.new(name, {humanize_name: humanize_name}, block)
end

def build(collection = [], output: nil, format: nil)
  exec_columns
  builder = case format
            when :csv
              CsvBuilder.new(columns, options, collection, output || "")
            else
              Builder.new(columns, options, collection, output || [])
            end
  builder.build
end

def exec_columns
  @columns = []
  instance_exec(&@block) if @block.present?
  columns
end
```

There are two main points of interest in this code: the column method and the build method.

The column method, which is what is actually called inside the DSL, creates a Column object that can calculate its header name and its data value. (There probably should be a way to limit the code so that no method other than column can be called via the DSL.)

The build method creates the CSV. It takes three arguments. The collection is the set of objects being converted into a report. The format method is the format of the output we use to determine which builder we get. The output argument is where the output goes. The default depends on the format. For the plain builder, the default output is an empty array. For CSV, it can be any object that accepts the shovel operator, <<. By default, it's an empty string, but it could also be a file or other stream. And, also rather usefully, it could be a Ruby Enumerator.

Inside the build method, exec_columns is called, which is where the code inside the block (meaning all those column calls) are executed.

After that, what happens depends on what builder you call. The plain builder converts the data into an array of hashes:

reporting/01/app/reports/report_builder.rb

```ruby
class Builder

  attr_accessor :collection, :output, :columns, :options

  def initialize(columns, options, collection, output)
    @columns = columns
    @options = options
    @collection = collection
    @output = output
  end

  def build
    build_header
    build_rows
    output
  end

  def build_header
    nil
  end

  def build_rows
    collection.each do |resource|
      output << build_row(resource)
    end
  end

  def build_row(resource)
    result = {}
    columns.each do |column|
      result[column.name] = encode(column.value(resource), options)
    end
    result
  end

  def encode(content, options)
    if options[:encoding]
      content.to_s.encode(options[:encoding], options[:encoding_options])
    else
      content
    end
  end

end
```

The builder calls a method to generate the header row, and then another that
calls the rows one by one. Each row must be able to respond to the method
calls defined by each column. Eventually the column either uses send on a
symbol or string argument, or executes its block to determine a value.

```
reporting/01/app/reports/report_builder.rb
class Column

  attr_reader :name, :data, :options

  def initialize(name, options = {}, block = nil)
    @options = options
    options[:humanize_name] = true if options[:humanize_name].nil?
    @name = humanize_name(name, @options[:humanize_name])
    @data = block || name.to_sym
  end

  def humanize_name(name, humanize_name_option)
    if humanize_name_option
      name.to_s.humanize
    else
      name.to_s
    end
  end

  def value(resource)
    case data
    when Symbol, String then resource.send(data)
    when Proc then resource.instance_exec(resource, &data)
    end
  end
end
```

The CSV builder subclasses from the main builder because it is converting everything into strings using the core CSV library, and also because it only needs the values when generating each row.

```
reporting/01/app/reports/report_builder.rb
class CsvBuilder < Builder

  def add_byte_order_mark
    bom = options.fetch(:byte_order_mark, false)
    output << bom if bom
  end

  def build_header
    add_byte_order_mark
    return unless options.fetch(:column_names, true)
    headers = columns.map { |column| encode(column.name, options) }
    output << CSV.generate_line(headers, options)
  end

  def build_rows
    collection.each do |resource|
      row = build_row(resource)
      output << CSV.generate_line(row.values, options)
    end
  end
end
```

Although I don't show it here, it would be pretty simple to generate an Html-Builder to generate an HTML table (for instance, you could pass the main builder to a Rails template and loop through it within the Slim markup). The JSON builder is pretty much just calling the regular builder and calling to_json on the result, though if you want to be able to specify JSON formatting like, say, a root element, then you'd need a custom builder.

To use the columns DSL, you need to define a small wrapper that allows a class to convert itself to a CSV file. The wrapper can then be mixed into a class.

reporting/01/app/reports/reportable.rb
```
module Reportable

  def self.included(base)
    base.extend(ClassMethods)
  end

  module ClassMethods

    attr_accessor :report_builder

    def columns(options = {}, &block)
      self.report_builder = ReportBuilder.new(options, &block)
    end

    def to_csv(collection: nil)
      report_builder.build(collection || find_collection,
          output: "", format: :csv)
    end

    def to_json(collection: nil)
      result = report_builder.build(collection || find_collection)
      result.to_json
    end

    def to_csv_enumerator(collection: nil)
      Enumerator.new do |y|
        report_builder.build(collection || find_collection,
            output: y, format: :csv)
      end
    end
  end

end
```

The Reportable module uses a common pattern: the module is included into a file, triggering the self.included method. This method then uses base.extend to define class methods on the class doing the including.

The Reportable module defines four methods. The first, columns, is the one used in the class definition to define the CSV format for the class. It creates an instance of ReportBuilder and holds onto it. Next are two methods to get the data out: the to_csv method and the to_csv_enumerator method. The to_csv method calls build on our builder with a string argument, so it returns a string. It takes an optional collection argument. Again, if that argument is not used, it looks for a find_collection method on the class. The to_csv_enumerator method does the same thing, but embeds the csv_builder inside the body of an Enumerator's creation block. The effect of this is that the method returns the Enumerator, and successive calls to next on that enumerator return the CSV rows one at a time. This enables us to start using data lazily before the entire CSV file is generated. Finally, we add a to_json method that converts the data to an array of JSON objects.

Let's see how you would use this CSV builder to create a daily revenue report that gathers payment by day and returns a total revenue.

reporting/01/app/reports/daily_revenue.rb
```ruby
class DailyRevenue

  include Reportable

  attr_accessor :date, :payments

  def self.find_collection
    Payment.includes(payment_line_items: :buyable)
        .all.group_by(&:date).map do |date, payments|
      DailyRevenue.new(date, payments)
    end
  end

  def initialize(date, payments)
    @date = date
    @payments = payments
  end

  def revenue
    payments.sum(&:price)
  end

  def discounts
    payments.sum(&:discount)
  end

  def tickets_sold
    payments.flat_map(&:tickets).size
  end

  columns do
    column(:date)
    column(:tickets_sold)
    column(:revenue)
    column(:discounts)
  end

end
```

This report includes our Reportable module and defines a find_collection method. The find_collection method grabs all the payments, groups them by day, and creates a new DailyRevenue object for each day. We define a few aggregation methods on the DailyRevenue, and then at the bottom of the file, define a csv block that declares the four columns of the result. Now we can call DailyRevenue.to_csv and get our CSV file.

Let's see what that looks like when it is called from our controller.

We've set up a dedicated controller to keep a RESTful API. Behind the scenes, we need to add a route in the config/routes.rb files specifying this as a singular resource: resource daily_revenue_report. If you look at the site navigation, I've also put some admin-only links in the navbar.

The controller defines a show method, like this:

```
reporting/01/app/controllers/daily_revenue_reports_controller.rb
class DailyRevenueReportsController < ApplicationController

  def show
    respond_to do |format|
      format.html {}
      format.csv do
        headers["X-Accel-Buffering"] = "no"
        headers["Cache-Control"] = "no-cache"
        headers["Content-Type"] = "text/csv; charset=utf-8"
        headers["Content-Disposition"] =
            %(attachment; filename="#{csv_filename}")
        headers["Last-Modified"] = Time.zone.now.ctime.to_s
        self.response_body = DailyRevenue.to_csv_enumerator
      end
    end
  end

  private def csv_filename
    "daily_revenue_report-#{Time.zone.now.to_date.to_s(:default)}.csv"
  end

end
```

The show method uses the Rails respond_to idiom to split into two paths, the first of which is the HTML request, with the URL /daily_revenue_report. That HTML request uses the format.html {} branch and displays a regular show.html.slim template. I've made that template really simple; all it does is provide a link back to the /daily_revenue_report.csv.

```
reporting/01/app/views/daily_revenue_reports/show.html.slim
h2 Daily Revenue Report

= link_to "Download CSV", daily_revenue_report_path(format: :csv)
```

Clicking the .csv link goes back to the same controller method, but this time, the controller follows the block defined by format.csv. The first thing that happens in that block is that a bunch of HTTP headers are defined. My set of headers here is based on a couple of different suggestions about how best to do this—I'm not sure you need all of these. Here's what they do:

- The X-Accel-Buffering = 'no' header turns off a default behavior of a web server like Nginx. In many production configurations, our Rails server is behind a load-balancing server or web server. Under normal circumstances, that server would buffer the response, meaning it would hold onto the data and release it in chunks for better networking performance. Because we are streaming data, we don't want that, so we turn the buffering off.

- Cache-Control = no-cache prevents the browser from caching the response from the server, which is often done to prevent duplicate downloading of the same material. Again, that doesn't really work for us in streaming mode, so we turn it off.

- ["Content-Type"] = "text/csv; charset=utf-8" sets the MIME type of the result. We're doing that because the CSV output MIME type is not the Rails default.

- The Content-Disposition header tells the browser that we are downloading a file to be saved to the local filesystem and not rendered in the browser by declaring it an attachment. We also give it a default filename, which we define to include a timestamp to guarantee uniqueness.

- The Last-Modified header specifies when the server thinks the data changed last. Again this is for purposes of browser caching, and again, we don't want caching so we explicitly set that time to right now. It's possible that including the timestamp on the file and setting the last-modified header is redundant.

Alternatively, some of these headers have alternate ways of being set in Rails, such as setting them as arguments to the Rails render method. But here we're bypassing the render method and specifying the response body directly.

The last line of the csv block explicitly sets self.response_body = DailyRevenue.to_csv_enumerator. In Rails, if the response_body is set to an Enumerator, Rails assumes you want to stream the response. It repeatedly queries the Enumerator for its next element and sends that over the wire. Because the enumerator is set up such that every call to next returns the next row of the CSV file, the code will generate a row, pass it to the enumerator, stop, send the row to the client, generate the next row, pass it to the enumerator, stop, send the row to the client, and so on.

As a result, this CSV report heads to the client much faster than if you had sent it normally. Depending on your server configuration, this can make a big difference (especially if you are deployed to a platform like Heroku that has a fairly strict policy of timing out relatively quickly).

I know that this report will start to have other serious performance issues once the number of payments and the number of days increases, but more on that in a bit.

You can also use your CSV builder to create reports that don't depend on aggregates and aren't the ActiveAdmin report for the class. Here's the beginning of a report you might use for an official list of purchases:

reporting/01/app/reports/purchase_audit.rb
```
class PurchaseAudit

  include Reportable

  attr_accessor :payment, :user

  def self.find_collection
    Payment.includes(:user).succeeded.all.map do |payment|
      PurchaseAudit.new(payment)
    end
  end

  def initialize(payment)
    @payment = payment
    @user = payment.user
  end

  columns do
    column(:reference) { |report| report.payment.reference }
    column(:user_email) { |report| report.user.email }
    column(:user_stripe_id) { |report| report.user.stripe_id }
    column(:price) { |report| report.payment.price.to_f }
    column(:total_value) { |report| report.payment.full_value.to_f }
  end

end
```

This report combines purchase information and user information. Later you can add user address location and other partial payment information to make this work as a report of taxable information.

Speeding Up Performance and Data Preparation

One problem with running reports is that they tend to want to use a lot of data, which becomes increasingly problematic over time as more and more data is accumulated. The two CSV generators we've looked at are naive interpretations that will absolutely not scale. Slow-running reports can lead to excessive server load, which can even crowd out regular users. (For example, I've worked on an app where I could see in the New Relic response graph when the administrator was running reports.)

A few strategies can be employed to speed up reports: do less work at once, do work in the database, and don't duplicate work. These will work on any code, but reports are particularly data-intensive.

Use ActiveRecord to Spread Out Database Access

Once upon a time, I worked for a large daily-deals company whose name rhymes with a major brand of dijon mustard. (I could name the company; it's just that being oblique makes me feel like I have cool secrets to hide.) As part of our new developer orientation, we had a session that was effectively "things Rails tutorials will do that you can't do at our scale." Topmost on the list was User.all, which, when you have something like seven figures of user records, is effectively a self-inflicted denial-of-service attack.

Happily, Rails has a way around this in the ActiveRecord methods find_each and find_in_batches. The find_each method goes at the end of an ActiveRecord database call chain, typically in place of all. The method takes a block. Rather than grabbing all the records from the database, find_each grabs the records in batches. By default, the batches are 1000, but you can set that number to what you want. The method grabs a batch, loops through the block once for records in the batch, then goes back to the database for another batch when it's done.

There are a couple of advantages to using find_each. One is that it limits the amount of data coming from the database, so the process can start before all the data comes in. More subtly, when ActiveRecord reads data from a database, it locks the rows in question so that they can't be updated until the read is complete. By using find_each, that lock is relinquished more often, making it easier for other traffic to be served and not blocked behind the large report query.

Using find_each is just a matter of putting replacing all method when we find_collections for the report. Here's the code from the listing of all Payment records:

reporting/02/app/reports/purchase_audit.rb
```ruby
def self.find_collection
  Payment.includes(:user).succeeded.find_each.lazy.map do |payment|
    PurchaseAudit.new(payment)
  end
end
```

All I've done here is replaced all with find_each.lazy, and amazingly, this works. And by "this works," I mean we get the exact same CSV as before only with much better database and memory performance. Exactly what's going on here is a little subtle. The find_each method takes a block argument, but if it doesn't get one, it returns a Ruby Enumerator, like the one we just used to allow our CSV files to be generated one row at a time.

In this version of the find_collection method, find_each doesn't take a block argument, even though it kind of looks like it does. Instead, find_each takes advantage of one of the great features of Ruby Enumerators, which is that they can be chained. When enumerators are chained, the output of the first one becomes the input of the second.

Next, the enumerator returned is passed by find_each to the lazy method. The lazy method returns a new lazy enumerator, just like the one that received the method. In this case "lazy" is a technical term that means it only returns new values one at a time, as requested, rather than all at once. This is valuable to us because, although find_each prevents us from collecting jillions of records from the database at once, it does nothing to prevent us from building up an array of jillions of PurchaseAudit objects. By using lazy, we protect ourselves, and only create one PurchaseAudit object at a time, as needed, allowing older ones to be garbage-collected if possible, and potentially dramatically reducing the amount of memory used for this query. The lazy enumerator passes off to map, which finally does get the block argument, and handles the actual conversion of the data.

This gets even cooler when you combine it with the CSV builder. If you call to_csv_enumerable, you get the CSV as an enumerator:

```
[1] pry(main)> x = PurchaseAudit.to_csv_enumerator
=> #<Enumerator: ...>
[2] pry(main)> x.next
=> "Reference,User email,User stripe,Price,Total value\n"
[3] pry(main)> x.next
REDACTED
=> "0cf77512b5291a246078,buyer@cubs.com,,30.00,30.00\n"
```

This time each next call walks all the way back to the lazy enumerator, which calls map one record at a time. When we hit a batch of 1000, we walk back to find_each and grab the next records. It's an extraordinary amount of bookkeeping that Ruby and Rails manage for us.

There's one limitation to find_each: you can't control the order of the elements. Rails automatically uses id order. If that's not good enough, and you happen to be on Postgres, you can use the PostgreSQLCursor gem,[2] which enables you to put the items into any order and then use the each_instance method instead of find_each. The each_instance gives you effectively the same batching behavior as find_each, but using Postgres internals so that you can do them in whatever order you choose. The PostgreSQLCursor gem also defines an each_row method, which returns the row as a hash instead of an ActiveRecord instance. This can be significantly faster, especially in a case like this one where we're just passing the values on to another object anyway.

Aggregate Database Functions

Our other report, which calculates daily revenue, aggregates data from the database in a way that doesn't quite make it amenable to the find_each improvement. But there's still a way to make the database more efficient. As written, the code imports all the payments from the database, and does the aggregation and summation in Ruby. Databases can do that stuff way faster if we let them.

Standard SQL databases support the GROUP BY clause, which aggregates rows based on specified criteria. Here's a very quick overview of GROUP BY. The GROUP BY clause allows us to more or less squash a bunch of rows together based on a common attribute value. For example, you could say select user_id from payments GROUP BY user_id and you'd get one row for each distinct user_id in the system from the Postgres prompt (I don't have a lot of data in this database):

```
=# select user_id from payments GROUP BY user_id;
 user_id
----------
 76570549
(1 row)
```

Just displaying the value we're grouping by isn't helpful, so also include any of the SQL calculation functions, as in count, sum, avg, max, and min:

```
# select user_id, count(*), sum(price_cents) as total_price,
  max(price_cents) as biggest_sale from payments GROUP BY user_id;
 user_id  | count | total_price | biggest_sale
----------+-------+-------------+--------------
 76570549 |     1 |        3000 |         3000
(1 row)
```

You can also use a clause called HAVING, which is WHERE for grouped clauses, so you could say GROUP BY user_id HAVING total_price > 100000 or something.

---

2.   https://github.com/afair/postgresql_cursor

From a database prompt, or using SQL directly, GROUP BY and HAVING allow you a lot of flexibility to get combined data out of the database. ActiveRecord does not pass all that flexibility on to Rails, except in the sense that you can use ActiveRecord to execute arbitrary SQL. As a general design touchstone, Rails and ActiveRecord prefer to have business logic in Ruby code and not in SQL. Normally, that's great, but sometimes that gets in the way of optimizing some database-intensive calculations.

ActiveRecord makes a few things really easy, such as calculating an aggregate function such that there's only one value, as in

```
pry(main)> Payment.sum(:price_cents)
   (0.8ms)  SELECT SUM("payments"."price_cents") FROM "payments"
=> 3000
```

Or where there is one grouped attribute and one value per row, as in

```
pry(main)> Payment.group(:user_id).sum(:price_cents)
   (0.9ms)  SELECT SUM("payments"."price_cents") AS sum_price_cents,
    "payments"."user_id" AS payments_user_id FROM "payments" GROUP BY
    "payments"."user_id"
=> {76570549=>3000}
```

In this case, ActiveRecord returns a hash where the keys are the grouped attribute and the values are the aggregate.

ActiveRecord can also handle cases where the resulting columns have the same attribute names as the ActiveRecord class. This one is a little weird:

```
Payment.select("sum(price_cents) as price_cents, user_id").group(:user_id)
   Payment Load (0.6ms)  SELECT sum(price_cents) as price_cents, user_id FROM
    "payments" GROUP BY "payments"."user_id"
=> [#<Payment:0x007fa778a0bbb8 id: nil, user_id: 76570549, price_cents: 3000>]
```

In general, ActiveRecord acts strange when you specify the select clause. In this case, the return value is an array of Payment objects where the attributes match the aggregates assigned to them in the select call. This seems kind of dangerous to me, in that it's not really a Payment object. In an ActiveRecord call like this one, columns in the select clause that are not attributes of the original class are ignored.

With all that in mind, you can rewrite your daily revenue report to use the database for calculations, rather than Ruby. You can do this in a couple of different ways. Here's what I settled on:

reporting/02/app/reports/daily_revenue.rb

```ruby
class DailyRevenue

  include Reportable

  attr_accessor :date, :revenue, :discounts

  def self.find_collection
    ActiveRecord::Base.connection.select_all(
        %{SELECT date(created_at) as date,
        sum(price_cents) as price_cents,
        sum(discount_cents) as discount_cents
        FROM "payments"
        WHERE "payments"."status" = 1
        GROUP BY date(created_at)}).map do |data|
      DailyRevenue.new(**data.symbolize_keys)
    end
  end

  def initialize(date:, price_cents:, discount_cents:)
    @date = date
    @revenue = price_cents.to_money
    @discounts = discount_cents.to_money
  end

  columns do
    column(:date)
    column(:revenue)
    column(:discounts)
    column(:ticket_count)
  end

  def ticket_count
    PaymentLineItem.tickets.no_refund
        .where("date(created_at) = ?", date).count
  end

end
```

The previous version of this class gathered all the payment records and grouped them in Ruby based on the date; then each individual instance calculated the necessary sums. This one works a little differently.

The find_collection method now uses ActiveRecord's connection.select_all to make an arbitrary SQL call to the database. The return value of select_all is an array of hashes, with each hash corresponding to each row of the return value from SQL. The call itself uses sum and GROUP BY. You GROUP BY the date the purchase was created, using the PostgreSQL date conversion function. (Parenthetically, this code is making me think I should have included an effective_date as an attribute of Payment.) In the select clause, you ask for the date, the sum of all the prices, and the sum of all the discounts. You also need to handle the limitation to successful payments yourself, with WHERE payments.status = 1.

Once you have that result from the database, you once again convert each row into a DailyRevenue object. This time, however, rather than passing in a list of payments to DailyRevenue, the price and discount sums are passed in directly and converted to money objects in the constructor.

Our CSV columns are the same, but we do take advantage of ActiveRecord's aggregate shortcut when looking at the total ticket_count. In this case, you can think of this calculation as an aggregate returning a single value, so by limiting the PaymentLineItem rows to tickets that haven't been refunded, you can search for the particular date and then ask for just the count, which returns the number of rows matching the criteria.

Strictly speaking, calculating the ticket_count inside each DailyRevenue object is probably inefficient. There's probably a way to add it to the original SQL statement using joins, but combining joins and aggregate functions makes my head hurt, and I find hard to maintain. You also could have gotten all the ticket counts for every day at once and handed it off to each individual DailyRevenue instance, but that code seemed awkward.

At this point, the DailyRevenue record works and is probably more scalable over large amounts of data, but it also probably results in a lot of redundant calculation if it's going to be done frequently. However, there's another path we can take for performance purposes.

Cache Calculated Data

One of the key concepts of web performance is trying not to calculate the same data more than once, instead using caching to present precalculated pages. We can apply similar ideas to our reporting, precalculating data to make its eventual presentation happen more quickly and with less database impact.

As with many topics in the book, there are many different ways to precalculate this kind of report data, and depending on the exact nature of your application, one or the other may make more sense. I'll discuss the general principles, warn about pitfalls, and show one specific solution.

Basically we want to precalculate our report rows and store them someplace useful. Let's talk about the storage first. I'm going to show this off using an ActiveRecord model, mostly because doing so does not require us to set up new servers, which is a significant consideration when you are writing a teaching example, and maybe not as big a deal when you are working with a real production app. It's common to use an in-memory store like Redis for this kind of thing, because there's often not that much data being stored and because a schema-less database is genuinely more flexible in this case. Sometimes, storing the data in flat JSON or YAML files works well.

Let's start with a database migration that creates a table matching the revenue report we've been working on:

```
% rails generate model day_revenue day:date \
    ticket_count:integer price:monetize discounts:monetize
```

A rake db:migrate later and you're open for business.

Now you have two problems. You need to get data into this database table, and you need to convert the table to our CSV builder.

Getting data into the table is a bit more complicated than it might seem at first glance. The way I see it, there are three general options:

- You can incrementally change data every time a Payment record is saved.

- You can have a background task that runs periodically and recalculates some or all of the data.

- You can lazily calculate the data when the report is requested.

Unfortunately, we have two goals that kind-of conflict. We usually want this data to be up-to-date, which argues for the incremental change, but we also want the calculation of the report to be easily auditable and idempotent, meaning the calculation won't change if you rerun it. Though it's possible to make the incremental version idempotent, it's more complexity than we probably need.

The exact trade-off depends on the report. For the daily revenue report we're looking at, it's unlikely old data will change, but not impossible—there can be errors, and it's kind of useful to see up-to-the-moment data. A hybrid approach for the revenue data makes sense: use a background task to calculate any data older than yesterday, and then use aggregation functions for current data. (By keeping both today and yesterday out of the cached data, you make the report a little more robust against both the time it's run and any time zone weirdness between the server and the database.)

Let's see what that looks like in code. I haven't shown a test in a while, and for something like this, which has the potential for subtle off-by-one errors, tests are a good idea. I decided to implement the data generator as a background job, so the tests behave accordingly:

```
reporting/02/spec/jobs/build_day_revenue_job_spec.rb
require "rails_helper"

RSpec.describe BuildDayRevenueJob, type: :job do

  let!(:really_old_payment) { create(
      :payment, created_at: 1.month.ago, price_cents: 4500) }
  let!(:really_old_payment_2) { create(
      :payment, created_at: 1.month.ago, price_cents: 1500) }
  let!(:old_payment) { create(
      :payment, created_at: 2.days.ago, price_cents: 3500) }
  let!(:yesterday_payment) { create(
      :payment, created_at: 1.day.ago, price_cents: 2500) }
  let!(:now_payment) { create(
      :payment, created_at: 1.second.ago, price_cents: 1500) }

  it "runs the report" do
    BuildDayRevenueJob.perform_now
    expect(DayRevenue.find_by(day: 1.month.ago).price_cents).to eq(6000)
    expect(DayRevenue.find_by(day: 2.days.ago).price_cents).to eq(3500)
    expect(DayRevenue.find_by(day: 1.day.ago)).to be_nil
    expect(DayRevenue.find_by(day: Date.current)).to be_nil
  end

  it "runs the report twice" do
    BuildDayRevenueJob.perform_now
    BuildDayRevenueJob.perform_now
    expect(DayRevenue.count).to eq(2)
    expect(DayRevenue.find_by(day: 1.month.ago).price_cents).to eq(6000)
  end

  context "it calculates tickets" do
    let!(:ticket) { create(:ticket) }
    let!(:payment_line_item) { create(
        :payment_line_item, payment: really_old_payment, buyable: ticket,
                            created_at: 1.month.ago) }

    it "adds ticket count" do
      BuildDayRevenueJob.perform_now
      expect(DayRevenue.find_by(day: 1.month.ago).ticket_count).to eq(1)
    end

  end

end
```

The test creates enough sample data to verify that it aggregates multiple payments on the same day, it creates a record for two days ago, and it doesn't create a record for yesterday or today. The first test checks that you get all the data you need. The second test checks for idempotency by running the test twice and seeing that the values are the same. The third test adds in ticket count—it's a separate test because it creates more data that you don't need for the first test.

The job is similar to the CSV builder that used aggregates:

```
reporting/02/app/jobs/build_day_revenue_job.rb
class BuildDayRevenueJob < ApplicationJob

  queue_as :default

  def perform(*_args)
    DayRevenue.transaction do
      DayRevenue.destroy_all
      ActiveRecord::Base.connection.select_all(
          %{SELECT date(created_at) as day,
          sum(price_cents) as price_cents,
          sum(discount_cents) as discounts_cents
          FROM "payments"
          WHERE "payments"."status" = 1
          GROUP BY date(created_at)
          HAVING date(created_at) < '#{1.day.ago.to_date}'}).map do |data|
        DayRevenue.create(data)
      end
      DayRevenue.all.each do |day_revenue|
        tickets = PaymentLineItem.tickets.no_refund
            .where("date(created_at) = ?", day_revenue.day).count
        day_revenue.update(ticket_count: tickets)
      end
    end
  end

end
```

All the action is in the perform method. Inside, we wrap a transaction in case something goes wrong. We delete the existing DayRevenue objects, which gives us idempotency at the cost of a longer job runtime. (Another option would be to figure out which days have updated payments and just recalculate those days.)

We use an SQL aggregation function similar to the one we built for the CSV. It's different in that we use the attribute names of the new class, and also because we use the HAVING clause to limit the dates we calculate. We create a new DayRevenue object based on that data. Then for each DayRevenue object, we calculate the ticket count with the same ActiveRecord count call into the PaymentLineItem table. And again, there's probably a more efficient way to do that.

Let's go to the actual CSV report. I'd like to make the report object separate from DayRevenue itself, because it's specialized. Doing so allows us to write some tests. Here's a test that uses the enumerator version of the CSV to make sure you get the data you expect:

```
reporting/02/spec/reports/day_revenue_report_spec.rb
require "rails_helper"

RSpec.describe DayRevenueReport, type: :model do

  let!(:really_old_payment) { create(
      :payment, created_at: 1.month.ago, price_cents: 4500) }
  let!(:really_old_payment_2) { create(
      :payment, created_at: 1.month.ago, price_cents: 1500) }
  let!(:old_payment) { create(
      :payment, created_at: 2.days.ago, price_cents: 3500) }
  let!(:yesterday_payment) { create(
      :payment, created_at: 1.day.ago, price_cents: 2500) }
  let!(:now_payment) { create(
      :payment, created_at: 1.second.ago, price_cents: 1500) }

  before(:example) do
    BuildDayRevenueJob.perform_now
  end

  it "generates the expected report" do
    enum = DayRevenueReport.to_csv_enumerator
    expect(enum.next).to eq("Day,Price,Discounts,Ticket count\n")
    expect(enum.next).to eq("#{1.month.ago.to_date},60.00,0.00,0\n")
    expect(enum.next).to eq("#{2.days.ago.to_date},35.00,0.00,0\n")
    expect(enum.next).to eq("#{1.day.ago.to_date},25.00,0.00,0\n")
    expect(enum.next).to eq("#{Date.current},15.00,0.00,0\n")
  end
end
```

All these tests require a little more setup than I'd like, but I'm not sure I can take away the database items without making the test a lot more complicated.

The test creates the same batch of data we were looking at before. (Copy and paste is great because it lets you reuse test setups easily, but also bad because it makes it easy to create complex tests without realizing it.) It runs the job to put the data in DayRevenue objects, and then makes sure the line-by-line result does what we want.

Now, because the background job is doing most of the data munging, the report itself doesn't need to do much work:

```
reporting/02/app/reports/day_revenue_report.rb
class DayRevenueReport < SimpleDelegator

  include Reportable

  def self.find_collection
    result = DayRevenue.all.map { |dr| DayRevenueReport.new(dr) }
    result << DayRevenueReport.new(DayRevenue.build_for(Date.yesterday))
    result << DayRevenueReport.new(DayRevenue.build_for(Date.current))
    result.sort_by(&:day)
  end
```

```ruby
def initialize(day_revenue)
  super(day_revenue)
end

columns do
  column(:day)
  column(:price)
  column(:discounts)
  column(:ticket_count)
end
```

`end`

It grabs all the DayRevenue objects and converts them to DayRevenueReport objects, and then asks the DayRevenue class to build—not save—objects for yesterday and today, puts them all together, and sorts them. The actual DayRevenueReport class is just a SimpleDelegator wrapping DayRevenue; really the only thing that it does differently is define the CSV format.

This leaves us with just the DayRevenue class needing to be able to build for a specific day. Again, a test:

reporting/02/spec/models/day_revenue_spec.rb
```ruby
require "rails_helper"

RSpec.describe DayRevenue, type: :model do
  let!(:really_old_payment) { create(
      :payment, created_at: 1.month.ago, price_cents: 4500) }
  let!(:really_old_payment_2) { create(
      :payment, created_at: 1.month.ago, price_cents: 1500) }
  let!(:old_payment) { create(
      :payment, created_at: 2.days.ago, price_cents: 3500) }
  let!(:ticket) { create(:ticket) }
  let!(:payment_line_item) { create(
      :payment_line_item, payment: really_old_payment, buyable: ticket,
                        created_at: 1.month.ago) }

  it "builds data" do
    revenue = DayRevenue.build_for(1.month.ago)
    expect(revenue.price_cents).to eq(6000)
    expect(revenue.ticket_count).to eq(1)
  end
end
```

The test grabs in a subset of data compared to the other tests—I left in one payment object not of the same day to prove that the method limits to only data for that day.

Finally, the DayRevenue class has some similar database logic in it.

reporting/02/app/models/day_revenue.rb
```ruby
class DayRevenue < ApplicationRecord

  monetize :price_cents
  monetize :discounts_cents

  def self.for_date(date)
    find_by(day: date) || build_for(date)
  end

  def self.build_for(date)
    revenue = ActiveRecord::Base.connection.select_all(
        %{SELECT date(created_at) as day,
        sum(price_cents) as price_cents,
        sum(discount_cents) as discounts_cents
        FROM "payments"
        WHERE "payments"."status" = 1
        GROUP BY date(created_at)
        HAVING date(created_at) = '#{date}'}).map do |data|
      DayRevenue.new(data)
    end
    revenue = revenue.first
    tickets = PaymentLineItem.tickets.no_refund
        .where("date(created_at) = ?", date).count
    revenue.ticket_count = tickets
    revenue
  end

end
```

This code is a little sketchy. There are two duplications that I'm nervous about. The big SQL string is basically shared between the background job and the DayRevenue object. Conceptually, the probable fix is to have the background job call the DayRevenue object on a day-by-day basis, but that does add some database overhead. I'm also concerned that the background job and the report both need to know that today's and yesterday's data are not in the database. I'm not completely sure what the answer to that one is.

Next Up

Now that we've covered administration from a number of different angles, it's time to go back to our user-facing functionality and look at a couple of advanced topics. In the two chapters that follow, we'll look at adding fees and taxes on to purchases, and we'll cover making payments, as in affiliate programs.

## CHAPTER 11

Adding Fees and Calculating Taxes

The price is never the price. The ticket might cost $15.00, but there's a processing fee, and a shipping fee, and maybe sales tax. These fees range from "a nice way to make a few extra dollars if you are Ticketmaster" to "a way to make customers pay for extra incremental costs" to "legally mandated extra fees that you must collect and pay to the government."

We'll start this chapter by looking at a structure to manage all of the extra costs that go into a transaction. We'll first talk about extra fees in general, then go into the complexity of dealing with third-party tax information providers.

I'm sure I'm going to say this a few more times before we're through, but I'm neither a lawyer nor an accountant. If you are concerned about sales tax in your application, you should consult one of each.

Adding Nontax Fees

One day our buddies at the Snow Globe Theater come to us with two requests. First, they'd like to charge a processing fee because they'd just like to make some extra money for doing the same amount of work. Second, they get a bunch of requests to send tickets via the physical mail, and they'd like a way to add extra money to an order to cover the mailing costs.

As a quick aside, obviously the Snow Globe Theater is fictional, and I, the author, am setting out these tasks for you to do because I hope they show interesting things about financial applications. In this case, I want to have one automatic fee and one that only applies based on user choice. I also want to start dealing with addresses before we start dealing with taxes.

What I didn't realize completely was that adding the shipping fee, in particular, was a dramatic change in the user's workflow. Previously, users could see the tickets in the shopping cart, enter their credit card information, and just go. Now, however, they see the shopping cart page and still have another piece of information to potentially enter, and we need to then display the results of that choice in the form of an updated price before the users can approve the sale. (We already were doing this a little bit when we entered discount codes in Chapter 8, *Administration Roles*, on page 155, but the address and shipping method data entry is more elaborate.)

The upshot is, this wound up touching a fair bit more code than I initially thought, but it turns out to be a good place to discuss how to safely make these kinds of structural changes to your code.

Store Your Fees, Please!

The absolute most important consideration regarding extra fees and taxes is that no matter what business logic calculates them, you must always be able to re-create the exact amount of all the parts of the transaction as they were calculated at the time of sale. This seems easy, but let me give you an example that is in no way pulled from something that actually happened to me (except that, of course, it is).

The application launched with an identical processing fee attached to each transaction. So naturally I thought to myself, "Self, why should I duplicate the same fee in the database record for each purchase? That is a waste of hard drive space." So, I added PROCESSING_FEE = $2.00 to the code, and made sure that all the relevant calculations and reports knew about it.

Then the fee changed. And it was super easy to change the single constant in the code that drove purchases. But all my calculations of historical ticket prices were now wrong, which was a potentially a huge problem for reporting. I needed to go into the code and insert an awkward method for calculating the processing fee given the day of sale. It works, but it's not my most elegant moment as a coder.

Migrating Existing Data to a New Structure

The first thing we need to do to add these nontax fees is adjust our Payment records so that they can record arbitrary fees or partial payments. We're already doing this a little bit by saving the discount_cents as a separate field, but that's really not going to cut it. We could start adding new fields for processing_fee_cents, shipping_fee_cents, and so on, but that's quickly going to get tedious, and it would require a database migration to add a new fee.

In the past, I might have created a separate fees database table to normalize this data as an alternative to creating a new column for each fee. These days, though, the PostgreSQL json tables work fine. We can drop a Ruby Hash into them directly, and we can also query for specific fields.

This change does, however, affect existing data, because we want to move the existing discount_cents field into the new field. We don't want to lose any data, though, so we'll need a way to migrate the data.

The key points in this data migration are: (1) don't lose any data, and (2) don't break the app. Adding columns is unlikely to cause the app to raise exceptions in the purchase process, but removing database columns easily can.

To manage the data migration, the steps are as follows:

1. Back up the database so you have a pre-migration snapshot. If the worst happens, you can re-create the data from the snapshot.

2. Write the part of the database migration that adds new columns.

3. Write a separate Rake task outside the database migrations that converts the data the way you want.

4. Make all the code work with the new database changes.

5. Deploy.

6. Once you are sure everything works and you have not introduced new errors, write a new migration that deletes the unneeded columns.

7. Make sure the app still works even with the columns gone.

8. Deploy again.

There's really no hurry to get to step 7 other than the fact that it's a little confusing to have dead data and dead code floating around.

With the database backed up, write the migration to add the JSON columns:

tax/01/db/migrate/20160901212715_add_partial_prices_to_payment.rb
```ruby
class AddPartialPricesToPayment < ActiveRecord::Migration[5.0]
  def change
    change_table :payments do |t|
      t.json :partials
    end
  end
end
```

Once upon a time, it would have been common to add the data migration to the database migration, but Rails practice these days tends to discourage putting code in the data migration. The argument in favor of this is that it guarantees that the data is moved over in production when the migrations are run, and does not require the extra Rake task step that could be forgotten. The argument against this practice is that having data in the migration makes it harder to run migrations in general, but the bigger argument is that one-off scripts are never really one-offs, and being able to run them outside of migrations is usually valuable.

The script moves our discount data from the discount_cents field to our new partials field. It also copies line-item data to an entry in the partials called tickets. The idea here is that the entries in partials should re-create the entire price of the payment.

```
tax/01/lib/tasks/migrate_discount_to_partials.rake
namespace :snow_globe do
  task migrate_discounts: :environment do
    Payment.transaction do
      Payment.all.each do |payment|
        partials = {}
        if payment.discount_cents.positive?
          partial[:discount_cents] = -discount_cents
        end
        partial[:tickets].each = payment.tickets.map(&:price_cents)
        payment.update(partials: partials)
      end
    end
  end
end
```

Again, there's not much here. Ideally these scripts are really simple. Don't tell anybody, but sometimes I don't write automated tests here; I just run the script and eyeball the output. If there was logic that seemed at all complex, though, I'd write tests.

Now our new data is in place. We just need to use it.

Adding a Cart Workflow

The changes we're making to the workflow become a little more far reaching than you might expect (certainly more far reaching than I expected). Let's ground this a little by going over the actual requirements:

- A $1 processing fee is added to all orders where the user is charged. Free orders do not have a processing fee.

- Users can opt to have their tickets mailed to them. To do so, they need to specify the shipping address. We offer standard mailing for $2 and overnight mailing for $10.

The processing fee is the less data-intensive of the two fees. Because it's static (for now), all we need to do is make sure it's accounted for in the price calculations. The mailing fee, however, imposes some data changes. The user's address needs to be associated with the shopping cart and the eventual purchase. If the user sets a mailing preference, we need to record that as well.

To me, the fact that we need to save an address and a preference with the cart means it's time to make the shopping cart an ActiveRecord object with a database presence.

There are other options for dealing with the shopping cart. We are currently using the session for storing the active discount code; therefore, we could continue to use the session for mailing information, but the session is not an object that's really under our control, and I'd rather have the data in a model. In the model, the shopping cart behavior is easy to test, and easier to find when reading the codebase. In fact, I also moved the discount code into the shopping cart as part of this change.

Alternately, rather than creating a shopping cart object, we could just create a Payment object earlier in the workflow with a status of waiting and store the information there. This is a tempting option because when we support taxes, we may need the shopping cart to generate the payment reference. However, having a lot of uncompleted payments in the database may make reporting weird. I decided to keep the definition of Payment as something where money has been agreed to change hands, in part because I wanted to minimize changing existing code. But starting with a Payment would absolutely work.

There are a lot of moving pieces here. Here's the plan of attack:

1. The first thing to do is update the PriceCalculator. My theory in starting here is that the PriceCalculator has the most direct changes, and also that it can be tested in isolation from the data changes.

2. At that point, it makes sense to start making ActiveRecord changes. We need to create an Address class, and convert the ShoppingCart to ActiveRecord. This will break a few tests because the API to create a ShoppingCart will change.

3. Now we can address the user workflow. Moving the discount code form submission to place it in the ShoppingCart rather than in the session is an easy way to start. The feature and workflow tests don't change much here, but we will add a new, small workflow and some tests.

4. By now, I understand the UI well enough to write the Capybara test to enter an address.

5. Making this test pass will mean changing the controllers and workflows to take in the shopping cart and pass the correct information to the Payment and PriceCalculators.

6. Some of the details of the existing tests will need to change to match the new API for workflows, taking in a ShoppingCart object.

This will get a little overwhelming surprisingly quickly (at least it did for me). The best advice I have for keeping this kind of process under control is to try to do one thing at a time. Focus on the one test you need to write or the one failing test you need to fix. Try to only change existing code in response to a failing test. Try to only do refactoring and cleanup when the tests all pass.

Let's go through these steps in more detail.

Update the Price Calculator

I'll start with updating the price calculator because it has no relationship with ActiveRecord or the rest of the code, making the tests fast.

The PriceCalculator tests need two changes. First, we have to update existing tests to take into account the processing fee—because the fee applies to all purchases, all tests referencing a total price have to at least have that price updated. Also, I'll add the partial price breakdown for the calculator to figure out which will eventually get put in our new JSON database field.

Here's an update to an existing test:

```
tax/01/spec/services/price_calculator_spec.rb
describe "without a discount code" do
  let(:discount_code) { NullDiscountCode.new }

  it "calculates the price of a list of tickets" do
    expect(discount_code.multiplier).to eq(1.0)
    expect(discount_code.percentage_float).to eq(0)
    expect(calculator.subtotal).to eq(Money.new(3500))
    expect(calculator.discount).to eq(Money.new(0))
    expect(calculator.processing_fee).to eq(Money.new(100))
    expect(calculator.breakdown).to match(
        ticket_cents: [1500, 2000], processing_fee_cents: 100)
    expect(calculator.total_price).to eq(Money.new(3600))
  end
end
```

It's the same as it was, except that I've added a line to calculate the processing fee and a line for the breakdown. The idea is that all parts of the price should be in the breakdown, so the sum of all the pieces should equal the total price.

However, there's one special case. A free ticket doesn't have a processing fee; that gets its own test:

```ruby
describe "with a free ticket" do
  let(:discount_code) { DiscountCode.new(percentage: 100) }

  it "calculates the total price and discount with a promo code" do
    expect(discount_code.multiplier).to eq(0)
    expect(discount_code.percentage_float).to eq(1)
    expect(calculator.discount).to eq(Money.new(3500))
    expect(calculator.processing_fee).to eq(Money.zero)
    expect(calculator.breakdown).to eq(
        ticket_cents: [1500, 2000], discount_cents: -3500)
    expect(calculator.total_price).to eq(Money.zero)
  end
end
```

I made that test pass, but the code got a bit overwritten by the result of the next test, which added a shipping option:

```ruby
describe "with a shipping fee" do
  let(:calculator) { PriceCalculator.new(
      [ticket_one, ticket_two], discount_code, :standard) }
  let(:discount_code) { NullDiscountCode.new }

  it "calculates the price of a list of tickets" do
    expect(discount_code.multiplier).to eq(1.0)
    expect(discount_code.percentage_float).to eq(0)
    expect(calculator.subtotal).to eq(Money.new(3500))
    expect(calculator.discount).to eq(Money.new(0))
    expect(calculator.processing_fee).to eq(Money.new(100))
    expect(calculator.breakdown).to match(
        ticket_cents: [1500, 2000], processing_fee_cents: 100,
        shipping_cents: 200)
    expect(calculator.total_price).to eq(Money.new(3800))
  end
end
```

The shipping fee comes in as an argument to the constructor. (We are getting to the point where I might change to keyword arguments for more clarity.) And the shipping fee is calculated and added to the breakdown as an integer number of cents.

Here's the PriceCalculator code that makes this work:

tax/01/app/services/price_calculator.rb

```ruby
class PriceCalculator

  attr_accessor :tickets, :discount_code, :shipping

  def initialize(tickets = [], discount_code = nil, shipping = :none)
    @tickets = tickets
    @discount_code = discount_code || NullDiscountCode.new
    @shipping = shipping
  end

  def processing_fee
    (subtotal - discount).positive? ? Money.new(100) : Money.zero
  end

  def shipping_fee
    case shipping.to_sym
    when :standard then Money.new(200)
    when :overnight then Money.new(1000)
    else
      Money.zero
    end
  end

  def subtotal
    tickets.map(&:price).sum
  end

  def breakdown
    result = {ticket_cents: tickets.map { |t| t.price.cents }}
    if processing_fee.nonzero?
      result[:processing_fee_cents] = processing_fee.cents
    end
    result[:discount_cents] = -discount.cents if discount.nonzero?
    result[:shipping_cents] = shipping_fee.cents if shipping_fee.nonzero?
    result
  end

  def total_price
    subtotal - discount + processing_fee + shipping_fee
  end

  def discount
    discount_code.discount_for(subtotal)
  end

end
```

This code includes three new methods. The processing_fee applies the fee if the subtotal minus the discount is greater than zero. The shipping_fee converts the shipping fee options to amounts of money (that one might be better as a lookup table). The breakdown method converts all the pieces into a hash, only including fees that are actually there. (This method clearly has a pattern and might be refactorable, but I didn't come up with anything that was as easy to read as this version.)

Add ActiveRecord

Now that the PriceCalculator is calculating correctly, we can begin the process of connecting it to the workflows and to user data entry. We need to create some database models to do so. The users are going to give us an address, so we need to create an Address class, and we need to attach it to the Payment table.

Here's how:

```
tax/01/db/migrate/20160902020145_create_addresses.rb
class CreateAddresses < ActiveRecord::Migration[5.0]

  def change
    create_table :addresses do |t|
      t.string :address_1
      t.string :address_2
      t.string :city
      t.string :state
      t.string :zip

      t.timestamps
    end

    change_table :payments do |t|
      t.integer :billing_address_id
      t.integer :shipping_address_id
    end
  end

end
```

The Address class itself is minimal:

```
tax/01/app/models/address.rb
class Address < ApplicationRecord

  validates :address_1, presence: true
  validates :city, presence: true
  validates :state, presence: true
  validates :zip, presence: true

  def all_fields
    [address_1, address_2, city, state, zip].compact.join(", ")
  end

end
```

Here, we're validating on fields that are needed to mail something.

Similarly, because we've decided to store shopping cart data in the database, we require a matching database table. A ShoppingCart needs to know about the user—what the user purchased, the user's address, and the user's preferred shipping method.

tax/01/db/migrate/20160902113711_create_shopping_carts.rb
```ruby
class CreateShoppingCarts < ActiveRecord::Migration[5.0]

  def change
    create_table :shopping_carts do |t|
      t.references :user, foreign_key: true
      t.references :address, foreign_key: true
      t.integer :shipping_method, default: 0
      t.references :discount_code, foreign_key: true

      t.timestamps
    end
  end

end
```

And it turns out we'll want the Payment to have the shipping method, too, so that later, after the shopping cart is gone, we can still determine how users want their tickets sent to them.

tax/01/db/migrate/20160903180301_add_shipping_method_to_purchase.rb
```ruby
class AddShippingMethodToPurchase < ActiveRecord::Migration[5.0]

  def change
    change_table :payments do |t|
      t.integer :shipping_method, default: 0
    end
  end

end
```

The ShoppingCart class changes slightly to accommodate being an ActiveRecord:

tax/01/app/models/shopping_cart.rb
```ruby
class ShoppingCart < ApplicationRecord

  belongs_to :user
  belongs_to :address
  belongs_to :discount_code

  enum shipping_method: {electronic: 0, standard: 1, overnight: 2}

  def self.for(user:)
    ShoppingCart.find_or_create_by(user_id: user.id)
  end

  def price_calculator
    @price_calculator ||= PriceCalculator.new(
        tickets, discount_code, shipping_method.to_s)
  end

  delegate :processing_fee, to: :price_calculator
```

In the first line of the class, we declare it a subclass of ApplicationRecord, which is the Rails 5 thing we use instead of directly accessing ActiveRecord::Base. We then add the belongs_to for users, addresses, and discount codes. This code replaces the old constructor for ShoppingCart as well as the accessors for discount_code, all of which are handled by ActiveRecord now. We add an enum for the shipping method, with the default value set to the free option, which we're calling electronic. And we add a factory method that takes a user and returns their cart, creating one if it's not already there. When we associate the cart with a price calculator, we need to also pass the shipping method.

Other than that, the cart doesn't change. Callers to the cart need to change to use the for method rather than creating a new cart on the fly.

This breaks a couple of ShoppingCart tests, which will require minimal changes. The workflow tests also break, and need to be modified to use the ShoppingCart. Here's a representative change from the prepares_cart_for_stripe workflow:

```
tax/01/spec/workflows/prepares_cart_for_stripe_spec.rb
let(:shopping_cart) { create(
    :shopping_cart, user: user, discount_code: discount_code,
                    shipping_method: :electronic) }
let(:workflow) { PreparesCartForStripe.new(
    user: user, purchase_amount_cents: 3100,
    expected_ticket_ids: "#{ticket_1.id} #{ticket_2.id}",
    payment_reference: "reference", stripe_token: token,
    shopping_cart: shopping_cart) }
let(:attributes) { {
    user_id: user.id, price_cents: 3100,
    reference: a_truthy_value, status: "created",
    discount_code_id: nil,
    partials: {ticket_cents: [1500, 1500], processing_fee_cents: 100},
    payment_method: "stripe", shipping_method: "electronic",
    shipping_address: nil} }
```

This setup changes the workflow to use the shopping cart (before it was taking the discount code directly), and it changes the expected attributes to have a shipping method and the partial payments from the payment calculator. I won't go through all the minor changes to the tests; you can see them by comparing the reporting/02 code directory with the tax/01. We'll see the final changes to the workflow itself in a moment.

You may have noticed that we haven't touched the subscription shopping cart and haven't made it an ActiveRecord object. If this was a real project, we probably would also do that at the same time—a subscription would likely offer the same kind of shipping options. In our case, it's a distraction.

Update the Shopping Cart Fee Workflow

The next step is to allow the user to enter the shipping information as part of the checkout process. To be minimally disruptive to the current process, we'll have the user go to the same shopping cart page as before, but that page will have links to forms off of that page where the user can enter other information.

For example, in the code as it stood before we started messing with it, the user entered a discount code and the submission went to the PurchasesController, which had a special case for that submission. Instead, we're going to send the form request for entering the discount code to a DiscountCode controller, add the code to the shopping cart, and redirect back to the shopping cart.

Similarly, we will include a link to a new form for shipping information, and that form will be managed by an AddressController that will also redirect back to the shopping cart. One advantage here is that the AddressController can take care of validating the address so that we guarantee the validity of the address that reaches the shopping cart and the payment workflows.

Let's test with the display code. Our existing feature test in spec/features/payments/purchase_cart_spec.rb, which covers display codes, actually doesn't need to change since the user actions don't change. We can make the test fail, though, by changing the target of the form in the view code. To do this we need to add a resources :discount_codes to the routes file, and then change the form:

```
tax/01/app/views/shopping_carts/_credit_card_info.html.slim
h3 Payment Options

= form_tag(discount_codes_path, id: "discount-code-form") do
  .form-group
    .col-sm-2
      = label_tag(:discount_code, "Discount Code", class: "control-label")
    .col-sm-2
      input.form-control.valid-field(name="discount_code" id="discount_code")
    .col-sm-3
      = submit_tag("Apply Code", class: "btn btn-primary", id: "apply_code")
```

This suggests that we redirect to DiscountCodesController#create, which is minimal:

```
tax/01/app/controllers/discount_codes_controller.rb
class DiscountCodesController < ApplicationController

  def create
    workflow = AddsDiscountCodeToCart.new(
        user: current_user, code: params[:discount_code])
    workflow.run
    redirect_to shopping_cart_path
  end

end
```

Next, we add the discount code to the new shopping cart, which implies a new workflow and a new workflow spec:

```
tax/01/spec/workflows/adds_discount_code_to_cart_spec.rb
require "rails_helper"

describe AddsDiscountCodeToCart do

  let!(:code) { create(:discount_code, code: "TEST") }
  let(:user) { create(:user) }

  describe "adds a code to a new cart" do
    let(:workflow) { AddsDiscountCodeToCart.new(user: user, code: "TEST") }

    it "adds a code" do
      workflow.run
      cart = ShoppingCart.for(user: user)
      expect(cart.discount_code).to eq(code)
      expect(workflow).to be_a_success
    end

  end

  describe "is a no-op if the code doesn't exist" do

    let(:workflow) { AddsDiscountCodeToCart.new(user: user, code: "BANANA") }

    it "adds a code" do
      workflow.run
      cart = ShoppingCart.for(user: user)
      expect(cart.discount_code).to be_nil
      expect(workflow).to be_a_success
    end

  end

  describe "with an existing cart and code" do
    let!(:existing_code) { create(:discount_code, code: "EXISTING") }

    before(:example) do
      ShoppingCart.for(user: user).update(discount_code: existing_code)
    end

    context "with a real code" do
      let(:workflow) { AddsDiscountCodeToCart.new(user: user, code: "TEST") }

      it "overrides an existing code" do
        workflow.run
        cart = ShoppingCart.for(user: user)
        expect(cart.discount_code).to eq(code)
        expect(workflow).to be_a_success
      end

    end

    context "with a fake code" do
      let(:workflow) { AddsDiscountCodeToCart.new(user: user, code: "BANANA") }
```

```
    it "overrides a code" do
      workflow.run
      cart = ShoppingCart.for(user: user)
      expect(cart.discount_code).to be_nil
      expect(workflow).to be_a_success
    end
  end

  end

end
```

This workflow calls up the shopping cart for the current user and updates it:

tax/01/app/workflows/adds_discount_code_to_cart.rb

```ruby
class AddsDiscountCodeToCart

  attr_accessor :user, :code

  def initialize(user:, code:)
    @user = user
    @code = code
    @success = false
  end

  def shopping_cart
    @shopping_cart ||= ShoppingCart.for(user: user)
  end

  def discount_code
    @discount_code ||= DiscountCode.find_by(code: code)
  end

  def run
    @success = shopping_cart.update(discount_code: discount_code)
  end

  def success?
    @success
  end

end
```

Now we're finally ready to talk about the shipping method. We start by adding an end-to-end feature spec for the user actions involving shipping:

tax/01/spec/features/payments/purchase_cart_spec.rb

```ruby
context "can add a shipping method" do

  it "comes back to the cart with shipping" do
    tickets(:midsummer_bums_1).place_in_cart_for(users(:buyer))
    tickets(:midsummer_bums_2).place_in_cart_for(users(:buyer))
    login_as(users(:buyer), scope: :user)
    visit shopping_cart_path
    click_on "shipping_details"
    fill_in "address_address_1", with: "1060 W. Addison"
```

```
    fill_in "address_city", with: "Chicago"
    select "Illinois", from: "address_state"
    fill_in "address_zip", with: "60613"
    select "Overnight", from: "shipping_method"
    click_on "add_address"
    expect(page).to have_selector(
        ".active_shipping_method", text: "overnight")
    expect(page).to have_selector(".total", text: "$41")
  end
end
```

The logic here is similar to our other checkout features. We set up a shopping cart, the user follows a link to the address page and fills in data, and we verify that the user is redirected back to the shopping cart with the updated total. We expect from our other calculator tests that if the total is calculated properly, the workflow will use it.

Now we need to add shipping into the shopping cart, which means another small workflow and another small workflow spec:

tax/01/spec/workflows/adds_shipping_to_cart_spec.rb
```
require "rails_helper"

describe AddsShippingToCart do

  let(:user) { create(:user) }
  let(:address) { attributes_for(:address) }
  let(:workflow) { AddsShippingToCart.new(
      user: user, address: address, method: :standard) }

  it "adds shipping to cart" do
    workflow.run
    cart = ShoppingCart.for(user: user)
    expect(cart.address).to have_attributes(address)
    expect(cart).to be_standard
    expect(workflow).to be_a_success
  end

  it "fails gracefully if a field is missing" do
    address.delete(:zip)
    workflow.run
    cart = ShoppingCart.for(user: user)
    expect(cart.address).to be_nil
    expect(cart.shipping_method).to eq("electronic")
    expect(workflow).not_to be_a_success
  end

end
```

This spec checks for a positive case where the user has entered all of the required fields, and then checks for a case where the user hasn't. We want the negative case to be handled gracefully.

Here's the workflow:

`tax/01/app/workflows/adds_shipping_to_cart.rb`
```ruby
class AddsShippingToCart

  attr_accessor :user, :address_fields, :method

  def initialize(user:, address:, method:)
    @user = user
    @address_fields = address
    @method = method
    @success = false
  end

  def shopping_cart
    @shopping_cart ||= ShoppingCart.for(user: user)
  end

  def run
    ShoppingCart.transaction do
      shopping_cart.create_address!(address_fields)
      shopping_cart.update!(shipping_method: method)
      @success = shopping_cart.valid?
    end
  rescue ActiveRecord::RecordInvalid
    @success = false
  end

  def success?
    @success
  end

end
```

The workflow takes in the user, the address fields as a hash, and the shipping method. Inside a transaction, the workflow grabs the shopping cart for the current user and associates the address with the cart. Then the workflow updates the cart to include the shipping method. If the address fields are invalid, an ActiveRecord::RecordInvalid exception is thrown, which we catch and set @success to false.

The controller does our standard bit of creating a workflow and getting out of the way:

`tax/01/app/controllers/addresses_controller.rb`
```ruby
class AddressesController < ApplicationController
  def new
    @address = Address.new
  end
```

```ruby
  def create
    workflow = AddsShippingToCart.new(
        user: current_user, address: params[:address].permit!,
        method: params[:shipping_method])
    workflow.run
    if workflow.success?
      redirect_to shopping_cart_path
    else
      render :new
    end
  end

end
```

A successful address submission takes the user back to the shopping cart page and an unsuccessful one goes back to the address entry form. (I do not show the form here—it is boilerplate—but you can find it in the code at /code/tax/01/app/views/addresses/new.html.slim.)

At this point, some tests fail due to either changes needed in the test to reflect the purchase fee or a couple of missing connections between objects.

The PreparesCart workflow constructor changes slightly to take the shopping cart as a parameter, to read the discount code from the cart, and to pass the shipping method to the payment calculator:

```ruby
tax/01/app/workflows/prepares_cart.rb
attr_accessor :user, :purchase_amount_cents,
    :purchase_amount, :success,
    :payment, :expected_ticket_ids,
    :payment_reference, :shopping_cart

def initialize(user: nil, purchase_amount_cents: nil,
    expected_ticket_ids: "", payment_reference: nil,
    shopping_cart: nil)
  @user = user
  @shopping_cart = shopping_cart
  @purchase_amount = Money.new(purchase_amount_cents)
  @success = false
  @continue = true
  @expected_ticket_ids = expected_ticket_ids.split(" ").map(&:to_i).sort
  @payment_reference = payment_reference || Payment.generate_reference
end

delegate :discount_code, to: :shopping_cart

def price_calculator
  @price_calculator ||= PriceCalculator.new(
      tickets, discount_code, shopping_cart.shipping_method)
end

delegate :total_price, to: :price_calculator
```

Three classes call the constructor to PreparesCart: the subclasses PreparesCart-ForStripe, PreparesCartForPayPal, and PaymentsController. These classes need to make the same change to their invocation to pass the shopping cart instead of the discount code.

Finally, the workflow needs to send the new attributes to the Payment when it is created, and we have to remove the ShoppingCart once its data has been safely copied to the Payment. Here we add the partials and shipping_method to the payment_attributes and we destroy the shopping cart as part of the workflow:

tax/01/app/workflows/prepares_cart.rb
```ruby
def run
  Payment.transaction do
    raise PreExistingPaymentException.new(purchase) if existing_payment
    unless pre_purchase_valid?
      raise ChargeSetupValidityException.new(
          user: user,
          expected_purchase_cents: purchase_amount.to_i,
          expected_ticket_ids: expected_ticket_ids)
    end
    update_tickets
    create_payment
    clear_cart
    on_success
  end
rescue
  on_failure
  raise
end

def clear_cart
  shopping_cart.destroy
end

def payment_attributes
  {user_id: user.id, price_cents: purchase_amount.cents,
   status: "created", reference: Payment.generate_reference,
   discount_code_id: discount_code&.id,
   partials: price_calculator.breakdown,
   shipping_method: shopping_cart.shipping_method,
   shipping_address: shopping_cart.address}
end
```

Now, with all that as prologue, we can get users' addresses, we have a mechanism for changing our user workflow, and we have a way to save arbitrary parts of a price. Now we can talk about paying taxes.

Calculating Taxes

The first thing to say about taxes is that they are complicated. They are more complicated than I can get into here. If you are a U.S. business, you have to deal with dozens of different state and local tax laws that are arbitrary at best. If you are an international business, the problems are compounded, and I'm sorry, but I don't have the space to deal with those specifics here. Whether your Internet-based good or service is subject to tax law is a question for an accountant and a lawyer, not your friendly neighborhood technical author.

What I can do here is give you a sense of what using a third-party tax calculator might be like, what information the calculator might need, and how you might incorporate such a calculator into your payment process.

In this section we're going to look at TaxCloud,[1] which has the virtues of being free and having a Ruby gem that has an acceptable level of incidental complexity. Unlike some of the other technology choices made in this book, this is emphatically not an endorsement that TaxCloud will meet your needs. I have a need for free and simple. You may have a need for a paid service that has different offerings. Again, pick carefully.

Signing Up for TaxCloud

To start, sign up for TaxCloud by going to http://www.taxcloud.net and clicking the "Register Now" button. You are asked to enter your name, your company's name, an email address, phone number, and website. You can also choose if you are integrating with an existing third-party shopping cart solution—I entered Stripe. TaxCloud sends an email to verify your address, and once you verify, you will see a profile screen similar to the one shown here.

---

1.   http://www.taxcloud.net

You need to enter a few pieces of information to your profile as well as to the sections listed in the left sidebar. After entering your business name, "Entity Type" refers to what kind of legal entity is collecting taxes—a corporation, an LLC, a trust, or whatever. "Federal Tax ID" is something you would have if you were a real business (for example, your EIN or SSN). "NAICS code" is a classification of your business type. Code 454111 means "Web Retailer," and is the TaxCloud-provided default that we'll stick with for now. (If you don't think that code is accurate, TaxCloud lets you search for a more accurate code.) You also need to add your legal state of incorporation. None of this is particularly easy for a fictional business, but we'll manage.

The sidebar on the left side of the screen gives you access to some other useful information. The Transactions tab shows you a list of all the transactions you've sent to TaxCloud that you can filer and download. The Reports & Filings tab purports to give you reports that you can send to the government. (It's hard to evaluate that because it won't generate reports until we go live.)

We need to enter data into two of the tabs: Locations and Websites. We need to have at least one business location set to use TaxCloud, because that location determines what states we need to worry about in terms of taxes. In the Locations tab, we can enter one or more addresses.

TaxCloud wants you to enter a real address. As shown in the screen that follows, I entered 1060 W. Addison Street in Chicago, which as referenced in *The Blues Brothers*, is the address for Wrigley Field. (And yes, I said earlier that the Snow Globe Theater was based in Alaska. Alaska doesn't have sales tax, so we've moved the corporate office to Illinois so that we can pay sales tax—which is totally a thing that businesses do, except they do it to not pay taxes. This is why the Snow Globe is fictional.)

Once you have the business locations set up, the Tax States tab, shown in the figure on page 255, shows you a map of all the states you are responsible for collecting taxes from, and the Sales Tax Policy tab gives you a written policy for what you are collecting that you can paste and display on your website.

The Websites tab lets us add our website URL and e-commerce platform, if any, to get an API ID and API key. All websites at TaxCloud are in test mode until you explicitly make the website live, which requires a federal tax ID number, among other things.

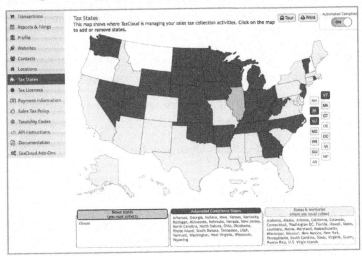

Integrating With TaxCloud

Once we're signed up, we can use the TaxCloud[2] gem to integrate our application with TaxCloud. Please note this gem is unofficial and does not seem to be under wildly active development, though it does still work. The underlying API calls are documented by TaxCloud.[3]

First, add the gem to our Gemfile:

```
gem "tax_cloud"
```

Then do a bundle install.

Next, we need to add our API keys to the secrets.yml file and then do a little bit of configuration in an initializer file:

tax/02/config/initializers/tax_cloud.rb
```
TaxCloud.configure do |config|
  config.api_login_id = Rails.application.secrets.tax_cloud_login
  config.api_key = Rails.application.secrets.tax_cloud_key
  # config.usps_username = 'your_usps_username' # optional
end
```

---

2. https://github.com/drewtempelmeyer/tax_cloud
3. https://dev.taxcloud.com/docs/versions/1.0/resources/taxcloud-us-main-apis and https://dev.taxcloud.com/docs/versions/1.0/resources/taxcloud-us-main-apis

In our Snow Globe Theater payment application, we need TaxCloud to do three things:

- Calculate tax given the items for sale. This has to happen for both shopping cart and payment. Because both of those objects use PriceCalculator, it makes sense that PriceCalculator is the main point of interaction with the tax system.

- Tell TaxCloud when a purchase has been completed so it can keep records. This needs to happen in our post-purchase workflows.

- Tell TaxCloud when a refund has happened so it can update records. This needs to happen in our refund workflow.

To accomplish these tasks, we're going to build up a TaxCalculator object to interact with TaxCloud.

Using the Tax Calculator

Our TaxCalculator object needs to integrate with TaxCloud, but for the most part, the rest of the system doesn't need to know that detail. The tax system needs the addresses of the seller and buyer, and information about the items being sold. In Illinois, admission fees to artistic events, such as performances by our theater company, are not taxed, but processing fees and shipping fees are, so our item list needs to include processing and shipment.

Let's start this process from the bottom up by building the TaxCalculator class and then inserting it into all the places that need to know about taxes.

The following spec makes sure our data is being translated into the API for the tax_cloud gem:

```
tax/02/spec/services/tax_calculator_spec.rb
require "rails_helper"

RSpec.describe TaxCalculator, :aggregate_failures, :vcr do
  let(:address) { build_stubbed(:address) }
  let(:user) { build_stubbed(:user) }
  let(:calculator) { TaxCalculator.new(
      user: user, address: address,
      cart_id: "1", items: [
          TaxCalculator::Item.create(:ticket, 1, Money.new(3000)),
          TaxCalculator::Item.create(:processing, 1, Money.new(100)),
          TaxCalculator::Item.create(:shipping, 1, Money.new(200))
      ]) }
  let(:transaction) { calculator.transaction }

  describe "creation" do
    it "creates a transaction properly" do
```

```
        expect(transaction).to have_attributes(customer_id: user.id, cart_id: "1")
        expect(transaction.origin).to have_attributes(
            address1: "1060 W. Addison", address2: nil,
            city: "Chicago", state: "IL",
            zip5: "60613")
        expect(transaction.destination).to have_attributes(
            address1: address.address_1, address2: address.address_2,
            city: address.city, state: address.state,
            zip5: address.zip)
        expect(transaction.cart_items.first).to have_attributes(
            index: 0, item_id: "Ticket",
            tic: "91083", price: 30.00, quantity: 1)
        expect(transaction.cart_items.second).to have_attributes(
            index: 1, item_id: "Processing",
            tic: "10010", price: 1.00, quantity: 1)
        expect(transaction.cart_items.third).to have_attributes(
            index: 2, item_id: "Shipping",
            tic: "11000", price: 2.00, quantity: 1)
    end

    it "handles a lookup correctly" do
      expect(calculator.tax_amount).to eq(0.3075.to_money)
      expect(calculator.itemized_taxes).to eq(
          ticket_cents: 0, processing_cents: 10.25, shipping_cents: 20.5)
    end
  end
end

end
```

The TaxCalculator is mostly a wrapper around the TaxCloud::Transaction object, and the bulk of the first test is just determining that the address and item data are correctly transferred to the underlying object.

There are two data modeling issues around how items are passed to the tax calculator. One issue is that the processing and shipping fees need to be treated as items, even though they are not line items in our current data model. The second issue is a little more subtle. When we have a payment with a discount code, we store it as, say, two $15 tickets and a $5 discount. TaxCloud wants us to structure that transaction a little differently and tell it that we have two $12.50 tickets.

In both cases, you could argue that we should change our underlying data model to make the fees line items in the database, or to calculate the price paid per ticket. That would give us a complicated refactoring that I've decided not to put us through, in the name of keeping focused on the payment logic.

What I have done is created an intermediate TaxCalculator::Item class, which takes a type, a quantity, and a price. The TaxCalculator expects those items, and it's the responsibility of the price calculator to create them. For tickets, we're just passing in the total ticket price—subtotal minus discount—as a single quantity of ticket. I'm not sold on this, but it does save us some floating point math.

The second test has us using the calculator to get the total tax amount and the partial amount per each line item, which is actually what we are going to store. This leads to one other modeling problem relating to our old friend, floating point math. TaxCloud returns the tax amounts as floating point dollars with fractional cents, as in 0.1025. I've decided to have our tax calculator cover the total amount to a Money object, but return the fractional amounts the tax as cents with decimals. I'm not in love with this choice, but it seems the safest way to store them to prevent rounding errors when adding them up to re-create the total sales tax. (I tried other options that all rounded more arbitrarily.)

The code that passes those tests goes in the TaxCalculator class:

tax/02/app/services/tax_calculator.rb
```
class TaxCalculator

  attr_accessor :user, :cart_id, :address, :items

  def initialize(user:, cart_id:, address:, items:)
    @user = user
    @cart_id = cart_id
    @address = address
    @items = items
  end

  def origin
    TaxCloud::Address.new(
        address1: "1060 W. Addison", city: "Chicago",
        state: "IL", zip5: "60613")
  end

  def destination
    TaxCloud::Address.new(
        address1: address.address_1, address2: address.address_2,
        city: address.city, state: address.state,
        zip5: address.zip)
  end

  def transaction
    @transaction ||= begin
      transaction = TaxCloud::Transaction.new(
          customer_id: user.id, cart_id: cart_id,
          origin: origin, destination: destination)
      items.each_with_index do |item, index|
        transaction.cart_items << item.cart_item(index)
      end
      transaction
    end
  end
end
```

```ruby
def lookup
  @lookup ||= transaction.lookup
end

def tax_amount
  lookup.tax_amount.to_money
end

def itemized_taxes
  types = items.map(&:type).map { |t| "#{t}_cents".to_sym }
  taxes = lookup.cart_items.map do |item|
    item.tax_amount * 100
  end
  Hash[types.zip(taxes)]
end
```

The initializer takes the user, a cart_id (an arbitrary identifier), an address, and the list of items. We convert the incoming address to a TaxCloud::Address object in the destination method, and have hard-coded Wrigley Field as our origin. If your situation is at all complex, then hard-coding the origin address won't be applicable.

The transaction method converts everything to a TaxCloud::Transaction, deferring the conversion of the item objects to code that we'll take a look at next. Then the tax_amount method does the lookup and conversion of the final amount, and the itemized_taxes method takes each item's tax and converts it to a Hash in the form we saw in the test.

I dealt with the individual items by nesting an Item class and some basic subclasses within the TaxCalculator as shown here:

tax/02/app/services/tax_calculator.rb
```ruby
class Item

  attr_reader :price, :quantity, :type

  def self.create(type, quantity, price)
    case type
    when :ticket then TicketItem.new(type, quantity, price)
    when :shipping then ShippingItem.new(type, quantity, price)
    when :processing then ProcessingItem.new(type, quantity, price)
    end
  end

  def initialize(type, quantity, price)
    @type = type
    @price = price
    @quantity = quantity
  end

end
```

```ruby
class TicketItem < Item

  def cart_item(index)
    TaxCloud::CartItem.new(
      index: index, item_id: "Ticket",
      tic: "91083", price: price.to_f,
      quantity: quantity)
  end

end

class ShippingItem < Item

  def cart_item(index)
    TaxCloud::CartItem.new(
      index: index, item_id: "Shipping",
      tic: "11000", price: price.to_f,
      quantity: quantity)
  end

end

class ProcessingItem < Item

  def cart_item(index)
    TaxCloud::CartItem.new(
      index: index, item_id: "Processing",
      tic: "10010", price: price.to_f,
      quantity: quantity)
  end

end

end
```

You may think that this is far too verbose. My goal was to avoid multiple case statements based on the type of object, and instead have one statement that creates a small object that knows how to convert itself to a TaxCloud::CartItem. The key part of each CartItem is that tic attribute, which is a code that TaxCloud uses to figure out which tax rate applies. The codes for tickets, processing fees, and shipping fees I got from the TaxCloud website, but as always, it is a good idea to consult with an expert before deploying.

Making Taxes Part of Prices

Now we need to enable the PriceCalculator to create and use a TaxCalculator. Once the PriceCalculator can do so, the various classes that use PriceCalculator will gain the tax calculations with little additional effort.

A test that includes taxes shows us what we need:

```
tax/02/spec/services/price_calculator_spec.rb
describe "with taxes", :vcr do
  let(:user) { build_stubbed(:user) }
  let(:address) { build_stubbed(:address) }
  let(:calculator) { PriceCalculator.new(
      [ticket_one, ticket_two], discount_code, :standard,
      user: user, address: address, tax_id: "cart_01") }
  let(:discount_code) { NullDiscountCode.new }

  it "calculates the price of a list of tickets" do
    expect(discount_code.multiplier).to eq(1.0)
    expect(discount_code.percentage_float).to eq(0)
    expect(calculator.subtotal).to eq(Money.new(3500))
    expect(calculator.discount).to eq(Money.new(0))
    expect(calculator.processing_fee).to eq(Money.new(100))
    expect(calculator.sales_tax).to eq(Money.new(31))
    expect(calculator.breakdown).to match(
        ticket_cents: [1500, 2000], processing_fee_cents: 100,
        shipping_cents: 200,
        sales_tax: {
            ticket_cents: 0.0, processing_cents: 10.25, shipping_cents: 20.5})
    expect(calculator.total_price).to eq(Money.new(3831))
  end
end
```

Here we set up the price calculator with the user, address, and tax_id, then let it calculate away, expecting to see taxes in the eventual breakdown and total.

Very Important Hand-Waving Note—I am assuming here that users only pay taxes if they enter a shipping method and an address. This is really arbitrary, but it gets us out of some validation code that would be distracting. In a real application you would need to ensure that you had the buyer's address if you are charging sales tax.

With that in mind, the PriceCalculator needs some extra fields to deal with taxes, namely an address, a user, and a federal tax ID, which is what will eventually become the cart_id for the TaxCalculator.

```
tax/02/app/services/price_calculator.rb
attr_accessor :tickets, :discount_code, :shipping, :user, :address, :tax_id

def initialize(tickets = [], discount_code = nil, shipping = :none,
    user: nil, address: nil, tax_id: nil)
  @tickets = tickets
  @discount_code = discount_code || NullDiscountCode.new
  @shipping = shipping
  @user = user
  @address = address
  @tax_id = tax_id
end
```

Then we use the TaxCalculator to calculate taxes (a radical idea, but I think we can make it work):

```
tax/02/app/services/price_calculator.rb
def breakdown
  result = {ticket_cents: tickets.map { |t| t.price.cents }}
  if processing_fee.nonzero?
    result[:processing_fee_cents] = processing_fee.cents
  end
  result[:discount_cents] = -discount.cents if discount.nonzero?
  result[:shipping_cents] = shipping_fee.cents if shipping_fee.nonzero?
  result[:sales_tax] = tax_calculator.itemized_taxes if sales_tax.nonzero?
  result
end

def tax_calculator
  @tax_calculator ||= TaxCalculator.new(
      user: user, cart_id: tax_id, address: address, items: tax_items)
end

def sales_tax
  return Money.zero if address.nil?
  tax_calculator.tax_amount
end

def tax_items
  items = [TaxCalculator::Item.create(:ticket, 1, subtotal - discount)]
  if processing_fee.nonzero?
    items << TaxCalculator::Item.create(:processing, 1, processing_fee)
  end
  if shipping_fee.nonzero?
    items << TaxCalculator::Item.create(:shipping, 1, shipping_fee)
  end
  items
end

def total_price
  subtotal - discount + processing_fee + shipping_fee + sales_tax
end
```

The tax_calculator method creates a new TaxCalculator object, using data that the price calculator already has, and using the tax_items method to build the internal items. We then use the tax calculation in two places: we calculate the sales_tax and add it to the total price, and we add the [:sales_tax] entry to the breakdown using the itemized taxes we just discussed.

At this point, we're surprisingly close to being done with actually calculating sales tax. But first we need to change the ShoppingCart to provide the necessary information to the calculators:

tax/02/app/models/shopping_cart.rb

```ruby
  def price_calculator
    @price_calculator ||= PriceCalculator.new(
        tickets, discount_code, shipping_method.to_s,
        address: address, user: user, tax_id: "cart_#{id}")
  end

  delegate :processing_fee, :sales_tax, to: :price_calculator

  def total_cost
    price_calculator.total_price
  end

  def tickets
    @tickets ||= user.tickets_in_cart
  end

  def events
    tickets.map(&:event).uniq.sort_by(&:name)
  end

  def tickets_by_performance
    tickets.group_by { |t| t.performance.id }
  end

  def performance_count
    tickets_by_performance.each_pair.each_with_object({}) do |pair, result|
      result[pair.first] = pair.last.size
    end
  end

  def performances_for(event)
    tickets.map(&:performance)
        .select { |performance| performance.event == event }
        .uniq.sort_by(&:start_time)
  end

  def subtotal_for(performance)
    tickets_by_performance[performance.id].sum(&:price)
  end

  def item_attribute
    :ticket_ids
  end

  def item_ids
    tickets.map(&:id)
  end

end
```

And to the PreparesCart workflow:

```
tax/02/app/workflows/prepares_cart.rb
def price_calculator
  @price_calculator ||= PriceCalculator.new(
      tickets, discount_code, shopping_cart.shipping_method,
      address: shopping_cart.address, user: user,
      tax_id: "cart_#{shopping_cart.id}")
end
```

Finally, there's a small bit of boilerplate needed to get the tax data to show in the shopping cart:

```
tax/02/app/views/shopping_carts/show.html.slim
- if @cart.sales_tax.nonzero?
  h4.active_code
    | Sales Tax: #{humanized_money_with_symbol(@cart.sales_tax)}
```

Now we're done with the calculation part.

Capturing Tax Data

At this point, we're calculating sales tax and probably holding on to enough information to create a report as required. However, TaxCloud also can generate reports for us, and all we need to do is tell it that a payment has been authorized.

We can do that via our TaxCalculator object:

```
tax/02/app/services/tax_calculator.rb
def authorized_with_capture(order_id)
  lookup
  transaction.order_id = order_id
  transaction.authorized_with_capture
end

def return(order_id)
  lookup
  transaction.order_id = order_id
  transaction.returned
end
```

This gives us an API method to tell TaxCloud when a payment has been authorized and one to use when a payment has been refunded—all we need to do is give it an order number. We're using our payment reference so that we can always associate a TaxCloud record with our database.

We can incorporate these calls into a workflow that takes a payment and calls these methods. First we need a payment to be able to create its own PriceCalculator and TaxCalculator, like so:

tax/02/app/models/payment.rb

```ruby
def price_calculator
  @price_calculator ||= PriceCalculator.new(
      tickets, discount_code, shipping_method,
      address: shipping_address, user: user,
      tax_id: "payment_#{reference}")
end

def taxes_paid
  partials.fetch(:sales_tax, {}).values.sum
end
```

Then the workflow:

tax/02/app/workflows/notifies_tax_cloud.rb

```ruby
class NotifiesTaxCloud

  attr_accessor :payment

  def initialize(payment)
    @payment = payment
    @success = false
  end

  def tax_calculator
    @tax_calculator ||= purchase.price_calculator.tax_calculator
  end

  def valid_amount?
    tax_calculator.tax_amount == payment.paid_taxes
  end

  def run
    if valid_amount?
      result = tax_calculator.authorized_with_capture(payment.reference)
      @success = (result == "OK")
    else
      raise TaxValidityException.new(
          payment_id: payment.id, expected_taxes: tax_calculator.tax_amount,
          paid_taxes: payment.paid_taxes)
    end
  end

end
```

What's tricky about this workflow is that the TaxCloud API doesn't seem to quite do what we want. The tax calculation for this payment has already been done (actually, it's probably already been done twice), but TaxCloud doesn't seem to have a simple finder API to retrieve the existing record (and even if the API has one hidden somewhere, the Ruby gem doesn't expose it). So our notification has to recalculate the taxes. We put in a pre-flight check to make sure the payments match, and if they do, we call the authorized_with_capture method to tell TaxCloud the payment happened.

Now the question is, how do we incorporate that workflow? My theory is that we don't want this notification to potentially crash a successful sale—by definition this has to happen after the sale completes. To me, this implies that each successful payment needs to trigger a background job:

```
tax/02/app/jobs/notify_tax_cloud_job.rb
class NotifyTaxCloudJob < ActiveJob::Base

  include Rollbar::ActiveJob

  queue_as :default

  def perform(payment)
    workflow = NotifiesTaxCloud.new(payment)
    workflow.run
  end
end
```

All the background job does is trigger the notification workflow. Alternately, we could not explicitly trigger a background job, but have a sweeper run every few minutes and identify purchases that haven't been sent to TaxCloud, which would have the advantage of not needing a change to existing workflows and the disadvantage of being harder to track down when something goes wrong.

We have three paths to creating payments: ExecutesStripePurchase, ExecutesPayPalPayment, and CashPurchasesCart. Each path needs a line like this in its success path:

```
NotifyTaxCloudJob.perform_later(payment)
```

Refunds work similarly. We create a workflow:

```
tax/02/app/workflows/notifies_tax_cloud_of_refund.rb
class NotifiesTaxCloudOfRefund

  attr_accessor :payment

  def initialize(payment)
    @payment = payment
    @success = false
  end

  def tax_calculator
    @tax_calculator ||= purchase.price_calculator.tax_calculator
  end

  def reference
    payment.original_payment&.reference || payment.reference
  end

  def run
    result = tax_calculator.refund(reference)
    @success = (result == "OK")
  end
end
```

This workflow is simpler because we don't need to compare the price information; we just pass the items that are being refunded and TaxCloud sorts it out. We do need to make sure we pass the reference of the original purchase. It should allow you to refund a different price than the one listed, to allow for partial refunds.

Next, we add a background job:

```
tax/02/app/jobs/notify_tax_cloud_of_refund_job.rb
class NotifyTaxCloudOfRefundJob < ActiveJob::Base

  include Rollbar::ActiveJob

  queue_as :default

  def perform(payment)
    workflow = NotifiesTaxCloudOfRefund.new(payment)
    workflow.run
  end

end
```

And add a similar line in the refund success path:

```
NotifyTaxCloudOfRefundJob.perform_later(payment_to_refund)
```

After all that, our tax calculations are fully incorporated into our workflow. Eventually, we'll need to report these taxes to the relevant government agencies. TaxCloud or your tax provider can help with that (again, I recommend a professional here), but you will be storing all the information necessary to create tax-related reports that you might need.

Next Up

In this chapter, we looked at how to add additional fees to our payment workflow, including both arbitrary fees and sales tax. The goal is to store enough information to re-create the purchase for reporting purposes, even if fee calculations change. We also need to be able to list taxes collected for reporting and auditing purchases.

Now we're going to take a look at relationships more complicated than buyer-seller and explore third-party selling options.

CHAPTER 12

Third-Party Sales with Stripe Connect

So far we've had a straightforward relationship with customers of the Snow Globe Theater: they are the buyers and we are the seller. They give us money in exchange for our services.

However, this relationship could become more complex. For example, we could build a storefront that allows third-party vendors to show their wares, like Etsy. In that case, the central application provides the shopping cart experience, but money is transferred to the provider of the good. A service provider like Uber behaves similarly: the central application provides the service, but the money received is split between the service and the driver. We could even build our own generic website or shopping cart tool, in which case users would incorporate our tool into their applications, letting our tool process transactions and transfer money.

Stripe provides a series of API tools that enables these kinds of third-party e-commerce interactions. Called *Stripe Connect*,[1] the API allows you to link your Stripe account with other Stripe accounts (and only other Stripe accounts) so that you can manage payments on behalf of that account and transfer funds accordingly.

In this chapter, we'll look at how to use Stripe Connect to handle payments on behalf of third parties. We'll send money from transactions their way, and we'll look at how to manage Stripe's verification process for those third parties. In order to learn this, we're going to build an affiliate program for the Snow Globe Theater, allowing users to have a URL code that causes a percentage of purchases to be transferred back to them.

There's one thing to note about the Stripe-managed accounts we are using here. Managed accounts for Stripe Connect are still in beta as I write this;

---

1. https://stripe.com/connect

however, Stripe claims it is being used in production by major clients. The API is subject to change, and it's also possible that different community best practices will emerge over time. Keep watching the skies, and by "the skies" I mean the Stripe Connect documentation.[2]

Creating Affiliate Accounts

To set up our Stripe account to deal with Stripe Connect, we need to decide how we are going to interact with affiliate accounts. Stripe allows for two different mechanisms, depending on whether or not the affiliate has its own Stripe account.

To prevent confusion over exactly which account needs to do what, let's start by defining our players:

- Player 1 is us, the Snow Globe Theater. We'll refer to our Stripe account as the *primary* account.

- Player 2 is the end user—the people buying a ticket, possibly via an affiliate link. We'll still call these folks *users,* and their interactions with us don't change.

- Player 3 is the intermediate users, who we'll call *affiliates*. We'll refer to their accounts as the affiliate accounts. In what we're building, these intermediate users are affiliates; in other contexts they might be called resellers or service providers, but regardless of what they are called, they'll all have similar Stripe relationships with us. We'll call them affiliates for consistency's sake.

We can create and interact with two types of affiliate accounts: stand-alone accounts and managed accounts. An affiliate who has its own Stripe account and interacts with Stripe on its own behalf is called a *stand-alone* account. A stand-alone account holder, crucially, has its own Stripe dashboard that it uses to manage its own charges and transfers. When a Stripe account onboards a stand-alone account, it uses the OAuth protocol with Stripe to get a token for further interactions with that account.

If we don't want the affiliate to interact with Stripe on its own, we can create what Stripe calls a *managed* account. As the primary account in a relationship with a managed account, we are responsible for making sure the affiliate gives us all the information needed to verify its identity and transfer its funds, and

---

2.   https://stripe.com/docs/connect

we are responsible for showing it our account information. Managed account users cannot access a Stripe dashboard.

Why should we use one type of relationship over another? There are three factors to consider:

- *How much code do you want to write?*

Although it's possible to start with both types relatively easily, stand-alone accounts require less custom code, as a managed account setup needs to provide some subset of the Stripe dashboard.

- *Who talks to your affiliates?*

If you want to control your affiliate's entire experience, managed is the way to go. If you think the Stripe dashboard is good enough for you so it's good enough for them, then a stand-alone account works well.

- *Who is responsible?*

In a managed account, we as the platform owner have more responsibility for fraudulent usage than in a stand-alone account.

For the Snow Globe Theater affiliate program, we're going to use managed accounts. The affiliates need a relatively small subset of the Stripe dashboard, so we won't be buried in code. In addition, we'd rather manage the entire affiliate experience, and we're fine with being responsible.

To prepare the primary account to use Stripe Connect in production, there's some activation we'll need to do. However, to activate managed accounts, we need to make our account live, even if it's just a test account. (We'll talk more about taking our account live in the next chapter.) For now, while in test mode Stripe will let us create and charge to managed accounts even if the account is inactive.

Our requirements for the affiliate program go something like this:

- Allow users to create affiliate accounts, and behind the scenes create Stripe managed accounts to handle the payments.

- Give each account a token that, when included in a URL, can be assigned to the current shopping cart.

- If there's an affiliate in the shopping cart, adjust the payment to send 5 percent to the affiliate account.

- Allow the affiliate to enter the necessary validation information to get paid.

Start by creating a managed account in Stripe that we can use for an affiliate.

Creating a Managed Stripe Account

I want to stress again that we are doing a minimal setup here so that we can focus on the account creation. We'll talk about the validation later in *Validating Affiliates*, on page 284.

We will start with some data. Here is the migration that declares our new Affiliate class:

```
connect/01/db/migrate/20160911221328_create_affiliates.rb
class CreateAffiliates < ActiveRecord::Migration[5.0]
  def change
    create_table :affiliates do |t|
      t.string :name
      t.references :user, foreign_key: true
      t.string :country
      t.string :stripe_id
      t.string :tag
      t.json :verification_needed
      t.timestamps
    end

    change_table :payments do |t|
      t.references :affiliate, foreign_key: true
      t.integer :affiliate_payment_cents, default: 0, null: false
      t.string  :affiliate_payment_currency, default: "USD", null: false
    end

    change_table :shopping_carts do |t|
      t.references :affiliate
    end
  end
end
```

Even though from Stripe's perspective, the term is "account," on our side, "affiliate" is the appropriate name. Affiliates have an optional name, and they belong to a user. Stripe requires that a country be set (we'll default to the United States). As with other bits of data in our system that interact with Stripe, we'll store a stripe_id to hold on to the connection. The tag is the URL tag we'll use to identify sales for this associate. And we'll get to the verification_needed attribute later on (we'll use that to track what fields Stripe says it needs for identity verification).

We'll also need to make some adjustments to our payments table. A payment can now potentially belong to an affiliate, and we'll record the payout and currency if it does.

There's not a lot of user interaction here; we can test this at the workflow level:

```
connect/01/spec/workflows/adds_affiliate_account_spec.rb
require "rails_helper"

RSpec.describe AddsAffiliateAccount, :vcr do

  let(:user) { create(:user) }

  describe "creates an affiliate from a user" do

    let(:workflow) { AddsAffiliateAccount.new(user: user) }

    it "creates an affiliate account with the required information" do
      workflow.run
      expect(workflow.affiliate).to have_attributes(
          name: user.name, country: "US",
          stripe_id: a_string_starting_with("acct_"), tag: a_truthy_value)
      expect(workflow).to be_a_success
    end

  end

end
```

This is a small test. It takes a user and creates an affiliate account workflow, and then verifies that the workflow creates an affiliate object. The key attribute of that affiliate object is the stripe_id, which needs to start with acct_, indicating that either it really came from Stripe or I'm faking the workflow. (Hint: I'm not faking the workflow.)

At this point, the workflow is also small, especially because we aren't dealing with data validation yet.

```
connect/01/app/workflows/adds_affiliate_account.rb
class AddsAffiliateAccount

  attr_accessor :user, :affiliate, :success, :tos_checked, :request_ip

  def initialize(user:, tos_checked: nil, request_ip: nil)
    @user = user
    @tos_checked = tos_checked
    @request_ip = request_ip
    @success = false
  end

  def run
    Affiliate.transaction do
      @affiliate = Affiliate.create(
          user: user, country: "US",
          name: user.name, tag: Affiliate.generate_tag)
      @affiliate.update(stripe_id: acquire_stripe_id)
    end
    @success = true
  end
```

```
  def acquire_stripe_id
    StripeAccount.new(
        @affiliate, tos_checked: tos_checked, request_ip: request_ip).account.id
  end

  def success?
    @success
  end

end
```

The run method creates one of our ActiveRecord Affiliate instances, grabbing the user and name from the inputted user and using the Affiliate class itself to gather the tag. Note that we have extra attributes in the constructor: tos_checked and request_ip. Those are some verification fields, and we'll talk about them more in a bit.

After the Affiliate is created, we call StripeAccount to register with Stripe. As with other Stripe objects in our system, StripeAccount is a wrapper around the Stripe gem's communication with Stripe.

The Affiliate class needs to generate a unique tag, which is extremely similar to generating a unique reference, so let's parameterize generate_reference and then use it in the Affiliate class:

connect/01/app/models/concerns/has_reference.rb
```
module HasReference

  extend ActiveSupport::Concern

  module ClassMethods

    def generate_reference(length: 10, attribute: :reference)
      loop do
        result = SecureRandom.hex(length)
        return result unless exists?(attribute => result)
      end
    end

  end

end
```

connect/01/app/models/affiliate.rb
```
class Affiliate < ApplicationRecord

  include HasReference

  belongs_to :user

  def self.generate_tag
    generate_reference(length: 5, attribute: :tag)
  end

end
```

Here we just changed generate_reference to optionally take a length and an attribute to check against. We defined the generate_tag as shorter (5 instead of 10) and pointing at the :tag attribute.

We need to deal with one more collaborating object: StripeAccount, which is our interface to the Stripe API for accounts.

```ruby
connect/01/app/models/stripe_account.rb
class StripeAccount

  attr_accessor :affiliate, :account, :tos_checked, :request_ip

  def initialize(affiliate, tos_checked:, request_ip:)
    @affiliate = affiliate
    @tos_checked = tos_checked
    @request_ip = request_ip
  end

  def account
    @account ||= begin
      if affiliate.stripe_id.blank?
        create_account
      else
        retrieve_account
      end
    end
  end

  private def create_account
    account_params = {country: affiliate.country, managed: true}
    if tos_checked
      account_params[:tos_acceptance] = {date: Time.now.to_i, ip: request_ip}
    end
    Stripe::Account.create(account_params)
  end

  private def retrieve_account
    Stripe::Account.retrieve(affiliate.stripe_id)
  end

end
```

There's a little bit of architectural tension in designing the API between the idea that you can deal with the StripeAccount without worrying about implementation details and also wanting to be kind of clear about exactly when the object is making a network call to Stripe for more information.

We create a StripeAccount by passing it one of our Affiliate instances. We talk to Stripe when we ask for an account. If the affiliate already has a Stripe account ID, we call for a retrieval; otherwise, we create an new account using a minimal set of information.

Integrating Affiliates into the Application

For the user to be able to create an affiliate account, we need to do some standard Rails actions.

Start by letting users sign up. To do this, add an option to the user#show page:

```
connect/01/app/views/users/show.html.slim
h1 User dashboard for #{current_user.email}

h2 Subscriptions

- current_user.subscriptions.each do |subscription|
  .subscription
    #{subscription.plan.plan_name} ending #{subscription.end_date}
    .btn
      = link_to("Cancel Subscription", subscription,
        method: :delete,
        confirm: "Are you sure you want to delete this subscription?")

h3 Affiliate

- if current_user.affiliates.empty?
  = link_to "Make me an affiliate", new_affiliate_path
- else
  h4 Affiliate Tags

  ul
    - current_user.affiliates.each do |affiliate|
      li= link_to(affiliate.tag, root_path(tag: affiliate.tag))
```

It's a link to the affiliate controller, then a list of affiliate accounts with their tag, and a sample customer-facing link using that tag, suitable to be passed on to customers. Clicking the affiliate controller link takes us to AffiliateController#new, which has no code in the controller, a simple form, plus…well, see for yourself:

```
connect/01/app/views/affiliates/new.html.slim
h1 Make Me an Affiliate

= form_for(Affiliate.new) do |f|
  .row
    .form-group
      .col-sm-1
        = check_box_tag(:tos, "1", class: "form_control")
      .col-sm-5
        = label_tag(:tos, class: "control-label") do
          | By registering your account, you agree to our Services Agreement
            and the
          = link_to " Stripe Connected Account Agreement ",
            "https://stripe.com/us/connect-account/legal"
  .row
    .form-group
      = f.submit("Make Me an Affiliate", class: "btn btn-default")
```

```
h2 Terms

| Payment processing services for affiliates on
  the Snow Globe Theater site are provided by Stripe and are subject to the
= link_to " Stripe Connected Account Agreement ",
  "https://stripe.com/us/connect-account/legal"
| which includes the
= link_to " Stripe Terms of Service ", "https://stripe.com/us/legal"
| (collectively, the "Stripe Services Agreement"). By agreeing to
  this agreement or continuing to operate as an affiliate for
  the Snow Globe Theater, you agree to be bound by the Stripe Services
  Agreement, as the same may be modified by Stripe from time to time.
  As a condition of the Snow Globe Theater enabling payment processing
  services through Stripe, you agree to provide the Snow Globe Theater
  accurate and complete information about you and your business, and you
  authorize the Snow Globe Theater to share it and transaction information
  related to your use of the payment processing services provided by Stripe.
```

Our form just includes a check box indicating agreement to the terms and services. (Remember, we're not doing identity verification at this point.)

We also have a bunch of legal text, which comes from Stripe's requirements. Stripe requires that we include a terms message that links to Stripe's Services Agreement. Again, you might want to consult a legal expert before you deploy.

Submitting this form takes us to the controller create method, which does a similar workflow dance as many of our other controllers and redirects back to the user page on success.

connect/01/app/controllers/affiliates_controller.rb
```ruby
class AffiliatesController < ApplicationController

  def new
  end

  def show
    @affiliate = Affiliate.find(params[:id])
  end

  def create
    workflow = AddsAffiliateAccount.new(
        user: current_user, tos_checked: params[:tos],
        request_ip: request.remote_ip)
    workflow.run
    if workflow.success
      redirect_to user_path(current_user)
    else
      render :new
    end
  end

end
```

Now that users can create affiliate accounts, let's make it so they can be credited for payments and get paid.

Transferring Payments to Affiliate Accounts

With the affiliate accounts created, we now need to pull them into our workflow so that our affiliates can get paid. The first step is to identify when an affiliate tag comes in via a URL so that we can associate the shopping cart with the affiliate. The expectation here is that the URL will be something like http://www.snowglobe.com/?tag=abcde, and we'll extract the "abcde" and associate the active shopping cart with the correct affiliate.

I wrote a few tests to cover the main case and some special cases:

connect/01/spec/workflows/adds_affiliate_to_cart_spec.rb
```ruby
require "rails_helper"

RSpec.describe AddsAffiliateToCart do

  let(:user) { create(:user) }
  let!(:affiliate) { create(:affiliate, tag: "tag") }

  it "adds tag to cart if cart exists" do
    workflow = AddsAffiliateToCart.new(tag: "tag", user: user)
    workflow.run
    expect(ShoppingCart.for(user: user).affiliate).to eq(affiliate)
  end

  it "manages if the tag doesn't exist" do
    workflow = AddsAffiliateToCart.new(tag: "banana", user: user)
    workflow.run
    expect(ShoppingCart.for(user: user).affiliate).to be_nil
  end

  it "manages if the tag is nil" do
    workflow = AddsAffiliateToCart.new(tag: nil, user: user)
    workflow.run
    expect(ShoppingCart.for(user: user).affiliate).to be_nil
  end

  it "correctly adds tag if the case is wrong" do
    workflow = AddsAffiliateToCart.new(tag: "TAG", user: user)
    workflow.run
    expect(ShoppingCart.for(user: user).affiliate).to eq(affiliate)
  end

  it "does nothing if there is no current user" do
    workflow = AddsAffiliateToCart.new(tag: "TAG", user: nil)
    workflow.run
    expect(ShoppingCart.for(user: nil)).to be_nil
  end
```

```
  it "does nothing if the affiliate belongs to the user" do
    affiliate.update(user: user)
    workflow = AddsAffiliateToCart.new(tag: "tag", user: user)
    workflow.run
    expect(ShoppingCart.for(user: user).affiliate).to be_nil
  end
end
```

The workflow expects to receive a tag and a user, presumably the current user. In the basic case, the shopping cart for that user gets associated with that affiliate. The primary special case is that a user can't associate with their own affiliate account. There are also a few error cases, such as when there is no user or when there is no tag.

Here's the workflow that passes those tests:

connect/01/app/workflows/adds_affiliate_to_cart.rb
```
class AddsAffiliateToCart

  attr_accessor :user, :tag

  def initialize(user:, tag:)
    @user = user
    @tag = tag&.downcase
  end

  def affiliate
    return nil if tag.blank?
    @affiliate ||= Affiliate.find_by(tag: tag)
  end

  def shopping_cart
    @shopping_cart ||= ShoppingCart.for(user: user)
  end

  def affiliate_belongs_to_user?
    return true unless affiliate
    return true unless user
    affiliate&.user == user
  end

  def run
    return unless user
    return if affiliate_belongs_to_user?
    shopping_cart.update(affiliate: affiliate)
  end
end
```

If there is an affiliate matching the tag, and a user, and the affiliate does not belong to the user, update the shopping cart to belong to the affiliate.

We ensure that check is run by making it a before_action in the ApplicationController:

connect/01/app/controllers/application_controller.rb
```
before_action :set_affiliate

def set_affiliate
  tag = params[:tag] || session[:affiliate_tag]
  workflow = AddsAffiliateToCart.new(user: current_user, tag: tag)
  workflow.run
  session[:affiliate_tag] = tag
end
```

There's one minor twist, which is that we normally expect the tag to come in via the params, but we'll store it in the session if we don't use it, and use the session if there is no param. That's to allow users to use an affiliate URL even if they aren't logged in—the system will take the tag from the URL and put it in the session, and will add the affiliate to the shopping cart once the user logs in.

We don't have to make many changes to our payment workflow in order to enable affiliate payments. However, there is one issue involving our interaction with Stripe to keep in mind. The Stripe tools are somewhat built around the idea that the primary account is taking only a small percentage of the fee, and that most of it will go to the connected account. In our case, though, our affiliates are getting the small percentage, and we're keeping most of it. That's not a deal breaker, but it will cause the Stripe interface to be a little awkward.

Specifically, Stripe's connection API says that we specify the total cost of the transaction, the dependent account, and the amount that is being reserved to go back to the primary account. In other words, rather than telling Stripe the transaction is a $20 sale, with $1 going to the affiliate, we tell Stripe the transaction is a $20 sale going to the affiliate with a $19 "application fee," which is certainly counterintuitive for our use case.

We need to allow our PriceCalculator to calculate the affiliate fee, which we are assuming is 5 percent of the sale:

connect/01/app/services/price_calculator.rb
```
def total_price
  base_price + processing_fee + shipping_fee + sales_tax
end

def base_price
  subtotal - discount
end

def discount
  discount_code.discount_for(subtotal)
end
```

```ruby
def affiliate_payment
  base_price * 0.05
end

def affiliate_application_fee
  total_price - affiliate_payment
end
```

The affiliate payment is based on the amount the user pays toward the actual good, whereas the application fee is based on the total price. So, a $20 transaction with a $1 processing fee has an affiliate_payment of $1 (5 percent of $20) and an affiliate_application_fee of $20 (the $20 price plus the $1 processing fee minus the $1 that goes to the affiliate). We don't need to put the affiliate fee in the breakdown attribute because it's a separate piece of data from the parts that make up the total price.

Now we need to add the affiliate information to our workflow. We're going to make this specific to Stripe payments, pretending for a moment that PayPal doesn't exist in this application. (Because the affiliate payments are to Stripe accounts, this mechanism won't work for PayPal.)

As far as testing goes, I started at the workflow level. The workflow test handles the integration, making sure we set up the Payment instance correctly. We need to test two different workflows. First, we test the PreparesCartForStripe workflow:

```ruby
connect/01/spec/workflows/prepares_cart_for_stripe_spec.rb
context "with an affiliate" do

  let(:affiliate) { create(:affiliate) }

  before(:example) do
    shopping_cart.update(affiliate: affiliate)
  end

  it "successfully handles the affiliate attributes" do
    workflow.run
    expect(workflow.payment).to have_attributes(
        affiliate_id: affiliate.id, affiliate_payment_cents: 150)
  end

end
```

This spec is inside the "successful credit card purchase" context of the file, meaning that the token is already set up and ready to go. The spec creates an affiliate, applies it to the cart, and gets going. We validate that two affiliate related attributes are set to nondefault values.

The change required to make this work is small. We just need to change the override of the payment_attributes method in PreparesCartForStripe:

connect/01/app/workflows/prepares_cart_for_stripe.rb
```ruby
def payment_attributes
  result = super.merge(payment_method: "stripe")
  if shopping_cart.affiliate
    result = result.merge(
        affiliate_id: shopping_cart.affiliate.id,
        affiliate_payment_cents: price_calculator.affiliate_payment.cents)
  end
  result
end
```

If the shopping cart has an affiliate, we set the necessary attribute based on the shopping cart and the price calculator.

Once the payment is set up, we also need to make changes to the execution of the payment to make sure we are sending the correct information to Stripe. For this part, we have both a workflow and a model test on the StripeCharge wrapper object. Here's the workflow test:

connect/01/spec/workflows/executes_stripe_payment_spec.rb
```ruby
context "with an affiliate fee" do
  let(:affiliate_user) { create(:user) }
  let(:affiliate_workflow) {
    AddsAffiliateAccount.new(user: affiliate_user) }
  let(:affiliate) { affiliate_workflow.affiliate }

  before(:example) do
    affiliate_workflow.run
    payment.update(
        affiliate_id: affiliate.id, affiliate_payment_cents: 125)
    workflow.run
  end

  it "takes the response from the gateway" do
    response = workflow.stripe_charge.response
    expect(workflow.payment).to have_attributes(
        status: "succeeded", response_id: a_string_starting_with("ch_"),
        full_response: response.to_json)
    fee = Stripe::ApplicationFee.retrieve(response.application_fee)
    expect(fee.amount).to eq(2375)
  end
end
```

The setup creates an affiliate. In this test we have to use the AddsAffiliateAccount workflow to register that affiliate with Stripe before the test gets cooking—we'll need a real account ID to have the actual charge approved.

We then run the workflow. In the aftermath, we're checking that the stripe payment succeeded, and we're parsing the response object from Stripe to determine that the application fee is set correctly. This is a $25 purchase, so $1.25 for the affiliate, which Stripe wants as a $25 purchase with a $23.75 application fee.

The code we need to change is in the StripeCharge, so we want a slightly different test for that one.

```
connect/01/spec/models/stripe_charge_spec.rb
context "with an affiliate fee" do
  let(:user) { create(:user) }
  let(:affiliate_user) { create(:user) }
  let(:affiliate_workflow) {
    AddsAffiliateAccount.new(user: affiliate_user) }
  let(:affiliate) { affiliate_workflow.affiliate }
  let(:payment) { Payment.create(
      user_id: user.id, price_cents: 3000,
      status: "created", reference: Payment.generate_reference,
      payment_method: "stripe") }

  before(:example) do
    affiliate_workflow.run
    payment.update(
        affiliate_id: affiliate.id, affiliate_payment_cents: 125)
  end

  it "calls stripe to get a charge" do
    charge = StripeCharge.new(token: token, payment: payment)
    expect(charge.charge_parameters).to match(
        amount: payment.price.cents, currency: "usd",
        source: token.id, description: "",
        destination: affiliate.stripe_id, application_fee: 2875,
        metadata: {reference: payment.reference})
    charge.charge
    expect(charge.response.id).to start_with("ch")
    expect(charge.response.amount).to eq(3000)
    expect(charge).to be_a_success
  end
end
```

Unlike the earlier tests for StripeCharge, this one can't easily use stubbed objects because we need a real Stripe account number to get the charge approved. Within the StripeCharge class, we've broken out a method called charge_parameters so we can easily verify that the proper fields are being sent to Stripe, particularly the destination field and the application_fee.

To do this, we need to make a few changes in the StripeCharge:

connect/01/app/models/stripe_charge.rb
```ruby
def charge
  return if response.present?
  @response = Stripe::Charge.create(
      {amount: payment.price.cents, currency: "usd",
       source: token.id, description: "",
       metadata: {reference: payment.reference}},
      idempotency_key: payment.reference)
rescue Stripe::StripeError => e
  @response = nil
  @error = e
end

def charge_parameters
  parameters = {
      amount: payment.price.cents, currency: "usd",
      source: token.id, description: "",
      metadata: {reference: payment.reference}}
  if payment.affiliate.present?
    parameters[:destination] = payment.affiliate.stripe_id
    parameters[:application_fee] = payment.application_fee.cents
  end
  parameters
end
```

Here, we have taken the hash that gets sent to Stripe::Charge.create and broken it out into its own method to better manipulate the data. If the payment has an affiliate, we set the destination to reflect the affiliate's Stripe account, and the application fee to refer to all the money in the account that we were going to take.

And that should have everything working. You can make affiliate transactions and trace them in the Stripe dashboard. It's odd—this transaction presents as a $25 payment to the affiliate and a $23.75 payment back—but the money does end up in the right place with the affiliate set up for a $1.25 transfer.

Validating Affiliates

Just setting up Stripe to make the transfer isn't enough. Stripe needs to verify the identity of the user you are transferring money to because of things like "not wanting to be defrauded" and "not wanting to violate the law." So, before Stripe will transfer money to a managed account, we need to provide Stripe with enough information to satisfy Stripe that the user is a real person, that the account exists, that the money is not going to be used for illegal purposes, and so on.

Stripe asks for different information based primarily on the country of origin and the amount of money being transferred. This process proceeds in multiple stages.[3] As we have seen, you can get started with almost no information. Quickly, though, Stripe will ask for more.

The first stage of verification includes not only the bank account information, but also basic information about the legal entity controlling the account. In the United States, that information includes the person's name and birth date, and the type of account. It's important in our case to provide basic information, as Stripe will block charges if an account exists without the first phase of identifying data. A blocked charge would mess up our charge workflow, and is a strong reason why we should include that information in the initial signup.

The second stage of verification, again in the United States, requires a valid address and the last four digits of a Social Security number (a business might have to provide a tax identification number). Later stages might include the entity's entire Social Security number or file uploads of identity documents, about which the Stripe documentation is maddeningly vague, but which I assume is some form of photo ID.

Learning What to Validate

Stripe does not provide exact guidance as to when an account triggers a new stage of verification, nor does it guarantee which fields are part of which stage. Instead, Stripe makes the list of needed fields part of the Stripe::Account object. When we create or update a Stripe::Account, the response gives us the new version of that account with an updated list of validation needs.

In addition, Stripe can send a webhook event called account.updated at any time it decides it needs more information—typically when a managed account has triggered some threshold amount.

The first thing we want to do is capture the validation data when the account is created. We'll need some more data fields for that locally. We've already got a verification_needed JSON field, but let's add a few more:

```
connect/02/db/migrate/20160923204055_more_affiliate_fields.rb
class MoreAffiliateFields < ActiveRecord::Migration[5.0]

  def change
    change_table :affiliates do |t|
      t.boolean :stripe_charges_enabled, default: false
      t.boolean :stripe_transfers_enabled, default: false
      t.string :stripe_disabled_reason
```

---

3. https://stripe.com/docs/connect/testing-verification

```
        t.datetime :stripe_validation_due_by
      end
    end

end
```

We want to keep track of two Booleans as to whether Stripe has enabled or disabled charges or transfers to this account. It's particularly important to know about the charges because if the affiliate account isn't taking charges, we don't even want to involve it in the transaction. We're also holding on to a string to capture Stripe's reason for disabling an account, and the due date by which Stripe needs validation information before it disables an account.

Now, to fill in that information we need to take it from the Stripe return value when we create an account. To do this, we first need to add a step to the AddsAffiliateAccount workflow:

connect/02/app/workflows/adds_affiliate_account.rb
```
def run
  Affiliate.transaction do
    @affiliate = Affiliate.create(
        user: user, country: "US",
        name: user.name, tag: Affiliate.generate_tag)
    @affiliate.update(stripe_id: acquire_stripe_id)
    account.update_affiliate_verification
  end
  @success = true
end

def acquire_stripe_id
  @account = StripeAccount.new(
      @affiliate, tos_checked: tos_checked, request_ip: request_ip)
  account.account.id
end
```

Here we're making one more method call on the StripeAccount, called update_affiliate_verification. That method takes the relevant information from Stripe and drops it in our affiliate instance:

connect/02/app/models/stripe_account.rb
```
def update_affiliate_verification
  Affiliate.transaction do
    affiliate.update(
        stripe_charges_enabled: account.charges_enabled,
        stripe_transfers_enabled: account.transfers_enabled,
        stripe_disabled_reason: account.verification.disabled_reason,
        stripe_validation_due_by: account.verification.due_by,
        verification_needed: account.verification.fields_needed)
  end
end
```

Most of this is just taking the Stripe naming conventions and translating them to our Affiliate naming conventions. The only thing that's a little bit weird here is that the account.verification.fields_needed is a list. This works for us because on our side, verification_needed is a JSON type object, so we can continue to treat it as a list.

Now that we are storing whether the affiliate is in good standing with Stripe, we can use that information to prevent making an affiliate transfer to an account that isn't in good standing.

First, we can allow the Payment instance to only return the affiliate if it's accepting charges. (We're less concerned if Stripe puts a hold on transferring money, because a hold on transfers doesn't affect our workflow.)

```
connect/02/app/models/payment.rb
def active_affiliate
  affiliate&.stripe_charges_enabled ? affiliate : nil
end
```

We can then use that method when we send off the charge to determine whether we use the affiliate.

```
connect/02/app/models/stripe_charge.rb
def charge
  return if response.present?
  @response = Stripe::Charge.create(
      {amount: payment.price.cents, currency: "usd",
       source: token.id, description: "",
       metadata: {reference: payment.reference}},
      idempotency_key: payment.reference)
rescue Stripe::StripeError => e
  @response = nil
  @error = e
end

def charge_parameters
  parameters = {
      amount: payment.price.cents, currency: "usd",
      source: token.id, description: "",
      metadata: {reference: payment.reference}}
  if payment.active_affiliate.present?
    parameters[:destination] = payment.affiliate.stripe_id
    parameters[:application_fee] = payment.application_fee.cents
  end
  parameters
end
```

Alternately, we could have chosen to block adding the affiliate to the shopping cart, but I think that blocking at the point of the charge is more robust.

Another weird quirk to the verification is that Stripe will sometimes decide, based on payment volume, that it needs more information. I assume that this decision is based on either the financial institutions requirements or its interpretation of the law, but from our perspective, it doesn't make much difference why Stripe is doing it, only that it is.

Stripe sends an account.updated webhook event when it needs more information. We've already got a way to handle webhooks—see *Setting Up Webhooks*, on page 131—and we just wrote a way to capture account verification information, so it's not much code to combine the two:

```
connect/02/app/workflows/stripe_handler/account_updated.rb
module StripeHandler

  class AccountUpdated

    attr_accessor :event, :success

    def initialize(event)
      @event = event
      @success = false
    end

    def account
      event.data.object
    end

    def affiliate
      Affiliate.find_by(stripe_id: account.id)
    end

    def run
      stripe_account = StripeAccount.new(affiliate, account: account)
      result = stripe_account.update_affiliate_verification
      @success = result
    end

  end

end
```

When we get the account.updated message, extract the local Affiliate object and the remote account object, and call the same update_affiliate_verification method to save the interesting information to our local database.

Obtaining Validation Information

Once Stripe has told us what information it needs to verify the account holder, we need to get that information from the account holder and send it back to Stripe.

What we've got here is the edit action for an Affiliate. I'm eliding some navigation to add this to the UI. We need to add some code to the AffiliatesController. This code finds the affiliate in question and passes it to the template:

connect/02/app/controllers/affiliates_controller.rb
```ruby
def edit
  @affiliate = Affiliate.find(params[:id])
end
```

Now there are design questions. We're storing the list of fields needed in our verification_needed field. Stripe cares about the answers to these questions, but we have no need to store them locally. For some of them, like bank account information, we actively don't want to store them locally. (Storing bank account information makes storing credit card information look tame. Don't do it.) Adding to the fun, the list of fields is presumably subject to change.

With all that, let's opt for a dynamic solution. This is on the quick-and-dirty side—I think there's some UI improvements that you'd want in a real app—but this will get us to a form and let us discuss the complications there.

In the Affiliate class, add some methods to convert the verification_needed list to a list of field names suitable for Rails:

connect/02/app/models/affiliate.rb
```ruby
class Affiliate < ApplicationRecord

  include HasReference

  belongs_to :user

  def self.generate_tag
    generate_reference(length: 5, attribute: :tag)
  end

  def verification_needed?
    verification_needed.size.positive?
  end

  def verification_form_names
    verification_needed.map { |name| convert_form_name(name) }
  end

  def convert_form_name(attribute)
    "account[#{attribute.gsub('.', '][')}]"
  end

end
```

So a field name from Stripe such as legal_entity.dob.day becomes account[legal_entity][dob][day]. This is some text manipulation that gives a set of field names that Rails will automatically turn into nested hashes, saving us some data manipulation on the server side.

Then we need a form that can take those names and give them all fields:

connect/02/app/views/affiliates/edit.html.slim

```
h1 Affiliate Validation

h2 Due by: #{@affiliate.stripe_validation_due_by}

= form_for(@affiliate, html: {id: "affiliate-form"}) do |f|

  - @affiliate.verification_form_names.each do |field_name|
    - if field_name == "account[external_account]"
      = render "affiliate/edit/bank_account_form"
    - else
      .row
        .form-group
          .col-sm-3
            = label_tag(field_name.humanize, field_name, class: "control-label")
          .col-sm-5
            = text_field_tag(field_name, "", class: "form-control")
  .row
    .form-group
      = f.submit("Make Me an Affiliate", class: "btn btn-default")
```

We're special-casing the external_account field (more on that in a just a little bit). For all the other fields, we're looping through and creating a label and text field, sort of hacking the label name from the field name. A more polished version would probably place the label names in an internationalization file and use the field name as the key. (A more polished version might also have some fields be select boxes rather than text fields.)

We're specializing the external_account because it maps to more than one field and it includes sensitive information that we don't want on our servers. So, we have some more Stripe.js and Stripe API features to explore.

Here's the partial that covers the bank account data:

connect/02/app/views/affiliates/edit/_bank_account_form.html.slim

```
.bank_account_form
  input(type="hidden" data-stripe="country" value="US")
  input(type="hidden" data-stripe="currency" value="USD")
  .row
    .form-group
      .col-sm-3
        = label_tag(:bank_routing_number, "Bank Routing Number",
          class: "control-label")
      .col-sm-5
        input.form-control.valid-field(data-stripe="routing_number"
          id="bank_routing_number")

  .row
    .form-group
      .col-sm-3
```

```
    = label_tag(:bank_account_number, "Account Number",
      class: "control-label")
  .col-sm-5
    input.form-control.valid-field(data-stripe="account_number"
      id="bank_account_number")
.row
  .form-group
    .col-sm-3
      = label_tag(:account_holder_name, "Account Holder Name",
        class: "control-label")
    .col-sm-5
      input.form-control.valid-field(data-stripe="account_holder_name"
        id="account_holder_name")
.row
  .form-group
    .col-sm-3
      = label_tag(:account_holder_type,
        "Account Holder Type (individual or company)",
        class: "control-label")
    .col-sm-5
      input.form-control.valid-field(data-stripe="account_holder_type"
        id="account_holder_type")
```

This looks a lot like the credit card form we created using Stripe.js back in Chapter 3, *Client-Side Payment Authentication*, on page 45. Again, we're not giving these input field name attributes; instead, we are giving them data-stripe attributes for processing by Stripe.js.

The plan is to use Stripe.js to authenticate the bank account information and give us a token to pass back to the server. This code is quite similar to the credit card processing code.

We start by adding the following line to app/assets/javascripts/application.js to add our new JavaScript file to the manifest:

```
//= require edits_affiliate
```

On page load, we simply look for the existence of the bank account form, and if it's there, we create a handler object:

connect/02/app/assets/javascripts/edits_affiliate.es6
```
$(() => {
  if ($(".bank_account_form").size() > 0) {
    return new AffiliateFormHandler()
  }
  return null
})
```

Like the credit card JavaScript, this code is in three parts: the AffiliateFormHandler, which looks for the submit event and passes it along; the BankAccountTokenHandler, which gets the response from Stripe after trying to validate the bank account; and the AffiliateForm, which is the thin DOM wrapper that knows all the form stuff.

The AffiliateFormHandler basically just waits for a submit button click:

connect/02/app/assets/javascripts/edits_affiliate.es6

```
class AffiliateFormHandler {

  constructor() {
    this.affiliateForm = new AffiliateForm()
    this.initEventHandlers()
  }

  initEventHandlers() {
    this.affiliateForm.form().submit(event => {
      this.handleSubmit(event)
    })
  }

  handleSubmit(event) {
    event.preventDefault()
    if (this.affiliateForm.isButtonDisabled()) {
      return false
    }
    this.affiliateForm.disableButton()
    Stripe.bankAccount.createToken(
        this.affiliateForm.form(), BankAccountTokenHandler.handle)
    return false
  }
}
```

Once clicked, control passes to handleSubmit, where we disable the submit button and call the relevant Stripe.js API call, Stripe.bankAccount.createToken. As with the credit card version, it takes two arguments. The first is either a JavaScript object bank account fields, or a jQuery form with a bunch of data-stripe fields. We've chosen the latter, and the data-stripe field names exactly match the object keys that Stripe.js is expecting. The second object is a callback, and again we've done the same pattern as the earlier code by making it a static method of a class, this time BankAccountTokenHandler.

The BankAccountTokenHandler expects a status code and a response object, and eventually calls the handle method:

connect/02/app/assets/javascripts/edits_affiliate.es6

```
class BankAccountTokenHandler {
  static handle(status, response) {
    new BankAccountTokenHandler(status, response).handle()
  }
```

```
  constructor(status, response) {
    this.affiliateForm = new AffiliateForm()
    this.status = status
    this.response = response
  }

  isError() { return this.response.error }

  handle() {
    if (this.isError()) {
      this.affiliateForm.appendError(this.response.error.message)
      this.affiliateForm.enableButton()
    } else {
      this.affiliateForm.appendHidden(
          "account[external_account]", this.response.id)
      this.affiliateForm.submit()
    }
  }
}
```

If the response is an error, we display the error and re-enable the button. If
the response is a success, we append a hidden field with the token, and
continue submitting the form. All this code depends on the AffiliateForm, a thin
wrapper around jQuery and the DOM:

connect/02/app/assets/javascripts/edits_affiliate.es6
```
class AffiliateForm {

  form() { return $("#affiliate-form") }

  button() { return this.form().find(".btn") }

  disableButton() { this.button().prop("disabled", true) }

  enableButton() { this.button().prop("disabled", false) }

  isEnabled() { return !this.button().prop("disabled") }

  isButtonDisabled() { return this.button().prop("disabled") }

  submit() { this.form().get(0).submit() }

  appendHidden(name, value) {
    const field = $("<input>")
      .attr("type", "hidden")
      .attr("name", name)
      .val(value)
    this.form().append(field)
  }

  appendError(message) {
    const field = $("<h2>").text(message)
    this.form().prepend(field)
  }
}
```

Most of these methods are just a semantic name around a jQuery call, and they are all similar to the credit card version.

Now we have all of this verification information, what shall we do with it? If you guessed "create another workflow," you're right!

Sending Verification Information

Once the verification form is submitted, we handle it in the controller with the more or less standard workflow pattern we've used so far:

connect/02/app/controllers/affiliates_controller.rb
```ruby
def update
  @affiliate = Affiliate.find(params[:id])
  workflow = UpdatesAffiliateAccount.new(
      affiliate: @affiliate, user: current_user,
      params: params[:account].permit!.to_h)
  workflow.run
  if workflow.success
    redirect_to user_path(current_user)
  else
    render :edit
  end
end
```

The workflow in question is called UpdatesAffiliateAccount. We pass it the affiliate in question, the current user, and the parameters. It's best to disable Rails strong parameters before we pass things along, because we don't know the exact list of parameters. Because of how Stripe is going to make us deal with that list, a mass-assignment problem seems unlikely. The workflow largely just passes the parameters off to the StripeAccount and says "you deal with it."

connect/02/app/workflows/updates_affiliate_account.rb
```ruby
class UpdatesAffiliateAccount

  attr_accessor :affiliate, :user, :params, :success

  def initialize(affiliate:, user:, params:)
    @affiliate = affiliate
    @user = user
    @params = params
    @success = false
  end

  def affiliate_belongs_to_user?
    return true unless affiliate
    return true unless user
    affiliate&.user == user
  end
```

```ruby
  def stripe_account
    @stripe_account ||= StripeAccount.new(affiliate)
  end

  def run
    Affiliate.transaction do
      return if user.nil? || affiliate.nil?
      return unless affiliate_belongs_to_user?
      stripe_account.update(params)
      @success = true
    end
  end

  def success?
    @success
  end

end
```

We do check to make sure the affiliate exists, the user exists, and that they belong to each other before passing the params to the stripe_account and its update method.

The Stripe Ruby gem does not allow us to mass-assign values, and the official way of updating an account is to update all the attributes individually and then save. But we have a hash of values, so we can do this:

`connect/02/app/models/stripe_account.rb`
```ruby
def update(values)
  update_from_hash(account, values)
  self.account = account.save
  update_affiliate_verification
end
private def update_from_hash(object, values)
  values.each do |key, value|
    if value.is_a?(Hash)
      sub_object = object.send(key.to_sym)
      update_from_hash(sub_object, value)
    elsif value.present?
      object.send(:"#{key}=", value)
    end
  end
end
```

The update_from_hash is a dynamic and recursive method that takes an object and a hash of values. Looping over the hash, if the key is a scalar data point, it dynamically calls the setter for that attribute object.send(:"#{key}="). If the key is a hash, it passes the hash into update_from_hash and goes from there.

With this method, we can take our nested hashes that have things like {"legal_entity" => {"dob" => {"day" => 22}} and convert that into a series of setter calls. On the first pass, we see that the legal_entity key has a hash value, so we grab account.legal_entity and call update_from_hash again. There, we see that dob has a hash value, so we call legal_entity.dob and call update_from_hash again. This time, we finally call day = 22, effectively winding up with account.legal_entity.dob.day = 22. If we call a key that doesn't exist in the Stripe account object, the whole thing errors out.

After updating all the values, the next step is to call account.save, which triggers a Stripe API call. The return value of that call is the newly updated account object, which has new verification information. Call update_affiliate_verification so that we can update our local information, removing the credit hold, or getting the remaining set of validation information needed so that the process can start over.

Eventually, Stripe may ask for a personal identification number, a Social Security number (in the United States), or a scanned photo of an identification document. The personal identification number is handled similarly to credit card information using Stripe.js.[4] The scanned photo is handled as a file upload, and the API exposes a Stripe::FileUpload object.[5] Both are documented in the Stripe developer documentation.

Next Up

In this chapter we created an affiliate program for our application using Stripe Connect to manage the third-party Stripe accounts. We created Stripe accounts for our users, and created a workflow to know when those accounts are being used so that we can make our Stripe charges aware of the managed account and send money to it. We also discussed how to determine what identifying information is needed and how to obtain it and send it to Stripe.

Now it's time to deploy our application to production and talk about a checklist of things we need to be aware of while we are in production.

---

4.   https://stripe.com/docs/stripe.js#collecting-pii-data
5.   https://stripe.com/docs/connect/testing-verification

## CHAPTER 13

Going to Production

Eventually, of course, your application goes live, and money starts coming in. In this chapter, we look at some of the issues involved in getting your application to that live state and beyond.

I'm not going to talk about the details of deployment and hosting. In my experience those are so specific to the budget, expertise, and other constraints on each individual project that limiting myself to only one option seems not to be helpful, and going through all the options is an entire book in itself.

That said, if you are not a server, operations, or security expert, and for whatever reason are tasked with having to set up the production server system for an application with important financial data, I recommend using a service like Heroku that will manage most of the hard things for you. Security is a notoriously challenging thing to teach yourself last minute.

In this chapter, then, is a series of tips that should be applicable to a wide variety of production environments. Let's get to it.

Going Live

Every third-party financial tool we looked at in this book has a checklist of information you need before you can take live payments. It's very important to review all the settings for each service before you go live so that there are no surprises.

To review the settings in Stripe, go to Your Account => Activate Account, where you will be asked for at least the following information:

- Your country of origin
- A description of your business

- Business account details, including your tax ID (if the business has one), business address, and website address

- The identity of a company representative (In the United States, this includes your legal name, date of birth, and last four digits of your Social Security number. You also can help verify this information by logging in with an account on Facebook, LinkedIn, or Google.)

- The name and phone number you want to appear on customer credit card statements

- The bank account into which you want money transferred

You should review and confirm these settings on Stripe before you go live:

- Whether you will require CVC number or zip code verification for payments

- How you want to handle failed subscription payments

- How often you want Stripe to transfer money to your account

- The URL endpoint for webhooks

- How you want to handle shipping and taxes on your account (Stripe allows you to add fees on the Stripe side, which I don't recommend if you can calculate them on your side.)

- When you want Stripe to send you email notifications

You also want to turn on Stripe Connect managed accounts, which you can only do after your account is active.

Any other service you use, including other gateways, like PayPal, or additional services, like TaxCloud, has similar lists of information you need to supply in order to allow money to flow through the system.

Finally, it's a good idea to refresh all of the API keys before you go live for the first time. Many services, including Stripe, have a optional feature where the old key is still good for 24 hours or so, to make it easier for you to change keys for a live application without losing connection to the API.

Way back in *Setting Up Our First Payment Gateway*, on page 23, we talked about keeping API keys in environment variables, and then having the secrets.yml file refer to those variables. Now that we are talking about the production machine, you have two options: You can continue to store API keys in environment variables, or you can actually hardwire them into the secrets.yml file that lives on the production machines and only on the production machines. (Some services, like Heroku, don't let you edit a custom secrets.yml in production. In that case, you'll put the API keys in environment variables.) As long as the production files aren't in any public source control, the API keys can be easier to manage if they are explicitly written out in a file.

Setting Up SSL/TLS Encryption

You absolutely, 100 percent must use the Secure Socket Layer (SSL) protocol (which is sometimes referred to as TLS, or Transport Layer Security, the newer name for the updated version) to encrypt all credit card or financial calls. I recommend using SSL/TLS for all traffic to and from your site.

SSL is a protocol for encrypting traffic between a client and a server. Like most Internet encryption, it relies on *public key encryption*. In a public key encryption system, a person who wants to send and receive encrypted information generates two keys: a public key and a private key. You may have seen these keys if you've ever looked at the .ssh directory of your computer—they are series of apparently random hex digits. Typically the public and private keys are generated together using a process that is easy to do but hard to reverse. (Often it's multiplying two prime numbers versus factoring the resulting very long number back into the original primes.)

You then distribute the public key to anybody who wants to send you a message, and the algorithm encrypts it in such a way that the associated private key is needed to decrypt. Using public key encryption can serve two purposes. Not only can it allow anybody to send you an encrypted message, but also it can be used to "sign" the message by validating that it came from the source with that particular private key.

When using SSL/TLS your server sends the public key out to browsers, which speak the same algorithm and use the public key to send encrypted data back and forth with the browser. Your server, then, uses the private key to encrypt them. You can't, however, define your own set of keys. Part of the SSL package is also the verification and validation part of public key encryption, and that comes about in part by requiring that SSL certificates are issued by a trusted authority.

It's not hard to find a trusted authority—there's a good chance your DNS registrar also offers SSL certificates, and there's a relatively new free and open certificate authority called Let's Encrypt.[1]

The certificate authority may provide multiple options, but what you want to look for is a 2048-bit private key. You also need to configure the certificate

---

1.   https://www.letsencrypt.org

when created to match the hostname, so typically, you might need a certificate that can handle access via the www subdomain, as well as access via just the stem of the domain name, as in http://snowglobe.com.

If you have a large or arbitrary number of subdomains, you can also get a *wildcard* certificate, which is set up to automatically apply to any subdomain. A wildcard certificate is generally only recommended where you really have one logical application with arbitrary subdomains, and not as a way to avoid purchasing separate certificates for different applications that happen to share a domain.

For more specific information about SSL configuration, refer to the website, Qualsys SSL Labs,[2] which provides a number of useful documents on SSL configuration, including a best practices guide.[3] If your server is public facing, SSL Labs can remotely test your SSL configuration, give you a letter grade, and let you know how your SSL setup can improve.

There is one more wrinkle. Many certificate providers may offer you the option of an *Extended Verification* (EV) certificate. The verification in question is more verification of your identity, not extra levels of encryption. Typically the certificate provider will ask you for some additional information about your organization, charge you more money, take a little more time to verify the certificate, and include extended information in the certificate. If you have an EV certificate, the browser will show something green in the URL bar that the user can click to verify the identity of the site and, in theory, prevent phishing. A quick walk through the web will confirm that most, though not all, major e-commerce sites have the green bar and use an EV certificate.

EV certificates are only available to business or other registered associations, so you probably can't get one for your personal site. They also don't have wildcard domains, again, to prevent phishing attacks.

Running Automated Security Audits

I don't intend this to be a full list of all the things you need to do to keep your site secure. That's a whole book in and of itself. I do want to mention a couple of automated auditing tools that can help you discover potential vulnerabilities in your site.

---

2.   https://ssllabs.com
3.   https://github.com/ssllabs/research/wiki/SSL-and-TLS-Deployment-Best-Practices

One cause of vulnerabilities is not your code, but the code in the gems you depend on and all the gems they depend on. The Bundler Audit[4] gem compares your Gemfile.lock against the Ruby Advisory Database (a list of security advisories affecting Ruby gems), and outputs a list of gems in your project known to have security issues. It also checks for gems sourced against nonsecure https sources.

To use bundler-audit, simply add it to your Gemfile. You probably want to put it in your development group:

```
gem "bundler-audit", group: :development
```

Then you can run it from the command line with bundle-audit. You can update the database that bundle-audit uses with bundle-audit update and you can check and update at the same time with bundle-audit check --update. (And yes, the gem is bundler-audit, and the command is bundle audit.)

```
bundle-audit
Insecure Source URI found: git://github.com/rails/sprockets.git
Insecure Source URI found: git://github.com/sinatra/sinatra.git
Name: actionview
Version: 5.0.0
Advisory: CVE-2016-6316
Criticality: Unknown
URL: https://groups.google.com/forum/#!topic/rubyonrails-security/I-VWr034ouk
Title: Possible XSS Vulnerability in Action View
Solution: upgrade to ~> 3.2.22.3, ~> 4.2.7.1, >= 5.0.0.1

Vulnerabilities found!
```

Huh. Looks like I've got an update to do. If I think that I've already worked around this issue and don't want to be bothered by it anymore, I can ignore it using the advisory name: bundle-audit check --ignore CVE-2016-6316.

If you want a tool that will find vulnerabilities in your own code, you can use the Brakeman[5] gem, which is also integrated into CodeClimate's static analysis tools.[6] Brakeman does code analysis of your Rails application and reports on the existence of a variety of security problems.

You can add Brakeman to your Gemfile like this:

```
gem "brakeman", :require => false
```

You probably want it in the development and test groups.

---

4.   https://github.com/rubysec/bundler-audit
5.   http://brakemanscanner.org
6.   https://codeclimate.com

You can run it with brakeman, although you get a slightly more readable report if you use brakeman -f plain. If I run it on my application now, I get the same warning about Rails 5.0.0, plus three other warnings. One of them is a case where I use permit! to whitelist parameters that are later broken up in work-flows, rather than used in mass-assignment.

The code that Brakeman doesn't like is from this snippet in RefundsController:

```
connect/02/app/controllers/refunds_controller.rb
VALID_REFUNDABLES = %w(Payment PaymentLineItem).freeze

private def load_refundable
  raise "bad refundable class" unless params[:type].in?(VALID_REFUNDABLES)
  @refundable = params[:type].constantize.find(params[:id])
end
```

The security issue is that I'm calling constantize on what Brakeman sees as an arbitrary parameter, params[:type]. That's bad because it could allow for remote code execution if somebody was clever. However, in this case, I took this possibility into account, and the code actually only runs that line if params[:type] is in VALID_REFUNDABLES. Brakeman is clever, but not that clever.

Brakeman allows you to ignore false positives with a config/brakeman.ignore file. The easiest way to get started with one is by running brakeman -I (for interactive). On the first run, it will create the brakeman.ignore file for you, and then it will allow you to go through each warning, presenting you with a list of options from the Brakeman docs:[7]

```
i - Add warning to ignore list
n - Add warning to ignore list and add note
s - Skip this warning (will remain ignored or shown)
u - Remove this warning from ignore list
a - Ignore this warning and all remaining warnings
k - Skip this warning and all remaining warnings
q - Quit, do not update ignored warnings
? - Display this help
```

After going through all the found vulnerabilities, it asks if you want to save the file, which it does, placing JSON metadata in config/brakeman.ignore. Future runs will ignore those vulnerabilities when encountered.

Brakeman isn't perfect. It doesn't know as much about your code as you do, so it will show up with false positives. It's worth taking it seriously, though, and confirming whether or not the alert is spurious.

---

7.   http://brakemanscanner.org/docs

Database Backups

Two useful database backup features, even for small sites that are just getting started, are regular (or snapshot) backups and read replicas. Depending on how your database was set up, your database service provider may make these features easily available.

Snapshot Backup

The snapshot backup is your basic database backup at a particular point in time. If you are using Amazon Web Services (AWS) or some other provider, you will typically be able to schedule both the frequency of backups and how long backups are stored. Back up frequently, keep things around as long as you can, and make sure you know how to restore a backup if the worst happens. However, make sure that the database backup process does not interfere with normal operations. Again, your database provider or devops team can help here.

Read Replica

A read replica is a little bit different. Unlike a snapshot, the read replica is a live database that is synchronized continuously with the main database. You can connect to this replica database and run queries against it, but you can't add, update, or remove data. Because the replica is alive and is usually less than a second behind the main database, having one gives you some interesting options.

A use of a read replica is to scale the database while avoiding synchronization problems. Because only one database instance gets written to, that instance becomes the source of truth, meaning you don't need to worry about consistency problems—data only flows one way. The replica databases are there, though, so they can handle requests, if you know they are read-only.

Although it can be challenging to tease out read-only requests, as it happens, we have one set of actions that are both read-only and use an unusual amount of data: reports. It'd be really nice if we could set up our application so that our report queries would go against the replica database and everything else went to the primary database.

Unfortunately, Rails makes this rather difficult. You can add a separate connection in the database.yml file and give it a name, but you still need to tell Rails to use it. By default, Rails allows you to specify database connections on a model-by-model basis, using the establish_connection method. Specifying database connections per model is great if you actually have two databases that each have a subset of your data, but it's not helpful in our use case.

A couple of gems are designed to allow ActiveRecord to use a replica database for writes: Makara[8] and Octopus.[9] For our purposes here, their functionality is pretty similar. They each allow you to define a primary and replica database, and have all SELECT statements go to the replica and INSERT and UPDATE statements go to the primary database.

That's not *quite* what we want; we'd really like for just our report data to go to the replica. Both gems offer mechanisms for specifying when you want the replica in use. Makara wants you to create a subclass of its ::Makara::Proxy base class and override a method called needs_master?. Octopus, which seems in general to be the more heavyweight of the two, offers a using extension to ActiveRecord, which takes the name of the connection to use and can either be chained on the end of an ActiveRecord call, as in Payment.includes(:user).succeeded.find_each.using(:production_replica), or in a block form, as in

```
Octopus.using(:production_replica) do
  Payment.includes(:user).succeeded.find_each
end
```

Neither of these solutions feels like a complete fit to me, and I suggest a slightly more radical solution: create a second, much smaller Rails application using the read replica as its database. That application would need little more than the report controllers and classes that we defined, and probably the definition of all the model classes and their relationships.

Arguments in favor of this solution:

- It's a little bit easier to set up in development mode because the development database for the report app can just point to your regular development database.

- Separation of concerns—report code can be completely separated out from transaction code.

- It gives more flexibility to your architecture over time.

Arguments against it:

- It involves much more overhead in your deploy. You need to deploy two apps, and your server-side setup needs to have some way to push URLs to one or the other.

---

8. https://github.com/taskrabbit/makara
9. https://github.com/thiagopradi/octopus

- Just having the second application implies some additional code overhead.

- There's coordination needed between the two applications when model definitions change, and there will probably be some duplicated code.

This is definitely one of those "your mileage may vary" situations, but it's worth having some kind of strategy for trying to separate out heavy read-only usage if your application loads become larger.

A very, very important caveat here. If your database contains cardholder data, or if you are bound by other privacy or data restrictions laws, such as HIPAA for medical information, or Sarbanes-Oxley, then you have legal constraints over what you can do with production user and transaction data and what servers that data can live on.

Running Periodic Tasks

There's a good chance you will want to have tasks run in the background on your servers at regular times. Just in this book we've discussed running meta checks on transaction data, pregenerating report tasks, possibly checking on subscription status—and your own business logic will likely lead to others.

If your application is on Heroku, you can use the Heroku Scheduler to run any task you can access from a command line—the convention is to use Rake tasks. You can schedule tasks to run daily, hourly, or at 10-minute intervals.

If you are not on Heroku, you have the ability to use cron, a long-standing Unix utility that enables you to schedule periodic tasks. Cron has a ridiculously arcane syntax, even by Unix standards.[10] Happily, though, there is a Ruby gem called Whenever[11] that gives a more friendly syntax.

Whenever is easy to integrate into your project. Add it to your Gemfile as gem 'whenever', :require => false. Then do two things from the command line:

```
$ bundle install
$ wheneverize .
```

The wheneverize command creates the file config/schedule.rb, which starts with some comments showing basic Whenever syntax.

There are two steps to using Whenever. First, we use Whenever's syntax to define jobs, and then add it to whatever our deploy process is so that the server's cron table is updated when you deploy the application.

---

10. http://www.adminschoice.com/crontab-quick-reference
11. https://github.com/javan/whenever

To define a task using Whenever, add it to the config/schedule.rb file. The basic syntax is as follows:

```
every <TIME> do
  <TASK>
end
```

The time can be specified in a few different ways:

- Using Rails ActiveSupport time methods, like every 1.day or every 15.minutes. The methods for minute, day, week, month, and year are supported.

- Using a shortcut defined by Whenever, such as every :day. Whenever defines :minute, :hour, :day, :month, :year, and :reboot, and a few synonyms like :annually.

- Using a day of the week as a symbol, such as every :sunday.

- Using actual Cron syntax, such as every 0 0 12 1/1 * ? * (which is not cryptic in the least).

You can augment the specified duration with an optional at, as in every 1.day, :at "1:00 am". You seem to have a fair bit of leeway in how you specify the at—the parser appears to be kind of forgiving. But I will tell you from experience that the comma in that line of code is easy to forget, and forgetting it will cause the at not to be parsed.

The job inside the block can be specified using one of three predefined job types or you can define your own. The simplest type is a command, which is a path to an executable on the server, as in command "/some/path/name". When a command event is triggered, Whenever executes the associated path.

You can also define a job as a Rake task, as in rake task_name, which Whenever parses and expands to "cd :path && :environment_variable=:environment bundle exec rake task_name --silent".

Finally, you can define a job as a string that can be eval-ed in the Rails environment, as in runner "DayReport.generate_data". Whenever expands this to cd :path && bin/rails runner -e :environment 'DayReport.generate_data'. I strongly prefer defining Rake tasks to doing string evals, for what it's worth.

You can also create your own job types in Whenever. In practice I find that I vastly prefer to specify everything as Rake tasks, which makes them easier to run as one-offs when needed.

Whenever also lets you log to arbitrary output files by specifying a log file. You can do this globally for all commands by putting a line like this at the top of your config/schedule.rb file:

```
set :output, "/www/shared/log/whenever.rb"
```

If the output is set, Whenever adds >> PATH 2>&1 to the commands, which makes sense if you speak Unix, otherwise it's enough to know that command specifies a log file. The argument to output can also be a hash with keys :error and :standard if you want to override standard out and standard error separately. Note that Rails.root is not available in the Whenever file, but Whenever.path is equivalent in most cases.

You can also specify :output as an optional argument to any command if you want to override logging on a command-by-command basis. (The Whenever docs and wiki have some other edge cases.)[12]

Once you have everything in the Whenever file, you can see the entire resulting Cron table with the command whenever. However, calling whenever with no arguments does not make changes to the server. If you are on the server and want to update the server's cron table, use whenever --update-crontab.

In practice, you don't want to do that manually; you want to add it to your deploy script. If you are using Capistrano, adding require whenever/capistrano will make updating the cron tab part of deploy. You can also add a :roles option to any command to limit that command to only servers that have a particular Capistrano role. Please note that there are some jobs that might only need to be run on one server if you have multiple servers, so you might want to tweak the roles to designate a server as the background task server.

Compliance

Let's close this out with a brief discussion of PCI compliance, or compliance with PCI DSS, which stands for Payment Card Industry Data Security Standard.[13] Compliance is a complicated topic, and if you need information beyond what's presented here, you should use the services of an approved PCI security expert.

First, let's define what the PCI DSS is. PCI DSS is not, in most U.S. jurisdictions, a legal standard, but is instead part of the agreement with credit card companies that allows you to process transactions. If you have any role in processing transactions, then you are subject to at least some of the PCI

---

12. https://github.com/javan/whenever/wiki
13. https://www.pcisecuritystandards.org

standards. How many of the standards depends on exactly how your application interacts with the banking system.

There are twelve top-level requirements in the PCI standard, each of which has many sub-requirements. These are subject to change every time the PCI group updates the standard. They are (slightly paraphrased):

- Install and maintain a firewall.

- Do not use vendor default passwords or security parameters.

- Protect stored cardholder data.

- Encrypt cardholder data when transmitted across open networks.

- Use and keep current antivirus software where needed.

- Develop secure applications and systems.

- Restrict access to cardholder data to people who need it for the business to run.

- Assign a unique ID to each person with access to systems.

- Restrict physical access to cardholder data.

- Monitor all access to network resources and cardholder data.

- Regularly test security processes.

- Maintain an information security policy.

As you see, this list runs the gamut from the quite hands-on to the rather theoretical.

To determine whether your application is compliant, the first step is to take a Self-Assessment Questionnaire (SAQ). There are multiple SAQs that check for different subsets of the requirements. Three SAQs are of interest to us:

- *SAQ A* is for e-commerce merchants who outsource all cardholder data to a third party, do not ever receive cardholder data to their servers, and only interact with that third party via a web page or iframe that is created entirely by a third party. SAQ A is by far the smallest set of requirements, and largely includes things you are likely doing already by virtue of having your cardholder data on a compliant third-party server.

- *SAQ A-EP* is like SQA A, but for e-commerce merchants who don't touch cardholder data, but interact with the third party via a page that contains elements from the merchant and elements from the third party. SAQ A-EP has a somewhat larger set of requirements, and is designed to prevent a malicious attack on cardholder data using compromised assets from the merchant's website.

- *SAQ D* is every other e-commerce merchant, even if you don't actually store the cardholder data, but it is sent to you (though if you don't store the cardholder data, then some of the requirements are trivial).

You really want to be in SAQ A. I want you to be there, the banks want you to be there, the payment gateways want you to be there, and your IT department wants you to be there. If you are a small e-commerce merchant, you want to be outsourcing hard security questions to companies that think about them all the time.

Looking at the Snow Globe Theater payment application we have built in this book, it is clear that the PayPal interaction, which takes place on PayPal's site, is SAQ A. It is less clear, but the Stripe iteration is as well, per Stripe.[14] The versions of stripe.js built after 2015 (the creation of the A-EP designation) were built in consultation with the PCI group. Behind the scenes, stripe.js creates a hidden iframe that handles interaction with the Stripe API, so that if you use stripe.js (or Stripe Checkout), and serve your pages with SSL/TLS, Stripe will certify that you qualify under SAQ A, and you can get a certification to that effect from your Stripe account if the account is live. (Stripe, or any gateway you might use, can validate the questionnaire because they run the systems that touch cardholder data—the questions do not apply to your application server.)

If you are using the server-side version of Stripe we looked at in Chapter 2, *Take the Money*, on page 21, then you are in SAQ-D territory, and even if you do not store the credit card data, as I read the standards, many of the questions apply to your application system because it touches cardholder data, albeit briefly.

The End

Now that we've looked at a few things that will make your production experience easier, it is time to come to the end. Writing and running an application that handles money can be stressful. I hope that the suggestions and recommendations in this book make the process easier for you and save you time and aggravation.

Thanks for your attention. I hope you build great things.

---

14. https://stripe.com/docs/security

Bibliography

[Rap14]   Noel Rappin. *Rails 4 Test Prescriptions*. The Pragmatic Bookshelf, Raleigh, NC, 2014.

Index

The Modern Web

Get up to speed on the latest JavaScript techniques.

Deliver Audacious Web Apps with Ember 2

It's time for web development to be fun again, time to write engaging and attractive apps – fast – in this brisk tutorial. Build a complete user interface in a few lines of code, create reusable web components, access RESTful services and cache the results for performance, and use JavaScript modules to bring abstraction to your code. Find out how you can get your crucial app infrastructure up and running quickly, so you can spend your time on the stuff great apps are made of: features.

Matthew White
(154 pages) ISBN: 9781680500783. $24
https://pragprog.com/book/mwjsember

Reactive Programming with RxJS

Reactive programming is revolutionary. It makes asynchronous programming clean, intuitive, and robust. Use the RxJS library to write complex programs in a simple way, unifying asynchronous mechanisms such as callbacks and promises into a powerful data type: the Observable. Learn to think about your programs as streams of data that you can transform by expressing *what* should happen, instead of having to painstakingly program *how* it should happen. Manage real-world concurrency and write complex flows of events in your applications with ease.

Sergi Mansilla
(142 pages) ISBN: 9781680501292. $18
https://pragprog.com/book/smreactjs

The Modern Web

Get up to speed on the latest HTML, CSS, and JavaScript techniques.

HTML5 and CSS3 (2nd edition)

HTML5 and CSS3 are more than just buzzwords –
they're the foundation for today's web applications.
This book gets you up to speed on the HTML5 elements
and CSS3 features you can use right now in your current projects, with backwards compatible solutions
that ensure that you don't leave users of older browsers
behind. This new edition covers even more new features, including CSS animations, IndexedDB, and
client-side validations.

Brian P. Hogan
(314 pages) ISBN: 9781937785598. $38
https://pragprog.com/book/bhh52e

Async JavaScript

With the advent of HTML5, front-end MVC, and
Node.js, JavaScript is ubiquitous—and still messy.
This book will give you a solid foundation for managing
async tasks without losing your sanity in a tangle of
callbacks. It's a fast-paced guide to the most essential
techniques for dealing with async behavior, including
PubSub, evented models, and Promises. With these
tricks up your sleeve, you'll be better prepared to
manage the complexity of large web apps and deliver
responsive code.

Trevor Burnham
(104 pages) ISBN: 9781937785277. $17
https://pragprog.com/book/tbajs

Secure JavaScript and Web Testing

Secure your Node applications and see how to really test on the web.

Secure Your Node.js Web Application

Cyber-criminals have your web applications in their crosshairs. They search for and exploit common security mistakes in your web application to steal user data. Learn how you can secure your Node.js applications, database and web server to avoid these security holes. Discover the primary attack vectors against web applications, and implement security best practices and effective countermeasures. Coding securely will make you a stronger web developer and analyst, and you'll protect your users.

Karl Düüna

(230 pages) ISBN: 9781680500851. $36

https://pragprog.com/book/kdnodesec

The Way of the Web Tester

This book is for everyone who needs to test the web. As a tester, you'll automate your tests. As a developer, you'll build more robust solutions. And as a team, you'll gain a vocabulary and a means to coordinate how to write and organize automated tests for the web. Follow the testing pyramid and level up your skills in user interface testing, integration testing, and unit testing. Your new skills will free you up to do other, more important things while letting the computer do the one thing it's really good at: quickly running thousands of repetitive tasks.

Jonathan Rasmusson

(254 pages) ISBN: 9781680501834. $29

https://pragprog.com/book/jrtest

Pragmatic Programming

We'll show you how to be more pragmatic and effective, for new code and old.

Your Code as a Crime Scene

Jack the Ripper and legacy codebases have more in common than you'd think. Inspired by forensic psychology methods, this book teaches you strategies to predict the future of your codebase, assess refactoring direction, and understand how your team influences the design. With its unique blend of forensic psychology and code analysis, this book arms you with the strategies you need, no matter what programming language you use.

Adam Tornhill
(218 pages) ISBN: 9781680500387. $36
https://pragprog.com/book/atcrime

The Nature of Software Development

You need to get value from your software project. You need it "free, now, and perfect." We can't get you there, but we can help you get to "cheaper, sooner, and better." This book leads you from the desire for value down to the specific activities that help good Agile projects deliver better software sooner, and at a lower cost. Using simple sketches and a few words, the author invites you to follow his path of learning and understanding from a half century of software development and from his engagement with Agile methods from their very beginning.

Ron Jeffries
(178 pages) ISBN: 9781941222379. $24
https://pragprog.com/book/rjnsd

The Pragmatic Bookshelf

The Pragmatic Bookshelf features books written by developers for developers. The titles continue the well-known Pragmatic Programmer style and continue to garner awards and rave reviews. As development gets more and more difficult, the Pragmatic Programmers will be there with more titles and products to help you stay on top of your game.

Visit Us Online

This Book's Home Page
https://pragprog.com/book/nrwebpay
Source code from this book, errata, and other resources. Come give us feedback, too!

Register for Updates
https://pragprog.com/updates
Be notified when updates and new books become available.

Join the Community
https://pragprog.com/community
Read our weblogs, join our online discussions, participate in our mailing list, interact with our wiki, and benefit from the experience of other Pragmatic Programmers.

New and Noteworthy
https://pragprog.com/news
Check out the latest pragmatic developments, new titles and other offerings.

Save on the eBook

Save on the eBook versions of this title. Owning the paper version of this book entitles you to purchase the electronic versions at a terrific discount.

PDFs are great for carrying around on your laptop—they are hyperlinked, have color, and are fully searchable. Most titles are also available for the iPhone and iPod touch, Amazon Kindle, and other popular e-book readers.

Buy now at *https://pragprog.com/coupon*

Contact Us

Online Orders:	*https://pragprog.com/catalog*
Customer Service:	*support@pragprog.com*
International Rights:	*translations@pragprog.com*
Academic Use:	*academic@pragprog.com*
Write for Us:	*http://write-for-us.pragprog.com*
Or Call:	+1 800-699-7764

CPSIA information can be obtained
at www.ICGtesting.com
Printed in the USA
BVOW04s0643200217
476648BV00003B/12/P

9 781680 501995